CW00829260

Study Commentary on Genesis
volume 2

A Study Commentary
on
Genesis

Volume 2: Genesis 25:19 – 50:26

John D. Currid

EVANGELICAL PRESS

EVANGELICAL PRESS
Faverdale North Industrial Estate, Darlington, DL3 0PH,
England

Evangelical Press USA
P. O. Box 825, Webster, New York 14580, USA

e-mail: sales@evangelicalpress.org

web: www.evangelicalpress.org

First published 2003

**British Library Cataloguing in Publication Data
available**

ISBN 0 85234 550 X

Printed and bound in Great Britain by Creative Print &
Design Wales, Ebbw Vale.

Contents

Glossary of linguistic terms

anacoluthon: a sentence or construction in which the expected grammatical sequence is absent

anadiplosis: using the same words at the end of one sentence or clause and again at the beginning of the next

antonomasia: the substitution of an epithet or title for a proper name

aposiopesis: the rhetorical device of suddenly breaking off in speech

asyndeton: the omission or absence of a conjunction between parts of a sentence

chiasmus (derivative **chiastic**): literary figure in which words, grammatical constructions, or concepts are repeated in reverse order, in the same or a modified form

epizeuxis: when a phrase is repeated but is separated by intervening words, which serve as a yoke, or joint, between the two

gemination: doubling or repeating (speech sounds)

hendiadys: the expression of a single idea by two words connected with 'and'

hysteresis: filling in the details of an event that had occurred a long time before

inclusio: a repeated theme which both introduces and concludes a passage, and thus encompasses the whole

litotes: an ironical understatement in which an affirmative is expressed by the negative of its contrary

meiosis — see litotes

merism: a pair of opposites that are all-inclusive

metonymy: the substitution of the name of an attribute or adjunct for that of the thing meant

peirastic (adj.): something that is done by trial or testing

pleonasm: the use of more words than are necessary to convey the meaning

polyptoton: the use of a verb and a cognate noun together, which acts as a superlative, giving great force and emphasis to the action

synecdoche: a figure of speech in which a part is made to represent the whole, or vice versa

zeugma: a figure of speech in which a word applies to two others in different senses, or applies to two words of which it semantically suits only one

8.The story of Jacob and Esau

(Genesis 25:19 – 36:43)

The birth of Esau and Jacob
(Genesis 25:19-26)

Abraham has died just prior to this story, and now the history of God's chosen seed is to be carried on through Isaac. Here we have a familiar beginning: Rebekah is barren, and the continuation of the promised seed is in jeopardy once again. How will God intervene in the situation and keep his promises?

25:19. And these are the generations of Isaac the son of Abraham: Abraham fathered Isaac.

The statement, **'And these are the generations of ...'** is an oft-repeated formula in Genesis (see 6:9; 10:1; 11:10,27; etc.). It serves two functions. First, it introduces genealogical data. And, second, it normally precedes a new block of narrative material — a new story is being introduced. (For the latter interpretation, see commentary on the passages listed above.) In addition, the verse serves as a contrast to Genesis 25:12 — there is striking similarity of language and contrast of purpose. The previous verse underscores Ishmael's descent, not from Sarah, but from Hagar, the Egyptian maid.[1] Isaac's direct descent from Abraham and Sarah is now accentuated and legitimized — that is, he is the true heir.

25:20-21. And it came to pass when Isaac was forty years old that he took Rebekah, the daughter of Bethuel, the Aramaean from Paddan-Aram, the sister of Laban the Aramaean, to be his wife. And Isaac prayed to Yahweh in front of his wife because she was barren. And Yahweh was entreated. So Rebekah his wife conceived.

In a general sense, this story parallels that of Abraham and Sarah. The latter were also subject to a long period of barrenness (see 11:30).[2] The length of barrenness for Isaac and Rebekah is twenty years (see 25:26); for Abraham and Sarah it appears to have been much longer. There is a major distinction between the two events, however: Isaac and Rebekah do not resort to concubinage to produce children. Rather, they seem to trust in the word and providence of God.

What Isaac does is to 'pray'. That verb is in the Qal stem, and when it appears that way in the Hebrew Bible, God is always the one being addressed. God responds by being **'entreated'** — that is the same verb as **'prayed'** in Hebrew, but it is in the Niphal pattern / stem. It is what is called a 'tolerative Niphal', signifying that the subject grants the request or prayer.[3] In the Bible this verb in this pattern is reserved for God's work.

It should also be observed that Isaac prays **'in front of'** Rebekah. That phrase is a substantive that is used almost exclusively to denote physical positioning.[4] Perhaps it signifies that Isaac is literally standing before his wife and interceding with God for her.

25:22-23. And the sons were crushing each other inside her. And she said, 'If it is so, why am I like this?' So she went to enquire of Yahweh. And Yahweh said to her:

> Two nations are in your womb
> And two peoples from your inward parts will be divided.
> And one people will be stronger than the other people
> And the older will serve the younger.

Here is the first indication of conflict between the two brothers who are soon to be born. They are **'crushing each other'** (Hithpael reflexive pattern) inside Rebekah. Such action reflects great animosity and enmity between the two children. Some of the rabbis explain that this verb really has the meaning of running or moving quickly, and so '… whenever she passed by the doors of the Torah (i.e. the Schools of Shem and Eber) Jacob moved convulsively in his efforts to come to birth, but whenever she passed by the gate of a pagan temple Esau moved convulsively in his efforts to come to birth'.[5] Although that story is apocryphal it reflects the bent of each child. In addition, the activity of crushing each other serves as a symbol representing the future history of the brothers' relationship.

Rebekah's verbal response demonstrates that something extraordinary is happening. Her question is brief and incomplete — it literally reads: **'If so, why am I?'** It may be that she is even going so far as to question her own existence in the light of the problem she is experiencing. But in the end she responds properly by going to Yahweh and enquiring of him. In that sense she imitates her husband, who had prayed earlier because of her barrenness.

Yahweh's answer to Rebekah is typical Hebrew poetry, and it consists of two pairs of lines, or, more technically, cola, in parallel.[6] The first is:

	a	b	
	Two nations	in your womb	
	a¹	b¹	c¹
	And two peoples	from your inward parts	will be divided

The construction is an incomplete synonymous parallelism in which the verb of the second line also applies to the first line — a feature that is typical of Hebrew poetical practice. The second couplet says:

a	b	c
And one people	than the other people	will be stronger
b¹	c¹	a¹
And the older	will serve	the younger

There is a clear reversal in the order of the elements: in the first line the one people — that is, the younger — is the subject; in the second line it is the other people, the older, that is the subject. This reversal serves to emphasize the point of the subservience.

This prophecy of Yahweh overturns the common practices of the ancient Near East. The first-born normally would receive the greater share of the inheritance and leadership of the family. In Mesopotamia, for example, the *māru rabū* (a term related to the Hebrew word for **'older'** used in this passage) inherits much more than the *marū ṣeḥru* (the latter term being related to the word translated **'younger'** above).[7] But in the case of Jacob and Esau it is God who predetermines that the situation will be different for the children of Rebekah.

The hostility between the two children is a symbol of enmity between two peoples. These two groups will be **'divided'**, which also carries the sense of 'separated' or 'incompatible', and strife will result. The fulfilment of the prophecy is clear: the people of promise, and ultimately the Messiah, will come through the lineage of Jacob, the younger son. Descendants of the elder son, Esau, become the Edomites, who stand outside the line of God's covenant promises. Indeed, there is considerable evidence regarding the conflict between Edom and Israel throughout biblical history (see 2 Sam. 8:14; 1 Kings 11:16; 1 Chr. 18:13).

25:24-26. And when her days were completed in order to give birth, behold, twins were in her womb. And the first came out ruddy, all of him, like a hairy cloak. And they called his name Esau. And afterwards his brother came out. And his hand was holding on to the heel of Esau, and so his name was called Jacob. And Isaac was sixty years old when she gave birth to them.

When Rebekah's pregnancy ends, she gives birth to twins. The first is born with a very unusual characteristic: he is born with hypertrichosis — that is, covered with hair. Many translations also add that it was 'red' hair (e.g., NASB, NIV); it probably is better to render that term as **'ruddy'** and to understand it as reflecting his complexion. The word is used of David in that way in 1 Samuel 16:12; 17:42.

The child is given the name **'Esau'**. This does not involve a word-play on any other term used in the story. It may be a derivative of the verb *'āsāh*, which means 'to press' 'squeeze' or 'crush'.[8] Thus its use may reflect the earlier incident of the children crushing one another in the womb (25:22).

The term translated **'hairy'** is *sē'ār* in Hebrew. Esau and his descendants later inhabit a land called Seir (32:3; 33:14,16; 36:8).[9] The territory probably receives its name from Esau's condition at birth. The reference to his hairiness also anticipates the story in Genesis 27 in which Isaac feels for the hairy arms of Esau in order to identify him (27:23).

The second child also appears in an unusual manner. His hand is grasping the heel of his brother. The symbol is obvious: the younger is holding on to the first, struggling, as if he is not going to allow his brother out before himself. This is a second indi-cation of conflict between them, and it signifies the future relationship of the twins. Jacob's name is the cognate verb of the noun **'heel'**; his name thus means 'one who takes by the heel'.[10] This translation is supported by the prophet Hosea, who said of Jacob, 'In the womb he took his brother by the heel' (Hosea 12:3).

Application

In the book of Romans, the apostle Paul makes mention of the story of the birth of Jacob and Esau. In Romans 9:10-13, he says the following: 'And not only this, but there was Rebekah also, when she had conceived twins by one man, our father Isaac; for though the twins were not yet born and had not done anything good or bad, so that God's purpose according to his choice might stand, not because of works but because of him who calls, it was said to her, "The older will serve the younger."' Paul uses the events recorded in Genesis 25 as an example to demonstrate God's work of election. Before the boys were born God made a distinction: he chose Jacob and his descendants to receive his revelation, to be the ones through whom the Messiah would come and to be his covenant people. Esau and his lineage would receive none of it. And this distinction was not made because of human merit or innate human goodness (was Jacob really a better person than Esau?). Rather, the distinction was made by the mercy of God.

The same still holds true today. People are of the covenant, not because of their own choosing, or because they somehow earned it, but simply because of the grace of God. Midlane tells the story of an unnamed minister in Scotland who was on his deathbed when a brother minister came to see him. The latter enquired, 'Well, my brother, what are you doing?' 'Doing?', answered the dying servant of God. 'Doing? I will tell you: I am gathering together all my prayers and sermons, all my good deeds and bad deeds, and am going to throw them all overboard together, and swim to glory on the plank of free grace!' Salvation is by God's grace alone. There is no other way.

Selling of the birthright
(Genesis 25:27-34)

The plot of the Jacob-Esau story was given in 25:23 with the prophecy of Yahweh. The prediction is that there will be animosity between the two brothers (and the peoples coming from them) and the older will serve the younger. That theme is now set in motion with Esau's selling of his birthright to Jacob.

Another primary point of the section is the careless and indifferent attitude of Esau regarding his birthright and the promises of God. This is underscored by the literary structure of the passage.[11] At the heart of the passage is a chiasmus:

A
Esau pleads for
food (25:30)

B
Jacob demands
that Esau sell
his birthright
(25:31)

C
Esau denigrates
the value of the
birthright
(25:32)

B¹
Esau sells his
birthright to
Jacob (25:33)

A¹
Jacob gives
Esau food
(25:34)

The crux of the chiastic unit, or its pivotal point, is verse 32. And that verse highlights the listless and disdainful nature of the character of Esau. His temper and demeanour will be further accentuated in other parts of the text.

25:27-28. And the young men grew. And it came to pass that Esau was a man knowing hunting, a man of the field. But Jacob was a man of peace, dwelling in tents. And Isaac loved Esau because [he put] game in his mouth; but Rebekah loved Jacob.

Further indications of conflict between the brothers are now provided. Contrasts in their occupations and characters are clear: Esau is aggressive and violent (see 27:40), an outdoorsman, whereas Jacob is a man of **'peace'**. The latter term probably reflects his quiet and retiring nature, as a person who works and stays near the tents.[12] Their dispositions are simply antithetical. Rashi puts it this way: 'So long as they were young they could not be distinguished by what they did and no one paid much attention to their characters, but when they reached the age of thirteen, one went his way to the houses of learning and the other went his way to the idolatrous temples.'[13]

Another sign of conflict is the fact that the family takes sides on the issue. **'Isaac loved Esau because [he put] game in his mouth.'** There is an ellipsis here — the verb is omitted — which places emphasis on the object. **'Game'** is what Isaac truly loves, and Esau receives love because he supplies it. Rebekah, on the other hand, loves Jacob. No reason is given. This split is to have dire consequences one day when the family is physically split from one another.

25:29-30. And Jacob boiled stew. When Esau came in from the field he was faint with hunger. And Esau said to Jacob, 'Let me swallow [some] of the red stuff, that red stuff, because I am faint with hunger.' Therefore his name was called Edom.

One day, Jacob does some cooking in the tent area. Esau then comes from hunting in the field and he is **'faint with hunger'**. That phrase is one word in Hebrew and it bears the idea of weariness due to physical exertion (see 2 Sam. 16:14; Judg. 8:4-5). Esau sees Jacob's stew and asks for some of it, but he employs crass terminology. He says, literally, **'Let me greedily swallow'** — this verb appears nowhere else in Scripture, but it clearly carries the idea of gulping down.[14] The Mishnah uses the Hebrew term for feeding cattle (Sabb. 155b). It demonstrates that Esau is simply an uncouth glutton.

Esau's vehemence is underscored by the figure called gemination (when a word is repeated in immediate succession).[15] In the Hebrew, Esau demands **'red stuff, red stuff'** — a reiteration like this is a powerful way of emphasizing the object. Esau wants the stew, and he wants it now! The Hebrew term for **'red stuff'** is *'ādōm*, and that is why Esau is named Edom. He receives this additional name because of this incident of gluttony and impatience. His name is 'Red stuff'!

25:31-32. But Jacob said, 'First sell your birthright to me!' And Esau answered, 'Behold, I am going to die! So what is the birthright to me?'

Aware of his brother's great desire for food, Jacob strikes up a deal. It is that Esau should exchange his birthright for something to eat. Birthright was a very important matter in the Bible, and in the ancient Near East in general. The one with the right of the first-born had preferential status in the family. First, he would receive a double portion of the inheritance (see Deut. 21:17) — a law well known in Levantine cultures.[16] Secondly, the right meant that when the father died, the first-born would assume headship of the family structure.

The Nuzi laws from Mesopotamia, dating to the mid-second millennium B.C., demonstrate that birthrights were transferable.[17] One case is mentioned in the literature of a man selling his birthright for a sheep.

Esau's reply is an expression of his careless and indifferent attitude. Apparently he attaches no importance to the rich promises of God through Abraham, Isaac and their descendants. He is short-sighted and materialistic. He is living for the immediate gratification of his physical desires. The things seen mean more to him than the promises of God! That is why the author of the book of Hebrews calls Esau an 'immoral' and 'godless person' (Heb. 12:16).

25:33-34. And Jacob said, 'First, swear to me!' And he swore to him. Thus he sold his birthright to Jacob. So Jacob gave to Esau bread and lentil stew. And he ate and he drank and he arose and he went. And Esau despised the birthright.

Although Esau appears to accede to Jacob's demand
in the previous verse, Jacob requires more: he wants
Esau to swear to it. Esau must give an oath, and an
oath in the Hebrew Bible is when one binds oneself
to a promise. An oath is a holy, unbreakable word in
testimony to a promise.

At the close of the passage there appears a staccato succession of five verbs: he **'ate ... drank ...
arose ... went'** and **'despised'**. These verbs are held
together by a series of conjunctions. This sentence
construction is called a polysyndeton, that is, many
'ands' stringing verbs together. Its purpose is to draw
'our attention ... to the deliberateness of Esau's
action... He did not fall under some sudden temptation, but ... he deliberately and wilfully "despised
his birthright".'[18]

Numerous translations end the passage by saying
that Esau hated '*his* birthright' (e.g., NIV, NASB) —
and the birthright is referred to as being his earlier in
the passage. In the Hebrew, however, there is no
personal pronoun on this last instance of the word. It
simply says that he despised **'the birthright'**. That is
an important distinction because the birthright no
longer belongs to Esau at the end of the passage, but
it has an existence apart from him.

Application

If the world considered these two men it would undoubtedly be
drawn more to Esau than to Jacob. Esau is the outdoorsman, the
real man, the 'macho' type. Jacob, on the other hand, is inclined
to be a mother's boy, staying near the tents and cooking! But we
must remember that God does not view things the way mankind
does: 'for he does not see as man sees, for man looks at the
outward appearance, but Yahweh looks at the heart' (1 Sam.
16:7).

To Esau, the things seen mean more than the very promises of God. Hebrews 12:16, therefore, calls Esau a 'godless' or 'profane' man. The same author, a chapter earlier, in contrast, calls Jacob an heir (with Abraham) 'of the same promise' (Heb. 11:9) — for Jacob had faith in 'the assurance of things hoped for, the conviction of things not seen' (Heb. 11:1). Jacob certainly was not sinless, but he was a man of faith, the one through whom the seed of the woman was to come.

Isaac in Gerar
(Genesis 26:1-17)

A famine now occurs in the land, and Isaac is forced to migrate to the area of Gerar in the Negev, which is close to the coastal plain. The story that unfolds there is a conscious echo by the author of Abraham's trip to Egypt during a similar famine (12:10-20). Both of them fear for their lives, and then attempt to pass off their wives as their sisters. The women are beautiful and obviously excite envy. Critical scholars believe this duplication to be an indication of multiple sources for the book of Genesis. But that does not seem to be the case: the present author is well aware of the earlier material in Genesis, and he even makes reference to it (see 26:1).

26:1. Then there was a famine in the land — besides the first famine that occurred in the days of Abraham — and Isaac went down to Abimelech, King of the Philistines, to Gerar.

Famine in Canaan was often due to lack of rainfall. In such conditions, nomads were forced to move to find water and pasturelands for their flocks. Abraham had gone to Egypt because of a famine (12:10) — an event referred to in the present passage. Isaac is probably near Beer-Lahai-Roi in southern Canaan (25:11) and then moves to the region of Gerar.

In Gerar, Isaac meets with Abimelech. There has been much speculation regarding whether this is the same person that Abraham had dealings with in

Genesis 20-21. Some argue that it is the same monarch because his military commander has the same
name, Phicol (26:26). On the other hand, royal
names in the ancient Near East frequently passed
from one generation to another. In Egypt, for
example, Dynasties 19-20 had at least eleven kings
named Rameses (1307–1070 B.C.). The Masoretes,
who put in the pointing of the Hebrew text (i.e., the
vowels, accents, etc.), believed the two rulers to be
different: in the present chapter the name **'Abimelech'** has a *daghesh* in it (a dot that doubles the 'm'
in the name), whereas 'Abimelech' in chapters 20-21
does not contain a *daghesh*. This is a device to in-
sinuate the idea of its being another Abimelech.[19]

The mention of the people called the **'Philistines'**
has often been regarded as an anachronism. For a
discussion and repudiation of this view, see commentary on 21:32 (vol. 1, p.385).

26:2-6. Then Yahweh appeared to him, and he said, 'Do not
go down to Egypt; settle in the land that I will tell you. Sojourn
in this land. And I will be with you, and I will bless you. For to
you and your seed I will give all these lands. And I will
establish the oath that I swore to Abraham your father. And I
will multiply your seed as the stars of the heavens, and I will
give to your seed all these lands. And all the nations of the
earth will be blessed by your seed, because Abraham
listened to my voice, and he kept my requirements, my
commandments, my statutes and my laws.' So Isaac lived in
Gerar.

The statement that **'Yahweh appeared'** to Isaac is the
language of a theophany (see commentary on 12:7, vol.
1, p.255). In this physical manifestation, he tells Isaac
to **'settle'** in the land; this is a verb that literally
means 'to camp' or '[pitch a] tent', and it underlines
Isaac's nomadic lifestyle. The command to **'sojourn'**

reinforces that idea because it demonstrates Isaac's status as an alien and sojourner in a foreign land.

The promises of the covenant given to Abraham are repeated here for Isaac.[20] Isaac will be blessed (cf. 12:2) even in times of famine. He receives the promises of an innumerable posterity (cf. 15:5; 22:17), as many as the stars of heaven; a land (cf. 15:7,18-21); and nations being blessed through him (cf. 12:3; 18:18). At the heart of these divine pledges is the 'Immanuel principle' — that is, God is with Isaac (cf. 17:8). This scene, then, is a renewal with Isaac, the promised seed of Abraham, of the covenant made with Abraham.

26:7. When the men of the place asked about his wife, he said, 'She is my sister,' because he was afraid to say, 'My wife.' [He thought], 'Lest the men of the place kill me on account of Rebekah because she is beautiful.'

Because Rebekah is **'beautiful'** (in Hebrew, literally 'good in appearance') the men of the city ask about her. Isaac is afraid — the particle **'lest'** is one of fear and precaution. So he uses the strategy of saying she is his sister and not his wife. Isaac is thus protected, but Rebekah is not.

This strategy was used by Abraham twice before — in Egypt (12:10-20) and at Gerar (20:1-18). The wife / sister episode involving Isaac is far less dramatic, however.[21] No kidnapping occurs, and the king himself does not appear to be involved in the activity; it is the **'men of the place'** who are interested in her. So the danger is not as threatening as it was for Abraham. On the other hand, Isaac's response is a downright lie; at least with Abraham, Sarah was indeed his half-sister.

Because of the element of duplication, modern commentators suppose that we are dealing with material written by various authors.[22] In other words, different ancient authors applied the same story to different people. On the contrary, duplicates are an essential feature of ancient Near-Eastern narrative, and they are often used for emphasis.[23] It is called an 'echo literary strategy' (see commentary on Genesis 19, vol. 1, p.338, for further discussion).[24] The point for the present study is that Isaac acts in the same way as Abraham: like father, like son. Although they are both the chosen ones through whom the seed is to come, they are both still sinful and often weak (even failing in similar ways!).

26:8-9. And it came to pass when he had been there for a long time that Abimelech, King of the Philistines, looked out of the window, and he saw that, behold, Isaac was caressing Rebekah his wife. Then Abimelech called for Isaac, and he said, 'Indeed, she is your wife! So how could you say, "She is my sister"?' And Isaac answered him, 'For I said, "Lest I be killed on her account."'

The ruse works **'for a long time'**. However, not by design, Abimelech is looking out of **'the window'** one day and he sees Isaac and Rebekah caressing. The fact that the word 'window' has a definite article probably signifies that it is a particular window, perhaps one that the king uses to look out over the city. The king is surprised by what he sees: **'he saw ... behold'** (a particle of exclamation). It is difficult to know what Abimelech sees. The verb **'caressing'** is the verb from which the name 'Isaac' derives: it means, literally, 'to jest / laugh / play'.[25] Whatever it is they are doing, it indicates to Abimelech that they are married.

Isaac is called to account for his actions. The king is incensed. He begins his accusation with the word, **'Indeed'** — this term has an asseverative force in Hebrew; it is an earnest affirmation that Isaac has

been lying to him and his people.[26] Isaac answers
honestly: he has been afraid for his life.

26:10-11. Then Abimelech said, 'What is this you have done
to us? One of the people might easily have slept with your
wife, and you would have brought guilt on us.' So Abimelech
commanded all the people, saying, 'Whoever touches this
man or his wife will certainly be put to death.'

Abimelech confronts Isaac with righteous indignation. He knows his own people, and that one of
them could **'easily'** have slept with Rebekah — it is a
hypothetical assertion, but one of likely occurrence.[27]
The king also realizes that even if it were done in
ignorance, the act would have been wrong. Isaac
would thus have brought **'guilt'** on the people of
Gerar. That term signifies the violation of a vow that
requires sacrificial recompense.[28] It would have been
a serious crime to have committed adultery, even in
ignorance.

Abimelech gives a royal command to his people.
They are not to abuse Isaac, perhaps as an act of
vengeance for lying to the Gerarites. And they are not
to molest Rebekah — a married woman is not to be
treated in such a way. The king announces a harsh
punishment for any who violate these commands:
they **'will certainly be put to death'**. This sentence
construction consists of an infinitive absolute followed by an imperfective stem of the same verb. It is
thus emphatic. Throughout the ancient Near East
the death penalty was a common sentence for adultery (Laws of Eshnunna no. 28; Code of Hammurabi
no. 129).[29]

26:12-14. So Isaac planted seed in that land. And in that year
he reaped one hundred-fold, because Yahweh had blessed
him. And the man grew wealthy, and he continued to grow
wealthy until he was very wealthy. And he had so many

flocks and herds and servants that the Philistines were jealous of him.

Because of the famine (26:1), Isaac is forced to do agricultural labour. Cultivation of the land was an exceptional activity for the patriarchs, who were primarily keepers of livestock, migrating with their herds from one grazing-land to another. Yet Isaac's involvement in arable farming should not be sur- prising, for most of these people were semi-nomadic: that is, they supplemented their herding with some agricultural production (e.g., 30:14).

God blesses Isaac's planting by causing it to produce **'one hundred-fold'**: this is an exceptional return even for times of prosperity. Here it occurs during famine! The nature of the crop is uncertain, although the word for **'-fold'** or 'measure' has the same Hebrew consonants as the word for **'barley'**.

Isaac continually increases his wealth and prop- erty. The verb translated **'he continued'** bears the idea of long and steady progress.[30] The regular in- crease eventually results in Isaac's becoming **'very wealthy'**. The rabbis comment on this by saying, 'Rather the dung of Isaac's mules than all Abime- lech's gold and silver.'[31] Such wealth also results in great envy on the part of the Philistines, the inhabit- ants of Gerar.

26:15-17. And all the wells that the servants of his father dug in the days of Abraham his father, the Philistines stopped them up and they filled them with dust. And Abimelech said to Isaac, 'Go away from us because you have become too mighty for us.' So Isaac left there, and he camped by the wadi of Gerar. And he lived there.

Envy motivates the Philistines to make Isaac's wells inoperative — these are the wells dug by Abraham in Genesis 21:25-30. Water, of course, is essential for

Isaac as he attempts to herd his flocks in a period of
famine. Famine is often due to drought, and so the
need for water is critical. So this is the method the
Philistines use to drive out Isaac from their company.

Isaac's yielding to the king's command underscores the fact that he is not a citizen of the land. He
has few rights and privileges as an alien and sojourner. So Isaac departs, and he makes camp **'by
the wadi of Gerar'**. Some modern versions translate
the main noun as 'valley' rather than 'wadi' (NIV,
NASB). The latter rendition is better, however, because it is the principal meaning of the term in
Hebrew.[32] In addition, it fits the context since Isaac is
looking for water and so camps near a stream-bed.[33]

Application

It is ironic that Isaac became so wealthy during times of famine.
Normally, at such times, people scrape by and struggle to
maintain a moderate level of existence. But we need to understand that God is not bound by nature, and certainly famine does
not control him. And so we read that, when Isaac planted seed,
'Yahweh blessed him,' and his crops increased one hundred
times. Is that not true of the church throughout history, that
sometimes God's greatest gifts and mercies come to his people
during times of great earthly peril?

One only need think of the American war between the states
when God brought great revivals among both the northern and
southern armies. That civil war was the bloodiest contest that
Americans have ever experienced. God, however, used such
danger and peril to bring about his grand purpose of bringing
many to himself.

Dispute over wells
(Genesis 26:18-25)

In verses 3-4 of the present chapter, God had promised Isaac at Gerar that 'To your seed I will give all
these lands.' Thus Isaac has the divine promise that
these lands will one day belong to his posterity. So,
although he had been driven from the region, he now
returns to re-dig the wells of his father Abraham.
This appears to be an attempt on Isaac's part to lay a
claim to wells, and perhaps to the land around them.
But the inhabitants do not co-operate. Therefore,
Isaac has the promise but he does not have land.

26:18. But Isaac returned and he re-dug the wells of water
which had been dug in the days of Abraham his father, which
the Philistines had stopped up after the death of Abraham.
And he called them by the same names that his father had
called them.

In times of famine, water and watering rights become
especially critical in the land of Canaan. It is clear
that the water from the wadi of Gerar is not enough to
supply the needs of Isaac's flocks. So he returns to the
Gerar area in order to restore the wells of his father
Abraham. He succeeds, and then proceeds to name
the wells as they had been named during the time of
Abraham. The naming of something often indicates
authority over the object. By giving them names, Isaac
is claiming ownership of the wells. A confrontation is
bound to ensue because the Philistines had stopped

up the wells in order to drive out Isaac from the
region.

26:19-20. When Isaac's servants dug in the wadi, they found
there a well of running water. So the shepherds of Gerar
quarrelled with the shepherds of Isaac, saying, 'The water
belongs to us.' Thus he called the name of the well Esek
because they contended with him.

Water is precious, especially during times of famine
and drought. And spring water is more valuable than
cistern water. It has a fresh, continual flow and is,
thus, highly desirable. No wonder there is a dispute
over ownership and water rights!

Because of the trouble between his shepherds and
those of the Gerarites, Isaac names the spring
'Esek'. That name derives from the verb used in the
same sentence, **'to contend'** — the subterranean
spring is called 'contention'. Both the noun and the
verb occur nowhere else in the Bible. The noun in
rabbinic times was a legal term regarding a dispute
over the ownership of something.[34] Isaac is pressing
his ownership status by naming the well (see 26:18).

26:21-22. So they dug another well, and they also quarrelled
over it. And he called its name Sitnah. Thus he moved from
there and he dug another well. But they did not quarrel over
it. And he called its name Rehoboth, for he said, 'For now
Yahweh has made room for us, and we will be fruitful in the
land.'

So the servants of Isaac dig another well. But similar
consequences develop: the shepherds of Gerar and
Isaac's shepherds **'quarrelled'** over ownership and
water rights. Because of the enmity Isaac names the
well **'Sitnah'**, which in Hebrew literally means
'hostility'.[35]

Isaac yields to the Gerarites, and he moves away. This act is prudent on his part because he is an alien in the land, one with few rights of citizenship (such as owning property). His servants then dig another well. This time the results are different: there is no quarrel. Consequently, Isaac names this well **'Reho-both'**, which means, 'open spaces'. That name de-rives from the verb of the clause, **'Yahweh has made room for us.'** This site is generally located at er-Ruhebe, approximately nineteen miles south-west of Beersheba.[36]

26:23-25. Then he went up from there to Beersheba. And Yahweh appeared to him that night, and he said, 'I am the God of Abraham your father. Do not be afraid because I am with you, and I will bless you, and I will multiply your seed on account of Abraham my servant.' So he built an altar there, and he called on the name of Yahweh. And he pitched his tent there. And Isaac's servants dug a well there.

Leaving Rehoboth, Isaac journeys to **'Beersheba'**. Abraham had named this site (21:31-33) because of an oath he had made with Abimelech at a well. He also lived there for a while (22:19). Here **'Yahweh appeared'** to Isaac: this is the language of theophany (see 12:7; 26:2). In the physical manifestation, God renews the covenant promises to Isaac. He begins with the covenantal formula of self-identification: **'I am'**.[37] The title **'God of your father'** is used here for the first time in the Bible, but it appears frequently in the remainder of the book of Genesis (28:13; 31:42; 43:23; 46:3; 49:25). Its purpose is to tie the covenant promises of God from one generation to the next.

God then recounts the essentials of the covenant promises to Isaac: the Immanuel principle (**'I am with you'**), great blessing and an innumerable pos-terity (see 26:2-4). Isaac responds by erecting an altar to Yahweh, and calling on his name in worship. Abraham had responded in the same way to the appearance of Yahweh (see commentary on Genesis 12:7, vol. 1, p.255).

Application

Isaac is here reminded that the fulfilment of the promise of a land would not come to him, but rather to his seed after him (see 26:3-4). He lives in a tent as a nomad, and he is driven from one watering spot to the next. He has no home, and he has few rights. He is like his father Abraham who 'by faith ... lived as an alien in the land of promise, as in a foreign land, dwelling in tents with Isaac and Jacob, fellow heirs of the same promise' (Heb. 11:9). And though he is on the receiving end of much hostility from the people of the promised land, Isaac nevertheless demonstrates a sound and sure faith in Yahweh. He is thankful that Yahweh has made room for him and his people, and so he builds an altar and calls on the name of Yahweh.

How could Isaac respond in such a way? One would have thought he would have been in despair. But the author of the epistle to the Hebrews tells us that Isaac and others '... died in faith, without receiving the promises, but having seen them and having welcomed them from a distance, and having confessed that they were strangers and exiles on the earth. For those who say such things make it clear that they are seeking a country of their own ... they desire a better country, that is, a heavenly one' (Heb. 11:13-14,16).

Treaty with Abimelech
(Genesis 26:26-33)

Abimelech appears to be anxious about having a prosperous and growing band of livestock farmers near the borders of Gerar. Indeed, Isaac has been aggressive by reopening the wells that the Gerarites had closed on him. And his flocks continue to increase so that water and pasturage become an issue of possible conflict. Abimelech realizes that Isaac is stronger than the Gerarites now, so he seeks an audience with Isaac in order to make a treaty with him.

26:26-27. Then Abimelech came to him from Gerar, with Ahuzzath his councillor and with Phicol the commander of his army. And Isaac said to them, 'Why have you come to me when you were hostile to me and you sent me out from you?'

Abimelech travels from Gerar to Beersheba to meet with Isaac. He brings with him Ahuzzath, **'his councillor'**: that term in Hebrew literally means 'his friend'. It can have a technical usage, however, such as 'adviser / councillor' (see 2 Sam. 15:37; 16:16; 1 Kings 4:5; 1 Chr. 27:33); it demonstrates the closeness of the two individuals. A similar title is used of close advisers to the king throughout the ancient Near East.[38] The monarch also has Phicol, his military leader, at his side. He is there to represent a military presence and perhaps a veiled threat.

Abimelech initiates the talks with Isaac. Evidently
the latter has become a threat to the Gerarites. This
is certainly true from an economic standpoint (see
26:12-14), but perhaps also from a military perspective. This is confirmed by Isaac's re-digging of the
wells in an area that he had previously been driven
out from. Abimelech is insecure and so he comes to
make a treaty with Isaac.

26:28-29. And they answered, 'We have certainly seen that
Yahweh has been with you. So we said, "Let us now have a
sworn agreement between us" — between us and you. So
now let us make [literally, "cut"] a covenant with you, that you
will not do wrong to us — as we have not touched you, but
we have done only good to you, and we sent you out in
peace. May Yahweh now bless you!'

The Gerarites have seen that Yahweh has been with
Isaac; the evidence, of course, is affluence. Isaac has
been very successful in agriculture (26:12), in animal
husbandry (26:14) and in locating sources of water
(26:19). Their use of the name **'Yahweh'** is certainly
to ingratiate themselves with the patriarch. Because
of Isaac's strength and wealth the Gerarites want a
'sworn agreement' with him; this term is normally
used of the curses of an oath, but it can also signify
the entire treaty with sanctions (see Deut. 29:20).[39] A
good example of its use in such a general fashion is
Genesis 24:41.

The picture painted by the Gerarites of past relations between themselves and Isaac is pristine. The
reality is somewhat different. Not only did they not do
'good' to him, but they did not send him out **'in
peace'**. He was ejected from the community, and
they quarrelled with him time and again over water
rights. He was not treated well at all.

The final statement is an emphatic blessing on
Isaac which serves as an invocation to the covenant

that is about to be established. The stress is evident
in the Hebrew, in which the literal sentence structure
is **'You, now, may Yahweh bless!'**

26:30-31. So he prepared a feast for them, and they ate and
they drank. When they arose in the morning they swore an
oath to one another. Then Isaac sent them out, and they
went from him in peace.

There are two parts to the covenant ceremony between Isaac and the leaders of Gerar. The first consists of a ceremonial meal which serves as a physical
rite of ratification for the treaty. This was a common
covenantal ritual.[40] The second element is an oath
sworn by both parties of the agreement: it may include the imprecation or curse mentioned in verse
28. In the treaty ceremony of Genesis 31:53-54, the
order of the two actions is reversed. Laban and Jacob
first swear an oath and then they enjoy a meal. This
arrangement is more common, although there is no
known reason why the order should not be reversed.

In verse 27, Isaac had accused the Gerarites of
being 'hostile' to him, and then of having 'sent [him]
out'. Now, in reverse, Isaac **'sent them out'** — this
time not in animosity, but **'in peace'**. This chiasmus
highlights the contrast between the two situations.

26:32-33. And it came to pass on that day that the servants
of Isaac came and told him about the well that they had dug.
And they said to him, 'We have found water.' So he called it
Shibah; therefore the name of the city is Beersheba to this
day.

The phrase, **'on that day'**, ties the current event to
the oath that had just been sworn by Isaac and the
Gerarites. That is important because Isaac names the
well **'Shibah'**, which is a word-play on the Hebrew

term for an 'oath'. **'Beersheba'** literally means 'the well of the oath'.

This is not the first time that the well and area have been named **'Beersheba'**. Abraham had previously dug a well here, made an oath with Abimelech and called the site 'Beersheba'. How are we to understand the relationship between these two accounts? Some scholars, like Von Rad, argue that they are two separate interpretations of the origin of the name.[41] Others suppose that there was only one incident but that separate authors have attributed it to two different patriarchs.[42] The reality is that Isaac digs up Abraham's earlier well at the site, and he gives it the same name. Verse 18 of the chapter confirms it, when it says, 'But Isaac returned and he re-dug the wells of water which had been dug in the days of Abraham ... and he called them by the same names that his father had called them.'

Application

When staying in Gerar, Isaac must have made it very clear that he was a follower of Yahweh. In the present episode, Abimelech and the other leaders of Gerar recognize that Yahweh has been with Isaac, and they even pronounce a blessing on him in the name of Yahweh! Even though he had lied to them, his life since that incident has displayed the blessings of God on him — it has been evangelistic. And, indeed, the life of the Christian can be a living sermon — that is, declaring the glory of God and the gospel of Jesus Christ. When Martin Luther gave the eulogy for Nicholas Hausmann, pastor of Zwickau, in 1522, he simply said, 'What we preach, he lives.' May all of our lives be a wonderful testimony to the truth of Yahweh!

The blessing
(Genesis 26:34 – 27:4)

The opening two verses of this section describe Esau's marriages to Hittite women, and how those women prove a burden to Isaac and Rebekah. The purpose of these verses is to serve as a bridge between the story of Esau's selling his birthright (25:29-34) and the stealing of his blessing by Jacob (27:1-40). They draw the reader back to that episode because they take up the theme of the flaws in Esau's character — both stories highlight his nature of indifference and rebelliousness.

In addition, Genesis 27:1-4 also takes the reader back to the earlier incident. Isaac still loves Esau, despite his character, and gives him preferential treatment. And, even though Esau has sold his birthright, Isaac still wants to give him the supreme blessing.

26:34-35. And it came to pass when Esau was forty years old that he married Judith the daughter of Beeri the Hittite and Basemath the daughter of Elon the Hittite. And they were a bitter spirit to Isaac and to Rebekah.

The contentious spirit of Esau is now seen in his marriage relationships. First, he is polygamous. Secondly, and perhaps this was the more heinous offence at that time, Esau marries Hittite women, not ones from his own clan or family structure.[43] These women apparently cause great problems for Isaac

and Rebekah: they are **'a bitter spirit'**. This may be
taken in one of two ways. Either they are a cause of
grief in the hearts of Isaac and his wife, or it is their
own spirits that are contentious and rebellious. In
either case, there is great animosity between the
wives of Esau and his parents.

Since Esau is forty years old when he marries,
Isaac is one hundred years old at the time (see
25:26). This fact sets the scene for the following story
in which Isaac is blind and appears feeble.

27:1. And it came to pass when Isaac was old and his eyes
were too faint to see that he called Esau his eldest son. And
he said to him, 'My son.' And he answered him, 'Here I am.'

Isaac is blind in his old age. The phrase literally says,
'His eyes were dim away from seeing' — the term
'away from' is the *min* of separation in Hebrew. It
has a pregnant force that indicates that Isaac cannot
see.[44] Rabbinic commentators provide many reasons
for Isaac's blindness: for instance, 'His eyes were dim
through the smoke raised by these women [i.e.,
Esau's wives] in offering incense to idols'; or 'When
Isaac was bound upon the altar and his father was
about to slay him, at that very moment the heavens
opened, the ministering angels saw it and wept, and
their tears flowed and fell upon Isaac's eyes which
thus became dim.'[45] The Scriptures, on the contrary,
indicate that Isaac's blindness is due to old age.

Isaac's blindness may not merely be physical. It
may also signify that he is unable to see the true
nature of his eldest son. Even with the fiascos of
Esau's marriages, Isaac appears still to favour him
over Jacob. It should also be noted that the author
does not call Esau the first-born son, but the eldest.
The fact is that Esau had sold that status of birthright to Jacob (25:29-34).[46]

27:2-4. And he said, 'Behold I am old; I do not know the day of my death. But, now, please, take your arms, your quiver and your bow, and go out to the field and hunt game for me. And make tasty food for me as I love. Then bring it to me so that I may eat — so that my soul will bless you before I die.'

Isaac's address to Esau is fiery. He employs five imperatives — **'take ... go out ... hunt ... make ... bring'** — and one cohortative, **'eat'**. Such language constructions emphasize greatly the assertiveness of the patriarch. In addition, in the Hebrew the volition that Esau should **'hunt game'** is a verb with a cognate noun — authors use that type of construction as a kind of superlative.

Isaac's preferential treatment of Esau takes us back to 25:28, where it says, 'Isaac loved Esau because [he put] game in his mouth.' Isaac's predilection for Esau continues into his old age, even though Esau has behaved poorly. The words **'love'**, **'hunt,'** and **'game'** appear in both passages in order to draw the reader's attention to the continuing moral blindness of Isaac. Indeed, the **'I love'** in the present passage is a durative stative perfect form of the verb that reflects an ongoing emotional response.[47]

The expression linking the **'soul'** with the act of 'blessing' another person is found three times in this passage (27:19,25,31). Its repeated presence may indicate that it is technical language for some type of ritual or ceremony.[48] The preparation of a meal, then, appears to be a part of the ceremony tied to the act of pronouncing the blessing.

Application

Isaac's blind treatment of Esau is hard for us to understand. Here is a son who is disobedient — one who marries Hittites and appears to be indifferent to life. He is quite callous. Yet, when we look into our own hearts and see how we treat our own children, Isaac's blindness is not so difficult to understand. How often we turn a blind eye to them. Do we really know where they are spiritually? Do we know if they are of the seed of the woman? Do we treat our children as if they can do no wrong?

In Jerusalem there is a monument called Absalom's Pillar in the Kidron Valley. According to Matthew Henry, it used to be common for foreign travellers 'to throw a stone to this heap, with words to this purpose: "Cursed be the memory of wicked Absalom, and cursed for ever be all wicked children, that rise up in rebellion against their parents."' It is a sobering matter to have such children — but let us not be guilty of compounding the problem by turning a deaf ear or a blind eye to their plight. May we minister to them and share the love of Christ with them. And may God be praised when he takes one of these sinners, changes his / her heart, and claims that son or daughter as his own.

Rebekah the trickster
(Genesis 27:5-17)

Rebekah, the wife of Isaac, is the principal character
in this next section. The theme is the plot of deception that Jacob will use to take the blessing from his
brother Esau. Rebekah is the prime motivator of the
action. She goads Jacob to carry out her plan —
even to the point of saying that she will take the
curse on herself if the plot fails. The author does not
reveal to us her intentions, apart from the obvious
result that Jacob will be the recipient of his father's
blessing.

27:5-7. And Rebekah was listening when Isaac spoke to
Esau his son. Then Esau went to the field to hunt game to
bring [back]. So Rebekah spoke to Jacob her son, saying,
'Behold, I heard your father speaking to Esau your brother,
saying, "Bring game to me, and make tasty food for me that I
may eat. Then I will bless you in the presence of Yahweh
before my death."'

Rebekah overhears the conversation between Isaac
and Esau. Of course, she wants to protect the interests of Jacob. The family division is quite evident
here: Esau is called **'his son'** and Jacob is called
'her son'. She then relates the conversation to Jacob. The major difference between the original dialogue and Rebekah's recital is that she adds the
words: **'in the presence of Yahweh'**. Certainly she is
attempting to impress on Jacob the importance and

solemnity of the act of blessing that is about to take place. It is one that requires divine presence and sanction.

27:8-10. 'And now, my son, listen to my voice, to that which I am commanding you: go, please, to the flock and take for me from there two choice young goats. And I will make them into tasty food for your father, as he loves. And you shall bring [it] to your father so that he may eat, in order that he may bless you before his death.'

Because of Rebekah's love for Jacob, she plots and conspires to pirate the blessing from Esau through stealth.[49] She is the principal active participant in the drama — she devises the plan, and then she 'commands' Jacob to carry it through. Rebekah's scheme is a cunning one. Jacob and his mother will prepare **'tasty food'** of the kind that Isaac has requested from Esau (see 27:4). Then Jacob is to take the meal to his father, pretending to be Esau, and thus receive the blessing Isaac had reserved for his eldest son.

27:11-12. But Jacob said to Rebekah his mother, 'Behold, Esau, my brother, is a hairy man and I am a smooth man. Perhaps my father will feel me, and I will be a mocker in his eyes. Thus I will bring on myself a curse and not a blessing.'

Jacob is cautious, and he responds to his mother with a caveat. Note that he does not complain about the morality of the act, but his concern is only whether he will be discovered in his deception. He would not be acting out of ignorance, but he clearly realizes it is an act of 'mockery', or deception. Jacob, in fact, calls himself a **'smooth man'** — ironically that term is used primarily of one who is slippery or seductive! (see Ps. 5:9; 55:21; Prov. 2:15; 7:5).

The contrast between the physical natures of Jacob and Esau comes to be enshrined in a geopolitical word-play.[50] Jacob says that Esau is a *sāʿir* man and he himself is a *ḥālāq* man. In the conquest account of Joshua it is said that Joshua captured all the land 'from Mount Halak *(ḥālāq)* that goes up to Seir *(sēʿîr)*' (Josh. 11:17). Mount Halak is part of the area that Israel captured, but Mount Seir remains under Edomite control (i.e., that of Esau's descendants). As in the story of Jacob and Esau, Israel hesitates to encroach on Edom's territory.[51]

27:13-14. And his mother said to him, 'Your curse be on me, my son. Just listen to my voice, and go, take [them] for me!' And he went and he took [them] and he brought [them] to his mother. And his mother made tasty food as his father loved.

Rebekah allays Jacob's fears by appropriating the curse to herself. In other words, if Isaac discovers the ruse, then Rebekah demands that the consequences should fall on her own head and not on that of Jacob. Yet it may be that she believes she is safe in taking this oath, remembering that God had promised that the older would serve the younger (25:23). She may have been acting on that promise.[52]

The word **'just'** is a restrictive adverb of instruction.[53] As such, it serves to restrict what has gone before. Even though the curse may fall on Rebekah as a result of the deception, *nevertheless* Jacob is to perform his duty. And he does his work in an efficient way. The staccato succession of verbs without objects attests to the character of his activity: **'he went ... he took ... he brought'**.

27:15-17. Then Rebekah took the precious clothes of her elder son Esau which were with her in the house, and she clothed Jacob her younger son. And the hides of the young goats she put on his hands and on the smooth portion of his neck. And she gave the tasty food and the bread she had made into the hand of Jacob her son.

The plot thickens. First, Rebekah makes Jacob put on Esau's **'precious clothes'** — this refers to dress probably reserved for ceremonial use.[54] It supports the idea that the giving of the blessing is an important ritual that is tied to a ceremony in Hebrew culture. Next, she covers the bare places on Jacob's body with the skins of the animals she had cooked. This action is, of course, also intended to deceive because Esau is a hairy man. And, finally, Rebekah gives Jacob the festive meal to take to his father; this is the meal that Isaac had requested from Esau. All of this is done at the behest of Rebekah — Rebekah, the trickster!

Application

Abraham and Sarah had displayed great impatience with the promises of God. God had declared that through them a son would be born to carry on the promised line of the seed. Abraham and Sarah then used various means in an attempt to bring about God's promise, such as adopting Eleazar of Damascus as an heir, and Abraham's fathering a son by Sarah's handmaid Hagar. They were apparently unwilling to wait on the timing of God. Rebekah, the daughter-in-law of Abraham and Sarah, now reflects their impatience. It appears that she plotted and connived against her husband in order to ensure that the promise of God would come on her son Jacob. Rather than waiting on the Lord, she sought to bring his work to fruition.

As if God were in need of us to bring about his promises! Some in the church today act as if God's kingdom will not be built unless they are building it. That is bogus — it is God who erects his own kingdom, and he has done that by sending his Son Christ. He may use us in kingdom-building, and sometimes even in our sinful ways, but he is not dependent on us. I once heard a pastor proclaim that 'God never violates man's sovereignty'! Wait a minute — who sits on the throne of the universe? May we proclaim with the apostle John: 'To him who sits on the throne, and to the Lamb, be blessing and honour and glory and dominion for ever and ever' (Rev. 5:13).

The blessing of Jacob
(Genesis 27:18-29)

Rebekah's plan is now executed by Jacob. As the plot unfolds, it is obvious that Isaac is inclined to be wary of what is going on in front of him. He resorts to various tests involving different senses in order to establish whether the son before him really is Esau. Jacob is able, through physical deception and downright lying, to overcome all of Isaac's objections and trials. Finally, Jacob receives the blessing meant for Esau.

27:18-19. And he came to his father. And he said, 'My father'. And he said, 'Here I am. Who are you, my son?' And Jacob said to his father, 'I am Esau your first-born. I have done according to what you said to me. Arise, now sit and eat from my game so that your soul might bless me.'

Jacob now puts Rebekah's plan into effect. He visits his father and begins the conversation by saying, **'My father'** — in Hebrew it is only one word. Perhaps Jacob is somewhat reluctant to address Isaac, or maybe he is attempting to conceal his voice from his father. Jacob's curt introduction ought to be compared with Esau's lengthy preface found later in verse 31.

Apparently Isaac does not recognize the voice as that of Esau. He may be blind, but he obviously has fairly good hearing! So Isaac asks Jacob who he is.

Here the deception becomes stark and blatant: Jacob answers, **'I am Esau.'** It is, of course, an outright lie.

27:20. And Isaac said to his son, 'How did you ever find [it] so quickly, my son?' And he answered, 'Because Yahweh your God caused it to happen to me.'

Isaac's response expresses astonishment. He is asking an animated question without really expecting a reply (this is called erotesis). In the Hebrew sentence construction there appears an enclitic particle which is being used for emphasis, and which we can translate as **'ever'**.[55] Isaac simply finds it hard to believe that his son could have trapped an animal and prepared it for eating in such a short time.

Jacob now invokes God's name in his lie. He declares that it was Yahweh who gave him good fortune, or success, in finding and preparing the game so quickly. Ironically, it is God who has chosen him as the one through whom the promised seed would come, but Yahweh is certainly not sanctioning Jacob's deception. Isaac would definitely have understood Jacob's answer because it is an idiom — one in fact that was used by Abraham's servant when looking for a wife for Isaac! (see 24:12). It is a standard formula reflecting the providence of God operating throughout the earth.

27:21-23. And Isaac said to Jacob, 'Please draw near that I might feel you, my son, [to know] whether you really are my son Esau or not.' So Jacob drew near to Isaac his father, and he touched him. And he said, 'The voice is the voice of Jacob, but the hands are the hands of Esau.' Thus he did not recognize him because his hands were hairy like the hands of Esau his brother. So he blessed him.

Isaac is intent on discovering if the man in his presence is truly Esau. The particle translated **'really'** is

zĕh in Hebrew, and it is being used in an emphatic
fashion. It is the same word that is translated **'ever'**
in verse 20, where it is also used to demonstrate
heightened inquisitiveness on the part of Isaac.

Because Isaac is blind he resorts to relying on his
other senses to tell if it is Esau who is before him.
Through the sense of hearing, Isaac senses that it is
Jacob — but through touch he senses it is Esau. The
latter sense impression carries more weight since
Isaac is convinced by it. He does not **'recognize'**
Jacob: that verb (in the Hiphil pattern) signifies more
than a mere physical recognition, but the fact that
Isaac does not perceive the true situation in general.[56]

The end of the verse says that Isaac **'blessed him'**.
This presents a problem because the blessing does
not take place until later in the section, and it is
obvious that Isaac does not bless Jacob twice. The
verb is imperfect and may, therefore, carry the idea
that Isaac is about to bless Jacob, but has not yet
done it. A suitable translation might be: **'So he was
about to bless him.'**[57]

27:24-25. And he said, 'Are you really my son Esau?' And he
said, 'I am.' So he said, 'Bring [it] to me so that I might eat
from my son's game, so that my soul might bless you.' Thus
he brought [it] to him, and he ate. And he brought wine to him
and he drank.

For the third time the particle *zĕh* appears in Isaac's
speech regarding the identity of his son. Here it is
translated **'really'**, and it is employed for stress.
Isaac is in a confused state, so he asks Jacob directly
whether or not he is Esau. Isaac is getting close to
the heart of the matter, and he is forcing Jacob to
answer one way or another. In Hebrew, Jacob gives a
one-word response. He is curt, to the point, and
answering with a downright lie.

Isaac then tests the situation with his sense of taste. He wants to make certain that the food has been prepared the way that Esau is known to prepare it (see 27:4). Thus far, Isaac has used his senses of hearing, touching and tasting to determine the identity of the son before him.

27:26-29. And Isaac his father said to him, 'Please draw near and kiss me, my son.' And he drew near and he kissed him. When he smelled the scent of his clothes, then he blessed him. And he said:

> 'See, the scent of my son
> is like the scent of the field
> that Yahweh has blessed.
> May God give to you the dew of heaven
> and from the fertility of earth
> and plentiful grain and new wine.
> May nations serve you
> and may peoples bow down to you.
> Be lord of your brothers
> and may the sons of your mother bow down to you.
> May the ones who curse you be cursed
> and the ones who bless you be blessed.'

Prior to bestowing the blessing, Isaac employs one further sense test: he smells the clothes worn by his son. Rebekah had, of course, given Jacob some of Esau's clothes to wear (27:15), and so he smells like his brother. Once this final test has been passed, Isaac proceeds to bless his son.

The blessing contains three general messages. First, Isaac calls for God to bring forth creation's produce for his son. In Scripture the granting of **'the dew of heaven'** often denotes the giving of great material blessing (see Deut. 33:13; Hag. 1:10; Zech. 8:12).[58] When combined with **'grain and new wine'** it is idiomatic for great fertility (Deut. 33:28).

The second part of the blessing calls for Jacob to have prominence and pre-eminence over nations and over his brothers. This is essentially the same as God's promise to Rebekah when the children were born: 'And one people will be stronger than the other people, and the older will serve the younger' (25:23). Naturally, this segment of the blessing is covenantal — it speaks to both Jacob and his progeny.

In this second section of the blessing, the term **'and'** seems superfluous. However, when lines in parallel have the identical meaning, the conjunction serves to intensify the poetry.[59] It is called a *waw emphaticum.*

The final two lines of the blessing sound familiar. When God first spoke to Abraham, he had said, 'And I will bless those who bless you, and the ones who curse you I will curse' (12:3). The present text essentially says the same thing, except that the grammatical construction is different. In Jacob's blessing, both lines of the parallel consist of a subject followed by a predicate. The identical word order, in reality, points to and underscores a contrast.[60] The parallel, therefore, is a severe antithesis.

Another grammatical point to consider is that in both lines there is a plural subject with a singular predicate. When this happens, 'Instead of the whole class of individuals, each severally is to be represented as affected by the statement.'[61] These lines, of course, fit into the overall theme and scheme of Genesis — that is, the enmity between the seed of the woman and the seed of the serpent. The Messiah will be descended from the line of Jacob.

Application

Back in Genesis 25:23, God had promised Rebekah that the older son — Esau — would eventually serve the younger son —

Jacob. In the present section, Jacob and Rebekah attempt to bring God's promise to pass by Jacob's securing the blessing of the first-born that Isaac was going to give to Esau. Jacob relies on cunning and deception throughout. On the one hand, God's purpose for Jacob is coming about, but, on the other hand, the Lord does not sanction or approve of Jacob's methods. It reminds us of the early life of Moses. The first act recorded of Moses' life is his killing of an Egyptian man. This murder led to his flight from Egypt. Yet God used that great sin to bring about his purposes for the nation of Israel — in the wilderness he prepared Moses to shepherd the Hebrews through that barren land. We should realize that God uses even the misdeeds of mankind to bring about his good purposes in creation. He is simply sovereign.

Do we really believe that our sin in some way will delay for one moment the plan of God? Even the devil in all his malevolent glory cannot postpone any work of God and, certainly, he cannot sway the redemptive decrees of God Almighty! As for Jacob, he used deceit to gain the blessing — and God made use of it in his redemptive plans to bring the promised seed through Jacob.

Esau's blessing
(Genesis 27:30-45)

Tension mounts in the story. Esau, unaware of what has happened, returns from the field and prepares a tasty dish for his father. He does all that Isaac has asked, yet he discovers that he is a victim of a heartless plot. The author portrays Esau as an innocent dupe, one who has been fooled by his brother's deceit. Esau is simply the victim of guile and treachery. Most telling, however, is the fact that the deed cannot be undone. Jacob has been blessed and, indeed, the blessing will stand.

27:30-31. And it came to pass when Isaac finished blessing Jacob, and Jacob had only just gone out from the presence of Isaac, his father, that Esau, his brother, came from his hunting. And he also made tasty food and he brought [it] to his father. And he said to his father, 'Let my father arise, and eat from his son's game, so that your soul might bless me.'

Esau, unaware of recent events, comes to his father's tent. He has done all that Isaac has asked, having prepared **'tasty food'** for him.[62] But the author emphasizes the problem at hand: he says, literally, that **'he made, also he'**. The word **'also'** is stressing the personal pronoun.[63] Esau has made the dish, but he is not the first to do so.

The author heightens the drama to fever pitch. The phrase **'just gone out'** is an infinitive absolute followed by a perfect of the same verb. It is used here to stress the immediacy involved in the timing of the events. With the addition of the particle **'only'**, the Hebrew writer is saying that one scene occurs after the other in rapid succession.[64]

27:32-33. And Isaac, his father, said to him, 'Who are you?' And he said, 'I am your son, your first-born, Esau.' Then Isaac trembled exceedingly, and he said, 'Who then was it who hunted game and brought [it] to me, and I ate all of it, before you came, and I blessed him? Indeed, he will be blessed!'

Isaac asks the same question that he had previously put to Jacob (27:18), except that he does not include the words, 'my son'. Obviously, Isaac is cautious that the one before him may be an impostor. He believes he has already given the blessing to Esau. Esau answers Isaac in much the same way as Jacob: **'I am your son, your first-born, Esau'** (see 27:19). Such parallels underscore the great contrast.

Isaac's first response is a physical one. The Hebrew literally says that he **'trembled a great trembling exceedingly'**. The severity of Isaac's reaction is highlighted by the use of the verb with its cognate noun. In addition, the term for **'exceedingly'** is frequently found in Hebrew to signify a superlative of degree.[65]

Isaac then asks a question expressing incredulity: **'Who, then ... ?'** When the particle **'then'** appears immediately after an interrogative it serves to give vividness to the question.[66]

Isaac's final response is to proclaim that even though the blessing was procured through deceit, it cannot be revoked.[67] The blessing has Yahweh's approval (see 27:7). The term in Hebrew for **'indeed'** serves to introduce an intensive clause — the blessing of Jacob will stand.[68]

27:34-35. When Esau heard the words of his father he cried out with an exceedingly great and bitter cry. Then he said to his father, 'Bless me, also me, my father!' And he said, 'Your brother came treacherously and he took your blessing.'

The grammatical construction of Esau's response is parallel to that of Isaac's reaction in verse 33. Here a verb with a cognate noun is used: **'he cried out ... cry'**, which is a condition that emphasizes the assertion. Next, the particles **'great'** and **'exceedingly'** are again used in order to denote the stress of the response. In addition, both father and son employ the Hebrew word *gam*, translated here as **'also'** and in verse 33 as 'indeed'. The term *gam* may, as Muraoka suggests, have no special emphasis, but the repetition of the term **'me'** in Esau's plea certainly does.[69]

There may be a word-play between **'bitter'** (Hebrew *mārāh*) and **'treacherously'** (Hebrew *mirᵉmah*). These similar-sounding words possibly point to a contrast between the characters of the two sons: one is ill-tempered and vulgar, and the other is deceitful and dishonest.

27:36-37. And he said, 'Is this the reason his name is called Jacob that he deceived me these two times? He took my birthright, and now, behold, he has taken my blessing!' And he said, 'Did you not reserve a blessing for me?' Then Isaac answered, and he said, 'Behold I have set him [as] lord over you, and all his brothers I have given to him as servants. And I have sustained him [with] grain and new wine. What then can I do for you, my son?'

In his state of discontent, Esau resorts to word-plays or puns to emphasize the striking nature of Jacob's actions. First, the name **'Jacob'** appears to be a cognate of the verb translated **'deceived'**. This verb literally means 'to follow at the heel', and its figurative sense is 'to assail insidiously'.[70] Esau's use of it here indicates that Jacob has rightly lived up to his birth-name.

A second word-play appears in the sentence, **'He took my birthright'** (Hebrew consonants *b-k-r*) **'and now behold he has taken my blessing'** (Hebrew consonants *b-r-k*). In addition, an alteration of elements appears in these two lines that serve as a chiasmus:

a   b

my birthright   he took

b¹   a¹

he took   my blessing

This introverted correspondence serves the purpose of making clear a precise meaning.

In Isaac's final question he uses the enclitic particle **'then'**; he had employed that word earlier (27:33). Its purpose is to give vividness and force to the question.

27:38-40. So Esau said to his father, 'Do you have only one blessing, my father? Bless me, also me, my father!' Then Esau lifted his voice and he cried. Then Isaac answered his son, and he said to him:

> 'Behold, away from the fertility of the earth will be your
>   dwelling-place,
> and away from the dew of heaven above.
> And you will live by the sword,
> and you will serve your brother.
> And it will be when you become restless
> that you will tear off his yoke from your neck.'

The Septuagint adds the statement, 'Isaac said nothing' between Esau's words of despair[71] and his lifting up of his voice. It is not, however, found in any early Hebrew manuscripts. Isaac's silence in regard

to Esau's request is obvious and it need not be
stated.

Isaac's pronouncement on Esau sounds more like
a curse than a blessing. Although the first two lines
appear to be similar to the blessing on Jacob in verse
28, there are some major distinctions. First, the two
lines are reversed, as following:

27:28   dew of heaven ———————> fertility of earth
27:39   fertility of earth ———————> dew of heaven

This alteration underscores the contrast between the
two.

Second, the preposition before these two elements
is a privative *min* (that is, it reflects being *without*
something).[72] Of course, a lack of fertility and water
characterizes the land of Edom where Esau's descendants eventually settle.

The final lines of the poem signify that one day
Edom will throw off the domination of Jacob and his
descendants. In biblical history, this development is
easily traced (see, for instance, the book of Obadiah).

27:41. Thus Esau bore a grudge against Jacob regarding the
blessing [with] which his father blessed him. And Esau said
in his heart, 'The days of mourning for my father draw near;
then I will kill Jacob, my brother.'

Esau realizes that Isaac, his father, will soon die. His
death will be followed by a period of mourning (see,
for example, 2 Sam. 11:27). Isaac will no longer be
head of the clan, and he will be unable to intervene
between the two brothers. So Esau decides that he
will kill Jacob at that time. The phrase **'said in his
heart'** does not mean that he kept it to himself.
Rather, it is a Hebrew idiom signifying that he has
made a resolution — it is a determination of his mind
and will.[73]

27:42-45. And the words of Esau, her eldest son, were told to Rebekah. Then she sent for and called for Jacob, her youngest son. And she said to him, 'Behold, Esau, your brother, is comforting himself concerning you [with a plan] to kill you. So now, my son, listen to my voice: arise, flee to Laban, my brother, to Haran! And stay with him for some time until your brother's ire subsides. When your brother's anger subsides against you, and he forgets what you have done to him, then I will send and I will take you from there. Why should I be bereaved of the two of you in one day?'

Esau clearly does not keep his thoughts to himself. His murderous plan is reported to Rebekah. She is alarmed and, therefore, plots a strategy.[74] She summons Jacob and with great intensity commands him to run away to Haran, to the safety of his uncle Laban. The verbs **'arise'** and **'flee'** are imperatives. Tied to the second verb by a *maqqef* (a Hebrew hyphen) is a preposition with a personal pronoun — it literally reads, **'Flee for yourself to Laban.'** The preposition with the pronoun is unnecessary in the sentence and it is often left untranslated; however, it is there 'to give emphasis to the significance of the occurrence in question *for* a particular subject'.[75]

Haran is in north-western Mesopotamia. It was to Haran that Terah and Abraham migrated after they had left Ur. Terah died there (11:31-32).[76]

Rebekah concludes her speech with a rhetorical question. In other words, she is not expecting an answer or wishing to obtain any information. It is an interrogative of affirmation or indignation. It is a change of speech pattern that accentuates her premonition of impending danger.

Application

Although Jacob secures the rights and privileges of the first-born, he does so in a deceitful way. And even though God had promised that 'The older will serve the younger', Jacob obtains that status through guile. Because of his sin, he receives temporal consequences. Esau desires to kill him, and he is forced to flee for his life to Haran. Later events of suffering in Jacob's life may also be identified as results of these early incidents of deception.

In true piety, the ends never justify the means. Jacob was simply seizing God's promise through sinful means. We too are like Jacob. Many in the church today have a desire to do good things for the glory of Christ and to obtain his promises for the church, yet are lax and careless as to how they are done. Often men professing faith follow the world rather than being prepared to trust in God that he will keep his word in his own way and timing.

Jacob departs
(Genesis 27:46 – 28:9)

Some commentators believe that this section is the work of a different author from the one who wrote the previous material in the account of Jacob. V. Mathews and F. Mims put it this way: 'Tone change comes with change of voice when the priestly (and thus more theological account) begins in Gen. 27:46. The new speaker's tone is distant and sanctimonious, revealing no discord, no anger, no deception. The story loses its drama and intensity, and the characters lose colour, emotional dimension, and individuality.'[77] Yet it must be recognized that change in tone is a very subjective rationale for positing the appearance of a new author. Every document has a certain amount of change in tone. As for lack of discord and drama, I would argue that they are here in abundance. Finally, as we shall see, the literary structure of the present material goes hand in hand with what has preceded it — it is a well-defined and well-thought-out passage.

27:46. And Rebekah said to Isaac, 'I hate my life because of the daughters of Heth. If Jacob takes a wife from the daughters of Heth, like these from the daughters of the land, why should I go on living?'

Rebekah must find a pretext for Jacob to go to her family in Haran. It would be unwise for her to share the true reason with Isaac, for her part in the plot

might be revealed. Also, because Isaac favours Esau
he might not intervene, or even allow Jacob to depart. In any event, Rebekah uses a secondary reason
for Isaac to send Jacob away. The daughters of Heth
(or Hittites) have already been mentioned, and they
have been a source of grief for both Rebekah and
Isaac (see 26:34-35). Rebekah argues that the problem will be exacerbated if Jacob marries someone like
them. Rebekah's unhappiness is also a source of
discord, and Isaac obviously must act upon the
situation.

The verb that Rebekah employs regarding her life
is quite strong. She says, **'I hate my life.'** That verb
means 'to abhor / loathe / have sickening dread'.[78] It
is a term used of the Hebrews' attitude towards
manna and quail in one instance of grumbling during
the Exodus (Num. 21:5), and of God's hatred of the
pagan practices of the Canaanites (Lev. 20:23).

28:1-2. So Isaac called for Jacob, and he blessed him. Then
he commanded him, and he said to him, 'Do not take a wife
from the daughters of Canaan. Arise, go to Paddan-Aram, to
the house of Bethuel, the father of your mother. And take for
yourself from there a wife from the daughters of Laban, your
mother's brother.'

Some have attempted to argue that there is no real
blessing in this encounter between Isaac and Jacob.
Rather, the term translated **'blessed'** simply means
to greet a person.[79] While that may be the case in
some instances, the present example does include
aspects of true blessing — especially verses 3-4.[80] It
is indeed a blessing, and its purpose is to confirm the
basic content of the previous blessing in 27:28-29.

28:3-4. 'And may El Shaddai bless you, and make you
fruitful, and multiply you so that you might be an assembly of
people. And may he give to you the blessing of Abraham, to

you and to your seed with you, so that you may possess the land of your sojournings, which God gave to Abraham.'

Isaac is directly linking this blessing with God's blessings of Abraham in Genesis 12 and 17. First, he uses the name **'El Shaddai'** as the one who is called on to bless Jacob. In Genesis 17:1, God revealed himself to Abraham by proclaiming, 'I am El Shaddai.' The precise meaning of **'Shaddai'** is difficult to determine, although many scholars, following Albright, argue that it is related to the Akkadian term *šadū*, which means 'mountain'.[81] Thus the Lord would be the 'God of the mountain' (perhaps anticipating Sinai?).

Second, this blessing of Jacob centres on the two ideas of nationhood and land. This is the first time the term **'assembly'** is used in the Bible. It is a word that almost always refers to the congregation of the people of Israel — this part of the blessing perhaps anticipates the founding of that group.[82] Both of these promises, a people and a land, were previously given to Abraham in Genesis 12 and 17.

The use of the term **'seed'** here confirms the fact that the line of the seed of the woman will be continued through the person of Jacob. It is through him and his descendants that the Messiah will come.

28:5. So Isaac sent Jacob, and he went to Paddan-Aram, to Laban the son of Bethuel the Aramaean, the brother of Rebekah, the mother of Jacob and Esau.

Rebekah's plan for Jacob's safety comes to pass. With Isaac's blessings and directives, Jacob travels to north-west Mesopotamia, to the family of Rebekah. Regarding the last phrase of the verse, **'the mother of Jacob and Esau'**, Rashi says, 'I do not know what the addition of these words is intended to tell us.'[83] In reality, what is important here is the order of the names — that is, the fact that Jacob is mentioned before Esau. It demonstrates the pre-eminence of status that Jacob now has over his elder brother. Jacob is, by all rights and privileges, the first-born — he has the birth-right and the blessing.

28:6-7. And Esau saw that Isaac blessed Jacob and [that] he sent him to Paddan-Aram to take to himself a wife from there, [and that] when he blessed him and commanded him, saying, 'Do not take a wife from the daughters of Canaan,' Jacob listened to his father and his mother, and he went to Paddan-Aram.

Esau sees that Jacob is obedient to the commands of his parents. Obviously he concludes that blessing must be tied to obedience. He himself has not been particularly obedient because of the women he has married — these wives are from outside the family, and they have been a snare to his parents. Esau will now seek to rectify the situation.

28:8-9. And Esau saw that the daughters of Canaan were displeasing in the eyes of Isaac his father. So Esau went to Ishmael, and he took for himself a wife — Mahaloth, the daughter of Ishmael, the son of Abraham, the sister of Nebaioth — in addition to his [other] wives.

Probably to put himself in good stead with his parents, Esau marries his cousin, the daughter of his father's brother. Her name is **'Mahalath**,' although in Genesis 36:3 she is called Basemath. Obviously, these are two names for the same person.[84] Esau's act in marrying her is a parallel to what Jacob will soon do — he will marry the daughter of his mother's brother.

The particle translated **'in addition to'** is a preposition of excess.[85] It means 'on top of that' — he has added another wife to those he already has. There is no sense from the text that the marriage solves any problems.

The opening of the account of the blessing began with the story of Esau taking two wives; now it ends with a similar episode. The structure of the passage, therefore, is bordered by an *inclusio*. In fact, the entire section dealing with the blessing is a masterful literary construction. It is a highly stylized piece, as follows:

A
Esau weds
(26:34-35)

B
Esau acts
(27:1-4)

C
Rebekah
plots
(27:5-17)

D
Jacob
receives a
blessing
(27:18-29)

D[1]
Esau
receives a
curse
(27:30-40)

C¹
Rebekah
plots (27:41
– 28:5)

B¹
Esau acts
(28:6-7)

A¹
Esau weds
(28:8-9)

Application

As we have seen, the pretext for Jacob's travel to Haran is so that he should not marry a Canaanite woman. Esau, of course, had married two of them, and they had become thorns in the flesh of both Isaac and Rebekah. They were a source of great conflict. There is an important lesson for the church here. F. Niedner once counselled a person about marriage by saying, 'Another thing that will keep your married life happy is that you are both of the same faith. This is very important. I know that in exceptional cases mixed marriages turn out to be happy marriages. But I want to insist that there is danger in mixed marriages. If both parties want to be absolutely loyal and true to their own faith and their own church in every way, there is bound to be conflict... Of course, it is possible to keep clear of any conflict by a compromise in these things, if each one gives up something for the other. But right there is the danger I am speaking of. A true and loyal member of the church cannot compromise. Loyalty knows no compromise.'

Jacob's dream
(Genesis 28:10-22)

The story of Jacob thus far has been, for the most part, a secular one. God has not figured in the account to any great extent. That is about to change. The section we are to look at now is a dream sequence in which Jacob has an encounter with the almighty God. On his journey to Haran, Jacob stops to rest, and there he sees the heavens opened, and there he receives the same promises that God had made to his ancestor Abraham. It is through Jacob that the seed will come! This story is pivotal in the life of Jacob.

28:10-11. So Jacob went out from Beersheba, and he went towards Haran. When he reached a certain place, he lodged there because the sun had gone down. And he took one of the stones of the place, and he set it under his head and he lay down in that place.

The place where Jacob rests on his journey is later revealed to be Bethel (28:19). From Beersheba to Bethel (then to Shechem and northern parts) is a well-known north-south travel route through Palestine. It is known as the 'spine' through the hill-country. It is the route by which Abraham travelled to Beersheba, and so Jacob is retracing his grandfather's journey from Haran.[86]

Bethel is called **'the place'** three times in these verses. Note that in the original Hebrew each

instance includes a definite article. The article in
Hebrew is used to denote a particular place.[87] The
term **'place'** also carries connotations of a sacred /
religious site. Later Jeroboam erects one of the
golden calves in Bethel (1 Kings 12:29). This place,
therefore, bears a long religious history and tradition.

28:12. And he dreamed; and, behold, a stairway was set up
on the earth. And its top was reaching to the heavens. And,
behold, the angels of God ascending and descending on it.

Dreams were common means of accessing a god's
will in the ancient Near East.[88] The difference here is
that Jacob is not attempting to divine the Lord's will
for him. In this dream, God is revealing himself to
Jacob. Yahweh is the source here, not Jacob or
divination.

What Jacob sees is a **'stairway'** going up from the
earth to the entrance of heaven.[89] Normally translated as 'ladder', this is the only occurrence of the
term, which stems from the verb *sālal*, signifying 'to
cast up a mound'.[90] It may be related to the Akkadian
word *simmiltu,* which means 'steps'. The picture is
that of a series of steps that lead into the entrance,
or gate, of the heavenly city.

Angels are going up and down the staircase. The
Hebrew word for **'angels'** simply means 'messengers'.
The obvious point of the picture is that God's retinue
leaves his presence in order to carry out his work on
earth and then returns to him for further directions.
In addition, the angels are seen to be there specifically to help Jacob, and to protect him and his
descendants.

28:13-15. And, behold, Yahweh was standing on it. And he
said, 'I am Yahweh, the God of Abraham your father and the
God of Isaac. The land on which you are lying, I have given it
to you and to your seed. And your seed will become as the

dust of the earth. And you will spread out to the west and to the east and to the north and to the south. And all the families of the land will be blessed on account of you and on account of your seed. And, behold, I am with you and I will guard you wherever you go, and I will bring you back to this land. For I will not leave you until I have done what I said to you.'

This theophany in a dream confirms Jacob as the true heir of Abraham. The promises God gives to Jacob here are very similar to the ones he made to Abraham in Genesis 13:14-17. In fact, much of the wording of the two exchanges is exactly alike.[91]

The opening phrase of this passage may be understood in two possible ways. The preposition with pronominal suffix translated as **'on it'** can be interpreted as meaning that Yahweh is standing on top of the staircase that Jacob is viewing. That preposition, however, often means 'next to / near' and the suffix can mean 'him' — so the phrase could read 'beside him' — that is, Yahweh is right next to Jacob. I have opted for the former translation because it fits the content of the dream in which Jacob is merely an onlooker.

28:16-17. And Jacob awoke from his sleep, and he said, 'Surely Yahweh is in this place, and I did not know [it].' And he was afraid, and he said, 'How awesome is this place! This is none other than the house of God and that is the gate of heaven.'

The dream makes a great emotional impact on Jacob. He has a highly charged reaction to the dream vision. He begins by saying, **'Surely,'** a particle that 'has a general emphatic sense'.[92] And then, the phrase, **'I did not know...'**, begins with the independent personal pronoun **'I'** — this is unnecessary in the sentence construction but it adds great weight to Jacob's

response of distress. The point of the latter phrase is
to say that if he had known God was in the place, he
would not have slept there. Obviously, Jacob believes
he has profaned the spot by sleeping, and thus
performing a mundane task, in the presence of the
transcendent and holy God.

The idea of a **'gate'** at the entrance to heaven is a
common motif in ancient Near-Eastern thought. For
example, one of the titles of the high priest of Thebes
in Egypt was 'The Opener of the Gates of Heaven'.[93]
In addition, the Egyptians believed that doors, or a
gateway, in the east opened into the Fields of Para-
dise.[94] The Sumerians understood the abode of the
underworld to be guarded by a gate.[95]

28:18-19. So Jacob arose in the morning, and he took the
stone which he had set under his head, and he set it up as a
pillar. Then he poured oil on top of it. And he called the name
of that place Bethel, although at the first the name of the city
was Luz.

Because of the dream he has had which included the
great promises of God, Jacob takes the rock upon
which he had slept and sets it up as a stone of commemoration. Such an act is a familiar concept in the
Bible (see 31:45-54; Josh. 24:27). Such pillars (Hebrew, *mazzēbōth*) carry inherent dangers, however;
they often become the subjects of idolatry — and for
that purpose they are later prohibited in Hebrew law
(see Deut. 12:3). There is no hint of any idolatrous
activity on the part of Jacob. His erection of the stone
is to honour a spiritual milestone — the appearance
of Yahweh to him in a dream!

The significance of Jacob's anointing of the rock is
ambiguous. Perhaps it is a covenantal exercise,
symbolizing or sealing the covenant relationship
between God and Jacob.

The changing of the place-name is important. **'Luz'** probably derives from a verb that means 'to turn aside' or 'depart', but when used figuratively it means 'to be crafty / cunning / devious'.[96] The name **'Bethel'** means 'the house of God'. The word-play involved may reflect the beginning of a change in Jacob's life — that is, he is now going to turn away from deception as a way of life and move to God. The event of the dream, therefore, appears to be the spiritual turning-point in the life of Jacob.

28:20-22. Then Jacob vowed a vow, saying, 'If God will be with me, and protect me on this journey which I am taking, and give me food to eat and clothing to wear, so that I return in peace to my father's house, then Yahweh will be my God. And this stone which I have set up as a pillar will be the house of God, and of all that you will give to me I will tithe a tenth to you.'

In two instances in this passage, a verb is tied to its cognate noun: he **'vowed a vow'** and **'I will tithe a tenth'** (or literally, 'I will give a tenth a tenth'). When this occurs, as we have seen repeatedly in the grammar of Genesis, a great emphasis is being placed on the assertion. So one proper translation of the first of these phrases would be 'Jacob solemnly vowed'.

The vow itself is structured as an 'if ... then' clause. If God cares for Jacob — by supplying bread, clothing and safety to Jacob on his trip — then Jacob will swear fealty to Yahweh. It is interesting to note that Yahweh has already promised these things to him in a dream (28:13-15). So if God keeps his word, then Jacob will swear exclusive loyalty and fidelity.

Jacob also promises to give a tithe to God. Some have suggested it is a one-off offering.[97] But that is unlikely because the verb 'to tithe' is in the Piel pattern which reflects a frequentive use, that is, it describes multiple acts.[98] Thus Jacob is probably making a lifetime commitment to Yahweh in the matter of tithing.

Application

In response to Nathanael's confession that Jesus is the Son of God and the King of Israel, Jesus tells him that he will see great things. He tells Nathanael, 'Truly, truly, I say to you, you will see the heavens opened and the angels of God ascending and descending on the Son of Man' (John 1:51). Jesus is making an allusion to the story of Jacob, and he is saying that he himself corresponds to the staircase in Jacob's dream. So, when Na-thanael looks at Jesus he 'will see "heaven opened" as Jacob did in his vision'.[99] It may also be suggested that Jesus is making the point that he alone is the gateway to heaven, and that dreams no longer supply such a vision. As the author of the epistle to the Hebrews says, 'God, after he spoke long ago to the fathers ... in many portions and in many ways, in these last days has spoken to us in his Son' (Heb. 1:1-2).

A. Ross draws another application from this story of Jacob. He says that the Christian experience is similar to that of Jacob: 'The effectual revelation of God's protective presence and promised blessings for Christians will inspire devout and faithful worship. Those who fully realize God's gracious provision, those whom the Word of God has powerfully impressed, will respond with consecration and commitment... Like the revelation to Jacob, the written revelation of God makes the believer aware of the Lord's presence and prompts him to a higher level of living.'[100]

Jacob meets Rachel
(Genesis 29:1-14)

The subject matter of this section is in many respects familiar. There are many similarities with the search for a bride for Isaac in Genesis 24. General scenes and specific language are alike in both stories. The major distinction, of course, is that in the earlier episode Isaac played no role in the choosing of his wife: Abraham sent a servant to Haran with camels loaded with articles of silver and gold and with garments. These the servant presented to Rebekah, the future wife of Isaac (24:53). Jacob, on the contrary, comes to Haran alone and apparently empty-handed (for he has to work for the hand of Laban's daughter). The later narrative of Moses' flight from Egypt in Exodus 2:15-21 appears to be structured on the basis of the Jacob story. The events involving Moses certainly took place, but the author is writing the account in such a way as to make the association, presenting Moses as a patriarch like Jacob.

29:1-3. And Jacob continued on his journey and went to the land of the sons of the east. And he looked, and behold, a well was in the field. And, behold, three flocks of sheep were lying down there next to it, because the flocks were watered from that well. Now the stone was large that was over the mouth of the well. When all the flocks were gathered there, then they would roll away the stone from over the mouth of the well, and they would water the flock. Then they would return the stone to its place over the mouth of the well.

After the astounding event at Bethel, Jacob proceeds on his trip to Haran. The phrase **'continued on his journey'** is literally 'He lifted up his feet' — this expression is found nowhere else in the Bible. However, it obviously is an idiom signifying that he arose from the sacred spot in Bethel and resumed his travels to Mesopotamia. Jacob's destination is **'the land of the sons of the east'**. This is a vague, general description used in the Bible of lands east of Canaan (see 25:6).

In one particular field, Jacob notices three flocks of sheep next to a well. Over the mouth of the well is a **'large stone'** — the rock apparently guarded or protected the well from either people or animals helping themselves to the water. As we have witnessed, wells belonged to individuals or groups (21:30; 26:18-22). The great dimensions of the stone serve as an important backdrop for the remainder of the story.

The word translated **'they'** is an indefinite personal pronoun — it signifies people in general. The Septuagint and other early manuscripts insert the word 'shepherds' here and, indeed, that is what is meant by the context.

29:4-8. And Jacob said to them, 'My brothers, where are you from?' And they said, 'We are from Haran.' Then he said to them, 'Do you know Laban, the son of Nahor?' And they said, 'We know [him].' Then he said to them, 'Is there peace with him?' And they answered, 'Peace. And, behold, Rachel his daughter is coming with the sheep.' And he said, 'Behold, it is still high day; it is not time for the livestock to be gathered. Water the sheep, and go, shepherd [them].' But they said, 'We are not able until all the flocks are gathered, and they roll away the stone from the mouth of the well. Then we will water the sheep.'

Jacob, never having been in Haran before, tries to find out where he is. He sees shepherds and asks them if they know **'Laban, the son of Nahor'**. In reality, Laban is the son of Bethuel and the grandson of Nahor (see 28:2). Certainly Jacob knows this, but he is using Nahor's name because the latter is well known and the patriarch of the clan. The workers answer with a curt, **'We know'** — there is no word in Hebrew for 'yes', so an affirmative response is generally expressed by repeating the emphatic word in the question.[101]

As they are speaking, Rachel, the daughter of Laban, appears on the scene leading sheep to the well. It may be ironic that Rachel's name means **'ewe'** in Hebrew.[102] In any event, Jacob obviously wants to talk with her alone, so he accuses the shepherds of shirking their duty. They are simply hanging about while the sun is still high, and there is time for work to be done. The shepherds, however, make excuses for their inactivity: all the flocks have not arrived to be watered, and the stone is too big to roll away.

29:9-10. While he was speaking with them, Rachel came with the sheep which belonged to her father, because she was a shepherd. And when Jacob saw Rachel, the daughter of Laban, his mother's brother, and the sheep of Laban, his mother's brother, Jacob drew near. And he rolled away the stone from the mouth of the well, and he watered the flock of Laban, his mother's brother.

When Jacob sees Rachel approach the well with her father's sheep, he springs into action. He rolls the stone away single-handedly — apparently it normally took more than one man to accomplish this task (see 29:8). His act highlights his prowess, that he is a man of strength. Rashi comments that Jacob does this *'as easily as* one draws the stopper from the mouth of a bottle — thus showing you how strong he was'.[103]

The phrase, **'his mother's brother'**, appears three times in these two verses for emphasis. It is there to remind the reader that Jacob has done exactly as he had been commanded by his mother (27:43) and his father (28:2). He has found the family of Laban.

29:11-12. Then Jacob kissed Rachel, and he lifted his voice and cried. And Jacob told Rachel that he was her father's brother, and that he was Rebekah's son. Then she ran, and she reported [it] to her father.

Jacob's taking action, first with the flock and then with Rachel, is underscored by an assonance between the verbs 'to water' *(y-sh-q)* and 'to kiss' *(y-sh-q)*. Some commentators argue that Jacob's kissing of Rachel is 'more affectionate than one would think proper under the circumstances'.[104] The act appears to be so bold that even Calvin questions the reliability of the text here because it calls into account Jacob's character.[105] In reality, this act is impulsive, but is natural and innocent on the part of one who has travelled so far and now suddenly meets a relative. If it were an unseemly act then we would expect the text to have made an issue of it, but it does not.

Jacob tells Rachel that he is her father's brother, when he is, in fact, her father's nephew, a cousin of hers. This is not a problem, however, because the Hebrew term for **'brother'** has a more generic function at times — it can simply mean a 'relative' (see 13:8).

29:13-14. And it came to pass when Laban heard the report about Jacob, his sister's son, that he ran to meet him. And he embraced him and he kissed him. Then he brought him to his home. And he recounted to Laban all these matters. And

Laban said to him, 'Certainly you are my bone and my flesh.' So he dwelt with him one whole month.

The first meeting between Jacob and his uncle Laban is congenial. After Jacob has disclosed **'all these matters'** — a phrase which certainly refers only to his journey and not to his previous deceptions — Laban recognizes that Jacob is a relative. The compound **'bone ... and ... flesh'** is idiomatic in Scripture for a family relationship (cf. 2:23; Judg. 9:2). No sense of deception or chicanery is evident at this time, but it will soon appear.

As a result of Laban's apparent acceptance of his nephew, Jacob remains with his uncle for **'one whole month'**. This expression literally reads, 'a month of days'. This is an example of apposition, which is defined as a 'collocation of two substantives to define more exactly the one by the other'.[106] Thus the phrase signifies that Jacob stays in Haran for the space of an entire month prior to the next recorded incident.

Application

Many of the elements of the story in the present section appear at first sight to be mere coincidence. Jacob happens to come across a field with sheep in it; the field happens to have some workers who happen to know Laban; then Rachel, the daughter of Laban, just happens to be coming to the well in *that very field* with sheep to be watered. Oh how we forget the providence of God when we read stories like this in Scripture! R. Cecil put it this way: 'We are too apt to forget our actual dependence on Providence for the circumstances of every instant. The most trivial events may determine our state in the world. Turning up one street instead of another may bring us in company with a person whom we should not otherwise have met; and this may lead to a train of other events which may determine the happiness or misery of our lives.'

At the time of the events, Jacob may not have seen them as the providences of God. As John Flavel so eloquently says, 'Some providences, like Hebrew letters, must be read backwards.' The same is true of any Christian life. One need only look back over time to see the hand of God working in even the most mundane and trivial matters of our lives.

Let's make a deal
(Genesis 29:15-30)

This section relates Laban's deception of Jacob in giving his daughters in marriage. It is the great hoax perpetrated by Laban, who offers the pitiful excuse for his behaviour that he is observing local custom. Most importantly, the tables have been turned on Jacob — the great deceiver is himself deceived!

29:15. And Laban said to Jacob, 'Is it because you are my relative that you serve me for nothing? Tell me what your wages should be.'

A superficial reading of the text gives the impression that Laban is greatly concerned for Jacob's welfare. Here Jacob has been working for Laban for at least a month and he has received nothing, or little, in return for his labour. Thus many commentators understand Laban's question as an attempt on his part to reward Jacob for the work he has so far carried out free of charge. But the reader must remember — a fact which will be further developed in the story — that Laban is a sly old fox. He does not appear to be the kind of person who gives wages to someone without receiving a substantial return on his investment. It may be that Jacob, as a distant relative, does not come under the full authority of Laban. But if Jacob agrees to work for Laban for payment, he will then become a hireling, under the jurisdiction of his employer. Laban may also be

setting a trap for Jacob, so that Jacob will end up
marrying his daughters!

29:16-18. And Laban had two daughters. The name of the
older was Leah, and the name of the younger was Rachel.
And Leah's eyes were soft, but Rachel was beautiful of
form and appearance. And Jacob loved Rachel. And he
said, 'I will serve you seven years for Rachel, your younger
daughter.'

The author does not immediately proceed to give
Jacob's answer to Laban's question; instead he
inserts a parenthetical break to provide information
necessary to the story. He relates that Laban has two
daughters, Leah (**'the older'**) and Rachel (**'the
younger'**). We know that Jacob loves Rachel and
that, of course, is the rub. In addition, the two sisters
are different in appearance.[107] Numerous translations
describe Leah as having **'weak'** eyes, which is often
understood as meaning that she had poor vision, or
that her eyes lacked lustre.[108] In reality, the Hebrew
word means 'soft / delicate / dainty'.[109] Leah has
pretty eyes. Rachel's beauty, on the other hand,
resides in her form and her whole appearance (literally, **'fair of form and fair of sight'**), not just in her
eyes. Some commentators have attempted to demonstrate a contrast between the physical characteristics
of the two sisters on the basis of the meaning of their
names: **'Rachel'** means 'ewe', and **'Leah'** may possibly mean 'cow'. The latter, however, is an uncertain
rendering of the Hebrew.
      Apparently Jacob has no bride-price to give for the
hand of Rachel. He did not come to Haran laden with
treasures or provisions. Thus Jacob offers to work for
seven years to earn her in marriage. This seems to be
an excessive amount of time — a view confirmed by
the lack of bartering on the part of Laban. Laban

comes best out of the deal and of course, he does even better later.

29:19-20. Then Laban said, 'It is better that I give her to you than that I give her to another man. Stay with me!' So Jacob served seven years for Rachel. And in his eyes they were like a few days because he loved her so.

Laban appears to be ecstatic about the deal. And, why not? Rachel will remain a member of Laban's family and under his authority. He has the benefit of his daughter's labour, as well as Jacob's labour, for seven years. Therefore, he responds to Jacob's offer by exclaiming with an imperative: **'Stay with me!'** The Hebrew term for **'with me'** stresses the idea of coming under a person's authority (compare verse 27 where the same expression is used for 'in my service' — NASB translation). Thus, both Jacob and Rachel remain under Laban's authority for seven years, and unbeknownst to them, for a further seven years also.

But because Jacob loves Rachel, the seven years of servitude feel **'like a few days'** to him. This is the same expression that was used back in 27:44, in which Rebekah had told Jacob to 'stay with him [Laban] a few days' (in my translation of that verse I render it with the more generic 'for some time'). Although Jacob stays with Laban for much longer than Rebekah had anticipated, it still seems like a short time to him.

29:21-22. Then Jacob said to Laban, 'Give me my wife, for my days are fulfilled, so that I may go to her.' So Laban gathered all the men of the place, and he made a feast.

After seven years of labour, Jacob demands from Laban **'my wife'**. The verb **'give'** is an imperative (in fact, that root appears only in the imperative in Hebrew), and here it has a hortatory usage — that is, as an exhortation. Jacob's omission of Rachel's name from his request portends the events that are about to occur: he will receive a wife, but it will not be Rachel.

Jacob's reference to Rachel as his **'wife'** prior to the wedding does not present a problem. In antiquity, a woman who was betrothed had the status of a wife (see Deut. 20:7; 22:23-24). The Mesopotamian Code of Hammurabi attests to this custom (paragraphs 130, 161).[110]

The phrase, **'go to her'**, in the Hebrew Bible often signifies the act of intercourse (see 16:2, for instance), and it appears to mean just that in the next verse (29:23). It sometimes has a more generic sense of denoting the act of cohabitation — that is, a husband and wife living together (which, of course, assumes intercourse).[111] Jacob is probably not being coarse or crass with his father-in-law, but he is asking for the uniting of himself and Rachel as husband and wife.

29:23-24. And it came to pass in the evening that he took Leah, his daughter, and brought her to him. And he went in to her. And Laban gave her Zilpah his handmaid as a handmaid for Leah, his daughter.

The only reasonable way to understand these verses is that Leah is veiled. Such covering of the face seems to have been customary for unmarried women in front of men (see 24:65). Veiling, then, is part of Laban's deception, as is his bringing her to Jacob in the darkness of **'evening'**. This cunning plot parallels Jacob's plot to steal the blessing from Esau: as Isaac was blind to Jacob's stealth, so now Jacob is blind to Laban's trickery.

The provision of a maid for the bride by the bride's father is attested in the Nuzi tablets of the second millennium B.C.[112] It may be part of the wedding arrangement to show that the marriage is legally binding. That and the fact that intercourse has taken place signifies that Jacob can in no way renege on the deal. Zilpah's being given to Leah also anticipates a later story in which she will bear two sons for Jacob (30:9-12).

29:25-27. And it came to pass in the morning that, behold, it was Leah! And he said to Laban, 'What is this you have done to me? Was it not for Rachel that I served with you? And why have you deceived me?' Then Laban said, 'It is not done so in our place to give the younger woman before the first-born woman. Finish the seven [days] of this one and we will also give you this one for the work you will do with me for another seven years.'

This entire scene drips with irony. First, in the morning after the giving of the bride Jacob realizes it is Leah, not Rachel — he has been tricked into taking the older before the younger. This is retributive irony because in his family the older will serve the younger. In addition, Jacob accuses Laban of 'deceiving' him. The cognate word of that verb is 'treacherously / deceptively', the term used by Isaac to describe Jacob's act of stealing Esau's blessing (27:35). What goes around, comes around!

Laban strikes up a further deal. If Jacob will complete **'the seven [days] of this one'** — probably a reference to the bridal week with Leah (cf. Judg. 14:12) — then he will receive the hand of Rachel in exchange for seven more years of labour. Jacob does not have to wait seven years for Rachel — Laban is too shrewd to suggest that — but he secures her immediately after the bridal week with Leah. It is interesting to note that later Hebrew law forbids a man from marrying sisters (Lev. 18:18).

The providence of God is at work here. Leah later bears six sons for Jacob: Reuben, Simeon, Levi,

Judah, Issachar and Zebulun (29:31-35; 30:16-20).
Of course, it is the lineage of Levi that becomes the
priesthood of Israel, and the descendants of Judah
produce the Davidic monarchy, which is fully realized
in the Messiah.

29:28-30. And Jacob did so, and he finished the seven [days]
of this one. And he gave him Rachel, his daughter, as a wife.
And Laban gave to Rachel, his daughter, Bilhah his handmaid to be her handmaid. And he [Jacob] came to Rachel.
And he loved Rachel rather than Leah. And he served him
yet another seven years.

Jacob agrees to the deal. And, in reality, he does not
fare too well in the bargain: for fourteen years of
labour he receives two wives and two handmaids. On
the contrary, when Rebekah came to marry Isaac,
she brought with her a nurse and several handmaids
(24:59-61). Jacob's acceptance without bargaining of
an apparently poor deal is to be explained by his love
for Rachel. In fact, he **'loved Rachel rather than
Leah'** — the preposition **'rather'** is a comparative
min of exclusion in Hebrew.[113] It is not that Jacob
loved Rachel more than Leah, but he loved Rachel
alone.

The flow of the passage is interrupted by the
inclusion of the fact that Bilhah is given as a maid;
this is similar to the interruption we noted in verse
24. The meaning of the name **'Bilhah'** is unknown.
She is important, however, because she becomes the
mother of Dan and Naphtali (30:3-8). At this point,
then, the four mothers of the twelve sons of Jacob /
tribes of Israel have been introduced.

Application

The principle of dramatic irony is clearly manifest in this story. The moral axiom that one's sins find one out, and return on one's own head in punishment, is commonly found in Scripture. We need only consider the example of the evil Haman in the book of Esther. There he erects gallows to hang the righteous Mordecai, only to be hung on those very gallows himself. The book of Psalms calls for the wicked to be found out by their sins: 'Hold them guilty, O God; by their own devices let them fall!' (Ps. 5:10); 'May his mischief return upon his own head, and his violence descend on his own pate' (Ps. 7:16).

The same principle operates in the world today. One thinks of Richard Nixon's attempt to become a famous president. He taped his White House conversations for future glory — but, of course, they revealed his deception, and they made him infamous.

And even though Jacob was a believer and the promised Messiah was to come through him, his sins found him out. They came back on his own head. Let us beware in the church today — we ought to flee from sin, for it has a way of rebounding on us if we use it for our own glory.

Jacob's sons
(Genesis 29:31 – 30:24)

This section reports the stories of the birth of the children of Jacob, the progenitors of the twelve tribes of Israel. The account narrates the birth to Jacob of eleven sons (and one daughter), and the birth of the twelfth son (Benjamin) is anticipated. So in a general sense, this passage serves as a genealogy that later results in the twelve tribes of Israel. These birth records also carry forward the motif of strife in the family of Jacob.[114]

29:31. And Yahweh saw that Leah was hated, so he opened her womb. But Rachel was barren.

In the entire story of Jacob's marriage to the daughters of Laban the name of God is never mentioned. He is clearly behind the scenes, running the entire drama with his providential hand — but he is nowhere directly acknowledged. Here, at the beginning of a large section of narrative material, Yahweh now becomes the subject. He is the active one: he **'saw'** and he **'opened'**.

Many Bible versions and commentators do not translate the Hebrew term as **'hated',** but rather as 'unloved'. The idea is that Leah is neglected, or receives little care from Jacob. Others argue that the word is actual legal terminology signifying a relative degree of preference that a husband has for one wife over another.[115] Such an understanding is based on its use in Deuteronomy 21:15. Even if such were the case, the word does bear a sense of aversion to something.[116] It is not merely that Jacob loves Leah less than Rachel, but he apparently does not love her at all.

29:32-35. And Leah conceived and she gave birth to a son. And she called his name Reuben because she said, 'For Yahweh has seen my affliction; indeed now my husband will love me.' Then she conceived again and she gave birth to a son. And she said, 'For Yahweh has heard that I was hated; so he gave me also this one.' And she called his name Simeon. Then she conceived again and she gave birth to a son. And she said, 'Now this time my husband will be joined with me because I have borne for him three sons.' Therefore his name was called Levi. Then she conceived again and she gave birth to a son. And she said, 'This time I will praise Yahweh.' Therefore, she called his name Judah. Then she ceased from giving birth.

The fruitfulness of Leah, the neglected wife, may be the chastisement of God against Jacob. Calvin explains it succinctly: 'Jacob's extravagant love [for Rachel] was corrected by the Lord.'[117] Leah deserves honour from her husband. And if he will not give it to her, then Yahweh will bestow glory on her because it is from her progeny that the chosen seed (i.e., the Messiah) will come.[118]

Each of the four sons receives a name that involves a word-play; each pun is explained in the text.[119] The first-born is **'Reuben'**, a name that literally means, 'Look, a son!' Leah explains the naming of the child as deriving from Yahweh's 'seeing' her need and thus providing a son. The second child's name, **'Simeon'**, also reflects Leah's relationship with God. His name derives from the Hebrew verb 'to hear' — he is so named because Yahweh **'has heard'** about Leah's distress. The third son is **'Levi'**, and his name is apparently related to the verb meaning 'to join / attach'.[120] Leah's hope is that a third son will bring Jacob and herself closer together as husband and wife. The name of the fourth son, **'Judah'**, again echoes Leah's relationship with the Almighty — it seems to have little to do with her relationship with Jacob — she is simply 'praising' God for providing another son.

Leah's hope that children would establish love and unity in her marriage to Jacob is obviously not realized. The statement, **'She ceased from giving birth,'** does not mean that she has become barren — she later gives birth to two more sons (30:17-19). What it probably means is that Jacob is no longer having sexual relations with her.

30:1-2. When Rachel saw that she did not bear children for Jacob, Rachel was jealous of her sister. And she said to Jacob, 'Give me children or I will die!' Then Jacob was angry with Rachel, and he said, 'Am I in the place of God who withheld from you the fruit of the womb?'

Leah's fruitfulness and Rachel's barrenness lead to domestic strife.[121] Rachel is unhappy and envious of Leah. In a culture that places great emphasis on a woman's value and worth through child-bearing, Rachel's lot is a pitiful one. Therefore, like Rebekah before her (25:22), she questions her very existence. Rachel then demands of Jacob that he **'give'** her **'children'** — this is an inappropriate request. She certainly should have gone to Yahweh in prayer, as had Isaac and Rebekah in a previous similar situation (25:21).

Jacob's response is a rebuke, and it is one filled with ire. He questions Rachel's understanding of the providence of God. God is the one who opens and closes the womb — why blame Jacob or ask of him things that he cannot deliver? It appears, however, that Jacob is not blameless here: he, too, does not approach God and seek his intervention as his father had done.

30:3. And she said, 'Behold, my handmaid Bilhah! Go to her that she might give birth on my knees, so that I, I too, might build [a family] from it.'

Because of her barrenness, Rachel resorts to concubinage — that is, she gives her handmaid to Jacob. He will sire children by the handmaid that will then belong to Rachel. This act is, of course, reminiscent of Sarah's giving Hagar to Abraham for the same purpose. In fact, Rebekah employs similar wording to that used by Sarah when speaking to Abraham: '... I might build [a family] from it' (16:2).

The act of placing a child on someone's knees was a well-known practice in the culture of the ancient Near East. To perform it was 'to acknowledge [the child] as one's own'.[122] It signified legitimization, and possibly even some form of adoption. Another example of this being carried out in the Bible is found in Genesis 50:23.

30:4-6. Thus she gave him Bilhah her handmaid as a wife, and Jacob went to her. And Bilhah conceived, and she gave birth to a son for Jacob. And Rachel said, 'God has judged me; that is, he has heard my voice, and he has given me a son.' Therefore, she called his name Dan.

The act of providing a new wife in the event of the original wife's proving barren was common in the ancient Near East. In the Nuzi texts from the fifteenth century B.C., the majority of texts dealing with marriage are concerned with childlessness and provisions for a new wife. For example, one document reads: 'Zike, son of Akkuya, gave his son Shennima in adoption to Shuriha-ilu, and Shuriha-ilu gave

Shennima all these fields. Should there be a son of
Shuriha-ilu, he will be the chief heir, and Shennima
will be secondary heir... And he gave Kelim-ninu as
wife to Shennima. If Kelim-ninu bears children,
Shennima will not take another wife, but if Kelim-
ninu does not bear children, Kelim-ninu will take a
slave-girl from the land of Nullu as wife for Shennima, and Kelim-ninu shall have authority over the
child [of the slave-girl]'.[123] It should be especially
noted in this text that the slave-girl is referred to as a
'wife'. The same is true in our biblical passage: Bilhah becomes a **'wife'** of Jacob. A concubine is a true
wife, although of a secondary rank. The major difference between the two is that no *mōhār*, or bride-
price, is paid for the slave-girl.

The bearing of a child by Bilhah is seen as vindi-
cation on the part of Rachel. She sees that her cause
has been undertaken by God. She then names the
child as a reflection of God's activity: **'Dan'** means
'judge', and it is a cognate of the verb used earlier in
the passage, 'judged'. It should be observed that
Rachel does not employ the name Yahweh, the very
personal name of God, but **'Elohim'**, a more generic
appellation.

30:7-8. Then she conceived again. And Bilhah, Rachel's
handmaid, gave birth to a second son for Jacob. And Rachel
said, 'I have wrestled the wrestlings of God with my sister —
indeed I have prevailed!' Thus she called his name Naphtali.

In response to the birth of a second son to Bilhah,
Rachel grandly proclaims that she has now bested
her sister Leah. She does so emphatically by using a
noun derived from the verb of the sentence: she has
'wrestled the wrestlings of God'. Then she employs
an intensive particle, *gam*, or **'indeed'**, to express the
concept of her having prevailed over her sister. The
force of the proclamation is underscored by its being

a prophetic oracle that is reflected in later literature (32:28).[124]

The expression **'the wrestlings of God'** may perhaps include a figure called enallage (that is, the exchange of one word for another), so that, rather than **'of God'** what is meant is actually 'great / mighty'.[125] Thus the divine name has an intensifying effect, or superlative force.[126] In other words, Rachel has had a great contest with Leah, and she now proclaims victory.

Rachel names the child **'Naphtali'**, which literally means 'my wrestling'. It is a word-play based on the two cognates earlier in the verse — 'wrestled' and 'the wrestlings of'.

30:9-13. And Leah saw that she had ceased bearing children; so she took Zilpah, her handmaid, and gave her to Jacob for a wife. Then Zilpah, Leah's handmaid, gave birth to a son for Jacob. And Leah said, 'By good fortune!' So she called his name Gad. Then Zilpah, Leah's handmaid, gave birth to a second son for Jacob. And Leah said, 'In my happiness! For women will call me happy.' So she called his name Asher.

The opening phrase takes the reader back to 29:35. Leah has stopped having children. It appears that she is discontent and perhaps jealous of her sister. So she responds, as Rachel had done before her, by giving her handmaid to Jacob as a wife in order to produce children through her.

The first son born to Zilpah is **'Gad'**. This is a name that literally means 'good fortune / luck'. Leah relishes in, and announces, her propitious circumstances in gaining another son. The name 'Gad' is an ancient Near-Eastern appellation for a god of good fortune and luck.[127] It may be used in Isaiah 65:11 regarding the libations given by pagans to such a

god. There is, however, no evidence to support the
idea that Leah is naming this child after the deity.

'**Asher**' means 'happy one'. It is a Hebrew word
semantically related to the words '**happiness**' and
'**happy**' used by Leah in her response to the birth of
Asher. Leah is simply ecstatic over the birth of this
child. In fact, she announces that '**Women will call
me happy,**' because of the event. The verb she uses
is an accidental perfective (or *perfectum confiden-
tiae*),[128] in which the speaker vividly and dramatically
expresses facts which 'are undoubtedly imminent,
and, therefore, in the imagination of the speaker,
already accomplished'.[129] In other words, Leah is so
certain of the outcome that she employs a verb that
reflects completed action!

In all of this, Leah does not mention Yahweh. As
Keil and Delitzsch comment, 'Leah did not think of
God in connection with these two births. They were
nothing more than the successful and welcome result
of the means she had employed.'[130]

30:14-15. Now in the days of the wheat harvest Reuben went
and he found mandrakes in the field. And he brought them to
Leah his mother. And Rachel said to Leah, 'Give me some of
your son's mandrakes!' But she said to her, 'Is it a small
matter that you took my husband, that you want to take my
son's mandrakes?' Then Rachel said, 'He may, therefore, lie
down with you tonight in place of your son's mandrakes.'

The continuing strife and conflict between Rachel
and Leah is very evident in the present incident. Here
they argue over '**mandrakes**' that Leah's son Reuben
brings in from the field. This plant carries a fruit that
looks like a small apple, and it was known throughout antiquity as an aphrodisiac.[131] It has an erotic
connotation because of its distinctive and beautiful
fragrance (S. of S. 7:13). It is possible that Rachel,
who is still childless, wants the fruit in order to

increase sexual desire and fertility. Ironically, she trades for the fruit by giving Leah a night with Jacob, and Leah becomes pregnant with another son.[132] Rachel, on the other hand, remains barren for approximately three more years.

30:16-18. And Jacob came in from the field in the evening. And Leah went out to meet him, and she said, 'Come to me for I have certainly hired you with my son's mandrakes.' So he lay down with her that night. And God listened to Leah, and she conceived, and she gave birth to a fifth son for Jacob. Then Leah said, 'God has given me my wage because I gave my handmaid to my husband.' So she called his name Issachar.

Leah bears a fifth son for Jacob, and she names him **'Issachar'**. His name means, 'There is a wage' *(kethib),* or 'He provides a wage' *(qere)*.[133] The name is a cognate of the two words, **'hired'** and **'my wage'**, spoken by Leah in the passage. The act of naming the child reflects two events: first, Leah's hiring of Jacob in exchange for her son's mandrakes; and, second, it is her payment for giving her handmaid to Jacob as a wife and one to bear children for her. Double puns of this type are frequent occurrences when the Hebrews name their children.

The second reason for naming the child Issachar seems to indicate that Leah is in some sense aware that it was not the aphrodisiac that helped produce her son. Rather, she recognizes the providence of God as the ultimate cause behind it.

30:19-21. Then Leah conceived again, and she gave birth to a sixth son for Jacob. And Leah said, 'God has endowed me with a good gift. Now my husband will honour me because I have given birth to six sons for him.' So she called his name Zebulun. Then afterwards she gave birth to a daughter, and she called her name Dinah.

Leah bears a sixth son, and she calls him **'Zebulun'**. There appear to be two reasons for giving him this name. First, it sounds very similar to the words for **'endowed'** and **'gift'** (they both derive from *zābad*) — the assonance is quite striking. Secondly, the name is probably a derivative of the verb *zābal* which Leah uses here when she says her husband will now **'honour'** her. Some translations render this latter verb as 'to dwell', but this is without linguistic justification.

Note that Leah uses the word **'now'** in her exclamation. It is an emphatic particle which signifies 'at last', 'finally', or 'this time'. Leah's great desire for her husband's approval and honouring of her is highlighted by her use of this term.

The birth of the daughter **'Dinah'** is reported, but the account contains little description. No explanation is given for the origin of her name. It is probably the feminine equivalent of the name 'Dan', both forms stemming from the verb 'to judge'. Her inclusion at this point in the narrative is merely anticipatory of the forthcoming incident concerning her in chapter 34.

30:22-24. And God remembered Rachel, and God listened to her, and he opened her womb. Then she conceived, and she gave birth to a son. And she said, 'God has removed my reproach.' So she called his name Joseph, saying, 'May Yahweh add to me another son!'

The statement that God **'remembered'** Rachel does not mean that he had forgotten her, or that he was in need of recall. It is a term which signifies that God is about to intervene and to take action in the situation (See the exposition of 8:1 — vol. 1, p.202).

Again we see a double source for the name of Rachel's first-born son, **'Joseph'**. It is related (either linguistically or phonetically) to two verbs used in the passage: **'removed'** (from the Hebrew *'āsaph*) and **'add'** (Hebrew *yāsaph*). The point that Rachel is making is that God has removed one thing and he has replaced it with another. In addition, the former is in the past tense, and the latter is in the future. The prophecy, of course, is fulfilled with the birth of Benjamin (35:16-18).

In her final exclamation Rachel employs the personal, covenant name of God — that is, **'Yahweh'**. This helps to form an *inclusio* for the entire narrative of the births that began in 29:31. In that verse, it was related that Yahweh opened Leah's womb to give birth. The point of this construction is to highlight the truth that Yahweh is the giver of life. He is the source of birth in contrast to, let us say, mandrakes!

Application

It is a simple but important statement to say that Yahweh is the source of human life. The psalmist declares:

> Know that Yahweh himself is God;
> It is he who has made us, and not we ourselves;
> We are his people and the sheep of his pasture
>
> (Ps. 100:3).

Such a truth points to his sovereign majesty, as Matthew Henry points out: 'Whatever we want, it is God that withholds it, a sovereign Lord, most wise, holy, and just, that may do what he will with his own, and is debtor to no man, that never did, nor ever can do, any wrong to any of his creatures. The keys of the clouds, of the heart, of the grave, and of the womb, are four keys which God has in his hand, and which (the rabbis say) he entrusts neither with angels nor seraphim.'

Jacob becomes prosperous
(Genesis 30:25-43)

This next episode occurs at the end of Jacob's fourteen-year-period of servitude under Laban. He has worked those fourteen years to earn his two wives. Now Jacob would like to return to the land of Canaan. Laban, however, does not want to lose Jacob's services — he has been materially blessed by the presence of Jacob. So the two of them make an arrangement — and in this text Laban's own greed and deceit now turn on his head, as Jacob's cunning earlier had come back on his own head.

30:25-26. And it came to pass when Rachel had given birth to Joseph that Jacob said to Laban, 'Send me out that I may go to my place and to my land. Give [me] my wives and my children for whom I have served you, so that I may go. For you know my service which I have rendered you.'

Jacob now wishes to obtain the dissolution of his status as a hired servant. He seeks his release from Laban by using a formula which occurs elsewhere in the Bible in the context of asking leave from someone to depart (see, for instance, 1 Kings 11:21).[134] In his request Jacob employs a figure called a hendiadys (that is, two terms are used but only one thing is intended). He says, **'... to my place and to my land'** — the figure intensifies the matter to a superlative degree. In addition, in the final sentence there is an independent personal pronoun before the verb, so that it literally reads, **'you, you know'**. The repetition underscores the point that Jacob has fulfilled his obligations to Laban. It is time to leave.

Jacob demands that his children be sent with him and his wives. This appears to be a problem because children born in servitude belong to the master and not the servant (see Exod. 21:4). The same was true throughout the ancient Near East, as is attested in the Nuzi documents. And Laban is also under that impression, as he later states: 'The children are my children' (31:43). Jacob, however, is stressing the fact that he is not an ordinary slave. He is Laban's son-in-law, and he has only been temporarily hired.

30:27-28. And Laban said to him, 'If indeed I have found favour in your eyes — I have divined that Yahweh has blessed me on your account.' Then he said, 'Name your wages [you want] from me, and I will give [it]!'

Laban's response is not an answer to Jacob's question at all. In fact, it is a conditional sentence in which the main clause is entirely suppressed. Many want simply to add the request: 'Please stay,' or 'Stay with me.' Gesenius argues that such conditional sentences are frequently found in such an abridged form.[135] On the other hand, it may be that Laban is so dumbfounded by the request that he is stumbling around for words to use.[136] His response may also merely be a formula intended to introduce a bartering session, such as is about to occur, and that is how I have translated it.

Laban then states that he has **'divined'** that **'Yahweh has blessed'** him because of Jacob's labours. That verb certainly reflects the practice of using omens to learn the divine will (see 44:5,15), one which was well known in the ancient Near East.[137] Some commentators want to tone down the direct meaning of the text by saying that Laban really

means, 'I have learned from experience' — but there
is no linguistic justification for this. Laban is merely
in a state of theological confusion. He knows that
Jacob serves Yahweh, and he tries to combine that
with his own pagan practices. He invokes the name
of Yahweh because he does not want to lose Jacob's
services, but he has in mind to continue the employer
/ employee relationship. He is a sly old fox and he will
employ any trick.

30:29-30. But he said to him, 'You know how I have served
you and how your animals have fared with me. Because the
little you had before I [came] has greatly increased. And
Yahweh has blessed you [wherever I have set] my foot. And
now what will I do, I also, for my household?'

Jacob does not respond to Laban's question regarding wages. He simply reminds Laban how richly the
latter has been blessed because of Jacob's presence.

Jacob begins his reminder by once again using the
independent personal pronoun **'you'** along with the
verb **'you know'** — this is a repetition for emphasis
(see 30:26).

Jacob then goes on to remind Laban of how greatly
his flocks have **'increased'** on account of Jacob. That
verb literally means 'to break forth / burst' from the
womb (see Exod. 1:12). And Jacob acknowledges that
it is **'Yahweh'** who is the source of this great increase. It is Yahweh who has blessed Laban, literally,
'at the foot of' Jacob. This is an idiom that signifies
that God's blessing is following Jacob wherever he
walks, or wherever he sets his foot.[138] The blessing
that Jacob stole from his brother Esau is partly
coming to pass here (27:28).

30:31-33. So he said, 'What can I give you?' And Jacob said,
'Do not give me anything. If you will do this [one] thing for me
[then] I will return, I will pasture, I will guard your flock. I will

pass through all your flock today, removing from there every speckled or spotted sheep, and every dark-coloured lamb among the lambs, and the spotted and speckled among the goats — and it will be my wages. So my righteousness will answer on my behalf one day when you come concerning my wages. All that are not speckled or spotted among the goats and dark-coloured among the lambs with me will be [considered] stolen.'

Laban now asks what Jacob wants in order for him to stay in hired servitude to him. Jacob responds in a similar way as did Abraham to the King of Sodom (14:24). Jacob simply refuses to take anything for nothing from the deceptive Laban.

Jacob proposes instead a plan by which he is willing to remain working for Laban. The staccato sequence of verbs highlights what Jacob is willing to trade: **'I will return, I will pasture, I will guard...'** The lack of conjunctions between the verbs draws our attention to the certainty of Jacob's actions. It is an elevated style that is further highlighted by the fact that **'I will return'** is a cohortative. In return, Jacob asks for something that appears to have little in it for him. For his continued labours, Jacob wants to receive the speckled and spotted animals from Laban's flocks (including those still to be born). It is important to note that these are rare colours for these animals: goats are normally dark-coloured and sheep are normally white.

Jacob is appealing to Laban's sense of greed and deception. Laban thinks that he is going to receive Jacob's labour and great blessing from Yahweh in exchange for a small price — a few oddly-coloured animals! Jacob, on the other hand, obviously realizes that on the surface he is getting a poor deal — yet he believes that his **'righteousness'**, or 'honesty' will be vindicated at a later time when the wages are called to account. That Hebrew term has a legal aspect to it.

It bears the idea that Jacob will eventually be paid justly and fairly for his labour — it is a matter of measure for measure; that is, of equality.

30:34-36. Then Laban said, 'Yes! May it be according to your word!' And he removed on that day the striped and spotted male goats, and all the striped and spotted female goats — each that had white on it, and all the dark-coloured ones among the sheep. And he gave them into the hands of his sons. Then he put three days' journey between himself and Jacob. And Jacob pastured the remaining flocks of Laban.

Laban is greatly pleased with the offer. His response, **'Yes!** [literally, "Behold!"]**, May it be...'** consists of two particles of exclamation followed by a jussive — Laban can hardly contain himself. He does not barter, but he perceives that this is greatly to his advantage. As Von Rad comments, 'Here Jacob seems to be playing a risky game, for every shepherd knows that unicoloured female animals seldom give birth to striped or spotted offspring.'[139]

Laban takes a precaution by segregating all the spotted, speckled and dark-coloured animals, and he places them in the care of his sons at a distance of three days' journey. He does this not only to cheat Jacob out of them, but he separates animals of different colours to prevent mating between them. Thus he attempts to ensure the continuation of his own flock! The figure of **'three days'** was used in the ancient Near East to denote a significant period of time, and thus three days' journey was a considerable distance.[140] There is, therefore, a major, indeed total, separation between the two flocks.

Some have argued that it is Jacob, not Laban, who is doing this separating, but that is frankly untenable. First, at the time Jacob's sons are too young to care for the flocks, the oldest being only six years old. Secondly, the final verse of the passage (30:36) continues with a third masculine singular **'he'**, and this obviously refers to Laban.

An interesting word-play occurs in the passage: the word **'white'** is *lābān* in Hebrew. So we have a pun on the name 'Laban'; it is as if each of these animals has Laban's name on it.

In any event, we see that Laban uses his human deceptive devices to ensure the increase and abundance of his own flocks. He is clever, taking as many unfair advantages as possible. Jacob, then, is left as shepherd of the unmarked, spotless flock of Laban, out of which he is to receive his wages of speckled, spotted and dark-coloured animals.

30:37-39. Then Jacob took for himself fresh sticks of poplar trees and almond trees and plane trees. And he peeled on them white stripes, laying bare the white on the sticks. Then he put the sticks which he had peeled in the troughs, [that is] in the watering troughs where the flock came to drink, directly in front of the flock. And when they were in heat they came to drink, and the flock mated in front of the sticks. And the flock gave birth to striped and speckled and spotted.

Jacob here institutes what is known as a maternal impression process — that is, he acts on the common belief that a vivid sight during conception or pregnancy will leave its mark on the offspring. Jacob thus takes peeled branches and lays them in the watering troughs, where the flocks come to water and to mate. The result is that the females of the flocks give birth to young that have the colour of the sticks!

Is there any evidence that such a prenatal influence theory has any basis in fact? Has it been scientifically proven to work? Absolutely not! It appears to be an old wives' tale or merely superstition. The law of genetics 'very definitely ascribes the colours of the offspring to factors present in the germ cells of both parents. The offspring will be spotted only when the parents, and more particularly the germ cells of the parents, contain factors for spotting.'[141] But if there is no real value to it, why did Jacob employ it? Calvin rightly believes that Yahweh revealed this animal marking system to Jacob, and then made it work just for him.[142] Later Scripture confirms Calvin's conclusion to be accurate (see commentary on 31:4-12). In other words, God intervenes to cause the animals to flourish. Thus the effort expended by Jacob is not the means by which the results are gained. Success does not come by questionable ancient customs, but only by the hand of Yahweh.

30:40-43. Then Jacob separated the lambs. And he set the faces of the flock in front of the striped and all the dark-coloured in the flock of Laban. Thus he set apart a herd to himself, but he did not put them near the flock of Laban. And it came to pass when the vigorous of the flock were in heat that Jacob set the sticks before the eyes of the flock in the troughs so that they might mate in front of the sticks. But when the flock was weak he did not put them [there]. And it came to pass [that] the weak ones belonged to Laban, and the vigorous ones belonged to Jacob. And the man increased exceedingly, and he had large flocks and hand-maids and male servants and camels and donkeys.

Jacob now turns to deal with the sheep of the flock. He employs a different method with them. He separates the speckled and spotted from the normal-coloured sheep. This prevents inbreeding between the two groups. Then Jacob returns to his old habit of maternal impression process in order to ensure the birth of speckled and spotted sheep. In addition, he makes certain that his animals will be strong and dominant because he only uses the method with the **'vigorous'** sheep. This term derives from a verb meaning 'to bind / league together', and it is probably related to the Akkadian word *gašrum*, which means 'sturdy / robust'.[143]

Jacob's activity is not a one-off or short-term deal. The first **'And it came to pass'** is a *tempora frequentativa* (that is, it is used to introduce actions frequently repeated).[144] Thus the events recorded here probably took a matter of years, rather than days or months.

Jacob becomes very prosperous — the Hebrew literally says that **'he increased very very'**; the repetition of the particle has a superlative force. The verb 'to increase' was used earlier when God promised Jacob that he would 'spread out / increase' over the earth (28:14). Now that promise has been partially fulfilled.

Application

Jacob's statement to Laban that 'Yahweh has blessed you' locates the source of prosperity in the right place. Believers need to recognize that any prosperity that they enjoy does not come from their own abilities, but from the hand of the Lord. A story appeared in the *Western Recorder* many years ago about two stock-buyers in the southern states. One day they spotted a fine milk cow grazing in the patch of ground by the home of an old black man. They went to see the man, and one of them said to him, 'We would like to buy that cow. Does she belong to you?' The old man replied, 'No, sah, boss, dat ain't my cow. Hit's de Lawd's cow. I'm jest a-keepin' her for him.' Certainly the old man grasped the meaning of stewardship, that everything that he had came from the hand of God and belongs to him.

The great escape
(Genesis 31:1-21)

The final drama between Jacob and Laban is now about to unfold. Because of his increased wealth, obtained at a great cost to Laban, Jacob senses grave danger. There is heightening tension between himself and his father-in-law, and Laban's relatives are talking and complaining about him behind Jacob's back. So Jacob makes plans with his wives to flee from Haran and to return to Canaan.

31:1-2. Then he heard the words of the sons of Laban, saying, 'Jacob has taken all that belonged to our father, and from that which belonged to our father he has made all his wealth.' Then Jacob saw the face of Laban and, behold, it was not towards him as it once had been.

Through the two senses of hearing and seeing, Jacob realizes that there is impending danger and trouble from Laban and his kin.

First, because of his great success in securing most of Laban's flock, Jacob **'heard'** that Laban's **'sons'** are spitefully speaking about him. One cannot be certain whether these 'sons' are actually the children of Laban or merely his kinsmen (see 31:23). The Hebrew word can have a broad usage: in verse 28 it is used with regard to Laban's male grandchildren.

Secondly, Jacob **'saw'** that Laban's **'face ... was not towards him'**. The latter phrase is a Hebrew idiom signifying a generally unfavourable attitude of one person towards another. Jacob is simply out of favour with Laban.

The clause, **'as it once had been'**, is literally 'as yesterday [and] the third day'. It is another Hebrew idiom, one that expresses the idea of 'formerly', or what used to be an ongoing situation.

31:3. Then Yahweh said to Jacob, 'Return to the land of your fathers and to your relatives, and I will be with you.'

Because of the great danger in remaining here, **'Yahweh'** commands Jacob to return to Canaan. Canaan is called **'the land of your fathers'** for the first time in Scripture, although later this becomes a common epithet for it (e.g., Josh. 1:6; 5:6). No matter how great the peril, Yahweh tells Jacob, **'I will be with you.'** God has made that announcement to him already (28:15), and it is a proclamation of divine protection.

31:4-7. So Jacob sent and called for Rachel and Leah to his flock in the field. Then he said to them, 'I see that the face of your father is not towards me as it once was; but the God of my father has been with me. And you know that with all my strength I have served your father, but your father has deceived me and he has changed my wages ten times. But God has not allowed him to do evil against me.'

After God's call to leave Haran, Jacob first summons his two wives to the field where he is guarding his flock. It is a safe place away from the hearing of Laban and his kinfolk — in addition, Jacob may be hesitant to leave his flock unguarded. In his speech, Jacob attempts to make a case for his departing secretly for Canaan. He wants to see if his wives are willing to go with him. He begins his argument by relating the deceptive actions of Laban, in contrast to his own reliance on God. Jacob, in other words, has not been the trickster in the family. It is Laban who has been the deceiver.

Jacob also insists that his wives are aware that what he is saying is true. He says to them, literally, **'you, you know'**. That independent personal pronoun with a verb is used to accentuate the fact of their knowledge and it demonstrates their strongly focused attention.[145]

Jacob employs the figure of anadiplosis here. It means to use the same words at the end of one clause / sentence and then again at the beginning of the next clause / sentence.[146] In the present passage it appears as **'your father, but your father'**. Its purpose is to emphasize the most important character in the passage: Jacob is focusing on how Laban has treated him. In fact, Laban has changed his wages **'ten times'** — this number may, in fact, be a round number indicating repetition and completeness.

31:8-9. 'If he spoke thus, "The speckled ones will be your wages," then all the sheep were born speckled. But if he spoke thus, "The striped ones will be your wages," then all the sheep were born striped. So God took away the herd of your father and he has given [it] to me.'

Jacob shares with his wives the manner in which God has frustrated Laban's treachery. Over this last period of servitude, Laban has changed Jacob's wages: here Jacob explains how Laban did it. Laban would simply say at one time that Jacob's wages would be the striped animals, and then, when those animals increased, he would alter the pay and say that Jacob would have the spotted animals instead. The verbs used in this section are *frequentive*, signifying that this activity on Laban's part occurred repeatedly.[147]

But Yahweh has protected Jacob. He **'took away ... and he has given [it] to me'**. This is well-known legal terminology in the ancient Near East in regard to the transference of property.[148]

This story is an example of hysteresis — that is, the filling in the details of events that occurred a long time before.[149] We knew earlier that Laban had been deceptive in his dealings with Jacob, but now Jacob tells his wives exactly how Laban had tried to dupe him.

31:10-13. 'And it came to pass when the flock was in heat that I lifted my eyes, and I saw in a dream, that, behold, the male goats that were mating with the flock were striped, speckled, or spotted. Then the angel of God said to me in the dream, "Jacob". And I said, "Here I am." Then he said, "Now lift up your eyes and see that all the male goats mating with the flock are striped, speckled, or spotted, because I have seen all that Laban has done to you. I am the God of Bethel, where you anointed a pillar and where you vowed a vow to me. Now arise, go out from this land and return to the land of your birth."'

In his continuing conversation with his wives, Jacob reports that God has appeared to him in a dream. God reveals to him that it is his providence that has been behind Jacob's success with the animals. In other words, it was not Jacob's 'stratagem, but the providence of God which had prevented him from falling a victim to Laban's avarice, and had brought him such wealth'.[150]

This dream calls to mind the original dream theophany at Bethel in 28:18-22. There Jacob had vowed a vow and he had anointed a pillar (as a sacred, covenantal ritual). Jacob must therefore follow God's commands. And his directive is given at the end of the passage: **'Go out from this land and return to the land of your birth.'** This, ultimately, is the reason for Jacob's desire to return home: God has mandated it!

31:14-16. Then Rachel and Leah answered, and they said to him, 'Do we still have a portion and an inheritance in our father's house? Are we not considered aliens by him? Because he has sold us, and he has certainly consumed our price. For all the wealth that God took away from our father it is for us and our children. And, now, all that God has said to you, do [it]!'

The response of Laban's daughters is decidedly animated. First, they open with a rhetorical question — a figure often used to emphasize a person's incredulity. And within the question they include a hendiadys, **'a portion and an inheritance'**, for the purpose of intensification.

Secondly, they accuse their father of having **'certainly consumed'** their dowry. That phrase literally says, 'He has eaten, also eating' — this type of construction denotes the climax of a series of situations.[151] Rachel and Leah are upset, and they are frankly charging their father with violating the family law of their country.[152] He has simply squandered their money — he is treating them as if they are **'aliens'** or 'foreigners'. The point of the heightened response by the daughters is that they give Jacob total leave and autonomy to act as he sees fit — that is, according to the word of God.

31:17-21. So Jacob arose, and he put his children and his wives on camels. And he drove all his herd and all his property which he had collected, his acquired herd, which he had collected in Paddan-Aram, to go to Isaac his father, to the land of Canaan. When Laban went to shear his flock, Rachel stole the household gods belonging to her father. Thus Jacob stole the heart of Laban, the Aramaean, by failing to tell him that he was fleeing. Thus he fled with all that belonged to him. And he arose and he crossed the river, and he set his face to the hill country of Gilead.

It is sheep-shearing season, a time of considerable work and feasting (see 1 Sam. 25). Laban and, obviously, many of his kinsmen go to the fields to shear the flock. It is a perfect time for Jacob to attempt an escape; in fact, Laban is so far removed that he does not hear of the escape for three days (31:22). The text says that Jacob **'fled'** and **'arose'**. Back in 27:43, Rebekah had used the same verbs to command Jacob to go to Laban — but she had said, 'Arise ... flee.' It is an *inclusio*, and the 'reversal of word order symbolizes reversal of direction'.[153]

Jacob's first order of business is to put his family on camels for the trip to Canaan. Some scholars argue that this is anachronistic because camels were not domesticated at such an early date. On the contrary, it appears that the domestication of camels began in the Levant by at least 2000 B.C.[154] The mention of camels at this point is also preparatory to the next episode in the story, in which Rachel hides idols under a camel's saddle (31:34).

Jacob takes with him all the property he had gained in Haran. The phrase **'acquired herd'** appears redundant, but its purpose is to highlight the fact that these things do indeed rightfully and legally belong to him. Rachel, however, takes some objects that do not belong to her: the **'household gods'** or 'teraphim'. It is difficult to be sure precisely what these objects are. Laban calls them **'gods'** (31:30). Some of them apparently had human shapes (1 Sam. 19:13,16). Their purpose was to obtain oracles (Ezek. 21:21). Why Rachel steals them is uncertain, although it may have been to prevent Laban from using them for divination — that is, to detect Jacob's escape route (cf. 30:27).[155] Others argue that possession of family gods symbolized title to family property in the ancient Near East, and so Rachel steals the gods to safeguard her inheritance.[156]

The consequence of Jacob's escape is that he **'stole the heart of Laban, the Aramaean'**. This is an odd expression in Hebrew. The phrase is perhaps to be understood as a double word-play: the word **'heart'** in Hebrew is *lēb,* and it echoes the name **'Laban'**; the term **'Aramaean'** evokes the stem *rāmāh,* which means 'to cheat'. Thus the idea is that 'Laban the heartless cheat has been beaten at his own game'![157]

The first topographical feature Jacob encounters is **'the river'**. This is a figure of speech called an antonomasia, that is, the change of a proper name for an appellative.[158] It is a reference to the Euphrates river (see Josh. 24:2; Ps. 72:8; Micah 7:12). After he crosses the river, he then heads towards the hill country of Gilead. **'Gilead'** is a region of Transjordan that lies south-south-east of the Sea of Galilee. It appears that Jacob is planning to take a Transjordanian route to the Arabah and, in particular, to Beersheba. This is a well-known route from antiquity.[159] On his way to Haran, Jacob had taken the usual route through the hill-country of Canaan — that is, the 'spine'; now he goes a different way, perhaps to keep Laban off his track.

Application

The story of Laban and Jacob is 'an honest if disturbing vignette of human history. It is a story of greed, lies, and feigned innocence which poisoned relationships and led to threats of violence. From Laban's deceit in giving his daughters to Jacob in marriage to Jacob's skilful manipulation of Laban's flocks and herds so that his holdings were increased at Laban's expense, the relationship had gone from bad to worse.'[160] It reflects the human predicament in a sinful world. It declares to the world, like a signpost, the brokenness of creation and humanity, in particular.

The story also demonstrates that humans have a need for that brokenness to be taken care of. A wicked man once asked Asahel Nettleton, 'How came I by my wicked heart?' 'That,' he replied, 'is a question which does not concern you so much as another, namely, How you shall get rid of it. You have a wicked heart, which renders you entirely unfit for the kingdom of God; and you must have a new heart, or you cannot be saved; and the question which now most deeply concerns you is, How shall you obtain it?' The fact is that all humans are truly broken like Laban and Jacob — and the only question is, how can it be taken care of? Jesus is the answer. And he makes the offer: 'Come to me, all who are weary and heavy-laden, and I will give you rest ... and you will find rest for your souls' (Matt. 11:28-29). Will you turn to him this day?

Laban pursues Jacob
(Genesis 31:22-35)

When it is reported to Laban that Jacob has fled with his daughters and all his flocks, he then immediately pursues Jacob. After a lengthy chase, Laban overtakes him in the hill-country of Gilead. There God warns Laban to be careful how he deals with Jacob. The next day, Laban and Jacob have their opening confrontation regarding Jacob's departure. Laban feels mistreated, especially because his gods have been stolen. He plays the part of one who has been deceived!

31:22-23. And it was reported to Laban on the third day that Jacob had fled. So he took his relatives with him, and he pursued after him [on] a journey of seven days and he overtook him in the hill-country of Gilead.

When Laban hears that Jacob has fled, he takes his **'relatives'** and goes in hot pursuit. The term for 'relatives' is literally 'brothers', but here it is being used as a synecdoche for his relatives in general. It takes them **'seven days'** to catch up with Jacob in the hill-country of Gilead. The number **'seven'** here is certainly a figure signifying a considerable length of time (see 2 Kings 3:9). From Haran to the region of Gilead is approximately 350 miles (as the crow flies) — for Jacob to have travelled that far in ten days, he, and all his flocks and property, would have had to average thirty-five miles per day. He could hardly have made it that far in so short a period. In any event, this is a time of great peril and danger for Jacob — Laban and his kin clearly have malice in their hearts.

31:24-25. Then God came to Laban the Aramaean in a dream at night. And he said to him, 'Guard yourself lest you speak with Jacob either good or evil.' Now Laban overtook Jacob when Jacob had pitched his tents in the hill-country. So Laban pitched [his tents] with his relatives in the hill-country of Gilead.

Obviously, Laban's intentions towards Jacob are hostile and, possibly, violent. In support of this enmity is the use of the verb 'to pitch'. It is not the common Hebrew verb used throughout the Bible to signify the pitching of tents *(nātāh)*. In fact, it is quite rare, employed elsewhere only in Jeremiah 6:3, where it occurs in the context of warring tribesmen (see, in particular, Jer. 6:4). Here, in the episode involving Jacob and Laban, the verb is being used to reflect a similarly antagonistic situation.[161]

God, however, intervenes so that the danger level is severely reduced. In a dream, he speaks to Laban, and he orders him to be careful in what he says to Jacob. The phrase **'either good or evil'** is a merism. The point is that God is warning Laban to take great care in how he speaks to Jacob about anything at all.

31:26-30. And Laban said to Jacob, 'What have you done that you stole my heart and drove off my daughters like captives of the sword? Why did you flee secretly and deceive me, and not tell me so that I might have sent you out in joy and with songs of tambourines and lyres? And you did not permit me to kiss my sons and my daughters. Now you have done foolishly. There is strength in my hand to do evil to you, but the God of your father last night spoke to me saying, "Guard yourself from speaking with Jacob either good or

evil." And now you have certainly left because you have
greatly longed for your father's house. Why did you steal my
gods?'

Laban's first words to Jacob are: **'What have you
done?'** This is a common form of accusation against
wrong-doers in the book of Genesis (see 3:13; 4:10).
It reflects Laban's indignation and expostulation. He
feels he has been wronged. In fact, Jacob himself
used that very question of Laban in Genesis 29:25
when he discovered that the woman he had married
was Leah and not Rachel!

Laban threatens Jacob with physical harm: he
says, literally, **'There is strength in my hand to do
with you evil.'** The Hebrew term translated **'there
is'** is a particle of existence, implying the idea that it
is in his power at that very moment to destroy Jacob
— and not only Jacob: the object **'you'** is a plural
pronoun — that is, all that are with Jacob. So the
danger is real and great. Yet Yahweh has intervened
and he has prevented Laban from hurting Jacob.
Laban now appears to understand why Jacob has
left: that fact is supported by the emphasis supplied
with two verbs and their infinitives. Laban literally
says, **'You have left leaving because you longed
longingly for your father's house.'** It is a typical
construction to denote intensity.

So far, everything that Laban has said is mere
reproach. But at the end of his speech he comes to
the point: **'Why did you steal my gods?'** This is the
true issue for Laban, and it will lead to his physical
inspection of Jacob's property.

31:31-32. Then Jacob answered, and he said to Laban,
'Because I was afraid, so I said, "Lest you take violent
possession of your daughters from me." With whomever you
find your gods, he will not live. In the presence of our relatives see if what belongs to you is with me, then take it to

yourself.' But Jacob did not know that Rachel had stolen them.

Jacob's reply is in two parts, in response to Laban's two-part accusation. In regard to his leaving clandestinely, Jacob admits that he was afraid. He feared that Laban would **'take violent possession'** of his daughters and take them away from Jacob. That verb in Hebrew is *gāzal*, and it is a harsh, severe term, signifying the act of 'tearing away with force'. Jacob does not employ the common Hebrew word for 'to steal' *(gānab)* because he knows that Laban has vicious intentions which involve physical violence.

Jacob then responds to Laban's accusation of stealing gods by taking a vow. He pronounces an imprecation on whoever has done this, that the person responsible will be subject to the death penalty. Capital punishment was rarely imposed for stealing in the ancient Near East — thus Jacob indicates that he takes the matter at hand very seriously. But it appears to be a foolish vow on his part. He, ironically and unwittingly, is in fact pronouncing the death sentence on his beloved wife Rachel.

31:33-35. So Laban came into Jacob's tent and into Leah's tent and into the tent of the two handmaids, but he did not find [them]. And he came out of Leah's tent and came into Rachel's tent. And Rachel had taken the household gods and she had put them in the saddle of the camel, and she sat on them. And Laban searched the whole tent, but he did not find [them]. And she said to her father, 'Let there not be anger in the eyes of my lord, for I am not able to rise before you — because I am in the way of women.' So he searched, but he did not find the household gods.

Despite Jacob's declaration, which would reflect innocence on his part, Laban begins his search with

Jacob's quarters. It is ironic that in Laban's eyes Jacob is the most likely culprit, so he searches his tent first — but the reader knows that Jacob is, in fact, innocent and that he has no knowledge of the incident! The drama, of course, heightens because the last tent in which he rummages belongs to the true villain of the piece, his daughter Rachel.

Rachel has taken the teraphim and she has hidden them beneath the saddle of her camel. Such saddles are known from reliefs of the ancient Near East.[162] Rachel then sits on the saddle in Laban's presence claiming that she cannot rise for she is in the **'way of women'** — an obvious reference to menstruation. According to ancient Near-Eastern law (see, e.g., Lev. 15:19-24) and custom, a woman in such a state was unclean / impure. Rachel is thus demonstrating the unholiness and worthlessness of Laban's gods by sitting on them and making them unclean. And, of course, the great irony is that Laban is deceived by his own daughter — his actions have come back on his own head, because he had acted deceitfully in the marriage episode.

Application

As the story of Jacob and Laban unfolds, we see a picture of great conflict, one that is on the brink of uncontrolled violence. It is the divine presence that restrains the hostility — a hostility that could easily have ended in fratricide. God simply restrains them in their sin. By nature, humans are totally self-absorbed and have their own self-interests in mind. But God does not leave people unchecked — he often curbs their desires and places divine fetters upon them. What a glorious thing that God does not allow humanity to operate unbridled, for if he did, then we would all soon be destroyed!

Jacob's defence
(Genesis 31:36-42)

Jacob's innocence in the situation is evident because Laban is unable to find the teraphim among his property. And even though Laban has the military superiority here, Jacob responds with righteous indignation. His reaction is not merely one of bitter resentment against the present situation, but his animosity spews forth in regard to the entire period of servitude under Laban. Special attention is paid in the section to the hardships that Jacob has endured.

31:36-37. Then Jacob became angry, and he strove with Laban. And Jacob answered, and he said to Laban, 'What is my transgression? What is my sin, that you hotly pursue after me? For you have searched all my goods, and what have you found of all the goods of your house? Place [it] thus before my relatives and your relatives, and let them decide between the two of us.'

Jacob responds in kind to Laban. Yet Jacob argues that he has legal rights and protection. He employs legal terminology in his speech: first, the verb translated **'strove'** is frequently used in a jurisprudential context.[163] Secondly, the idea that Jacob wants to put the matter in the hands of the relatives to **'decide'** has similar legal connotations — the term often simply means 'to judge'. The entire scene bears characteristics of a forensic context; we are witnessing legal proceedings.

31:38-40. 'These twenty years I have been with you, your ewes and your she-goats have not miscarried and I have not eaten the rams of your flock. I did not bring to you a torn animal; I bore the loss. You sought payment from me when something was stolen away by day or by night. [When] I was in the day, the heat consumed me and the cold in the night; and my sleep fled from my eyes.'

Jacob now claims that he has kept his side of the bargain with Laban. Then he proceeds to recite his grievances staccato fashion — there is an acute lack of conjunctions in his speech; he lists his grievances rapidly, one after the other.

One of Jacob's complaints is that he did not make Laban bear the loss when an animal from his flock was torn apart by a wild beast. Instead, Jacob paid for it — although in ancient Near-Eastern law the shepherd was not generally held accountable for such a loss. The Code of Hammurabi, for instance, reads: 'If a visitation of god has occurred in a sheepfold or a lion has made a kill, the shepherd shall prove himself innocent in the presence of the god, but the owner of the sheepfold shall receive from him the animal stricken in the fold' (Law no. 266).[164] The fact of the matter is that Jacob has gone beyond what is required of him by the law.

Laban, on the other hand, has been unreasonable. The fact that he required Jacob to make good the value of animals stolen under his care seems to have been legal; however, Jacob's use of a merism, **'day or night'**, indicates that Laban made such claims even when Jacob was not with the flock. Apparently Jacob was under obligation seven days a week, twenty-four hours a day!

31:41-42. 'These twenty years I was in your house: I served you fourteen years for your two daughters and six years for your flock. And you changed my wages ten times. Except that the God of my father and the Awe of Isaac was with me, certainly now you would have sent me out empty-handed. My affliction and the toil of my hands, God has seen, so he judged last night.'

Jacob goes on to argue that Laban did not keep his side of the bargain. In reality, he altered Jacob's pay many times, an accusation that Jacob had already related to his wives (31:7). Jacob is also under no illusions regarding how Laban would have dealt with him in the future: Laban would not have sent him away 'in joy and with songs of tambourines and lyres' (31:27), but **'empty-handed'**. Thus, Jacob would have worked all those years for Laban for *nothing*.

Jacob also realizes that it is God who has shielded him from disaster. He uses a form of hendiadys when speaking of God — **'the God of my father and the Awe of Isaac'** — for the purpose of intensification. It is this God who has delivered him, and no other! The first title is a common epithet for God, going back to 26:24 (see commentary on that verse). The second is used only here, and perhaps in verse 53, in the entire Bible. The word **'Awe'** is a metonymy standing for the one who is held in awe, or revered.[165] The name may reflect the ordeal of Isaac reported in Genesis 22.[166]

In verse 37, Jacob had dared Laban to lay the stolen objects before all their relatives and 'let them decide between the two of us'. The verb for 'decide' is the same one used here saying that God has already **'judged'**. In other words, the fact of God's speaking to Laban in a dream the night before demonstrates that God has already made his mind up regarding whom he supports: it is Jacob and not Laban. So Jacob has both human and divine support.

Application

Jacob recognizes that it is 'the God of my father and the Awe of
Isaac' who has protected him from the treacherous hand of
Laban. We need to be clear that Laban had malicious intent and
ill-will against Jacob — who knows what would have happened to
Jacob apart from God's protecting shield?

The missionary John G. Paton awoke one night to find the
natives of the New Hebrides burning down the church next to his
home. In his autobiography he describes the scene: 'They yelled
in rage and urged each other to strike the first blow, but the
Invisible One restrained them. I stood invulnerable beneath His
invisible shield. At this dread moment a rushing and roaring
sound came from the south like the noise of muttering thunder.
They knew from previous hard experience that it was one of their
awful tornadoes of wind and rain. The mighty roaring of the wind,
and the cloud pouring in torrents awed them into silence. Some
began to withdraw from the scene, all lowered their weapons of
war, and several, terror-struck, exclaimed: "That is Jehovah's
rain! Truly their Jehovah is fighting for them and helping them.
Let us away!"'

In Jesus' first sermon he proclaims that he has come to
deliver his people. He reads from the prophet Isaiah and applies
the words to his own ministry:

> The Spirit of the Lord is upon me,
> Because he anointed me to preach the gospel to the poor.
> He has sent me to proclaim release to the captives,
> And recovery of sight to the blind,
> To set free those who are oppressed,
> To proclaim the favourable year of the Lord
>
> (Luke 4:18-19).

The covenant between Laban and Jacob (Genesis 31:43-55)

The dispute between Laban and Jacob now draws to a conclusion. Laban offers a covenant agreement to Jacob, a treaty of peace and non-aggression. This covenant is typical of many that have been found from the ancient Near East.[167] The provisions of the treaty deal with some family matters and issues which could potentially lead to future disputes — the latter are taken care of by the erection of boundary markers.

31:43-44. Then Laban answered, and he said to Jacob, 'The daughters are my daughters, and the sons are my sons, and the flock is my flock, and all that you see belongs to me. But what can I do to these my daughters today or to their sons which they have borne? So, now, come, let us make a covenant, I and you, and he will be a witness between me and you.'

The beginning of Laban's response lacks tact. He states directly and without hesitation or reservation that everything that Jacob has really belongs to him. He does not waver in his moral stance regarding these matters. Yet it is interesting that Laban does not mention the teraphim — a point which causes one to wonder whether the stolen household gods were not merely an excuse for Laban to pursue Jacob. What Laban really wants is to recover all his possessions!

Nevertheless, Laban relents and offers to enter into a covenant agreement with Jacob. His rationale for making such a treaty is that he does not want to harm his daughters or grandchildren. Included in the covenant will be a witness, or testimony to its validity. Many translations say, 'it will be a witness', understanding the 'it' as referring to the covenant itself. The problem with that rendition is that the word **'covenant'** is a feminine noun and the verb here for **'will be'** is in the third person masculine singular.[168] Thus, for the sake of agreement, the phrase ought to be translated as **'he will be a witness'**, and the pronoun is a reference to Yahweh. Thus Laban and Jacob are about to make a treaty with God as the one who testifies to its validity.[169]

31:45-46. So Jacob took a stone and he set it up as a pillar. And Jacob said to his relatives, 'Pick up stones.' So they took stones and they made a heap. Then they ate there next to the heap.

Jacob proceeds at once to enact his father-in-law's proposal. He first takes a single stone and sets it up as a *mazzeboth,* that is, a **'pillar'**. The act is reminiscent of the scene described in 28:18-22, the commemorative display at Bethel. Jacob may consciously be performing a similar act to demonstrate the presence of God as witness to the ratification of the covenant.

Jacob then commands his relatives (the verb for **'pick up'** is a plural imperative) to gather stones, and they make a heap out of them. This heap and the pillar both serve as physical witnesses to the compact — the ceremony thus involves a double sign, certainly for the purpose of intensification.[170]

The preposition translated **'next to'** often simply means 'upon', so it has been suggested that Jacob and his relatives use the heap as a table at which they eat the covenantal meal.[171] That is unlikely, however, for the preposition is simply being used in a contingent locational sense (that is, to mean 'beside / near'.[172]

31:47-50. And Laban called it Yegar-Sachadutha, but Jacob called it Galeed. Then Laban said, 'This heap is a witness between me and you today.' Therefore, he called its name Galeed and Mizpah, for he said, 'May Yahweh keep watch between me and you when we are separated one from another. If you mistreat my daughters, or if you take wives besides my daughters, [even though] no man is with you, see [that] God is a witness between me and you.'

Laban calls the pile of stones by the name **'Yegar-Sachadutha'**, literally 'the heap of stones', in his native Aramaic tongue. Jacob calls it **'Galeed'**, which means exactly the same thing in the Hebrew language. Laban also names it **'Mizpah'**, a name that means 'height' or 'tower' — obviously reflecting the stature of the monument. In later parts of Scripture, there is an important site called Mizpah of Gilead (Judg. 10:17; 11:11,29). The etymology of that site name is being recorded here in the story of Jacob.

Laban spells out a few of the stipulations of the treaty. First, the condition that Jacob should not take any more wives is typical of many marriage documents from Mesopotamia, such as at Nuzi.[173] Secondly, Jacob is not to **'mistreat'** Leah or Rachel. That Hebrew verb covers a wide range of ways in which people can be afflicted, so it is clear that Laban is consciously using a term which is broad in its application.[174] He simply does not want his daughters mishandled in any way, shape, or form.

The phrase, **'[even though] no man is with us, see'**, has been repointed in the Hebrew by some scholars so that it reads, '[even though] no man of our people is watching'.[175] This latter reading would highlight the lack of trust between Laban and Jacob. Such a revision is linguistically possible, but the repointing would involve the use of a very rare form. Thus I have adopted the more common translation.

Covenants in the ancient Near East normally contained a witness clause. Often the witnesses to the treaty were the gods of the land.[176] Yahweh is serving as the one who testifies to the treaty between Laban and Jacob; this demonstrates divine sanction.

31:51-53. **Then Laban said to Jacob, 'Behold this heap and behold the pillar which I have set between me and you. This heap is a witness and the pillar is a witness that I will not pass by this heap to harm you, and you will not pass by this heap or this pillar to harm me. May the God of Abraham and the god of Nahor, the gods of their father, judge between us.' So Jacob swore by the Awe of his father Isaac.**

Not only do the heap and the pillar serve as earthly, physical symbols of the covenant between the two men, but they also appear to be boundary markers. Jacob and Laban agree not to pass by these markers with malicious intent. It is to be noted that in later history Gilead becomes an area of dispute between Israel and Aram (see 1 Kings 22:3; 2 Kings 9:14).

Verse 52 is a solemn oath that Laban and Jacob agree to and then pronounce. This is confirmed by the use of the Hebrew term *'im* in front of the personal pronouns **'I'** and **'you'**. It is left untranslated, but its purpose is to act as a signpost to the utterance of an oath.[177]

The verb **'judge'** is in the plural, probably indicating that the **'God of Abraham'** and the **'god of Nahor'** are separate deities. The first is the guardian of the covenant on the side of Jacob, the other the protector of Laban. **'Nahor'** was, in fact, the grandfather of Aram, the progenitor of the Aramaeans. So Laban calls upon his basic polytheistic understanding of the universe as a witness to the covenant. Note, however, that Jacob responds by swearing only by the name of the Awe of Isaac! (For commentary on the latter epithet, see 31:42.)

31:54-55. Then Jacob offered a sacrifice in the hill-country, and he called to his relatives to eat food. And they ate food, and they spent the night in the hill-country. When Laban awoke in the morning, he kissed his sons and his daughters and he blessed them. Then Laban left, and he returned to his place.

Jacob then prepares a sacrificial meal, and he calls his relatives to partake. Apparently Laban and his people are included. The feast serves as a seal to the agreement between the two men (see commentary on 26:30).

Laban is obviously appeased. He bids his family farewell and then departs peaceably. Laban consequently returns **'to his place'** — according to 24:10 that place is 'the city of Nahor'. So ends a twenty-year period and relationship between Jacob and Laban.

Application

Jacob is presented in a good light in this concluding episode with Laban. He reflects a fine, upstanding, godly character. He is quick to make peace — it is an easy conciliation. Although he has endured many serious and grievous wrongs at the hand of Laban, Jacob stretches forth his hand in peace. It is Jacob who sets up the pillar first, and who orders his relatives to build the heap. He does not do it begrudgingly, and his lack of resentment is quite astonishing. Oh that the people of the church would act the same way! Richard Whately once commented, 'To cherish, or to gratify, haughty resentment, is a departure from the pattern left us by him who "endured such contradiction of sinners against himself", not to be justified by any offence that can be committed against us. And it is this recollection of him who, faultless himself, designed to leave us an example of meekness and long-suffering, that is the true principle and motive of Christian forgiveness. We shall best fortify our patience under injuries by remembering how much we ourselves have to be forgiven, and that it was "while we were yet sinners, Christ died for us".'

Yet it should also be observed that Jacob, even in forgiveness, does not compromise the truth. He does not swear superstitiously or imprudently. As Calvin says, Jacob 'did not assent to the preposterous form of oath dictated by his father-in-law; as too many do, who, in order to gain the favour of the wicked, pretend to be of the same religion with them'.[178]

Jacob prepares to meet Esau
(Genesis 32:1-23)

After solving and putting behind him the problems of one stormy relationship, Jacob soon finds himself encountering another. He has left Haran and is now travelling to Canaan. But that is where Esau resides — the brother who had announced that he would kill Jacob. And even though twenty years have passed, Jacob is well aware of the deep-seated hatred on Esau's part because of their prior relationship. How will Esau respond to Jacob's arrival? Jacob does not know, so he makes detailed preparations for their meeting.

32:1-2. Then Jacob went on his way, and the angels of God met him. And Jacob said when he saw them, 'This is the encampment of God.' So he called the name of that place Mahanaim.

On his way to Haran, many years earlier, Jacob had an encounter with the angels of God (28:12). The purpose of that vision was so that Jacob would be encouraged on his journey, knowing that he was protected by God's messengers. Now Jacob is on his way back to Canaan from Haran, and angels appear to him again. It is probably for the same reason: Jacob is about to meet Esau, and he thus needs hope and comfort.

Jacob declares that the place is **'the encampment'** of God, and he calls it **'Mahanaim'**. The latter

term is the Hebrew word for 'encampment', except
that it is a dual form meaning 'two camps'. The
change from a singular to a dual anticipates Jacob's
separating his people and goods into two 'companies'
(32:7-8). In fact, the word 'company' is the same word
as 'camp' in our present verses.

Mahanaim is an important city in later Israelite
history. It is appointed a Levitical city in the territory
of Gad (Josh. 21:38). Ishbosheth, the son of Saul, is
made king here (2 Sam. 2:8-9). It is near this town
that the army of David defeats the host of Absalom
(2 Sam. 17-18). One of the twelve chief officers of
Solomon resides there (1 Kings 4:14).

32:3-5. **Then Jacob sent messengers before him to Esau his
brother, to the land of Seir, the country of Edom. And he
commanded them, saying, 'Thus you will say: ' "To my
master Esau: Thus says your servant Jacob, I have been
sojourning with Laban and I have remained [there] until now.
And I have oxen and donkeys, sheep, and male and female
servants; and I have sent to tell [it] to my master in order to
find favour in your eyes." '**

Jacob has set things right with Laban; now he intends to be reconciled with his brother Esau. But,
obviously, he does so with great fear and trepidation.
So he makes detailed preparations and safeguards
for meeting Esau. His first act is to send messengers
to Esau to scout out the situation, in order to determine Esau's demeanour towards him. Certainly
Jacob believes that Esau still maintains great hostility and enmity towards him. The first sentence of the
passage reminds the reader of that earlier series of
conflicts: the name **'Seir'** brings to mind the hairiness of Esau (25:24-26); the reference to the **'country'**, or 'field', recalls the incident in which Jacob
secured the birthright (25:27-30); and **'Edom'**, of
course, is a term which owes its origin to Esau's

eating of the red stew that Jacob had made (25:29-30).

Jacob's first act of sending *mal'ākīm* (**'messengers'**) is in response to his seeing the *mal'ākīm* ('angels') of God. Curtis comments on this parallel: 'Given what we know of Jacob at this point it seems likely that the repetition of the word *mal'ākīm* is intended to make the point that Jacob was trying to do the same thing that God was doing.'[179] In other words, Jacob is depending on his own ways, power and efforts to solve the problem at hand.

Jacob's message to Esau has a conciliatory tone. Numerous translations (e.g., NIV, NASB) do not include the phrase, **'To my master Esau'**, in the content of Jacob's message, but merely as part of the instructions to the messengers. But surely Jacob would not refer to Esau in such a way in private. In addition, we know that there was a common ancient Near-Eastern epistolary formula that read: 'To my lord X say, thus speaks your servant Y.'[180] For example, the Lachish letters are addressed by an inferior ('your servant', as in our text) to a superior ('my master / lord', also as in our text).[181] That point underscores what Jacob is doing here: he is placing himself in a subordinate position in relation to Esau. That, of course, is ironic because previously Jacob had pilfered Esau's birthright and blessing.

Finally, Jacob lists various possessions he has accumulated during his time at Haran. It has been suggested that Jacob does this in order to alert Esau that he is willing to give a substantial gift in return for peace and safety.[182]

32:6-8. And the messengers returned to Jacob, saying, 'We came to your brother, to Esau, and, indeed, he is coming to meet you, and 400 men are with him.' So Jacob was very frightened and distressed. Thus he divided the people who were with him, and the flocks and the cattle and the camels,

into two companies. And he said, 'If Esau comes against one
company and strikes it, then the remaining company will be
able to escape.'

The report which the messengers bring back to Jacob
is not clear as to whether Esau is coming in amity or
enmity. Jacob, however, senses great danger. The
number of men that Esau is bringing with him appears to be excessive and ominous — 400 men also
seems to have been a standard size for a militia in
antiquity (see 1 Sam. 22:2; 25:13; 30:10,17).[183] What
are Esau's intentions?

Jacob takes some defensive measures. He divides
his people and his possessions into two **'companies'**,
or 'camps'. He does this so that if Esau attacks, then
Jacob will not lose everything. It should be noted that
'camels' were not mentioned among Jacob's possessions in his message to Esau: perhaps they were
too precious a commodity to have been included in
that list. He does, however, end up presenting thirty
of them to Esau (32:15).

32:9-12. Then Jacob said, 'O God of my father Abraham,
and O God of my father Isaac, O Yahweh, who said to me,
"Return to your land and to your relatives, and I will cause
you to prosper," I am small in relation to all the covenant
loyalty and faithfulness you have done to your servant —
because I crossed this Jordan with [only] my staff, but now I
am two companies. Deliver me, please, from the hand of my
brother, from the hand of Esau, because I am afraid of him
— lest he strike me, the mothers with [their children]. But you
said, "I will certainly cause you to prosper. And I will establish
your seed like the sand of the sea, which cannot be counted
for multitude."'

Jacob now responds to his trying circumstances by
turning to God in prayer. His prayer consists of five
parts. The opening of it is an *invocation*, in which the

one who is being addressed receives great praise and honour. The second part is a *recitation*: here Jacob recalls what God had previously promised him (based on 28:12-15 and 31:3). Then follows Jacob's *confession*. Here he employs a comparison of capability (the expression translated, **'in relation to'**) in order to demonstrate his own inadequacy in comparison with God's love towards him.[184] The phrase, **'I am small in relation to'** is idiomatic for the idea that 'I am unworthy'. The two characteristics of **'covenant loyalty and faithfulness'** serve as a hendiadys for the purpose of intensification of the concept conveyed. The fourth part of the prayer is a *petition* — Jacob seeks Yahweh's intervention in his present trying circumstances. And, finally, Jacob uses a second *recitation* so that God would certainly act upon the promises he made to the patriarch. The expression, **'like the sand of the sea'** becomes proverbial in Scripture in order to signify an innumerable multitude (22:17; 41:49).

32:13-15. And he lodged there in that night. Then he took from what belonged to him as a present for Esau, his brother: 200 female goats and twenty male goats; 200 ewes and twenty rams; thirty nursing camels and their offspring; forty heifers and ten bulls; twenty female donkeys and ten male donkeys.

Jacob spends the night at Mahanaim. But prior to resting, he decides to give a **'present'**, or 'gift', to Esau before they meet. That word in Hebrew has the consonantal structure *m-n-ḥ-h*, and there appears to be an intentional assonance with the Hebrew word meaning 'camp / company / Mahanaim' (*m-ḥ-n-h*). This play on words may indicate that Jacob is willing to part with a 'present', but not with one of his 'companies'.

Provision of tribute from someone of lower status to one of higher rank was common in the ancient Near East. It was a polite custom. However, Jacob's list is too lavish even by those standards: it consists of 550 animals that are of breeding age. The gesture undoubtedly reflects the magnitude of Jacob's fear at the thought of meeting his brother — his purpose, of course, is to ameliorate the situation.

32:16-20. So he gave [them] into the hand of his servants, herd by herd by themselves. Then he said to his servants, 'Cross before me, and put an interval between one herd and another herd.' And he commanded the one in the lead, saying, 'When my brother Esau meets you, and he asks you, saying, "To whom do you belong? And where are you going? And to whom do these [animals] belong that are before you?", then you shall say, "To your servant, to Jacob: it is a present sent to my master, to Esau. And, behold, he is coming after us."' He also commanded the second, also the third, also all who went after the herds, saying, 'According to this word you shall speak to Esau when you go out to him. And you shall also say, "Behold, your servant Jacob is coming after us."' For he said, 'I will pacify him with the present going before me; and afterwards I will see his face — perhaps he will be gracious to me.'

The expression translated **'herd by herd'** reads literally in the Hebrew 'herd, herd' — the repetition of the noun is a common construction signifying a *distributive* sense.[185] Jacob's plan is to send individual herds as a present to Esau with time lapses between the arrival of each. Obviously, he wants to appease Esau's anger in stages, and to overwhelm him with his generosity. Jacob hopes that by doing this he **'will pacify him'** — a similar idiom appears in Exodus 32:30, and there it certainly carries the idea of atonement.[186] He clearly desires to have a reconciliation with his brother, and a covering over of past deeds and enmity.

Jacob's hope is that Esau will, literally, **'lift my face'**. This is a Hebrew idiom that means to confer favour on another person.[187] In addition, in the final verse the word **'face'** appears four times in the Hebrew, and then again in the next verse (32:21). The reason for this is anticipation: the next story, Jacob's wrestling with the angel, occurs at Peniel, a Hebrew term that means 'the face of God'.

32:21-23. And the gift passed before him, but he lodged that night in the camp. Then he arose in that night, and he took his two wives and his two handmaids and his eleven sons, and he crossed the ford of the Jabbok. And he took them and he sent them across the river, and he sent across all that belonged to him.

Jacob does not follow immediately behind the gifts that he presents to Esau, but he spends the night in the camp. Yet he is uneasy and restless, because fear overtakes him. So he takes another guarded measure: he gives up the idea of two camps and places everyone and everything on the north side of the river — perhaps at Mahanaim.[188] Esau is coming from the south, so Jacob takes up a defensive position, putting the river between the two of them.

The reason why Dinah is excluded (see 30:21) and only the eleven sons are mentioned is anticipatory. In the next episode Jacob is given the name of Israel and, of course, it is his sons who become the fathers of the tribes of Israel.

Application

Prior to this present incident, there has been little evidence of Jacob's relying solely upon God in any situation. He appears

basically as a self-sufficient person, one who trusts in his own
ways to get what he wants. There was some breakdown of his
self-reliance in the episode with Laban, but it was only a partial
dependence. That is the case in the present story as well —
there is a certain degree of dependence when he prays to God,
yet he employs all his own ways and means to protect himself
from Esau. It is once again only a partial reliance. In whom does
Jacob trust?

The same question is true for all of us. J. C. Ryle put it this
way: 'The bankrupt who asks a bankrupt to set him up in business again is only losing time. The pauper who travels off to a
neighbour pauper, and begs him to help him out of difficulties, is
only troubling himself in vain. The prisoner does not beg his
fellow prisoner to set him free. The shipwrecked sailor does not
call on his shipwrecked comrade to place him safe ashore. Help
in all these cases must come from some other quarter. Relief in
all these cases must be sought from some other hand... So long
as you seek it from man, whether man ordained or man not
ordained, you seek it where it cannot be found.'

Wrestling with God
(Genesis 32:24-32)

This present section is a mysterious and perplexing narrative. Its obscurity primarily stems from the question of the identity of the adversary with whom Jacob wrestles. Many interpretations have been given regarding this issue, and they range from the rational to the bizarre.[189] It has been argued that the foe is Jacob's guardian angel, or Esau,[190] or Isaac. Others see Jacob wrestling with himself, with his fear, guilt and shame. Maimonides says it is merely a dream. Some see the adversary as some sinister character, such as a nocturnal demon or a Canaanite god.[191] It has even been argued that this story has nothing to do with Jacob, but rather that it reflects the tensions of the exile community of the Jews in Babylon.[192]

32:24-25. So Jacob was left alone, and a man wrestled with him until daybreak. When he saw that he did not prevail against him, he touched the socket of his hip. So the socket of Jacob's hip was dislocated when he wrestled with him.

Jacob finishes sending all his people and possessions to the other side of the Jabbok river. Now he stands alone. Then a mysterious figure appears and **'wrestles'** with Jacob all night until the rising of the sun. That verb in Hebrew is *'abāq;* it occurs only in this passage, where it serves as an important word-play on the sounds of the two names, Jacob and Jabbok.[193]

Who is this man with whom Jacob wrestles? First, it must be noted that it is a **'man'**; however, as we know from earlier episodes, divine beings may appear as men. So the 'three men' who visit Abraham are, in reality, two angels and Yahweh (18:1-2). In fact, the later prophet Hosea concludes that it is an 'angel' that wrestles with Jacob (12:4). The rabbis explain it as Jacob's guardian angel (*Gen. R.*77).[194] But that explanation is insufficient because Jacob says in verse 30, 'I have seen God face to face.' Apparently this figure is none other than 'the Angel of the Lord' who in Scripture is at times identified with God and speaks as if he is God (see, especially, Exod. 3:2-6; Judg. 13:17-22). Some commentators argue that this figure is the pre-incarnate Christ, the Second Person of the Trinity. As Calvin says, 'But let us enquire who this Angel was? ... The ancient teachers of the Church have rightly understood [it to be] the Eternal Son of God in respect to his office as Mediator.'

The fact that the wrestling match occurs at night has two purposes. First, the darkness conceals the identity of the adversary. It is likely that Jacob would have immediately recognized his authority and power if he had seen him in daylight. Secondly, night is particularly associated with self-examination, meditation and solitude. It is the time when fear grips a person. One often faces reality and truth then.

The turning-point in the match comes when the adversary touches the socket of Jacob's thigh and dislocates it. Why does the Angel of Yahweh do this? Perhaps it is to show Jacob that he is not prevailing in and of his own power. He is still standing only because God is allowing him to stand. The truth is that no man can strive with God and prevail, unless God so wills it. Does Jacob, the trickster, truly believe he is standing under his own power?

32:26-29. Then he said, 'Let me go because it is daybreak.'
But he said, 'I will not let you go unless you bless me.' And
he said to him, 'What is your name?' And he said, 'Jacob.'
Then he responded, 'Your name will not be called Jacob
again, but rather Israel; because you have struggled with
God and with men, and you have prevailed.' Jacob then
asked, and he said, 'Now tell me your name.' But he said,
'Why do you ask my name?' Then he blessed him there.

As the day breaks and the sun begins to rise, Jacob
still holds on, unwilling to let go unless the adversary
gives him a blessing. At this point Jacob must have
realized the identity of the adversary. The prophet
Hosea says that Jacob not only grappled with him,
but he wept and pleaded for a blessing (Hosea 12:4).
He also draws a parallel between Jacob's tenacity in
grasping the angel and in grasping Esau's heel in
Genesis 25:26 (Hosea 12:3) — in both instances the
context is the struggle for blessing.[195]
    The wrestler then asks, **'What is your name?'** It
is, of course, an obvious rhetorical question in order
to set the scene for the name-change that is to follow.
No longer is his name to be **'Jacob'** ('one who takes
the heel'), but now it will be **'Israel'**. The exact
meaning of this name is uncertain, although it appears to be related in some way to the verb translated **'you have struggled'**. The change of name may
perhaps point to a character change in Jacob: he is
no longer deceiver or supplanter, but now he is the
resolute warrior.[196] Thus it may be a purging of some
of Jacob's unsavoury character traits. In addition, he
is now to serve as the patriarch of a nation to be
named after him.
    Another important aspect of the renaming of Jacob
is an assertion of the adversary's authority and power
to impart a new status to Jacob (cf. 2 Kings 23:34;
24:17). This is no mere ordinary man. Conferring a

new name on someone is often a kingly prerogative in
Scripture.

Jacob then attempts to turn the tables by asking,
'Now tell me your name.' The Angel of Yahweh
responds with another rhetorical question — Jacob
already knows with whom he is wrestling. Then
Jacob is given a divine blessing. It is likely, although
not directly stated in the text, that it is a similar
blessing to the ones that had been given to Abraham
and Isaac, one that culminates in the coming of the
promised Messiah.

32:30-32. Then Jacob called the name of the place Peniel
because 'I saw God face to face, yet my life has been
delivered.' And the sun came up on him as he passed by
Penuel, and he was limping because of his hip. Therefore,
the children of Israel do not eat the tendon of the thigh
attached to the socket of the hip — to this day — because he
touched the socket of Jacob's hip on the tendon of the thigh.

Because of the magnitude of the event, Jacob gives a
name to the spot where the wrestling match took
place: **'Peniel'.**[197] It literally means 'the face of God'.
Jacob has struggled with God face to face, but, most
importantly, he has survived the encounter. Humans
do not live through such a meeting unless by divine
grace and dispensation (see Exod. 19:21; Judg.
6:22-23).

As the sun rises, Jacob is limping. As he turns
now to face Esau, he has the very event of the encounter with God imprinted on his flesh. It was no
mere dream, no mere illusion!

The last verse is an editorial note from Moses that
explains a dietary restriction which originated from
this episode. This is the first time **'the children of
Israel'** are mentioned in Scripture — this is not a
reference to the immediate progeny of Jacob, but to
the later people of Israel. The use of the expression,

'to this day' confirms this understanding — Moses is describing a law not found in the Sinaitic code, but one that was practised in his day.

Application

In this encounter, God is, first and foremost, attempting to assure and encourage Jacob. Jacob is about to meet Esau, who is coming with 400 men. From every appearance, Jacob is staring defeat and death in the face. But God graciously appears to Jacob, wrestles with him, causing him to prevail, and to receive the blessing. He is blessed, and made to see that he and his line will continue. Indeed, after such a meeting, Jacob is fully prepared to encounter Esau!

The wrestling match is also an attempt to break Jacob of his self-reliant attitude. Up to this time he has mostly relied on his own skill and craftiness. But God fights with Jacob to show him that the blessings of God come only through the gracious provision of God, and not from anything else. They do not come from human strength or cunning. So, as Jacob goes to meet Esau, he carries in his very flesh the sign that God provides, and that Jacob need not rely on his own wily ways. We, of course, ought to learn from the example of Jacob. To live our lives as Christians we must depend on God. We cannot rely on our own ways, means and strength. And if we do not depend on him, God may bring us to a point, as he did Jacob, where he shows our self-sufficiency to be insufficient. As Martin Luther remarked, 'And so we have this noble chapter, in which you see the marvellous dealing of God with his saints for our comfort and example, so that we may daily ask ourselves if he is also at work with us and be prepared for it.'

The encounter with Esau
(Genesis 33:1-20)

After all the anxiety and preparations on the part of Jacob, he is about to meet his brother Esau. What awaits him? Is it hostility or reconciliation? This section is divided into two parts: the first is the actual meeting between the brothers (33:1-11) and then their disengagement and departure (33:12-20).

33:1-2. And Jacob lifted his eyes and looked and, behold, Esau was coming and 400 men with him. Then he divided the children among Leah, Rachel and the two handmaids. So he put the handmaids and their children in front, then Leah and her children next, then Rachel and Joseph last.

Immediately after Jacob's encounter with Yahweh, the patriarch sees Esau coming at a distance. Esau's intentions are still unknown, yet the situation appears potentially dangerous because of the 400 men with him. So Jacob makes a precautionary move. He divides his wives and their children into units. The order of separation is proper — that is, the first wife Leah, the second wife Rachel and the two hand-maiden wives. Sarna judges that this act is not precautionary on Jacob's part: 'The present act is solely a matter of arranging mothers with their respective children for formal presentation to Esau.'[198] I disagree. When Jacob sets them in order in verse 2, he places Rachel (and Joseph) last in line. If there is hostility, she will have the best chance of escape. As the rabbis declare, 'The more behind — the more beloved' (*Gen. R.* 78).

33:3-4. Then he passed before them, and he bowed to the ground seven times until he drew near to his brother. But Esau ran to meet him, and he embraced him and he fell on his neck and he kissed him. Then they wept.

Jacob now places himself between Esau and his family. And as he approaches his brother he bows down to the ground. This is an act of submission that is well known from the ancient Near East, particularly from the Amarna Letters. Bowing seven times indicates complete submission on Jacob's part — normally one bow would be sufficient (23:12; 42:6). Jacob's action is also an ironic reversal of 27:29, in which Isaac had blessed him by saying, 'May the sons of your mother bow down to you.'

Esau's response to seeing his brother shows that Jacob's apprehensions and precautions have all been unnecessary. Their meeting of reconciliation is related with a rapid staccato of five verbs: **'Esau ran ... he embraced ... he fell ... he kissed... They wept.'** That is reminiscent of 25:34 when a series of five verbs in a similar succession demonstrated hostility and discord between the brothers.[199]

In the Masoretic text there are markings placed over each letter of the Hebrew verb translated **'and he kissed him'**. These are scribal markings called *puncta extraordinaria* ('extraordinary points'), and they may mean that the word / letters ought to be deleted.[200] Yet the idiom, 'He fell on his neck and he kissed him,' is known from ancient Near-Eastern texts.[201] There really is no good reason to amend the text as we have it. In addition, the act of kissing is another example of irony in the text — in 27:26 Jacob's theft of Esau's blessing was accompanied by a kiss.

The reconciliation and forgiveness in the episode are astounding. Some commentators do not like this. One late Jewish Midrash changes the words, 'and he kissed him,' to 'and he bit him'![202] Some simply do not want to accept the concept of conciliation and absolution between Israel / Jacob and Edom / Esau.

33:5-7. And he lifted his eyes and he saw the women and the children, and he said, 'Who are these with you?' And he said, 'The children that God has graciously given your servant.' Then the handmaids, they and their children, drew near and they bowed down. And Leah and her children also drew near and they bowed down. Then afterwards Joseph and Rachel drew near and they bowed down.

After embracing Jacob, Esau looks up and sees the women and children. He asks Jacob who they are. We must remember that Jacob had left Canaan empty-handed; now God is bringing him back with a large family and many possessions. And Jacob acknowledges that such prosperity has come from the hand of **'God'**.

Jacob addresses Esau calling himself **'your servant'**. He thus continues to play the subservient role. And then Jacob's family is presented to Esau (as to one who stands in the superior position). They are introduced in order of affection — and that is probably why Rachel is presented last. In the other instances, the mothers appear before the children, but not Rachel — she is the one Jacob truly adores.

33:8-11. And he said, 'What do you mean by all this company that I have encountered?' And he responded, 'To find favour in the eyes of my lord.' Then Esau said, 'I have much, my brother; let it be for you what belongs to you.' But Jacob answered, 'No, please, if I have found favour in your eyes, then take my gift from my hand; for therefore I have seen your face like the appearance of the face of God, and you

have accepted me. Please take my blessing that has come
to you because God has been gracious to me, and because I
have plenty.' And he pressed him, so that he took [it].

Esau now questions Jacob regarding all the droves of
animals that he had met along the way. Jacob calls
these **'my gift'**, and urges Esau to accept them. He
refuses to take no for an answer — in fact, he says
'no' to Esau.[203] Later in the conversation, Jacob
refers to these things as **'my blessing'**. The term
'blessing' has an idiomatic meaning of 'gift' or
'bounty' (see 1 Sam. 25:27); however, its use here
may be an ironic comment on 27:30-40 in which
Jacob stole Esau's 'blessing'.

Jacob's statement to Esau that **'I have seen your
face like the appearance of the face of God, and
you have accepted me,'** draws a parallel with his
wrestling match with the Angel of Yahweh (32:24-32).
There Jacob met God face to face, and yet he was
spared. The same is true here: Jacob meets Esau
face to face, and yet Esau does not destroy him, as
he could so easily have done.

33:12-15. Then he said, 'Let us take our journey and let us
go; and I will go with you.' But he answered him, 'My lord
knows that the children are weak and the flocks and the
herds which are nursing are under my care. And if they are
severely driven one day, then all the flocks will die. Now
please let my lord pass before his servant. Then I will gently
travel by stages according to the pace of the expedition
before me and according to the pace of the children until I
come to my lord, to Seir.' And Esau said, 'I will place some of
my people with you.' And he responded, 'Why is this? Let me
find favour in the eyes of my lord.'

Esau now offers to travel with Jacob. Jacob hesitates, however, and he provides excuses for them not
to travel together. He claims that all the children are

'weak', or 'frail', and the animals are **'under my care'** (literally, 'upon me'). Jacob then employs a jussive with the particle **'please'** in order to urge Esau forward; the construction reflects an urgent request. Obviously, Jacob does not fully trust Esau; he is afraid that the latter might yet change his mind.

Jacob then announces to Esau that he will follow him to Seir. But he will **'travel by stages'** — this is a verb that means to journey from one watering station to another.[204] He will be able to travel only at the speed of the **'expedition'**; this is a term that literally means 'work / occupation', but at times may indicate possessions. The problem here is that Jacob does not follow Esau to Seir, and probably never had any intention of doing so. Apparently Jacob is deceiving Esau so that he may be free to go on his way. The character of Jacob still retains elements of his old nature of craftiness.

33:16-20. And Esau returned that day on his way to Seir. But Jacob travelled to Succoth, and he built a house for himself and he made shelters for his livestock. Therefore he called the name of the place Succoth. Then Jacob came safely to the city of Shechem which is in the land of Canaan, when he came from Paddan-Aram — and he camped in front of the city. And he bought the plot of the field on which he had pitched his tent, from the hand of the sons of Hamor, the father of Shechem, for 100 pieces of money. Then he erected an altar there, and he called it El Elohe Israel.

Esau departs for Seir and, for the most part, he leaves the story of the book of Genesis — he is mentioned once again at the burial of Isaac, but that is all. Jacob does not follow Esau to the south but rather travels west to the site of Succoth. Succoth is perhaps to be identified with Tell Deir 'Alla, a site located directly west of Peniel where the Jabbok river runs into the Jordan valley.[205] There Jacob builds

'shelters' for his animals; that term in Hebrew is *succōt*, thus signifying the etymological significance of the site's name. He also constructs a **'house'** for himself — the nature of the structure is unknown because the word can mean either a permanent or a temporary structure, and at times refers to a tent.[206]

Subsequently Jacob journeys to Shechem, a site further west and in the middle of the hill-country of Canaan. It is the first time this site is mentioned in Scripture, and it becomes an important place in the history of Israel — here, for example, Joshua addresses the tribes of Israel for the last time, and here is where Joseph has his final resting-place (Josh. 24:1,32).[207] The biblical author comments on the trip to Shechem by saying that Jacob came **'safely'**, and the term can mean 'to be safe and sound'. However, it also means to be 'guileless / loyal' — it is an antonym of the words for craftiness and deception.[208] Perhaps it signifies that Jacob is coming back to the land in the opposite manner from that in which he had left it.

Jacob buys a plot of ground in a similar way to Abraham (23:17-18). Then he erects an altar there, and he names it **'El Elohe Israel'**, literally, 'God the God of Israel'. The term **'Israel'** here refers, of course, to Jacob. This act is in commemoration of God's bringing him safely back to Canaan. Many years earlier Jacob had declared that Yahweh would be his God if he brought him safely back to Canaan (28:20-21). So now he worships his God.

Application

It is clear that at this point in the story Jacob is a believer, and he is in covenant with the Holy One of Israel. He serves Yahweh, and he serves him alone. Yet, at times, Jacob reverts to his old ways of craftiness and deceit. Some may ask, 'How can this be?'

How can he still act that way if he is a true believer? The answer for us is to make certain that we do not mix up two theological concepts — justification and sanctification. Justification 'is a judicial act of God, in which He declares, on the basis of the righteousness of Jesus Christ, that all claims of the law are satisfied with respect to the sinner'.[209] In other words, the sinner has received forgiveness of sins and restoration to the divine favour. This act takes place once and for all; thus Jacob is in the state of justification.

Sanctification, on the other hand, is an ongoing, gradual process that occurs in a believer after he or she is justified. As the *Westminster Confession of Faith* says, 'This sanctification is throughout in the whole man, yet imperfect in this life: there abideth still some remnants of corruption in every part: whence ariseth a continual and irreconcilable war, the flesh lusting against the spirit, and the spirit against the flesh' (Ch. XIII, 2). This is what we see in the person of Jacob: elements of corruption remain, yet, through the power of the Holy Spirit, Jacob is overcoming — that is, he is growing in grace and increasing in holiness.

The scandal concerning Dinah
(Genesis 34:1-31)

The final verse of chapter 33 mentions the name of God and the first verse of chapter 35 also refers to him. But the name of God is nowhere to be found in chapter 34. I believe this omission highlights the very secular and seedy nature of the present chapter. Without God, mankind easily falls prey to sin and malice.

Also of great importance is the concept of the sedentarization of the Hebrews in Canaan — that is, the process of their moving from a semi-nomadic existence to one of settlement in one area. The chapter points out one of the great dangers involved in this: the problem of intermarriage with the Canaanites.[210] In other words, how are the Hebrews to deal with assimilation into the local cultures?

34:1-3. And Dinah, the daughter of Leah who was born to Jacob, went out to look on the daughters of the land. Then Shechem, the son of Hamor the Hivite, the prince of the land, saw her; and he took her and he lay down with her and he defiled her. And his soul clung to Dinah the daughter of Jacob, and he loved the girl and he spoke to the girl's heart.

In the previous chapter Jacob purchased a piece of land in the northern highlands of Canaan, near the city of Shechem. Shechem at the time was a large and important Canaanite town; Jacob, as a semi-nomad, must have been drawn to the urban centre for obvious reasons, such as social advantages, trade, and so forth. His attempt to settle, however, has dire consequences.

Dinah, the eldest daughter of Jacob, is intrigued by the Shechemite women; she is clearly attracted by their ways and manners. So she sallies forth into the big city as an apparently innocent and inexperienced girl. Why Jacob allows her to do this unchaperoned is not stated; perhaps he sees nothing wrong with it — these people are his neighbours!

Shechem, the son of an important figure in the city of Shechem, takes her and violates her. The act is obviously rape as the verbs in verse 2 increase in severity: **'he took ... he lay with ... he forced'**. The last of these verbs normally means 'to afflict' or 'humiliate', and it is purposely used to signify great social disgrace for a girl who has sexual relations prior to marriage.[211] There is no evidence from the text that Dinah is in any way a willing participant in the act.

After debasing her, Shechem, **'clung'** to Dinah. That verb is used in Genesis 2:24 regarding the marriage relationship created by God prior to the Fall. In the present episode, it is perverted: we see it used of a forced intimacy which is a clear violation of God's moral law. Note, in addition, that the three verbs in verse 3 are set in opposition to those of verse 2:

| 34:2 | he took | he lay with | he defiled |
| 34:3 | he clung | he loved | he spoke to the heart |

The real situation is described in verse 2; what Shechem hopes for is in verse 3![212]

34:4-7. Then Shechem spoke to Hamor his father, saying, 'Take this girl for me as a wife!' And Jacob heard that he had sexually defiled Dinah his daughter. But his sons were with his livestock in the field. And Jacob was silent until they came back. Then Hamor, the father of Shechem, came to Jacob to speak with him. And the sons of Jacob came from the field when they heard [about it]; and the men were grieved, and they were very angry because he did a disgraceful thing against Israel to lie down with the daughter of Jacob — it is a thing not to be done.

Shechem's response to the situation is to speak to his father to arrange a marriage with Dinah. Marriage contracts were instigated and put into effect by the parent on behalf of a son. But Shechem has clearly put the cart before the horse: he rapes Dinah, and then seeks her hand in marriage. And he demands, using an imperative form, that Hamor should **'take'** Dinah to be his wife. Ironically, that same verb is used in verse 2 of Shechem, where it states that he 'took' her.

Before any negotiations occur, however, Jacob hears that Dinah has been **'sexually defiled'** (see Ezek. 18:6,11,15; 22:11; 33:26). Jacob responds by remaining **'silent'**; some believe him to be displaying prudence at this point. Yet, throughout the entire episode, he appears passive — is he reluctant to confront the people of Shechem, those with whom he has recently made a deal?

While Jacob is waiting, Hamor arrives to enter into marriage negotiations with him. Subsequently the sons of Jacob come in from the field having heard about **'the disgraceful thing'** — this term in Hebrew is used of the most serious kind of sexual evil; it is a profane and moral outrage (see Deut. 22:21; Judg. 20:6).[213] Their reaction is to be incensed about the crime. First, they are **'grieved'**. This verb is in the Hithpael pattern in Hebrew, and it appears in this form in only one other instance in the Old Testament — in Genesis 6:6, in which God has great sorrow

regarding mankind's sin. Secondly, they feel great
anger — anger that will be acted on later in the
chapter.

The brothers see the act as an abomination
against **'Israel'**. Since there is no nation of Israel at
the time of the event, the person of Jacob is being
denoted here. Yet Moses is writing Genesis for the
people of Israel and, thus, there must be an application to the nation. So this defilement is not only
against Dinah but against Jacob and, ultimately,
against the people of God.

The reactions to the rape are varied. It does not
appear that the Shechemites see it as a moral issue.
Jacob is passive, and he appears to be afraid of what
the Shechemites might think or do. The sons of
Jacob are enraged and hostile.

34:8-10. And Hamor spoke with them, saying, 'My son
Shechem has a great desire for your daughter. Please give
her to him as a wife! And intermarry with us. You shall give
your daughters to us, and take our daughters for yourselves.
And you shall dwell with us, and the land shall be before you.
Dwell in it and travel in it and get property in it.'

Hamor offers enticement to Jacob's family by saying
that this marriage will only be the beginning of a
close and prosperous relationship between the
Shechemites and the Hebrews. The marriage between
Shechem and Dinah, in other words, will be the first
in a bond of *connubium* (that is, the right to intermarry). In addition, Hamor offers the Hebrews the
privileges of owning property and of having unlimited
grazing rights. It appears to be an offer of citizenship
— no longer will Jacob's family be aliens and sojourners in a foreign land! No longer will they have to
be nomads, but they will be able to settle and dwell
with the Shechemites. This offer is made by Hamor,
who says, literally, **'and with us you shall dwell'** —

the personal pronoun leads the construction of the sentence because it is to be emphasized. The point of the entire section is to lure the Hebrews into believing that they will be one with, or the same as, the people of the land.

But the true intent of Hamor is different. When he speaks to his own people in verse 23, he argues for the relationship because, he says, 'Will not their livestock and their property and all their animals belong to us?' He is lying to the Hebrews in order to acquire possession of their goods. Clearly, no good can come from an agreement with the pagan Shechemites.

34:11-12. Then Shechem said to her father and to her brothers, 'If I have found favour in your eyes, whatever you say to me, I will give [it]. Make a very large bride price and gift request of me, and I will give it as you have said to me. Then give me the girl as a wife.'

Shechem himself now enters into the discussion. He pleads with Jacob and his sons for an arrangement so that he might marry Dinah. He begins by saying, **'If I have found favour in your eyes...'** — although this is an idiom often used in negotiations, it is my opinion that it reflects a hardness, arrogance and irreverence on Shechem's part. Indeed, in his entire statement there appears to be no sense of remorse or repentance regarding his dastardly deed. It is almost as if Shechem expects Jacob's family to say, 'Oh yes! Why shouldn't we favour you? All you did was rape our sister — how could we hold that against you?'

Shechem's insatiable desire for Dinah is underscored by his willingness to pay whatever bride-price Jacob lays on him. This is the *mōhār*, a payment made by a prospective husband in return for the bride. There would usually be a set price in a community, but Shechem is willing to go way beyond it.

In addition, he wants to give a **'gift'** to Jacob's family over and above the bridal price. Shechem seems to be under the impression that he can buy his way out of the present difficulty.

34:13-17. But the sons of Jacob answered Shechem and Hamor his father deceitfully and they spoke [to them] because he had defiled Dinah their sister. And they said to them, 'We are not able to do this thing, to give our sister to a man who is uncircumcised, because it is disgraceful to us. Only on this condition will we give our consent to you: if you will become like us, so that every male among you will be circumcised. Then we will give our daughters to you, and we will take your daughters to ourselves. And we will dwell with you, and we will be as one people. But if you do not listen to us to be circumcised, then we will take our daughter and we will go.'

It looks as though the brothers already have a plan for revenge in their minds prior to this conversation. The author says that they responded **'deceitfully'**. This term is first found in Genesis 27:35, in which Isaac claims that Jacob came 'deceitfully' to steal Esau's blessing. Apparently Jacob taught his sons well! Instead of confronting the issue head-on, as they certainly have a right to do, they act craftily — like father, like son! It should also be observed that Jacob is a passive party to their treachery; he in no way calls them to account.

The thrust of their argument presented to the Shechemites is that the Hebrews cannot be **'one people'** with them unless all are circumcised. Such an agreement would be **'disgraceful'** without circumcision. There is an irony about this comment in the light of verse 7, in which the truly 'disgraceful' thing is the act of Shechem in raping Dinah. The plot of the brothers is then presented as an 'if ..., then ...' statement. **'If'** the Shechemites agree to be circumcised,

'**then**' the Hebrews will enter into a covenant with
them. If they refuse, then the Hebrews will depart and
'**take**' their sister (cf. the use of the verb 'take' in
verses 2 and 4).

It is astounding that the brothers attempt to cloak
their maliciousness behind the sign of circumcision.
This is the sign of the covenant between God and
mankind (Gen. 17) which represents a person's turning to God in faith. Here it is used to deceive the
Shechemites. On the other hand, it is dramatic irony
that the very physical instrument used by Shechem to
rape Dinah is now to be cut off. The circumcision will
cause the downfall and disgrace of the Shechemites!

The Hebrews need to be careful not to show their
hand. It is clear that when Shechem took the girl he
must have kept her (see 34:26). The situation is a
very dangerous one for all involved.

34:18-19. And their words were good in the eyes of Hamor
and in the eyes of Shechem, the son of Hamor. And the boy
did not hesitate to do the thing because he had great delight
in the daughter of Jacob. And he was held in honour more
than anyone in his father's house.

Both Hamor and Shechem respond favourably to the
demands of the Hebrews. Shechem is so blinded by
his love for Dinah that no hindrance is large enough.
He refuses any delay, but he swallows the Hebrews'
bait hook, line and sinker! In addition, Shechem is
held in such high esteem by the community that the
author leaves little doubt but that others will follow
his lead. Shechem has great sway and influence over
them.

34:20-23. So Hamor and Shechem his son came to the gate
of their city, and they spoke to the men of their city, saying,
'These men are peaceable with us. Let them dwell in the
land, and travel in it, for the land is very wide before them.

We will take their daughters as wives for ourselves, and we will give our daughters to them. Only on this condition will the men consent to us, to dwell with us, to be as one people: every male among us must be circumcised just as they are circumcised. Their livestock, their possessions and all their animals — will they not belong to us? Only let us consent to them, and they will dwell with us.'

The two men go to the gate of Shechem to present the proposal. In antiquity the city-gate was the place of assemblies and meetings (see Ruth 4:1). Archaeologists have uncovered gates from the biblical period that include benches on the inside.[214]

The proposition made by Hamor and Shechem to the Shechemites highlights the advantages of their acceptance of the agreement. It is primarily an economic benefit: the Shechemites stand to gain all the property of the Hebrews. Yet these men are deceiving their own people: first of all, they omit the promises they have given to the Hebrews — that is, the rights and privileges of owning property. In addition, they say nothing regarding the situation with Dinah and all its ramifications. Hamor and Shechem are simply painting a rosy picture for their people. There is no sense of danger or foreboding.

34:24. All who go out of the city gate listened to Hamor and to Shechem his son. Thus every male, all who go out of the city gate, was circumcised.

The ones who listen to Hamor and Shechem are **'all who go out of the city gate'** (the expression appears twice in the verse). The phrase is idiomatic for the men who participate in the decision-making process. So in Genesis 23:10,18 Abraham, in his attempt to buy a burial plot for Sarah, negotiates with 'all who go in at the city gate'. Yet the verbs of the two clauses are different: here it is 'go out' and in the earlier passage it was 'go in'. The Hebrew verb 'to go out' carries military overtones (i.e., to go out to war). Thus the idiom may define these men not only as decision-makers for the community, but also as males of military age. That it is only the able-bodied men is confirmed by verses 25 and 29, in which they are the only ones killed by the Hebrews.

These men trust the words of Hamor and Shechem. The verb 'to listen' in Hebrew not only means 'to hear', but 'to agree to something and then to obey it'.[215]

34:25-26. And it came about on the third day when they were in pain that the two sons of Jacob, Simeon and Levi, Dinah's brothers, each took his sword, and they came on the unsuspecting city. And they killed every male. And they killed Hamor and his son Shechem by the edge of the sword. Then they took Dinah from the house of Shechem, and they went out.

On the third day after the agreement, all the Shechemite men have been circumcised and they are **'in pain'** — that is, in their weakest state. They are incapacitated and unable to protect themselves or their city. At this point two of the sons of Jacob, Simeon and Levi, act on their adversaries' incapacitation. The reason why these two sons take the situation in hand is because they are full brothers of Dinah, all three having been born to Jacob and Leah (29:33-34; 30:21). They would have suffered the greater humiliation. The two men **'took'** their swords: there is an irony about this because Shechem 'took' Dinah (34:2).

Simeon and Levi then arrive at the **'unsuspecting'** city. This term is not an adjective agreeing with **'city'**, but rather a substantive that perhaps refers to the city. However, it may also apply to the two brothers in the sense of their being 'unopposed'.[216] Either way, the men of the city are unable to defend it, and the Hebrews have free rein to do what they will.

The last line uses the two verbs **'they took'** and **'they went out'**. The story of Dinah began with those very same verbs but in reverse order: she 'went out' (34:1) and 'Shechem ... took her'.[217] This form of chiasmus serves as an *inclusio* for Dinah's having left the fold of the Hebrews but eventually being brought back into it.

34:27-29. The sons of Jacob came on the dead bodies and they plundered the city that defiled their sister. And they took their flocks and their herds and their donkeys and that which was in the city and that which was in the field. And they captured and they plundered all their wealth and all their little ones and their wives; [even] all that is in the house.

The **'sons of Jacob'** here do not include Simeon and Levi because these two would not have **'[come] on the dead bodies'**. So it must mean the other sons: Hebrew often expresses the idea of 'other' through mere juxtaposition, as in the present case.[218] The text tells us that they then pillage the city, not for the sake of mere plunder but because the Shechemites have disgraced their sister. But why kill all the Shechemites and plunder the entire city? Obviously, the Shechemites are willing accomplices of Hamor and Shechem — there had been no sense of outrage on their part.

The extent of the pillaging is sweeping. The two words **'city'** and **'field'** serve as a merism to show that everything is included. In addition, the list of plunder that includes flocks, herds, children and women is used elsewhere in Scripture to reflect the total ravaging of a site (see Num. 31:9). This is poetic justice because the Shechemites had planned on seizing all the wealth of Jacob — now all their wealth belongs to Jacob!

The final statement that they plunder **'[even] all that is in the house'** is peculiar because of the use of the singular, 'house'. One may argue that it is simply being used in a collective sense. On the other hand, it may refer to one particular building: the Hebrew term *bayit* can be used of a monumental structure, such as a temple or palace. We know that the Canaanites at Shechem had a pagan temple called 'the house of Baal Berith' (see Judg. 9:4). It has been excavated at the site of Shechem, and its incipient use was during the Middle Bronze Age (*c.* 1650 B.C.).[219] It is possible that this is the building that the Hebrews plunder.

34:30-31. Then Jacob said to Simeon and to Levi, 'You have troubled me by causing me to stink among the dwellers of the land, among the Canaanites and the Perizzites. And I am few in number. And should they join against me and strike me, I and my house will be destroyed.' But they answered, 'Should he treat our sister like a prostitute?'

Jacob, who has remained passive throughout most of this episode, now reappears on the scene to rebuke Simeon and Levi. The other brothers, who take plunder, are not chided. Jacob is worried about two things: first, his standing with the pagan peoples of the land; and, secondly, how he can protect his people. Thus he demonstrates little concern about the morality of the brothers' actions, but he is fretting about the possible consequences.

When Jacob later gives prophecies about his sons, he combines Simeon and Levi into one oracle, which says:

Simeon and Levi are brothers;
Their swords are implements of violence.
Let my life not come into their council;
Let not my glory be joined into their assembly.

Because they killed men in their anger
And they destroyed oxen in their pleasure.
Cursed is their anger because it is strong
And their wrath because it is harsh.
I will divide them in Jacob
And I will scatter them in Israel

(49:5-7).

The biblical writer is not as judgemental as Jacob.
He allows the two brothers the final word. They
respond to their father with a question of incredulity
— no answer is expected because it is all too obvious.
Simeon and Levi seem to be much more concerned
about the morality of the situation than Jacob,
caring more about right and wrong. The author
leaves the question hanging, as if he is in agreement
with the brothers.[220]

Application

The allurements of the world are many and delusory. In the
words of C. H. Spurgeon, 'One of Aesop's fables says, "A pigeon
oppressed by excessive thirst saw a goblet of water painted on a
signboard. Not supposing it to be only a picture, it flew towards it
with a loud whirr and unwittingly dashed against the signboard
and jarred itself terribly. Having broken its wings by the blow, it
fell to the ground and was killed by a bystander." The mockeries
of the world are many, and those who are deluded by them not
only miss the joys they sought but in their eager pursuit of vanity
bring ruin on their souls. We call the dove silly to be deceived by
a picture, however cleverly painted, but what epithet shall we
apply to those who are duped by the transparently false allurements of the world?'

In Genesis 34, Jacob is too concerned with his acceptance in
the world, how he would be treated — he wants to offend no one.
Thus he is guilty of false compromise. The apostle John encour-
ages Christians to rely on God's Word, not the ways of the flesh:

'Do not love the world nor the things in the world. If anyone loves the world, the love of the Father is not in him. For all that is in the world, the lust of the flesh and the lust of the eyes and the boastful pride of life, is not from the Father, but is from the world. The world is passing away, and also its lusts; but the one who does the will of God lives for ever' (1 John 2:15-17).

Jacob at Bethel again
(Genesis 35:1-15)

Jacob does not remain in the area around Shechem for very long. Instead God commands him to move to Bethel, the place where God had revealed himself to Jacob in an earlier theophany. Before he departs Jacob enlists his people in various acts of purification. He is about to go to Bethel to worship the one true God.

35:1. And God said to Jacob, 'Arise, go up to Bethel, and dwell there. And make there an altar to God who appeared to you when you fled from before Esau your brother.'

God now commands Jacob to leave the Shechem area. Obviously one of the reasons is for his protection because of the offence created among the inhabitants of the land by the events recorded in the previous chapter. God directs him to **'Arise, go up'**: these two imperatives may in fact echo the topographical features of the land. The site of Bethel is much higher in the hill-country than Shechem, and one must go up to get there. In addition, the verb 'to go up' often signifies to go on a pilgrimage (see 1 Sam. 1:3; Ps. 122:4).[221] Jacob is making a holy trek to the site where God first appeared to him on his way to Haran — there he had set up a pillar to commemorate that experience (28:22). What a contrast to the impious and profane activity of chapter 34!

Jacob's return to Bethel serves as an *inclusio* for his entire trip to Haran and back. In 28:10-22 he had stopped at Bethel on his way to Haran, and there he met God. Now God will appear to him again at Bethel (35:9-15).

35:2-3. Then Jacob said to his household and to all who were with him, 'Remove the foreign gods that are in your midst, and purify yourselves, and change your clothes. Then let us arise and go up to Bethel. And I will make an altar there to God who answered me in the day of my distress and who has been with me wherever I have gone.'

In 28:20-21, Jacob had vowed that Yahweh would be his only God if Yahweh protected him and brought him back to Canaan safely. Jacob is now in Canaan, having arrived unharmed and with great wealth. So Jacob keeps his word and he makes all who are with him stop using, literally, **'the gods of foreignness'**. These deities may include ones brought by the people from Haran, as well as some brought by the captured Shechemites. They may also include the teraphim that Rachel had stolen from her father (31:19,30,34).

Jacob not only commands his people to get rid of their idols, but, with an imperative (Hithpael pattern), he orders them to **'Purify yourselves!'**, and to change their garments. In other words, they are to prepare for a religious observance; they are going up to Bethel, where God will meet with Jacob. Such preparations are known from other passages in the Old Testament when people go forth to meet God (see Exodus 19:10 in which Moses directs the Israelites to consecrate themselves and to wash their clothes before the meeting with God at Sinai).

35:4. And they gave to Jacob all the foreign gods that they had and the earrings in their ears. Then Jacob buried them under the oak tree near Shechem.

Not only do the people hand over the gods to Jacob, but they give him their **'earrings'** as well. No doubt these are amulets bearing images of foreign gods.[222] Such things are well known from antiquity.[223] It was believed that jewellery in that form had magical deterrent power.

Jacob then takes all of these idolatrous objects and buries them beneath **'the oak tree'** near Shechem. This is the famous landmark where God appeared to Abraham in Genesis 12:6, and the patriarch responded by erecting an altar there. In that earlier passage it is called 'the oak of Moreh'. It appears to have been a venerated spot. Why does Jacob do this? Perhaps it is a renunciation of the tree as an object of veneration. It could not be used by a monotheist with all those gods buried there. It may also be part of the ritual of purification prior to Jacob's ascending to worship at Bethel.[224] But it is more likely to be an example of a *favissa*: this is a repository for discarded cultic objects, and such discarding was a common practice in ancient times. Burying the objects is thus a burial of the veneration of them. In later codified Hebrew law, the Israelites were to destroy such cultic artefacts (see Deut. 7:5,25).

35:5. Then they travelled. And the terror of God was on the cities that were around them. Thus they did not pursue after the children of Jacob.

Jacob and his people leave Shechem. But Jacob's fears that he will be attacked by the inhabitants of the area are unwarranted (see 34:30). God has promised to protect Jacob, and he does so: his **'terror'** inspires the surrounding cities with great fear and restrains them from taking action against Jacob.[225] This is certainly the same type of 'terror' that God sends before the Israelites into the promised land in the time of Moses: 'I will send my terror ahead of you, and throw into confusion all the people among whom you come, and I will make all your enemies turn their backs to you' (Exod. 23:27).

35:6-7. Now Jacob and all the people who were with him came to Luz (that is, Bethel) in the land of Canaan. And he built an altar there. And he called the place El Bethel because there God revealed himself to him when he fled before his brother.

After years of absence, Jacob finally returns to Bethel **'in the land of Canaan'** (Luz was the earlier name of the city — 28:19). God has kept his promises to Jacob (28:15). So Jacob honours God by building an altar to him; in the previous episode at Bethel Jacob had erected a pillar, but not an altar. He then re-names the site: he had earlier named it Bethel ('the house of God' — 28:19), but now he calls it **'El Bethel'**, literally, 'the God of the house of God'. This new name comes from the occasion recorded in Genesis 31:13 when God commands Jacob to leave Haran and return to Canaan: there God says, 'I am El Bethel.'

One grammatical problem needs to be considered. The verb **'revealed'** in the Hebrew is a third person plural, although it is referring to the one true God. Some commentators argue that it is a 'polytheistic form of expression' — that is, a vestige of paganism.[226] That is untenable. Perhaps it refers not to God but to 'divine beings' — the Hebrew term *Elohim*, normally used of God, is known to sometimes signify heavenly beings (Ps. 8:5; Heb. 2:7). In the first meeting at Bethel, it was not only God, but the heavenly host, who met with Jacob. On the other hand, the name of God with the plural of the predicate is found elsewhere in the Old Testament. But in all those cases, one being is clearly intended.[227]

35:8. And Deborah, Rebekah's nurse, died. And she was
buried under the oak tree beneath Bethel. And its name was
called Allon-Bacuth.

As an aside, the biblical author tells us that Rebekah's nurse Deborah has died and has been buried
near Bethel. The only connection with the account of
Jacob appears to be one of location — in other words,
Jacob is worshipping at Bethel, and that is where
Deborah is buried. She is mentioned by name nowhere else in Genesis, although 24:59 may refer to
her. It is puzzling why she is even mentioned in
connection with Jacob. One possibility is based on
the fact that the oak tree near Bethel is a famous
landmark. In the Hebrew the object **'oak tree'** has a
definite article prefixed to it, indicating that it is a
recognized landmark and well known.[228] So the writer
may be explaining why this site is so famous: Deborah, Rebekah's nurse, is buried here.

35:9-10. Then God appeared to Jacob again when he came
from Paddan-Aram. And he blessed him. And God said to
him, 'Your name is Jacob, but your name shall no longer be
called Jacob; but your name shall be Israel.' So he named
him Israel.

This is the second appearance of God to Jacob in a
theophany since the patriarch left Haran. The first
was the wrestling match at the Jabbok river (32:30).
And, as on that earlier occasion, God once again
blesses Jacob (cf. 32:29), and he repeats the announcement that his name is to be changed to Israel.
Why is this event reiterated? The reason is that the
first theophany occurred in Transjordan, when Jacob
was not yet in the promised land. But now he is
actually standing in Canaan and God's promise of a
land is validated — it is directly under Jacob's feet!
In addition, the following two verses will give detail to

his change of name: a people called Israel will descend from Jacob to possess this land. So we are not
witnessing two alternative versions of the same story,
but rather two distinct episodes in which the second
confirms the promises made during the first.

35:11-12. Then God said to him, 'I am El Shaddai. Be fruitful
and multiply. A nation and a company of nations will come
from you. And kings will come forth from your loins. And the
land that I gave to Abraham and to Isaac, I will give it to you.
And to your seed after you I will give it.'

This pronouncement of God to Jacob is essentially
the same as that which God had spoken to Abraham
in Genesis 17:1-8. The reader should consult the
commentary on that passage. The following similarities are obvious:

Component of Gen. 35		*Parallel in Gen. 17*	
1.	Introduction: 'I am El Shaddai'	1.	17:1
2.	'Be fruitful and multiply'	2.	17:2,6
3.	'Nations will come from you'	3.	17:4, 5, 6
4.	'Kings will come forth from your loins'	4.	17:6
5.	'the land'	5.	17:8
6.	'to your seed'	6.	17:8

The conclusion to be drawn here is that the covenant
promises to Abraham are renewed in their totality to
Jacob. Jacob's change of name to Israel further
signifies that the promises of God are to come to pass
through the person of Jacob: he is the promised seed
through whom the people of God are to come, a
descent that finds its climax in the person of the
Messiah.

35:13-15. Then God went up from him in the place where he
had spoken to him. Then Jacob erected a pillar in the place
where he had spoken to him, a pillar of stone. And he poured
a libation on it; then he poured oil on it. And Jacob called the
name of the place where God had spoken to him Bethel.

The theophany now disappears. The verb **'went up'**,
or 'ascended', is commonly used of the departure of
an appearance of God (see, e.g., Judg. 13:20). That
same verb is used back in Genesis 17 when God's
presence departed from Abraham after establishing a
covenant with him (17:22). Thus the two stories are
tied together again.

The site of the theophany is described three times
in the text as **'the place where he / God had spoken to him'**.[229] Some authors see either a dit-
tographic error, conflation, or duplication here.[230]
Such reiteration, on the other hand, is clearly emphatic. The reason why Jacob responds with worship
is that Yahweh had truly made himself known to the
patriarch, and it occurred in this very place!

Jacob's reaction to the theophany is to erect a
stone pillar, and to pour a drink offering and oil on
top of it. These actions are the same as those which
he performed at his first encounter with Yahweh at
Bethel in 28:18-19, with the exception of the libation.
This parallel has caused some commentators to
believe that this second event is merely an episode of
rededication. In other words, it is the same pillar as
before, but now a second ceremony takes place in
connection with it.[231] Documents of the ancient Near
East confirm that rededication of monuments did
occur. For instance, a portion of Sennacherib's Bit
Kutalli inscription reads: 'When that palace shall
have become old and ruined, may some future prince
restore its ruins, look upon the stele with my name
inscribed [on it], anoint it with oil, pour out a libation
upon it, and return it to its place.'[232]

The added dimension of the **'libation'**, or 'drink-offering', underscores the nature of Jacob's actions as acts of worship. Drink-offerings throughout the entire ancient Near East were for purposes of worship. On one occasion, for example, the Canaanite deity Baal demands that people 'pour a peace offering in the heart of the earth' in order to honour and worship the goddess Anat.[233]

Application

In this marvellous story of Jacob we see him demanding that his people lay down their idols, and that there should be a turning to the one true God at Bethel. I have been asked what lesson there might be for today since few in the West worship stone or wooden idols. That is true, but idols certainly may appear in more ways than that! Herbert Schlossberg, in his powerful work *Idols for Destruction*, defines idolatry in the following manner: 'Idolatry in its larger meaning is properly understood as any substitution of what is created for the creator. People may worship nature, money, mankind, power, history, or social and political systems instead of the God who created them all' (p. 6). It is turning away from the worship of God and turning to something else in his place. Frankly, idolatry dominates our culture. We need to lay down our gods and bury them, as did Jacob, and then turn to worship the only God.

The sons of Jacob
(Genesis 35:16-29)

Now Jacob is faced with a series of tragedies. First, his beloved wife Rachel dies in childbirth. Next, his first-born son Reuben violates one of Jacob's concubines. And, finally, his father Isaac dies. These are all cryptically related in the passage before us. But not all is grim: all twelve sons of Jacob are now on the scene, and, of course, they are the progenitors of the tribes of Israel. Even in the midst of great tragedy, God's promises of a seed continue to be fulfilled.

35:16-17. Then they travelled from Bethel. And it came to pass while there was some distance to go to Ephrath that Rachel began to give birth. And she had difficulty in her labour. And when her labour was at its most difficult the midwife said to her, 'Do not be afraid, because this one is also a son for you.'

Jacob and his family move from Bethel to Ephrath (which 35:19 tells us is Bethlehem), which lies seven miles to the south of Jerusalem. But while still **'some distance'** from Ephrath Rachel goes into labour. That measurement is literally in the Hebrew 'a stretch of land', and the distance is uncertain.[234] It is a rare term in Hebrew, yet its other occurrence in 2 Kings 5:19 indicates the distance to be short.

The expression, **'when her labour was at its most difficult'**, is a prime example of the elevative use of the Hiphil pattern of the Hebrew verb.[235] In other

words, that pattern / stem takes the verb to its greatest height and emphasis. It is, therefore, at the most
extreme point of pain and labour that the midwife
speaks soothingly to Rachel, announcing that a son is
being born to her.[236] This is a great comfort because it
is what she had prayed for when she named Joseph
after his birth: 'May Yahweh add to me another son!'
(30:24). God has indeed answered her request.

35:18-20. And when her spirit went out (because she was
dying) she called his name Ben-Oni. But his father called him
Benjamin. And Rachel died, and she was buried on the way
to Ephrath — that is, Bethlehem. So Jacob erected a pillar
over her grave; that is the pillar of Rachel's grave even to this
day.

As Rachel breathes her last during this severe
labour, she is able to name the child. She calls him
'Ben-Oni'. This is a compound name in Hebrew. The
first part literally means 'the son of' (construct state).
The second part of the name is problematic because
it possibly derives from one of two roots. It may come
from a noun that means 'strength / vigour', and so
she may be calling him 'the son of my vigour'.[237] It is
more likely that it stems from a noun meaning 'sorrow' or 'misfortune' and, that she is, therefore, naming him 'the son of my sorrow'.[238] Name-giving in the
Hebrew Bible often has a prophetic aspect to it, and
that is why Jacob changes the child's name so
quickly. It may be that Jacob saw Rachel, inadver-
tently or not, as placing a negative oath on the child
— so he rectifies it.

Jacob renames the child **'Benjamin'**, which literally means 'the son of my right hand'.[239] The right
hand throughout Scripture is the position of primacy,
pre-eminence and strength. It is associated with good
fortune. Thus it appears that Jacob changes the

child's name in order to pronounce the exact opposite of what Rachel had spoken.

At the site of Rachel's grave, or tomb, Jacob erects
a pillar as a landmark. It does not appear to be
anything more significant than that — and it becomes a famous marker during the history of Israel
(see 1 Sam. 10:2). The pagans in Canaan, on the
other hand, believed that the spirit of the dead was
present in the stone. They would honour that spirit
by anointing the stone or by presenting offerings to
the dead.[240] That is totally lacking in the episode
involving Jacob; there is no sense of religious ritual
or ancestor worship here.

35:21-22. Then Israel travelled on and he pitched his tent
beyond Migdal-Eder. And it came to pass when Israel was
encamped in that land that Reuben went and he slept with
Bilhah, his father's concubine — and Israel heard [about it]...

Jacob and his company travel near to **'Migdal-Eder'**,
a name that literally means 'the tower of the flock'. It
probably relates to a stone structure used by shepherds that later came to serve as a marker identifying
a particular site. The location of the site is unknown.
There Jacob sets up a tent encampment.

In a terse and concise statement we read that
Reuben violated Bilhah, one of his father's concubines, the handmaid of Rachel and the mother of
Dan and Naphtali (30:3-8). The purpose of this act is
not mere lust;[241] it actually serves a number of social
and political purposes.

First, the violation ensures that Bilhah cannot
ascend to the position of chief wife. That position
belongs to Leah, Reuben's mother (29:32).

Secondly, Reuben may be challenging his father's
authority. It was a well-known and widely adopted
practice in the ancient Near East that the eldest son
should inherit the concubines of his father (see

2 Samuel 16:22, in which Absalom challenges David's kingship). Reuben may have been asserting himself as the true heir of Jacob — however, it was a premature claim, and it backfired. In 1 Chronicles 5:1 we read, 'Now the sons of Reuben the first-born of Israel (for he was the first-born, but because he defiled his father's bed, his birthright was given to the sons of Joseph the son of Israel ...)'

The account of Reuben's act also serves a literary purpose, providing a backdrop to the conflict between Reuben and the sons of the concubines in chapter 37. Reuben desires to have compassion on Joseph, whereas the other brothers want him murdered.

The episode ends abruptly with the statement which says literally, **'and Israel heard'**. It stops right in the middle of verse 22. This is not unheard of: the scribes place a paragraph marker at this point in the Masoretic Text. This signifies a break in content.[242] The point is that Jacob does not immediately respond to his eldest son's abominable act — however, he does eventually curse him for it in 49:3-4. In that passage it is clear that because Reuben attempts to snatch pre-eminence he ends up losing it!

35:22-26. ... And the sons of Jacob were twelve: the sons of Leah: Reuben, the first-born of Jacob, and Simeon and Levi and Judah and Issachar and Zebulun; the sons of Rachel: Joseph and Benjamin; and the sons of Bilhah, the handmaid of Rachel: Dan and Naphtali; and the sons of Zilpah, the handmaid of Leah: Gad and Asher. These are the sons of Jacob who were born to him in Paddan-Aram.

With the birth of Benjamin, all twelve of Jacob's sons whose descendants will constitute the tribes of Israel have been born. It is appropriate to provide a list of sons in full. The final sentence is a concluding

statement of apposition for the purpose of expla-
nation.²⁴³ It is an emphatic summary statement.

The listing of the wives is in a chiastic form:

Leah ———————————— Bilhah
Rachel ——————————— Zilpah

This formula is adopted in order to denote that all
the wives and sons are accounted for; in other words,
it acts as a summary.

The inclusion by the author of Benjamin in the
statement that these are the ones **'born to him in
Paddan-Aram'** is not a problem. The statement is a
synecdoche in which a collective is put for a singu-
lar.²⁴⁴ It is a proposition that is being loosely
employed.

35:27-29. Then Jacob came to Isaac his father at Mamre
near Kiriath Arba — that is, Hebron — where Abraham and
Isaac had sojourned. And the days of Isaac were 180 years.
So Isaac expired and he died. And he was gathered to his
people, old and full of days. And Esau and Jacob, his sons,
buried him.

Since Jacob's departure for Haran, Isaac's company
has moved from Beersheba (28:10) to Hebron. Here is
where Isaac dies. Yet the information given is somewhat cryptic — the fact is that Isaac did not die until
Jacob had been at Hebron for some twelve years.²⁴⁵
Genesis 49:29-32 tells us that Esau and Jacob
buried him in the cave of the field in Machpelah, in
which Abraham, Sarah, Rebekah and Leah were all
eventually interred.²⁴⁶

Little information is provided regarding the death
of Isaac, except his age at the time. The manner in
which it is recorded appears to follow a standard
formula, as most of the same elements are found in
the obituary of Abraham (see commentary on 25:8).

Application

Jacob suffers three major blows in this short passage: his beloved wife dies, his father dies and his first-born son heinously violates one of his concubines. It is a great period of adversity and suffering. By it we are called to understand that into every life such things fall, as Jesus said: 'For he causes his sun to rise on the evil and the good, and sends rain on the righteous and the unrighteous' (Matt. 5:45). But unlike the unbeliever, no matter how severe the affliction, there is one thing the believer can count on: suffering will never destroy the child of God. It cannot and will not claim victory over the godly. As Paul so eloquently says:

> Who will separate us from the love of Christ? Will tribulation, or distress, or persecution, or famine, or nakedness, or peril, or sword? Just as it is written,
>
> > 'For your sake we are being put to death all day long;
> > We were considered as sheep to be slaughtered.'
>
> But in all these things we overwhelmingly conquer through him who loved us. For I am convinced that neither death, nor life, nor angels, nor principalities, nor things present, nor things to come, nor powers, nor height, nor depth, nor any other created thing, will be able to separate us from the love of God, which is in Christ Jesus our Lord
> (Rom. 8:35-39).

Esau's legacy
(Genesis 36:1-43)

This section serves as the conclusion to Esau's part in the book of Genesis. It traces his migration to the land of Edom, his immediate lineage and the clan structure that arises from his line. It is the fulfilment of God's promise to Rebekah when the twins were born: 'Two nations are in your womb; and two peoples from your inward parts will be divided' (25:23). It also serves as a parallel, and perhaps a foil, to the line of Jacob, and its division into the twelve tribes of Israel, beginning in the very next chapter of Genesis.

36:1. And these are the generations of Esau, that is, Edom.

Here is the common introductory formula for genealogies in the book of Genesis (see 5:1; 10:1; 11:10,27; 25:12). It often also denotes a new block of narrative material (see 2:4; 6:9; 25:19; 37:2). In the present chapter it has both purposes: the section relates Esau's final move into Edomite territory, and it catalogues his posterity.

The name **'Edom'** signifies three different things in the chapter. First, it is used of the person of Esau (36:1); second, the inhabitants of Seir are called by the title Edom (36:9); and, finally, the territory itself is described as the land of Edom (36:31).

36:2-5. Esau took his wives from the daughters of Canaan: Adah, the daughter of Elon the Hittite; and Oholibamah, the daughter of Anah and the granddaughter of Zibeon the Hivite; and Basemath, the daughter of Ishmael, the sister of Nebaioth. And Adah bore for Esau Eliphaz, and Basemath bore Reuel, and Oholibamah bore Jeush, Jalam and Korah. These are the sons of Esau who were born to him in the land of Canaan.

At the close of chapter 35, we were presented with a list of the sons of Jacob (35:22-26). They were catalogued according to their mothers. The same method is now used to record the sons of Esau: they are registered according to the identity of the mother. Here, however, the author emphasizes that these wives, in contrast to Rachel and Leah, are **'daughters of Canaan'**. In addition, the contrast is further heightened by the author's use of the formula: **'These are the sons of Esau who were born to him in the land of Canaan'** — the same expression was used of Jacob in 35:26, except that in that verse it says 'in the land of Paddan-Aram'.

This genealogy agrees with verses 9-14 later in the chapter. Some commentators argue that these are 'conflicting compilations, evidently by different researchers'.[247] In reality, they are similar accounts with different emphases: verses 2-5 are from the perspective of the mothers and who gave birth to whom; in verses 9-14, the sons are being stressed, and their descendants.

The names of the wives of Esau as they are listed in the present section are different from the names given to them in 26:34 and 28:9. A comparison of the two lists is set out below:

36:2-5	*26:34; 28:9*
1. Adah the daughter of Elon the Hittite	1. Judith the daughter of Beeri the Hittite

2. Oholibamah the   2. Basemath the daugh-
    daughter of Anah   ter of Elon the Hittite
3. Basemath the   3. Mahaloth the daughter
    daughter of Ishmael   of Ishmael

In the case of the last pair we are obviously given two names for the same person — instances of multiple names for the same individual were common in the ancient Near East. The opening two pairs have names that are so distinct from one another that it is hard to imagine that they do not refer to separate wives of Esau. Of course, multiple marriages were also common in the ancient Near East.[248]

36:6-7. And Esau took his wives and his sons and his daughters and all the people of his household and his herds and all his animals and all his possessions which he had acquired in the land of Canaan, and he went to a land away from his brother Jacob. For their possessions were too much for them to dwell together, and the land where they sojourned was unable to sustain them because of their herds.

Esau migrates from Canaan because of both economic and social forces. First, he and Jacob have both increased in flocks to such a great extent that the land cannot sustain both of them. The Hebrew employs an elative particle here, an absolute comparative that expresses a quality of too high a degree.[249] Secondly, Jacob obviously has the right to remain where he is because of his inheritance rights that he received after the death of Isaac. His status as first-born gives him priority of choice. An interesting contrast may be seen in the story of Lot and Abraham: although by right Abraham should have been accorded first choice of land, he allows Lot to choose first.

36:8. Thus Esau dwelt in the land of Seir; Esau, he is Edom.

In verse 6 we were told that Esau migrated 'to a land away from his brother Jacob'. The particular land was not specified in that verse, but now it is given definition: Esau has left Canaan and now lives in **'the land of Seir'**. Esau had been living there previously (32:3) but, apparently, he had returned after the death of Isaac. Now he will make a permanent separation from Canaan.

The final phrase is a clause of identification. The personal pronoun **'he'** is pleonastic (it is unnecessary in the Hebrew sentence construction).[250] The writer could simply have said, 'Esau is Edom.' Yet the personal pronoun serves as a *copula* — that is, a connecting link that makes the relationship more concrete.[251]

36:9-14. And these are the generations of Esau, the father of Edom, in the hill-country of Seir. These are the names of the sons of Esau: Eliphaz the son of Adah, the wife of Esau; Reuel the sons of Basemath, the wife of Esau. And the sons of Eliphaz were Teman, Omar, Zepho and Gatam and Kenaz. And Timna was a concubine of Eliphaz the son of Esau, and she bore Amalek for Eliphaz. These are the descendants of Adah the wife of Esau. And these are the sons of Reuel: Nahath and Zerah, Shammah and Mizzah. These are the descendants of Basemath the wife of Esau. And these are the descendants of Oholibamah the daughter of Anah, and the granddaughter of Zibeon, the wife of Esau: and she bore Jeush and Jalam and Korah for Esau.

Not all the names of Esau's descendants listed here are recognizable, although some of them are, and these play an important role in biblical history. The first grandson of Esau mentioned is **'Teman'**. That title later becomes a designation for a region in Edom (Jer. 49:7,20; Ezek. 25:13). And the people of that district are called Temanites (see 36:34 below).

Another grandson of Esau through his son Eliphaz is **'Kenaz'**. Some commentators have tried to tie this name with the Kennizzites of Genesis 15:19, a group whose land God promises to Abraham. The nature of the connection between the two is unknown, if there is any at all.

Eliphaz's concubine, a certain Timna, bears him a son named **'Amalek'**. He is obviously the progenitor of the group called the Amalekites in the Bible. They are traditional enemies of Israel (see Exod. 17:8-16; Deut. 25:17-19; 1 Sam. 15:1-33; 30:1-20). The fact that the Amalekites are descended from Esau through a concubine is a disparagement of their status in relation to the Edomites. They are thus to be seen as inferior to — the 'poor cousins' of — the Edomites!

36:15-19. These are the clans of the descendants of Esau. The descendants of Eliphaz, the first-born of Esau: clan Teman, clan Omar, clan Zepho, clan Kenaz, clan Korah, clan Natam, clan Amalek. These are the clans of Eliphaz in the land of Edom. These are the descendants of Adah. And these are the descendants of Reuel, the son of Esau: clan Nahath, clan Zerah, clan Shammah, clan Mizzah. These are the clans of Reuel in the land of Edom. These are the descendants of Basemath the wife of Esau. And these are the descendants of Oholibamah the wife of Esau: clan Jeush, clan Jalam, clan Korah. These are the clans of Oholibamah, the daughter of Anah, the wife of Esau. These are the descendants of Esau — that is, Edom — and these are their clans.

Numerous Bible versions render the Hebrew term *'allūph* as 'chief' rather than adopting our translation of **'clan'**. This is a word that is related to a common Hebrew word meaning 'a thousand', 'a company' or 'a group'. And, as Speiser points out, 'Individuals would not be so described.'[252] Indeed, in every instance of its use the best meaning for it is 'clan' (see Zech. 9:7; 12:5-6). It should also be noted that the word is always used of early Edomite clans, except in the passages from Zechariah just mentioned, where it refers to clans within Judah.[253]

36:20-30. These are the sons of Seir the Horite who lived in the land: Lotan and Shobal and Zibeon and Anah and Dishon and Ezer and Dishan. These are the clans of the Horites, the descendants of Seir, in the land of Edom. And the sons of Lotam are Hori and Heman; and the sister of Lotam is Timna. And these are the sons of Shobal: Alvan and Manahat and Ebal, Shepho and Onam. And these are the sons of Zibeon: Aiah and Anah; that is the Anah who found the water in the desert when he was shepherding the donkeys of Zibeon his father. And these are the sons of Anah: Dishon and Oholibamah, the daughter of Anah. And these are the sons of Dishon: Hemdan and Eshban and Ithran and Keran. These are the sons of Ezer: Bilhan and Zaavan and Akan. These are the sons of Dishan: Uz and Aran. These are the clans of the Horites: clan Lotan, clan Shobal, clan Zibeon, clan Anah, clan Dishon, clan Ezer, clan Dishan. These are the clans of the Horites according to their clans in the land of Seir.

This section is a listing of the Horites who had lived in the land of Seir. According to Deuteronomy 2:12, the Horites of Seir were displaced by the descendants of Esau. It says, 'And the Horites formerly dwelt in Seir but the sons of Edom dispossessed them and they destroyed them from before themselves and they settled in their place.' The fact that the Horites have an inferior status to the Edomites is evident from the fact that **'Timna'**, mentioned here as **'the sister of Lotam'**, is the concubine of Esau's son Eliphaz (see 36:12).

The figure of **'Anah'** is famous because of a particular discovery. What he found is uncertain. Numerous

translations say that he stumbled on 'hot springs' in
the desert — that translation appears as early as the
Vulgate but there is no linguistic support for it.[254] The
Hebrew consonantal term is *h-y-m-m*: it occurs only in
this passage and its meaning is dubious. In reality,
what we may be seeing is a scribal transposition of two
of the word's consonants — perhaps it should be read
h-m-y-m, which means 'the water'. And, indeed, it
would be a great feat to find water in the desert!

The beginning of verse 26 literally reads, **'And
these are the sons of Dishan.'** The name here
should not be Dishan, but Dishon, and our translation reflects this change (1 Chr. 1:41 also confirms
this reading). The appearance of the name Dishan at
this point in the Masoretic Text reflects some form of
scribal dittography.

36:31-39. And these are the kings who ruled over the land of
Edom before a king ruled over the children of Israel: Bela the
son of Beor ruled over Edom, and the name of his city was
Dinhabah. And Bela died. Then Jobab the son of Zerah from
Bozrah ruled in his place. And Jobab died. Then Husham
from the land of the Temanites ruled in his place. And
Husham died. Then Hadad the son of Bedad, who struck
Midian in the country of Moab, ruled in his place, and his city
was Avith. And Hadad died. Then Samlah from Masrekah
ruled in his place. And Samlah died. Then Shaul from Reho-
both of the river ruled in his place. And Shaul died. Then
Baal-Hanan the son of Acbor ruled in his place. And Baal-
Hanan the son of Acbor died. Then Hadar ruled in his place,
and the name of his city was Pau. And the name of his wife
[was] Mehetabel, the daughter of Matred, the daughter of
Me-Zahab.

The author now inserts an Edomite king-list that
enumerates a series of monarchs that reigned **'before a king ruled over the children of Israel'**. This
introductory comment conveys the fact that Edom

develops faster than Israel — the older grows quicker than the younger! So what we have before us is a catalogue of Edomite kings prior to the ascension of Saul to the throne of Israel.[255] Various dates have been given regarding the compilation of the list, anywhere from the late second millennium B.C.[256] down to as late as the sixth century B.C.[257] There is little reason to question the early and authentic origination of the document.

Most of the names and kings listed are unknown to us from anywhere else in the Bible or in ancient Near-Eastern literature.[258] The first king, **'Bela son of Beor'**, sounds like the figure of Balaam son of Beor in Numbers 22:5, but this is probably mere coincidence. The one name we are certain of is **'Bozrah'**: it is the site of Buseirah, located to the east of the Dead Sea, approximately four kilometres from the King's Highway. Pottery from the site dates from as early as the Iron I period (beginning of the thirteenth century B.C.), although the exact nature of this early settlement is unknown.[259]

After the reigns of these kings, Israel begins to subjugate the Edomites: the older serves the younger. That subjection begins with Saul (1 Sam. 14:47) and becomes severe under the monarchy of David (2 Sam. 8:2-14; 1 Kings 11:14-17).

36:40-43. And these are the names of the clans of Esau, according to their families and according to their regions, by their names: clan Timnah, clan Alvah, clan Jetheth, clan Oholibamah, clan Elah, clan Pinon, clan Kenaz, clan Teman, clan Mibsar, clan Magdiel, clan Iram. These are the clans of Edom according to their settlements in the land of their possession. This is Esau the father of Edom.

Now the author provides a summary list of the various clans that have settled in the land of Edom. Not only are these names of clans, but they appear to denote specific geographic regions. Eleven clans are catalogued, and the same list appears in 1 Chronicles 1:51-54.

We are able to identify with various degrees of certainty at least four of the names. **'Elah'** perhaps refers to Elath, which lies at the head of the Gulf of 'Aqaba. It is mentioned several times in Scripture in relation to the territory of Edom (see Deut. 2:8; 2 Chr. 8:17). For example, 1 Kings 9:26 reports that Solomon built a navy at Ezion-geber which is 'near Elath on the shore of the Red Sea, in the land of Edom'.

The next title, **Pinon**, is probably to be identified with the copper-smelting site of Feinan on the east side of the Wadi 'Araba.[260] Ceramic remains from the Late Bronze, Iron I and Iron II periods have been found at the site. It is a site also mentioned in the travel itinerary of the Hebrews out of Egypt in Numbers 33:42-43.

The two other sites have been mentioned previously in chapter 36. **'Teman'** is a district of Edom (see commentary on 36:9-14). It has been suggested that the term **'Mibzar'** is to be identified with Bozrah (see 36:31-39) or what is modern-day Buseirah.[261]

This section comprises the final comments in Genesis on the story of Esau. It is truly ironic that it concludes with a comment on the **'possession'** of the Edomites. The verbal form of that word appeared in the very first incident involving Jacob and Esau, when the former came out from the womb 'holding / possessing' the heel of Esau. The issue of what land belongs to what people serves as an *inclusio* to the entire story!

Application

The purpose of this genealogical chapter is to trace Esau's settlement in the land of Edom, his immediate succession and his progeny that inhabits the land of Seir. The Edomites, of course, become Israel's mortal enemies. In fact, during the wilderness wanderings when Moses set down these genealogies in writing, it is Edom who 'refused to allow Israel to pass through his territory; so Israel turned away from him' (Num. 20:21). Thus the writer is chronicling the line of Esau for an important point: know your enemy!

The genealogy also serves to demonstrate that the seed of the serpent, the non-covenanted people, are alive and well on the planet earth. They are increasing and being fruitful. And the question we are left with now is: how will God take care of his elect? How will he fulfil his promises to the seed of the woman?

9. The story of Joseph

Genesis 37:1 – 50:26

A story of jealousy
(Genesis 37:1-11)

Here begins the story of the patriarch Joseph. The remainder of the book of Genesis describes his life, except for the inclusion of the stories of Tamar (ch. 38) and Jacob's blessings upon his sons (ch. 49). It, therefore, constitutes the longest single passage in the entire book.

The present section relates the dissension and division that arise between Joseph and his brothers, in particular the sons of Bilhah and Zilpah. In a sense it mirrors the disputes that had previously occurred between Jacob and Esau. Here we see a growing animosity and hatred by the brothers towards Joseph.

37:1. And Jacob dwelt in the land of his father's sojournings, in the land of Canaan.

This verse serves as a transition from the previous genealogical material relating to the line of Esau. The author now turns to consider the descendants of Jacob. He presents us with a contrast: Esau had left the land of Canaan (36:6), but Jacob remains **'in the land of Canaan'**. The enmity between the two brothers and between their two posterities is accentuated in this manner.

37:2. These are the generations of Jacob: Joseph was seventeen years old when he was shepherding sheep with his brothers, and he was a helper to the sons of Bilhah and to the sons of Zilpah, his father's wives. And Joseph brought their slanders against him to their father.

The contrast between Jacob and Esau is further emphasized by the use of the introductory formula: **'These are the generations of...'** This is a common heading in Genesis proclaiming the beginning of a new section of narrative material (see commentary on 2:4 — vol. 1, p.96). That formula had just previously introduced the genealogy of Esau (36:1), and now it announces the lineage and history of Jacob's descendants.

The term translated **'helper'** is the common Hebrew word meaning 'boy / youth'. However, in a number of instances it signifies one who is an attendant, aid, or retainer.[1] The context requires the latter interpretation.

The sons are not identified by name, but only by reference to their mothers. This may underscore an underlying problem and tension in the story. Bilhah and Zilpah were handmaids / concubines given to Jacob by his two wives, Rachel and Leah (30:3-7,9-12). They bore the sons Dan, Naphtali, Gad and Asher. Joseph, on the other hand, is the son of Rachel, the beloved wife of Jacob. Rachel had been barren (29:31) until God opened her womb to bear Joseph (30:23-24). In the present verse, Joseph is pictured as serving the sons of the concubines.

Another indicator of discord is narrated at the end of the verse. Joseph tells his father of the slanders of his brothers against him. Many translations render this clause as if it is Joseph who is maligning the others. For example, the NIV says that 'He brought

their father a bad report about them.' On the contrary, the Hebrew here is probably to be understood
as a subjective genitive 'in the sense that Joseph
reported to his father *their* slander against him'.[2]
Although the precise nature of the reports is not
stated, this nevertheless highlights the growing
animosity among the brothers in the family.

37:3. Now Israel loved Joseph more than all his sons because he was the son of his old age. And he made for him a
tunic with long skirts and sleeves.

A third indicator of tension and conflict appears in
this verse in the fact that Jacob loves Joseph to a
greater extent than the rest of his sons. Jacob shows
partiality to Joseph because Jacob was old when
Joseph was born, and Joseph is the first-born of
Rachel, whom Jacob deeply loved. The separateness
of Joseph is accentuated by the use of a comparative
min here, which in Hebrew means 'more than'. It
places Joseph in a singular position, one that is
distinct from, and superior to, the others.[3]

The common translation of the garment that Jacob
made for Joseph as 'a coat of many colours' is con-
jecture. The Hebrew phrase *kᵉtōnēt pāssîm* is used
elsewhere in the Old Testament only in 2 Samuel
13:18-19, where it refers to the clothes commonly
worn by the virgin daughters of Israel. The term
kᵉtōnēt simply means 'tunic / coat / robe'. The word
pāssîm is more difficult, perhaps being related to the
noun *pās*, which means 'flat of hand or foot'.[4] Thus it
is likely that Joseph's coat is one that is long and
flowing. That interpretation does not detract from the
special nature of the clothing. In an extra-biblical
text from Mesopotamia a *kutinnū pišannu* is mentioned.[5] It refers to a ceremonial robe that was
wrapped around an idol and was decorated with gold

rings. That use underscores the distinctive nature of such a robe in antiquity.

37:4. And his brothers saw that their father loved him more than all his brothers, and they hated him and they were not able to speak to him in peace.

The Hebrew word order of the opening clause is inverted in order to emphasize the object. It literally reads, **'And his brothers saw that him their father loved.'**

The final clause of the verse is unique because it employs an infinitive with a noun suffix (i.e., the verb **'to speak'** with **'him'** attached). How the two elements relate to each other is difficult to know: perhaps it means 'to speak to him', or possibly 'to speak about him'. The latter rendition would fit better with the interpretation of verse 2 given above. In any event, the attitude of the brothers to Joseph is one of great animosity and discord. This is a fourth indicator of conflict.

37:5. And Joseph dreamed a dream. When he told [it] to his brothers they hated him even more.

Dreams possessing oracular power were a common medium in the ancient Near East. Collections of dream omens are well known from ancient Egypt, Mesopotamia and Ugarit.[6] The idea of Joseph's being a dreamer and interpreter of dreams is not a problem because Yahweh is clearly the source of both (see 41:16). The author of the epistle to the Hebrews tells us that God 'spoke long ago to the fathers in the prophets in many portions and in many ways' (Heb. 1:1).

The dream and its meaning turn out to be a fifth indicator of discord between Joseph and his brothers. The brothers end up hating him **'even**

more' — the Hebrew substantive used here expresses continuance, persistence, repetition and heightening.[7]

37:6-7. And he said to them, 'Listen, please, to this dream which I have dreamed: behold, we were binding sheaves in the field, when, behold, my sheaf rose up and it stood upright; and, behold, your sheaves gathered around it and they bowed down to my sheaf.'

This is the first of two dreams that Joseph relates to his brothers in this chapter. And he is quite earnest and insistent in sharing the dream with his kin. In relaying the contents of the dream, Joseph uses the word **'behold'** *(hĭnneh)* three times — it is a demonstrative particle making the narrative graphic and vivid.[8] He also opens his speech with the particle of entreaty *nā'*; often left untranslated, it can mean 'please'.[9]

Joseph's dream is allegorical. Allegory is typical of ancient Near-Eastern dream omens. For example, in ancient Egypt, the most important collection is the Chester Beatty Papyrus III, which comes from Dynasty 19.[10] The manuscript is divided into dreams experienced by the Sons of Seth and the Sons of Horus. Over columns listing various dreams are written the words, 'If a man sees himself in a dream.' Adjoining columns provide interpretations. For example:

If a man sees himself in a dream:
Seeing a large cat   Good: It means a large harvest will come to him.
Seeing his face in a   Bad: it means another wife.[11]
mirror

In Joseph's dream, the sheaves symbolize the sons of Jacob, and the fact that one day they will all humble themselves before their brother Joseph.

37:8. And his brothers said to him, 'Will you really rule over us? Or will you really reign over us?' And they hated him even more on account of his dreams and on account of his words.

The brothers respond vehemently to Joseph's dream. First, they ask the same question in different words — a common Hebrew construction to express a question more emphatically. The two verbs of the questions, **'rule'** and **'reign'**, are 'semantically closely related'12 — in other words, they are synonyms. Both verbs are imperfective forms preceded by infinitive absolutes. The infinitive absolutes have an intensifying effect on a question.

In addition to the strong spoken reaction of the brothers, they also harbour a growing animosity towards Joseph. The phrase, **'They hated him even more'**, is a repetition of verse 5, and it forms an *inclusio* for the first dream sequence. It is the third time the word **'hated'** has been used in the passage to describe the brothers' feelings towards Joseph (37:4,5,8). That recurrence possibly reflects the increasing intensity of their hatred as time passes.

The hostility towards Joseph is based upon two things: **'his dreams'** and **'his words'**. The latter expression probably refers to verse 2 above, in which Joseph had told his father about his brothers' slanderous ways.

The dream is in no need of interpretation — its lesson is quite obvious. The lack of an interpreter for the dream contrasts with the dreams of the Egyptians later in the story of Joseph (40:5-13; 41:1-8).

37:9. And again he dreamed another dream, and he recounted it to his brothers. And he said, 'Behold, again I dreamed a dream. And, behold, the sun and the moon and eleven stars were bowing down to me.'

Joseph's second dream uses different symbols from the first one, but it retains the same theme. Dream sequences throughout the Joseph story appear in pairs (see chapters 40 and 41).[13] Such repetition reflects the certainty of the dream's fulfilment. In Genesis 41:32, Joseph says to the King of Egypt, 'And concerning the second dream unto Pharaoh repeating, it is because of the certainty of the matter from God, and that God will quickly do it.'

Joseph's second dream has the same theme as the first, yet it extends the application of the message conveyed. Here the sun and moon represent Joseph's parents (see 37:10), whereas they were not part of the first dream.

37:10. And he recounted it to his father and to his brothers. And his father rebuked him, and he said to him, 'What is this dream you have dreamt? Will we really come, I and your mother and your brothers, to bow down to you to the ground?'

The statement that Joseph recounted the dream **'to his brothers'** is redundant. He had already done so in verse 9. Therefore, the Septuagint deletes the clause. However, it probably belongs here and is repetitive for a purpose: it may highlight the fact that Joseph is inclined to be haughty or pompous in relating his dream. He is narrating it a second time in the presence of his brothers. This idea is supported by the statement that Jacob **'rebukes'** him. That verb often signifies the correction given to the proud or foolish (Ps. 119:21; Prov. 13:1,8; 17:10; Isa. 17:13).

Jacob's reference to Joseph's mother poses a problem because Rachel has long since died (35:19). Possibly the dream sequence is to be placed earlier in the story, prior to Rachel's death. However, in verse 9 Joseph speaks of eleven stars as representing his brothers, and so Benjamin must have been born by this time. Rachel died giving birth to Benjamin (35:18).[14] Maybe the reference is to one of the other wives of Jacob who took the position of first wife or most beloved.

37:11. And his brothers were jealous of him, but his father kept the matter [in mind].

The repetition of the dreams underscores the gravity of the message. Anger is not the only response of the brothers; now they are **'jealous'**, or envious, of Joseph. This reaction demonstrates that the brothers do not offhandedly discount the message of Joseph's dreams. Jacob, too, reacts in a more sober manner: he, literally, 'keeps', or 'guards', the matter or thing — this is a Hebrew idiom conveying the idea of treasuring something in the memory (cf. 1 Chr. 29:18; Prov. 4:21).

Application

Although this section appears to be purely secular, centring on the human drama of brother against brother, something greater is taking place. It is an example of the divinely ordained course of human history. The hatred of the brothers leads to the selling of Joseph into Egypt. His slavery eventually leads to all Israel dwelling in Egypt and, ultimately, to the deliverance of the Hebrews during the period of the Exodus. All of that comes to pass according to the promise of God to Abraham in Genesis 15:13-14 many years before the story of Joseph.

The incident also points out that God uses man's sinful ways and deceitfulness to bring about his own good purposes. All events, in heaven above or on the earth beneath, unfold according to his will. He is simply sovereign.

Joseph's sale into slavery
(Genesis 37:12-36)

The author now narrates the details of how the other
sons of Jacob conspire to destroy Joseph. An opportunity to act out their hatred is given to them as they
are in the fields with the flocks far away from their
father's oversight. Joseph arrives to check on their
welfare. It is at this point that the hostility of the
brothers results in the physical abuse of Joseph.

37:12. And his brothers went to shepherd the flock of their
father in Shechem.

As semi-nomads, Jacob and his family would continually move their flocks from one area to another.
They did this in order to provide grazing land and
water for the animals. Shechem was a town located
in the central hill-country of Palestine.[15] It was situated in a region that had rich soil and abundant
water supplies.[16] Shechem was a very important site
in the history of the patriarchs: it was the first city in
Canaan visited by Abraham (12:6); Jacob himself
purchased a plot of land here, and he erected an
altar to God on the spot (33:19-20). Here Joseph
found his final resting-place (Josh. 24:32).

Verse 14 informs us that Jacob and Joseph are in
the Valley of Hebron while the brothers are in
Shechem. The former was a region around the city of
Hebron that lay about twenty miles south of Jerusalem. It was also the scene of much patriarchal

activity (see 23:17-20; 35:27). It is important to note that the distance between Shechem and Hebron was approximately fifty miles — and, therefore, it is no wonder that Jacob is not able to intervene in the following episode.

37:13. And Israel said to Joseph, 'Are not your brothers shepherding in Shechem? Come, and I will send you to them.' And he said to him, 'Here I am!'

In the light of the recent troubles between Joseph and his brothers it seems strange that Jacob should be sending Joseph to them at so great a distance. Perhaps Jacob (**'Israel'**) is not fully aware of the extent of the animosity among the members of his family. No less odd is Joseph's unquestioning will-ingness to go. He replies to his father's advance with, **'Here I am!'**, a demonstrative particle with a first person singular pronominal suffix. It is used in the Old Testament especially in response to a call; thus it underscores the readiness of Joseph to obey (cf., 22:1,11; 27:1,18; 31:11). He is eager. Joseph himself may be unaware of how deep-seated is the hatred of his brothers.

37:14. And he said to him, 'Go now, see if there is peace with your brothers and peace with the flock, and bring back word to me.' And he sent him from the Valley of Hebron and he came to Shechem.

Three of the words Jacob uses in this command to Joseph were similarly employed in verse 4 above. In that previous hostile situation Joseph's brothers 'saw' and they were not able to speak a 'word' of 'peace' to him, or about him. Ironically, the use here of the same words highlights the tragedy that is about to occur.

37:15-17. And a man found him and behold he was wandering about in the field. And the man asked him, saying, 'What are you seeking?' And he said, 'I am seeking my brothers. Please tell me where they are shepherding.' And the man said, 'They have travelled from this [place] because I heard them saying, "Let us go to Dothan."' And Joseph went after his brothers and he found them in Dothan.

This brief scene portrays Joseph as one who shows great persistence and determination. He is a man of his word by being diligent in finding his brothers. That intensity is highlighted by the sentence construction of Joseph's reply to the man: the Hebrew word order reads: **'My brothers I am seeking.'** This is a structure in which priority of position gives emphasis to the object.[17]

The man obviously knows Joseph's brothers, sufficiently well to be able to quote them about where they are going. Dothan was about thirteen and a half miles directly north of Shechem. It was an area of extensive pasturelands, and it was situated in a broad valley. One of the most important highways in antiquity passed near to the city, leading from the Samarian Hills into the Jezreel Valley. Extensive excavations were carried out at Dothan in the 1950s-1960s.[18]

37:18. When they saw him from a distance, and before he had drawn near to them, they craftily plotted against him to kill him.

Now that the brothers are in Dothan, they are even further from Jacob's oversight than when they were in Shechem. The sight of Joseph coming from a distance evokes feelings of hatred among the brothers. Because Joseph is still far away, they have time to plot his destruction. The verb for **'craftily plotted'** derives from the root that means 'to be clever /

deceitful / cunning'.[19] It is a plural verb in the Hithpael pattern (reflexive) which signifies that the brothers are plotting *together*.

*37:19. And they spoke, a man to his brother, 'Behold, here
comes this lord of dreams!'*

The title given to Joseph by his brothers is usually
translated as 'this dreamer'. However, the genitive
bă'ăl appears in the clause: it means 'master / owner
/ possessor of'. By describing Joseph as the **'lord of
dreams'**, the brothers are mocking and insulting
him. The festering anger of the brothers is reaching a
crescendo, which will find its climax in their physical
attack on Joseph.

*37:20. 'And now, come and let us kill him and toss him into
one of the pits; and we will say, "A fierce animal ate him."
Then we shall see what will become of his dreams.'*

The evil and determined intent of the brothers is
clearly evident in this verse. First, the verb translated
'come' is a plural imperative, and it denotes the
volitional mood of the brothers to carry out the
dastardly act. Secondly, the cohortative **'let us kill'**
derives from a verb that implies 'ruthless violence'.[20]
It is rarely used of judicial killing, but most often of a
private vendetta.

There were many reasons in antiquity for digging
pits. They served as grain storage receptacles, cis-
terns, latrines, refuse dumps and robber pits.[21] The
pits were often fairly large, reaching a width of ten
feet (or three metres), and a depth of sixteen feet (or
nearly five metres). Because of their size they were
known to have been used for the temporary incarceration of humans — for example, the prophet
Jeremiah was imprisoned in a pit (Jer. 18:20-22;
38:6-13). The bodies of murder victims were also

thrown into pits. The men who murdered King
David's son Absalom threw his body into a pit
(2 Sam. 18:17). After the Babylonian destruction of
Jerusalem in 586 B.C., seventy supporters of
Gedaliah, the puppet ruler of Judah appointed by the
Babylonians, were murdered and thrown into a royal
pit (Jer. 41:7-9). The pit into which Joseph will be
thrown by his brothers is a cistern (37:24).

37:21. When Reuben heard, he then delivered him from their
hands. And he said, 'Let us not strike him, [to the point of
taking his] life.'

Reuben, Jacob's first-born, takes advantage of his
status to intervene and to save Joseph from the
murderous hands of his brothers. His authority is
unquestioned, as none of the others raises an objec-
tion to Reuben's demand. Some scholars want to
change the name 'Reuben' to 'Judah' because otherwise they see the next verse (37:22) as redundant.[22]
But that emendation misses the point: the repetition
of the demand is to underscore its importance and
insistence on the part of Reuben. He will get his way,
and Joseph is not killed.

In the Hebrew, Reuben's statement ends with a
double accusative, saying literally, **'Let us not strike
him, life.'** A second accusative serves to define more
precisely the intent of the action — the striking is to
the point of taking a life.[23]

37:22. And Reuben said to them, 'Do not shed blood! Throw
him into this pit that is in the wilderness! But do not stretch
out [literally, "send forth"] a hand against him!' — so that he
might deliver him from their hand to return him to his father.

To express a negative imperative in Hebrew, authors
often use the negative *'al* with a non-perfective verb.
It appears twice in this verse: **'Do not shed ...'** and

'**Do not stretch out...**' (literally, 'Do not send forth...'). Between these two there is a positive imperative form: '**Throw him...**' All three verbs are in the plural: this demonstrates that it is Reuben against the other brothers. They are not, at this point, acting with one accord.

By adding the phrase '**in the wilderness**', Reuben is probably playing on his brothers' desire to kill Joseph.[24] Being left in a pit out in the wilderness is a sure recipe for death as a result of exposure to the elements. Reuben, however, plans to rescue Joseph at a later time and return him to Jacob. Reuben's desire to save Joseph may stem from a hope to regain his father's favour. Back in Genesis 35:22, Reuben had slept with Bilhah, Jacob's concubine and, thus, he was certainly not in his father's good graces. It may also be that Reuben and the sons of Bilhah do not see eye to eye because of that previous situation; and the sons of Bilhah are instigators of the hatred towards Joseph (37:2).

37:23. And it came to pass, as Joseph came to his brothers, that they stripped Joseph of his tunic, the tunic with long skirts and sleeves that was on him.

The first thing the brothers do when meeting Joseph is to strip him of the ornamental robe that their father had given to him. It is a symbol of Jacob's special favour to Joseph, and now the brothers remove it from him. The verb for '**stripped**' is in the Hiphil, or causative, pattern — that is, the brothers are the cause and origin of the cloak's removal.

A construction of apposition appears in this verse: '**his tunic, the tunic with ...**'. The apposition defines the precise nature of the tunic, and this is important for the development of the story. Later, in verse 33, it is this very tunic that identifies the victim as Joseph to his father.

37:24. And they took him and threw him into the pit. And the
pit was empty; there was no water in it.

The brothers physically seize Joseph. They then cast
him into an empty cistern, in accordance with Reuben's demand in verse 22. The fact that the cistern is
empty is stated to show that Joseph will not drown,
but is to be imprisoned in the pit.

37:25. And they sat down to eat food. And they lifted their
eyes and they looked, and behold a caravan of Ishmaelites
was coming from Gilead. And their camels were bearing
spice and balsam and myrrh, and they were walking to go
down to Egypt.

The callousness and crassness of the brothers is
demonstrated by their sitting down to a meal immediately after abusing Joseph. While they are eating, a
company of Ishmaelites is seen passing by. The name
'Ishmaelites' denotes various tribes that are descended from Ishmael, the son of Abraham (16:11). It
is probably a generic title for many different tribal
peoples in the Levant (see 25:18). Later we are told
that the specific tribal group that bought Joseph was
the Midianites (37:28). The two groups are elsewhere
identified as one and the same (see Judg. 8:22-24).[25]

The Ishmaelites are a caravan of traders who are
travelling from **'Gilead'**. Gilead was a mountainous
district on the eastern side of the Jordan river, and it
was well known for its rich pasturelands.[26] They are
carrying many goods to trade in Egypt, including
'spice and balsam and myrrh'. It is ironic that these
same three items are mentioned in 43:11, in which
Joseph's brothers bring him presents while he is in
Egypt. Two of the words, **'spice'** and **'myrrh'**, are
found only in these two places in the entire Old
Testament.

37:26-27. And Judah said to his brothers, 'What profit that we kill our brother and conceal his blood? Come and let us sell him to the Ishmaelites. And may our hands not be on him because he is our brother, our flesh.' And his brothers listened [to him].

Judah now assumes a leadership role in the question of Joseph's fate. He is the fourth son of Jacob by Leah (29:35). From this point on Judah takes on an increasingly prominent role in the family: for example, it is he who becomes the mediator between Jacob and Joseph later in the story (43:3,8; 44:14, etc.). Judah's ascendancy to leadership in the family reflects the history of the tribes of Israel. Judah and his descendants are promised a position of rulership by Jacob in Genesis 49:8-12.

Judah's motivation for wanting to sell his brother to the Ishmaelites is complex. On the surface, it appears that he has a simple desire for monetary gain because of his brother's misfortune. The term for **'profit'** is very negative, reflecting the idea of 'making gain by violence' — Judah uses a word that is callous and one that points to selfish plundering. On the other hand, he is saving Joseph from certain death; whether or not he does this because of some admirable trait is uncertain. It actually may be in order to justify what they have already done, and to clear themselves of guilt (at least in their own minds). It is truly ironic that Judah says, **'And may our hands not be on him'** — when in fact their hands have already seized Joseph and thrown him into a pit!

37:28. And [the] Midianite traders were passing by. So they dragged and raised up Joseph from the pit. And they sold Joseph to the Ishmaelites for twenty [shekels] of silver. And they brought Joseph to Egypt.

Speiser argues that the appearance of the name **'Midianites'** demonstrates that the first sentence of this verse is 'manifestly from another source'.[27] One would rather expect the name 'Ishmaelites', as it is found in verse 25 and later in the present verse. However, as was stated previously, it is obvious that the Midianites were a specific tribal grouping within the overall population grouping generically called Ishmaelites.[28] So the names are being used interchangeably.

Speiser further argues that the subject of the verbs **'they dragged'** and **'they sold'** refers to the Midianites — that is, the Midianites kidnapped Joseph and sold him to travelling Ishmaelites. That is probably incorrect. The **'they'**, of course, refers to the brothers in verses 26-27 who were conspiring to sell Joseph to the Ishmaelites. Genesis 45:5 confirms this when Joseph says to his brothers, 'And now do not be grieved or angry with yourselves, because you sold me here.'

There was a significant substratum of foreign slaves in Egypt at any given time. Many came as booty from war, but there also was a large slave trade. So many of them came from Asia (i.e., Palestine, Hatti, Mesopotamia, etc.) that 'The generic word "Asiatic" *('amu)* became synonymous with "slave".'[29]

The amount paid by the Ishmaelites for Joseph was the usual price for a male between five and twenty years old. And twenty shekels is the value of a slave in the Code of Hammurabi (Laws nos. 116, 214, 252).[30]

37:29. And Reuben returned to the pit and, behold, Joseph was not in the pit. And he tore his clothes.

Obviously Reuben had no part in the selling of Joseph to the Ishmaelites. The text tells us that he had gone off somewhere — perhaps tending the sheep.

When he returns he sees the empty pit, and he assumes the worst. He believes Joseph to be dead, and so he rips apart his clothing. To tear / rend one's clothing in the Old Testament is a sign of extreme grief and sorrow. It is sometimes used to signify grief for someone who has recently died (2 Sam. 13:31). Jacob responds with the same action when he learns of Joseph's supposed death (37:34).

37:30. And he returned to his brothers, and he said, 'The boy is not [there]! And I? Where am I going?'

After his discovery, Reuben seeks out his brothers. They have left the scene after the sale of Joseph. Reuben's remarks to them underscore his great grief, fear and confusion. His first statement literally says, **'The boy is not!'** It may be a reference to his belief that not only is Joseph not in the pit, but perhaps he is not alive. Reuben then responds with an emphatic personal pronoun: **'And I?'** He is questioning what the death of Joseph might mean for him; it must be remembered that Reuben is the first-born and the one with the principal resposibility for his brother. **'Where am I going?'** sounds as if he is thinking of fleeing — how can he tell his father such sad news?

37:31. And they took Joseph's tunic. And they slaughtered a he-goat. And they dipped the tunic in the blood.

Now proceeds the first step in the cover-up. The plan that the brothers had concocted to hide their terrible deed when they first planned to kill Joseph goes into effect (see 37:20). It is indeed ironic that Jacob had deceived his father by using a goat and a garment (27:9-16), and now his own sons deceive him using similar methods.[31]

37:32. And they sent the tunic with long skirts and sleeves, and they caused [it] to be brought to their father. And they said, 'We have found this. Please examine the coat: is it your son's or not?'

The first two verbs, **'they sent'** and **'they caused [it] to be brought'** (Hiphil causative), indicate that the brothers send the blood-soaked coat to Jacob by the hand of others. Either they are feeling extremely guilty, or else they are attempting to distance themselves from the dastardly deed. In any event, they are obviously afraid to confront their father directly — his reaction would certainly be too much to bear.

The brothers ask Jacob to **'examine'** the coat. This verb has the basic meaning, 'to recognize / regard / pay attention'. It also ties the story back to Jacob's deception of his father Isaac in chapter 27. There, because of the goat-skins and robe, we are told that Isaac 'did not recognize' Jacob (27:23).

37:33. And he examined it. And he said, 'My son's tunic! A ferocious animal devoured him. Joseph has certainly been torn to pieces!'

Jacob thus takes a look at the coat. He recognizes it immediately as the one he had previously given to Joseph because he loved him. The father then observes the blood on the coat, and concludes that a beast must have killed Joseph, and that he must have been ripped to shreds. So the evil designs of the brothers come to pass: Jacob's response is precisely what they had hoped for (see 37:20).

Jacob's deep emotion and reaction are reflected in the grammatical construction of his final statement. The sentence revolves around a repetition of the same verb, 'to tear to pieces': a Pual perfect is preceded by an intensifying infinitive. The repetition is for emphasis, and it means that 'Without a shadow of a doubt he has been torn to pieces.'[32]

37:34. So Jacob tore his clothes and he put sackcloth on his loins. And he mourned over his son many days.

Jacob's response to Joseph's presumed death is typical of expressions of grief in Old Testament times. The tearing of one's clothes was a symbol of the measure of the person's grief — a physical sign of mourning (see 37:29). **'Sackcloth'** — probably garments made of goat's hair — was worn to cause discomfort and as a sign of suffering. Periods of mourning could last from a week to many weeks (see, for instance, Deut. 34:8).

37:35. And all his sons and all his daughters arose to comfort him, but he refused to be comforted. And he said, 'Indeed, I will go down mourning for my son to Sheol.' And his father cried for him.

The only daughter of Jacob of whom we have heard thus far in Genesis is Dinah (30:21). The reference to **'daughters'** may be to other daughters who have not been mentioned in the text, or perhaps to daughters-in-law. The sons, alongside the daughters, try to give comfort to their grieving father. The deceit of the sons is thus compounded after their acts of seizing and selling Joseph. It is all a ruse.

Jacob's statement does not mean that he 'will make a ritual descent into the underworld'.[33] The term **'Sheol'** most often simply means 'grave'. Jacob is announcing that he will be inconsolable in this life: he will mourn and grieve for his son as long as he lives.

The final sentence of the verse is vague because neither **'his father'** nor **'him'** is identified. Although it may be assumed that these terms refer to Jacob

and Joseph respectively, they may possibly refer to
Jacob and his father Isaac. Indeed, Isaac would still
have been alive at this time, according to the biblical
genealogies.[34]

**37:36. And the Midianites sold him into Egypt to Potiphar, an
officer of Pharaoh, captain of the guard.**

Joseph is finally sold to an Egyptian of some means
named Potiphar. In Egyptian the name Potiphar
literally means, 'He whom Re gives.' Because the
name Potiphar was not commonly used in Egypt
prior to the tenth century B.C., some scholars call
into question the veracity of the story of Joseph.
There are, however, a number of possible solutions to
the problem.[35] To posit the unhistorical nature of the
Joseph episode on the basis of the name Potiphar is
unnecessary and misleading.

The Hebrew word for **'officer'** often signifies a
'eunuch'. It is unlikely that Potiphar was a eunuch.
The fact that he was married weighs against such a
conclusion, although it is not a decisive factor. Married eunuchs are attested in ancient oriental contexts.[36] The Hebrew word also denotes some type of
court official / courtier / chamberlain — and Potiphar probably held an aristocratic office of this kind.

The precise meaning of the title **'captain of the
guard'** is unclear. It is a general designation in
Hebrew that could translate into a number of Egyptian offices. The Hebrew root for **'guard'** can be used
in reference to guarding the king (2 Kings 25:8-20),
cooking (1 Sam. 9:23-24) and slaughtering animals
(Exod. 22:1). It thus appears to be a broad term
designating officials or courtiers of sundry ranks and
titles.

Application

The name of God does not appear in this entire chapter. Its absence is not to secularize the chapter in any way, however. The writer's purpose is rather to encourage the reader to ask the question: why is God's name not found here? It is a didactic or teaching technique that, in reality, highlights the sovereignty of God. We know that God is behind the picture, that he is working all things out for the good of his people. Although God is not mentioned, his providence is the central theme of the story!

Judah and the levirate law
(Genesis 38:1-30)

The biblical author now interrupts the story of Joseph. He relates an episode in the life of Judah, in which he leaves his family, lives with the Canaanites and marries one of the pagan women. He is then trapped in a story of deceit and sexual immorality. Why is this story here?[37]

First, it is to serve as a foil to the account concerning Joseph that is to follow. Here Judah marries a Canaanite, and after his wife's death he has sexual relations with a woman he thinks is a prostitute. Joseph, on the contrary, does not fall victim to sexual temptation.

Secondly, it is a story that demonstrates a development of character in Judah: he begins the chapter doing malicious, sinful things; by the end of the chapter he sees some of his faults. This is important because Judah is ascending to a position of leadership in the clan structure of Jacob — that will become clear in Genesis 44-50.

Finally, the story ends with the birth of Perez and Zerah, and the former is the ancestor of both David and the Messiah. And the point is that God will carry out his purposes of Genesis 3:15 and a coming seed no matter how his people act. Even though they may be greatly unfaithful, God will accomplish his will for the creation.[38]

38:1. And it came to pass at that time that Judah went down from his brothers and he turned aside to an Adullamite man, and his name was Hirah.

The phrase, **'at that time'**, has been understood to coincide with the sale of Joseph into Egypt. It is not very precise, however, but is often used as a formula to denote a general period of time (see 21:22; Num. 22:4). Thus it could easily be rendered, 'about that time'.

Judah leaves his brothers, and he takes his flocks into the area of Adullam. This was located to the west of Hebron and the hill-country, lying in the foothills, or Shephelah region, of Canaan (Josh. 15:35). The use of the verb **'went down'** is purposeful on the part of the author because the Shephelah had a significantly lower altitude than the area of Hebron.[39]

Judah then **'turned aside'** to a man named Hirah who was from Adullam. This Hebrew verb is rarely used in the context of visiting a person or a place. Perhaps it is being employed here because it is often used figuratively of someone's deviating from the path of loyalty or righteousness (Exod. 23:2; Judg. 9:3; 1 Kings 2:28). It is probably a criticism of Judah's abandonment of his brothers and his seeking out the Canaanites.

38:2-5. Then Judah saw there a daughter of a Canaanite man, and his name was Shua. And he took her, and he went in to her. So she conceived, and she gave birth to a son. And he called his name Er. Then she conceived again, and she gave birth to a son. And she called his name Onan. Then she increased again, and she gave birth to a son. And she called his name Shelah. And it was in Chezib when she gave birth to him.

Judah marries a Canaanite woman. Her name is not given in these early verses. In verse 12, she is called 'the daughter of Shua', which in Hebrew is 'Bath-Shua'. 1 Chronicles 2:3 tells us that is her name: 'Bath-Shua the Canaanitess'. She bears three sons for Judah: Er, Onan and Shelah. The meaning of their names is uncertain. **'Er'** perhaps carries the idea of someone 'rousing himself to activity'. **'Onan'** probably means 'vigorous'. And **'Shelah'** may denote one who has been 'drawn out' (of the womb). It ought to be noted here that Judah only names the first-born son and not the others.

Bath-Shua gives birth to the last son in **'Chezib'**. This is probably to be identified with the site of Achzib, located in the Shephelah, or foothills, near the cities of Mareshah and Lachish (see Josh. 15:44; Micah 1:14). The name of the city seems to derive from a Hebrew verb meaning 'to lie / to be deceptive'. In that regard it may anticipate what soon happens: Judah promises Shelah, who is born in Chezib, to Tamar, but he does not give him to her (38:14). Judah simply deceives Tamar.

38:6-7. Now Judah took a wife for Er his first-born, and her name was Tamar. And it came to pass that Er, the first-born of Judah, was wicked in the eyes of Yahweh; so Yahweh put him to death.

Judah, as is the custom of the day, selects a bride for his son. Her name is **'Tamar'**, which literally means 'palm-tree / date palm'. It is used in Scripture as a symbol of a person with graceful stature (S. of S. 7:7-8). A beautiful sister and daughter of Absalom during the period of the united Israelite kingdom have the same name (2 Sam. 13:1; 14:27). The current Tamar is a Canaanite from the city of Enaim (38:14,21).

Er, however, **'was wicked in the eyes of Yahweh'**. The verb of that clause is stative, thus expressing a general condition of evil nature. Er's particular acts of evil that derive from his nature are not stated, but are suppressed. The rabbis speculate that he commits the same act as Onan in verse 9. And why would he do that? 'So that she [Tamar] should not bear children and her beauty thereby become impaired' (Jeb. 34b).[40] The verb 'to be wicked' in Hebrew has the consonants *r-'*. It is a word-play on, and an inversion of, the name **'Er'**, in Hebrew *'-r*. That inversion of consonants 'may symbolize his disordering of nature'.[41] His name signifies one's being roused to activity, and his activity is wicked.

38:8-9. Then Judah said to Onan, 'Go in to your brother's wife, and perform the duty of the widow's brother-in-law to her. And raise up a seed for your brother.' But Onan knew that the seed would not belong to him. So whenever he went in to his brother's wife he spilled [his semen] to the ground so that he would not produce a seed for his brother.

Judah's first-born has died, so Judah orders the second son, Onan, to raise up seed in his brother's name by marrying Er's wife. Here it is called to **'perform the duty of the widow's brother-in-law'**; this verbal form is known only here and in Deuteronomy 25:5,7.[42] It refers to the levirate law of antiquity (the Latin *levir* means 'a husband's brother'). The purpose of this law has been disputed. Here and elsewhere (Deut. 25:6; Ruth 4:10) it is for the preservation of the dead brother's name and family. In addition, the law is one of inheritance so that the dead man's property will remain in the extended family. Finally, it is for the protection of the widow so that she should not have to sell herself for debt or have to marry outside the clan.

Onan publicly obeys the law by having sexual relations with Tamar. The clause, **'whenever he went'**, is frequentative, and not a one-off event.[43] But, in secret, **'he spilled [his semen] to the**

ground' — that verb literally means 'to waste / spoil / corrupt', and it may serve as a moral judgement on his activity.[44] His motive for neglecting his duty is selfishness: the progeny would not be his, nor would the inheritance of his brother. He thus employs trickery because of his uncharitableness.

38:10-11. And what he did was wicked in the eyes of Yahweh, so he put him to death also. Then Judah said to Tamar, his daughter-in-law, 'Live as a widow in your father's house until Shelah my son grows up.' For he thought, 'Lest he also die like his brothers.' So Tamar went and she lived in her father's house.

The reason for divine wrath coming on Onan is clearly because he does not perform his fraternal duty. He is required to keep the levirate law, but he disobeys and, therefore, receives God's judgement. He disobeys in secret, but God knows the deepest secrets! This leaves Judah in a perplexing situation: he has lost his two eldest sons, yet the levirate law is in effect because his youngest son Shelah is alive. According to law, Shelah must now take Onan's place (and Er's).

Judah seems to fear that there is a curse on Tamar. Anyone whom she marries dies. He is hesitant to allow his youngest son to marry her lest he too die. His thoughts are introduced by the word **'lest'**, which at the beginning of a clause expresses fear and precaution.[45] He is superstitious. So to prevent the evil which he fears, Judah comes up with a pretext: Shelah is too young to marry Tamar at this time. This is trickery on Judah's part because he has no intention of ever giving Shelah to her.

Judah tells Tamar to go and live in her father's house. It is not near to the people of Judah, so it is a case of 'Out of sight, out of mind'. But Tamar is not going to let it pass. She is not a true widow, and is

not free to marry another, as long as the levirate law
remains in effect.⁴⁶

38:12-13. After many days passed, Bath-Shua, the wife of
Judah, died. And when Judah was comforted, he went up to
Timnah to the ones shearing sheep, he and his friend Hirah
the Adullamite. And it was reported to Tamar, saying, 'Behold, your father-in-law is going up to Timnah to shear his
sheep.'

After an indeterminate period, Judah's Canaanite
wife Bath-Shua dies. This fact is included as anticipatory: Judah is vulnerable, and he may be easily
coaxed by a prostitute. Judah is **'comforted'**, or
'consoled', after his wife's death — this is a technical
verb referring to the various rituals associated with
mourning. These days of grief have now ended.
    Judah decides to go to sheep-shearing (cf. 31:19).
This is a once-a-year activity that includes days of
festivity. A contrast to the period of mourning, it is a
time of great joy. The location of the sheep-shearing
is in **'Timnah'**, which was located in the hill-
country.⁴⁷ The directional verb **'he went up'** is appropriate since he is travelling from the foothills up
to the highlands (cf. 38:1). Ironically, between the
place where Judah mourns his wife and Timnah is
the site of Enaim (38:14). Enaim is the home of
Tamar, and it is 'on the road to Timnah'.
    Tamar is told that Judah is on the way to Timnah.
The one who brings the report begins with the exclamation, **'Behold'**; here it is being used as a particle
of vivid immediacy.⁴⁸ If Tamar is going to act, she
must do so quickly.

38:14. So she removed her widow's clothes, and she covered herself with a veil and she disguised herself. And she
sat at the entrance of Enaim, which is on the road to Timnah.

For she saw that Shelah had grown up, and she had not
been given to him as a wife.

Tamar now realizes the truth: Judah has no plans to
fulfil the levirate obligation by giving her to Shelah.
So she cleverly sets a trap for Judah. This highlights
the fact that the ultimate responsibility for the levirate law belongs to the father. Her first step is to
remove her **'widow's clothes'**. Apparently, the widow
at this time wore mourning clothes for the rest of her
life, her marital duties enduring long after the death
of her spouse.[49] A contrast is evident with verse 12,
in which Judah's period of mourning had ended.
Tamar's situation, on the other hand, is unresolved.

Tamar then puts on a veil and disguises herself as
a cult prostitute (see 38:21 below — the Hebrew word
is *qādēshāh*). 'Temple prostitution was a common
practice the Canaanites used to gain the gods' good
will. According to this custom, male and female
harlots were attached to central religious sanctuaries
and shrines. Members of this ritual order were
known in the Old Testament and Canaanite literature
as the *qadēshîm*, quite literally, "the set-apart ones".
They were individuals "set apart" for the special
function of ritual prostitution. The Canaanites
thought that committing acts of whoredom ... would
guarantee the fertility of all their people, land, and
animals.'[50]

Tamar, dressed as a cult prostitute, then sits at
the **'entrance'** of Enaim. It does not say that she is
in the gate area; perhaps she is at a road junction
that leads into the town of Enaim. Judah, on his way
to Timnah, will soon pass the spot as he travels along
the road. It is ironic that the town-name **'Enaim'**
literally means 'eyes': the act that is to take place is
carried out in stealth, yet because of it Judah's eyes
will be opened.

38:15-16. When Judah saw her, he thought she was a prostitute because her face was covered. So he turned aside to her by the road, and he said, 'Come now, let me go in to you,' for he did not know that she was his daughter-in-law. Then she responded, 'What will you give to me that you might come in to me?'

Judah passes the road to Enaim, and he sees a woman whom he believes to be a prostitute: her veiled face and the place where she is sitting are indications of her profession. He is unsuspecting of Tamar's identity because of her veiling. The biblical author is clear that Judah would have had nothing to do with her if he had known who she was. But he does not recognize her. So the two of them begin to strike a deal for her services. These are what the Bible often refers to as the 'earnings of the harlot' (see Hosea 2:12; 9:1; Micah 1:7).

38:17-19. Then he said, 'I will send a young goat from the flock.' And she answered, 'Will you give a pledge until you send it?' And he responded, 'What is the pledge that I shall give you?' And she said, 'Your seal and your cord and your staff which is in your hand.' Then he gave [them] to her. So he went in to her, and she conceived for him. Now she got up and left, and she took off her veil and she dressed in her widow's clothes.

Judah responds enthusiastically to Tamar: the personal pronoun **'I'** begins his answer, and in Hebrew grammar that adds force to his assertion. In Judges 15:1, Samson also brought a goat to his wife in order to have sexual relations with her. Tamar replies to Judah that a pledge is needed — that is, something must be given in deposit or in security so that he is bound to her and his promise.

Tamar asks for items of personal identification. First, she wants Judah's **'seal'** and his **'cord'**: this is probably a hendiadys that refers to the same item. The first part is the cylinder seal that bears an impression identifying the owner — these were often used in antiquity to seal documents.[51] Ancient Near-Eastern seals were normally perforated for suspension on a 'cord' around a person's neck. The staff, or rod, was also an important object for identifying the owner; it was a symbol of power and authority in the ancient Near East.[52] The Greek writer Herodotus tells us that every 'Babylonian carries a seal ring and an artfully carved staff and every staff bears an emblem of an apple, a rose, a lily, an eagle, or something. For no one may carry a staff without a distinctive symbol.'[53] Tamar is asking for clear and distinct proof of the identity of the person who is giving her a pledge and a promise.

At the close of the passage, a series of verbs appear in a rapid staccato: **'he went ... she conceived ... she got up ... left ... took off ... dressed'**. This chain of verbs in quick succession accentuates the methodical, almost clinical, actions of the players in the story.

38:20-21. Then Judah sent a young goat by the hand of his friend the Adullamite in order to take the pledge from the woman's hand. But he did not find her. So he asked the men of her place, saying, 'Where is the cult prostitute who was in Enaim near the road?' And they said, 'There is no cult prostitute in this place.'

Judah now attempts to fulfil his promise to **'the woman'**. No name is given to her; apparently Judah did not bother to find one out. It underscores the point that his act was merely one of obtaining sensual pleasure in exchange for payment. Judah sends his gift by an emissary, his friend Hirah. It is likely that a man of his stature would not be involved personally in such a demeaning task as retrieving his pledge. Or, perhaps he does not want any further contact which might indicate an ongoing relationship.

Hirah calls her a **'cult prostitute'**. He understands her to be such because of the way she was dressed and where she was seated. It is interesting to note that, in verse 15, when Judah saw her he thought she was a mere 'prostitute / harlot' — this is a different noun in Hebrew that is devoid of any religious connotation. Perhaps Judah did not recognize this subtle difference, although Hirah clearly sees it.

38:22-23. So he returned to Judah, and he said, 'I did not find her. And the men of the place also said there is no cult prostitute in this place.' And Judah said, 'Let her keep it for herself, lest we become an object of scorn. Indeed, I sent this young goat, but you did not find her.'

Hirah reports to Judah his failure in finding the woman. Tamar has disappeared without a trace. What is Judah to do? He decides that no further search should be made for her. His rationale begins with the particle of caution **'lest'**. Judah is afraid that a search would reveal his wanton act, and he does not want to be a victim of slander. It may appear that he did not even pay her! He reasons that he has tried and that is enough.

38:24. And it came to pass after three months, that it was reported to Judah, saying, 'Tamar your daughter-in-law has prostituted herself and, in addition, behold, she is pregnant through fornication.' So Judah said, 'Bring her out that she might be burned!'

After a three-month period, Tamar's pregnancy has become apparent. So **'it was reported'** to Judah — this is the same phrase that is used in verse 13 regarding how Tamar knew that Judah was passing

by Enaim. This double usage indicates that there is
no direct contact between Judah and Tamar; Judah
has created a great distance between them.

Judah's response to the news is one of severity.
According to her legal standing, Tamar remains
bound to the levirate law. She is still legally Er's wife.
And, therefore, an extra-marital sexual relationship
is deemed as adultery. Ancient Near-Eastern law
required that the adulterer should be put to death
(Lev. 20:10; Deut. 22:22; Code of Hammurabi no.
129). Burning as a means of judgement, however,
appears to have been mandated only in extreme
cases of sexual misconduct (Lev. 20:14; 21:9). Thus,
we see Judah being quite willing to act as judge in
this matter of Tamar. He is a biased and severe
judge: he does not even allow her to defend herself,
but makes a quick judgement. His family has been
violated!

The entire scene is one of dramatic irony. Judah is
really the one who has violated the law by not fulfilling his responsibility in the matter of the levirate law.
In addition, he himself has just participated in har-
lotry, and now he condemns his daughter-in-law for
the same act. Judah is thus about to be caught in
his own sin.

38:25-26. As she was being brought out she sent to her
father-in-law, saying, 'I have become pregnant by the man
who owns these things.' Then she said, 'Please, examine
[them]. To whom belong these things, the seal and the cord
and the staff?' So Judah examined [them]. Then he said,
'She is more righteous than I, because I did not give her to
Shelah my son.' And he did not have sexual relations with
her again.

At the critical moment of the episode, just before the
execution, Tamar reveals the true story. Her accusation is indirect, however; she has his pledges, the

clear-cut evidence, taken before Judah. It is now public, and there is no way he can deny complicity. He cannot deflect the responsibility, and he has no one else to blame. Judah must now admit his guilt: he did not give her to Shelah according to the levirate law of the land.

Judah claims that Tamar is **'more righteous than I'** (using the Hebrew comparative), and he is correct. She did what was left to her to do. Yet the biblical writer makes no judgement about her himself — it is as if her deed of trickery simply cannot be sanctioned. It should also be noted that the text leaves many unanswered questions. Most importantly, there is no mention of whether or not the levirate law is enforced, and Tamar given to Shelah.[54] That may underscore the point that this episode is not primarily about the levirate law, but rather about Judah and his seed.

38:27-30. And it came to pass when it was time for her to give birth that, behold, twins were in her womb. And as she was giving birth, one put out a hand; so the midwife took a scarlet thread and she tied it on his hand, saying, 'This one came out first.' But it came to pass as he drew back his hand that, behold, his brother came out. Then she said, 'How you have broken through and made a breach for yourself!' So he called his name Perez. Then afterwards his brother came out who had the scarlet thread on his hand; and he called his name Zerah.

Tamar now gives birth to twins. The event may be seen by Judah as 'compensation for his two deceased sons'.[55] His naming of them may reflect their substitutionary positions. The fact that there are two children may also be an outpouring of God's goodness on Tamar — that is, a grand compensation for her heroism. She had no sons, and now she receives two at the same time.

Verse 27 is almost a verbatim repetition of Genesis 25:24. There Rebekah gave birth to twins, and they too struggled, like Perez and Zerah, to get out of the womb first. As in the earlier story, the present one is prescient: the contention between the two anticipates the pre-eminence that Perez and his descendants will have in the tribe of Judah (see 1 Chr. 2:4-8). Although Zerah's hand comes out first, it is Perez's whole body that 'breaks through', forcing its way past Zerah to get out first. And, indeed, it is from the line of Perez that David is born (Ruth 4:18-22) and, ultimately, so is the promised Messiah (Luke 3:33).[56] The story of Tamar has some interesting ties to the book of Ruth in this regard.[57]

The name **'Perez'** means 'breach', or 'burst', and it derives from the verb used by the midwife, 'to break through'. **'Zerah',** on the other hand, comes from the verb meaning 'to rise / to come forth': it is a verb that denotes a natural emergence.[58] Perhaps the author is highlighting Perez's forcefulness, even in the womb, in leading the descendants of Judah.

Application

There is no question that Judah acts sinfully in the present episode. He turns from his family, and he turns from righteousness. He marries a Canaanite woman, and he refuses to fulfil his obligations to the levirate law. All these deeds are well planned and thought out on his part. They are simply premeditated. Yet, as the book of Proverbs says, 'The mind of man plans his way; but Yahweh directs his steps' (Prov. 16:9). And, thus, we see that out of the wicked plans and acts of men, God brings about his good and just purposes. It is through Judah and his illicit relationship with his daughter-in-law that God brings to Israel its greatest earthly king, David, and its only divine king, Jesus Christ. Despite mankind's wickedness, God's promise of a seed will come to pass.

Is this not how God uses his people in all ages? When Joseph reveals himself to his brothers they are afraid because of the horrible things they have done to him. Joseph responds, however, by saying, 'Do not be afraid, for am I in God's place? And as for you, you meant evil against me, but God meant it for good in order to bring about this present result, to preserve many people alive' (50:19-20). This biblical principle applies even to the arrest, trial and crucifixion of Christ. As some of the disciples commented in Acts 4, 'For truly in this city there were gathered together against your holy servant Jesus, whom you anointed, both Herod and Pontius Pilate, along with the Gentiles and the peoples of Israel, to do whatever your hand and your purpose predestined to occur' (Acts 4:27-28). Even the evil deeds of these men were used by God to bring about victory through the death and resurrection of Christ!

Temptation
(Genesis 39:1-10)

The author abruptly returns to the story of Joseph. And almost immediately Joseph is subjected to sexual temptation from Potiphar's wife. In this regard Judah, as portrayed in chapter 38:1-5, serves as a foil, or contrast, to Joseph. Whereas Judah succumbs to the allurements of the Canaanites, Joseph refuses to give in.

39:1. Now Joseph had been taken down to Egypt. And Potiphar, an officer of Pharaoh, captain of the guard, an Egyptian, bought him from the hand of the Ishmaelites who had brought him there.

This resumption of the account of Joseph begins with a summary of where the narrative had ended in chapter 37. As a sequel, when a perfect verb is used 'it is generally to be rendered in English as a pluperfect' — thus the translation **'had been taken down'** is a proper one.[59]

39:2. And Yahweh was with Joseph, so he was a man who prospered. And he was in the house of his master the Egyptian.

The phrase, **'Yahweh was with Joseph'**, is used four times in this chapter (39:2,3,21,23). Its repetition underscores its purpose as a key or foundational concept in the story of Joseph. It means that, even with all the tragedy in Joseph's life — his abuse at the hands of his brothers, his sale into slavery, and his bondage — God is still in control of all these events. Everything is unfolding according to his good purposes.

The second clause begins with a *waw* conversive and an imperfective verb: that construction normally indicates temporal sequence, or logical succession from what went before it. And, thus, it should be understood that the prosperity of Joseph is because of Yahweh's presence with him. Joseph is not succeeding because of his own ability or prowess, but God is causing him to succeed.

Joseph is not a common field slave. Rather, he is **'in the house of his master'**. That position is evidence of what God is doing: Joseph is gaining great benefit and advantage because God is with him. Yet even in great success there is great danger. Joseph's position places him in daily contact with Potiphar's wife.

39:3. And his master saw that Yahweh was with him, and [how] everything he was doing Yahweh was causing to prosper by his hand.

The manner in which Joseph carries out his duties and his success in doing them serve as a testimony to Yahweh. In other words, the proficiency by which Joseph does his tasks is visible proof of Yahweh's blessing on him. And Potiphar recognizes that it is Yahweh who is the source of Joseph's welfare and prosperity. Joseph is thus a powerful witness to the omnipotence of God.

39:4. And Joseph found favour in his sight, and he served him. And he appointed him over his house, and everything belonging to him he gave in his hand.

Because of Yahweh's blessing on Joseph, Potiphar
holds the young man in high esteem and regard.
And, so, Joseph **'served him'**. That verb is not the
common Hebrew term meaning 'to serve', but it really
means 'to minister to' in a position of high service.[60]
Some commentators translate the verb as if it were
transitive, as follows: 'And he [Potiphar] made him
[Joseph] his personal attendant.' Either way, Joseph
is promoted in his service to the Egyptian.

Joseph's promotion is then defined. He is made
overseer of Potiphar's entire household. This is the
position of a private household manager, or steward.[61] It is perhaps to be equated with the Egyptian
office of *mr pr wr* — that is, 'high steward',[62] a job
which involved administering all the estates of the
master.

39:5. And it came to pass, from the time that he appointed
him over his house and over everything that belonged to him,
Yahweh blessed the house of the Egyptian on account of
Joseph. And the blessing of Yahweh was on everything that
belonged to him in the house and in the field.

The Egyptian Potiphar, who is outside the covenant
people of God, nevertheless reaps the benefits of
Joseph's service. Note that the source of the prosperity is mentioned again (twice) — it is the blessing of
Yahweh. The extent of Yahweh's favour is accentuated by repetition of the phrase, **'everything that
belonged to him'**. In addition, the final clause of the
verse, **'the house and the field'**, is a figure of speech
called a merism, indicating that absolutely everything
belonging to Potiphar is thriving.

39:6. And he left everything that belonged to him in the hand
of Joseph. And he did not concern himself about anything
except the food which he ate. And Joseph was handsome of
form and appearance.

The favour bestowed on Joseph by Potiphar is sum-
marized in the first line of the verse: for the third
time it is said that **'everything that belonged to
him'** is given over to Joseph's care. Joseph's oversight is so comprehensive that Potiphar, literally, **'did
not know anything'** about his own affairs. The only
exception is regarding food, and that may be because
of special Egyptian dietary restrictions or customs.
One such restriction is mentioned in 43:32.

The final clause of the verse is transitional and it
serves as important information for the episode
which follows. Joseph is deemed to be a man who is,
literally, **'fair of form and fair of sight'** — that is, he
is well-built and handsome. Exactly the same description is made of his mother Rachel in Genesis
29:17, although it is often translated somewhat
differently.

39:7. And it came to pass after these things that his master's
wife looked longingly at Joseph, and she said, 'Lie down with
me!'

The opening phrase, **'And it came to pass after
these things'**, is what Redford calls 'plot retardation'.[63] It is a common, staple writing device that
heightens the suspense of the plot. Much is left out
and passed over in order to arrive at the basic sense
of the episode.

When the author says that Potiphar's wife, literally, **'lifted her eyes to Joseph'**, he is employing an
idiom that is employed elsewhere in the literature of
the ancient Near East. The identical expression is
found in *The Epic of Gilgamesh.* Tablet VI, lines 6-7
say:

Glorious Ishtar raised an eye at the beauty of
    Gilgamesh:
'Come, Gilgamesh, be thou [my] lover!'[64]

Potiphar's wife makes a similar brazen demand. There are no preliminaries to her remark, but just a mere imperative: **'Lie down with me!'** The fact that the wife is not named adds to the crudity and im- morality of her behaviour.

Adultery was certainly frowned on in ancient Egypt. Certain instructions, or teaching texts, from the New Kingdom period warn that a man who com- mits adultery is probably to be killed by the woman's husband.[65] However, no official, state-enforced sanc- tion of the death penalty was applied to adultery in Egypt; that is why Potiphar is later able to send Joseph to prison.

39:8-9. But he refused. And he said to his master's wife, 'Behold, my master does not know what is in the house with me [around], and everything that belongs to him he has given into my hand. No one is greater in this house than I. And he has not withheld anything from me except you, because you are his wife. How then could I do this great evil, and sin against God?'

Joseph flatly refuses to consider the woman's de- mand. Such a response is dangerous because he is a slave. Joseph takes time to explain to her why he will not comply. He gives three reasons. First, he runs the entire household, and he has been entrusted with everything of Potiphar's. However, secondly, Potiphar has specifically withheld his wife from Joseph. How could Joseph go against the authority of his earthly master? And, finally, Joseph understands that such adulterous activity is sin against God. Adultery, thus, not only has a negative horizontal impact against one's fellow man, but it also has a negative vertical impact against Almighty God. It is breaking his law. Joseph is an upright, moral, godly figure.

Note that the name 'Yahweh' is not used here. Joseph is speaking to an Egyptian, so he employs the more generic name, *Elohim.*

39:10. And it came to pass as she spoke to Joseph day by day that he did not listen to her to lie down next to her to be with her.

The temptation is not an isolated incident. Potiphar's wife is relentless, constantly coaxing and luring Joseph into an adulterous affair. Repetition of the word **'day'** underscores that idea: it expresses entirety, that is, each and every day she spoke to him. It is an incessant enticement.

The phrase, **'to be with her'**, is probably idiomatic, a euphemism for sexual intercourse (see, for example, 2 Sam. 13:20). The wife's actions are thus to be seen as coarse and brazen.

Application

Joseph's witness before the Egyptians in the conduct of his life is certainly worthy of our deliberation. MacLaren once commented that 'The best advertisement of Christianity is a good life. People read us a great deal more than they read the Bible.' This does not mean that one does not orally proclaim the truth of the God of the Bible — and we shall see later that Joseph does exactly that — but one can testify to the truth of God by the way one lives.

Day of reckoning
(Genesis 39:11-18)

The drama of the story now rises to a crescendo. Potiphar's wife seizes an opportunity and forces the issue with Joseph. And when it fails, she plots and connives so that all blame and responsibility falls on Joseph. Here is a story of the righteous being caught in the web of the unrighteous.

39:11. And it came to pass one day that he came to the house to do his work, and there was no one from the men of the house there in the house.

The term for **'one day'** in the Hebrew language is literally 'this day' — it is the Hebrew way of expressing a certain, particular day. It is to be seen in contrast to the 'day by day' of verse 10.

In any event, on a particular day Joseph enters Potiphar's house to do work, the nature of which is unspecified; it is not important to the story-line. No other workers are in that part of the house. Joseph is apparently alone.

39:12. So she grabbed his garment, saying, 'Lie with me!' But he left his garment in her hand, and he fled and went outside.

The daily enticement of Joseph by Potiphar's wife has not succeeded in wearing him down. There is no evidence that he is in any way lured by her wiles. The woman, therefore, resorts to a physical assault by seizing him by his clothes. Joseph has no inclination to comply with her demands, and so he runs from the house. Unfortunately, he leaves his garment behind — that, of course, will prove to be part of his undoing.

The Hebrew consonants for **'garment'** are *b-g-d*. The word is a homonym to the verb *b-g-d*, which means 'to deal treacherously in marriage relations'.[66] The author may be employing a play on words to highlight the deceitfulness of the adulterous activity of Potiphar's wife.

39:13-15. And it came to pass when she saw that he left his garment in her hand and fled outside, that she called to the men of her house. And she spoke to them, saying, 'See, he has brought to us a Hebrew man to make sport of us! He came to me to lie with me, but I called out in a loud voice. And when he heard that I raised my voice and I cried out, he left his garment next to me, and he fled, and he went outside.'

The woman now needs to arrange a cover-up for what has happened. She calls to her other servants in the house, who are apparently Egyptians. In sarcasm, she blames her husband for bringing Joseph and setting him over the entire household. Egyptian servants certainly would have resented having a foreigner placed over them. Potiphar's wife taps into their emotions of resentment.

The name **'Hebrew'** has a limited range: it is used only when Israelites speak of themselves to foreigners, or when foreigners use it to speak of the Israelites.[67] Potiphar's wife seems to employ it as a form of name-calling, a derogatory epithet against Joseph's heritage.

39:16. So she laid down his garment next to her, until his master came to his house.

The woman lays the cloak down right next to her. She is not letting the evidence out of her sight. Physical evidence is more convincing than mere reports or gossip. The clause **'next to her'** was used in verse 10 as the place where the woman demanded that Joseph should lie, but he refused. Now the incriminating evidence is placed in that very spot.

She waits until **'his master'** comes home. The text does not identify Potiphar as her husband. The reason for this is probably to point out Potiphar's authority over his slave, and his being in a position to deal with the matter.

39:17-18. And she spoke to him according to these words, saying, 'The Hebrew slave, whom you brought to us, came to me to make sport of me. And it came to pass as I raised my voice and I cried out, that he left his garment next to me. And he fled outside.'

The woman is wily in reporting the incident to her husband. First, she calls Joseph the **'Hebrew slave'**. When she related the episode to her servants in verse 14 she called him a 'Hebrew man'. She certainly did not want to upset her other servants, but now she emphasizes Joseph's true position in the household. He is a slave. In addition, when she told the story to the servants she spoke in the first person plural, saying that Joseph came 'to make sport of us'. Now with Potiphar, her statement is in the first person singular: he came **'to make sport of me'**. The wife does this to raise the level of indignity in her husband: this slave has tried to sleep with a free Egyptian woman, one who is the wife of an important official. Who does he think he is?

Application

There are some in the church today who teach that if someone has enough faith, or is godly enough, then that person will not suffer or be subject to persecution. What a false teaching! The truth is that the exact opposite seems to predominate. As Bowes comments, 'There is no saint in the Bible, of whose history we have any lengthened record, who was not called to endure trouble in some form; and very frequently the most eminent saints were most tried. Those who were called to important services, were generally trained in the school of affliction.' And Jesus promised his disciples that 'A slave is not greater than his master. If they persecuted me, they will also persecute you' (John 15:20).

Temporal punishment
(Genesis 39:19-23)

Joseph's life moves from one tragedy, enduring slavery, to another — that of imprisoment. Potiphar's wife is vindictive. She did not get her way, and so she seeks to destroy Joseph. Potiphar, however, does not respond by killing Joseph; he is more lenient and puts him into jail.

39:19. And it came to pass when his master heard the words of his wife which she spoke to him, saying, 'According to these things your slave did to me,' his anger burned.

When Potiphar returns home, his wife relates to him her concocted story. Potiphar is seething. The Hebrew uses an idiom to display his anger: literally, **'his nostrils'**, or nose, **'are burning'**. It perhaps reflects a snorting or flaring of the nostrils in the same way as an enraged bull reacts. However, the object of his emotion is not stated — it is likely that he is enraged at the entire situation, not just at Joseph. He will lose a good worker. In addition, he probably knows his wife's tendencies quite well.

39:20. So Joseph's master took him and put him into the jail, where the prisoners of the king were incarcerated. And he was there in the jail.

Imprisonment in a jail is a punishment unknown in the law codes of the ancient Near East, including biblical legislation. However, it is well attested in Egyptian documents and, thus, the story rightly reflects the culture of ancient Egypt.[68]

Egyptian literature includes the account of a false accusation of adultery called 'The Story of Two Brothers'.[69] One brother accuses the other of forcing a sexual relationship on his wife. The wife really was the deceitful one, but blames her brother-in-law. The ending is different from the story of Joseph: the husband kills both his brother and his wife, the latter having been found out.

39:21. And it came to pass that Yahweh was with Joseph, and he extended lovingkindness to him. And he gave him favour in the eyes of the officer of the jail.

Joseph's life has hit rock-bottom. Not only has he been attacked by his brothers, thrown into a pit, sold to travelling merchants and made a slave in Egypt, but now he has been falsely accused of adultery and put into prison. Psalm 105:18 explains that he is placed in shackles, the jailers afflicting 'his feet with fetters', and laying him 'in irons'. How much worse can it get?

Yet the author tells us that, despite all the hardship Joseph endured, **'Yahweh was with Joseph.'** And in the midst of such dire circumstances, Yahweh is extending his **'lovingkindness'** to Joseph. That word in Hebrew is *ḥĕsĕd*, and it bears quite a complex meaning. It generally signifies faithfulness and steadfast love in a relationship.[70] But it also applies specifically to the superior party in the relationship and the protection offered to the inferior party.[71]

39:22. And the officer of the jail put in Joseph's hand all the prisoners who were in the jail. And everything that was being done there, he was doing [it].

As God had caused Joseph to rise in standing in Potiphar's house, so now he causes him to attain status in the prison. Joseph's specific position is not stated; however, just as in Potiphar's house, Joseph has been given authority over **'everything'**.

39:23. The officer of the jail did not oversee everything in his hand because Yahweh was with Joseph, and whatever he did Yahweh made prosperous.

The chief jailer does not have to look after everything in the jail: such matters are in Joseph's capable hands. This situation parallels what went on in Potiphar's house. Joseph also ran things there, and Potiphar paid little attention to the operation of the household (39:6). The reason why Joseph is so capable is vividly stated here: **'because Yahweh was with Joseph'**. The term translated **'because'** is a preposition followed by a relative pronoun in Hebrew, and it is causal. Yahweh is the source of Joseph's success.

Application

Corrie Ten Boom once said that 'There is no pit so deep enough, that He is not deeper still.' And that is certainly true of the life of Joseph (even in a literal sense!). Even after all the terrible things that happened to that biblical saint, Yahweh was with Joseph.

James Hastings tells the story of one Captain Allan Gardiner who went to preach the gospel to the people of Tierra del Fuego. Because of a very harsh winter, Gardiner and his companions all starved to death. Their bodies were found at the entrance to a cave. On the entrance to the cave, Gardiner had scrawled the following lines: 'My soul trusts still upon God.' And in his diary were found his last words, 'I know not how to thank God for His marvellous loving-kindness.' Even in the midst of such a death, God was with Allan Gardiner. May we realize that he is with us, even in the midst of the most dire and trying circumstances of life.

The cupbearer and the baker
(Genesis 40:1-4)

The author now provides a detailed account of one particular incident in the jail. It is an event that leads to the deliverance of Joseph, and to his elevation to the court of Pharaoh. The incident is the imprisonment of Pharaoh's chief officers, the cupbearer and the baker.

40:1. And it came to pass after these things [that] the cupbearer and the baker of the King of Egypt offended their lord, the King of Egypt.

The opening of the verse is another example of plot retardation, as was explained in the commentary on 39:7. It expresses an indefinite time period. We do know, however, that Joseph is twenty-eight years old at this time. He will be brought before the pharaoh two years after these events (41:1), and at that time he will be thirty years old (41:46). Thus Joseph has been in Egypt, either as a slave in the house of Potiphar or in jail, for the last eleven years (37:2).

Two high officials of the pharaoh are the **'cupbearer'** and the **'baker'**; in verse 2 these men are identified as 'chiefs' or 'heads' in the Egyptian government. In any event, these two high-standing courtiers have **'offended'** the king. That verb in Hebrew really means 'to sin', but here it is used in a secular context and it simply signifies some type of misdeed. The precise nature of the acts committed by

the officials is not stated, perhaps because this
information is unnecessary to the flow of the story.

In the ancient Near East, the position of cupbearer
was one of a high advisory capacity in relation to the
king. Often it denotes the responsibilities of a gover-
nor or prime minister.[72]

**40:2. And Pharaoh was angry with his two officials, with the
chief cupbearer and with the chief baker.**

The title **'Pharaoh'** is now given to the King of Egypt.
It derives from the Egyptian *pr*, which means 'house'
or 'palace'. It did not originally refer to the Egyptian
king, but to his residence. Not until the middle of the
Eigteeenth Dynasty (c. 1550-1070 B.C.) was it employed as an appellative of the ruler.

Repeating the individual identities of the two
officials may be for the purpose of separation. In
other words, the author wants to make it clear that
each of them had committed a separate offence
against Pharaoh and, of course, they are dealt with
differently in the subsequent story.

**40:3. And he put them in prison, in the house of the captain
of the bodyguard, into the jail, the place where Joseph was
imprisoned.**

The clause translated **'in prison'** is literally 'in
keeping'. It signifies that the two officials are being
held in custody, or temporary confinement, until
their cases have been decided. Since written, codified
law was at a minimum in Egypt, it was Pharaoh who
would dispose of their cases. Pharaoh's word was
law, and thus they are waiting on his decree.

The place of imprisonment is called three different
things in this verse. This has led some commentators
to argue that these are insertions by later editors.[73]
In reality, it is more likely that the author is making

a deliberate attempt to avoid any ambiguity over the fact that this place is the very same prison as that in which Joseph is confined.

40:4. The captain of the bodyguard assigned them to Joseph. And he served them. And they were in prison for a long time.

The title **'captain of the bodyguard'** probably refers to Potiphar, as he was previously given that epithet (see 37:36; 39:1). Joseph is thus not removed from under the authority of his Egyptian master — he still serves Potiphar even in his confinement. Joseph is both prisoner and slave!

The clause rendered **'for a long time'** is literally the plural noun 'days'. Such a simple plural can often denote a long period of time.[74]

Application

The imprisonment of the baker and cupbearer by Pharaoh would on the surface seem to be an action based on the whim of Pharaoh. But how untrue! Even the very deeds of Pharaoh unfold according to the providence of God. It is this event that will lead to Joseph's deliverance, and he is unaware of the fact. Yet he clearly trusts in a sovereign God.

Hanns Lilje, a German Lutheran bishop, was thrown into a German prison camp during World War II. He describes what happened when Allied bombers began bombarding areas around the prison camp — everyone scattered, including the guards. He comments, 'When the guards had fled and we were alone up there in the darkness, we felt as if their power had been removed; for a few moments, at any rate, we felt the pressure of their authority lifted, and we knew ourselves to be in the hands of the Lord of life and death, whose sovereignty was exercised over them and us alike.' Indeed, the unbeliever does not understand that it is God who 'causes his sun to rise on the evil and the

good, and sends rain on the righteous and the unrighteous'
(Matt. 5:45).

We must be aware of our dependence upon God's providence in everything. Cecil once said, 'We are too apt to forget
our actual dependence on Providence for the circumstances of
every instant. The most trivial events may determine our state in
the world. Turning up one street instead of another may bring us
in company with a person whom we should not otherwise have
met; and this may lead to a train of other events which may
determine the happiness or misery of our lives.'

Dreams
(Genesis 40:5-8)

One particular night, both the baker and the cup-bearer have dreams. The Egyptian background to this event is important. The ancient Egyptians believed that one of the prominent ways that they received communications from the gods was through dreams. It was also an important medium by which one could foresee the future. Both of these officials are very interested in what the future holds, whether it will be life or death.

40:5. The two of them — the cupbearer and the baker of the King of Egypt who were imprisoned in the jail — dreamed a dream in the same night. Each dream had its own interpretation.

At least as early as the Middle Kingdom in Egypt (beginning *c.* 2040 B.C.) the Egyptians believed that dreams were a medium of the gods to reveal the future to humans.[75] Thus dreams have oracular power — that is, they can predict the future. That point is underscored in the present verse when it declares that **'Each dream had its own interpretation.'** The Hebrew term for **'interpretation'**, in either verbal or noun form, is only found in Genesis 40-41 in the entire Bible. It literally denotes 'meaning' or 'significance' — in other words, each dream has its own message regarding the future.

The genitive **'of the king'** is a periphrastic expression in Hebrew to state possession.[76] The point is that the chief cupbearer and the chief baker belong to Pharaoh, and he may dispose of their cases, and their persons, in any manner he pleases.

It is ironic that Joseph's dreams recorded previously (ch. 37) led to his immediate downfall (even though they were dreams of exaltation), but these present dreams will lead to his elevation.

40:6. And Joseph came to them in the morning. And he saw them, and behold they were dejected.

The response of the two high officials to their dreams accentuates the seriousness of dreams and the import that they had for the ancient Egyptians. They are **'dejected'**; that is, they are distraught and show a haggard face (the verb is used that way in Daniel 1:10). The reason for their worry is not only because they have no interpreter (see 40:8), but because they both dreamed a similar dream on the same night. It cannot be a coincidence!

40:7. And he asked the officers of Pharaoh who were with him in custody in the house of his master, saying, 'Why are your faces unpleasant today?'

Having served the chief cupbearer and the chief cook for some time, Joseph sees immediately that something is wrong by the look on their faces. The word translated **'unpleasant'** is a derivative of a noun that commonly means 'evil'; however, it can also reflect something that is in distress or in misery. Obviously the officials of Pharaoh are very concerned about the dreams and the absence of an interpreter.

The phrase **'in the house of his master'** again highlights the direct authority that Potiphar has over Joseph. Apparently Potiphar is the officer / captain of the bodyguard that houses the king's prisoners (see 40:3).

40:8. And they said to him, 'We have dreamed a dream. And there is no one to interpret it.' And Joseph said to them, 'Do not interpretations belong to God? Please tell [them] to me.'

As has been mentioned, dream omens in ancient Egypt were a means of receiving information from the next world. They were widely employed as a means of knowing the divine will. However, the ancient Egyptians also believed that it was necessary to have diviners who were skilled in the arts of interpreting dreams. Joseph is correcting that idea here by saying that not only are the dreams themselves communications from above, but so too are the interpretations of the dreams. He is thus denying the magical, mystical power of Egyptian magicians.

Joseph does not use the name 'Yahweh' when speaking of God, but *Elohim*. The latter is a more generic name for the deity and it would be less offensive to the Egyptians than the name Yahweh. The latter name is identified particularly with the Hebrews as a people.

Application[77]

In the Old Testament, God revealed himself to his people in a variety of ways. He revealed himself through many mighty acts, such as the creation, the plagues on Egypt and the dividing of the Red Sea. He also gave his people a divine word. This was done both orally, such as the giving of the Decalogue on Sinai, and in written form, such as the Book of the Covenant. Often Yahweh employed prophets to speak his word to the people. In addition, God revealed himself and the future through the means of dreams (41:1-37). The casting of lots was a common means of receiving revelation in the Old Testament. Gideon even laid out a fleece so that God would make known to him his will (Judg. 6:36-40). There were other methods as well.

People in the church today are often troubled by these various means by which God spoke to his people in Old Testament times. They want to know if God speaks in these ways today. And, if not, why not? Or, if he does, does he speak to each one of us in these ways? Are these methods still applicable to the church? The writer of the epistle to the Hebrews answers these questions in the very opening passage of his book when he says, 'God, after he spoke long ago to the fathers in the prophets in many portions and in many ways, in these last days has spoken to us in his Son, whom he appointed heir of all things, through whom also he made the world' (Heb. 1:1-2). The author is pointing out that the fulness of revelation is now complete and final in the coming of Jesus Christ. No further revelation is needed. He is the final revelation. As F. F. Bruce points out, 'The story of divine revelation is a story of progression up to Christ, but there is no progression beyond Him.'[78]

The dream of the chief cupbearer
(Genesis 40:9-15)

The chief cupbearer is the first to relay his dream to Joseph. Joseph interprets the dream, and then he asks for a favour from the official.

40:9-11. So the chief cupbearer related his dream to Joseph. And he said to him, 'In my dream, behold, a grape-vine before me. And on the grape-vine were three branches. And when it was sprouting its blossoms arose — its clusters grew ripe grapes. And Pharaoh's cup was in my hand. So I took the grapes and I squeezed them into the cup of Pharaoh. Then I gave the cup into Pharaoh's hand.'

The most important collection of dream omens from ancient Egypt is the Chester Beatty Papyrus, which comes from Dynasty 19 (thirteenth century B.C.).[79] The manuscript is divided into dreams experienced by the Sons of Seth and the Sons of Horus. Four basic characteristics of the dreams are:

1. In each dream the dreamer sees himself doing something.
2. The dreams have oracular power, that is, they can predict the future.
3. The dreams are allegorical.
4. 'Very commonly, the principle of similars is used, either similars of sound, that is, puns, or similars of situation.'[80]

The dreams of the chief cupbearer and the chief baker include all four of these essential elements.

In the present verses, the chief cupbearer is an active participant in his dream. He views himself grasping and squeezing a cluster of grapes into the cup of Pharaoh.

40:12-13. And Joseph said to him, 'This is its interpretation: the three branches are three days; in three days Pharaoh will lift up your head, and he will restore you to your office. Then you will put Pharaoh's cup in his hand, as was the previous custom when you were his cupbearer.'

The second and third characteristics of an Egyptian dream are found in these verses. First, the cup-bearer's dream is allegorical: the three branches signify three days. Symbols of the number three are also seen in verse 11 in which the name 'Pharaoh' and the word 'cup' are employed three times each. Second, the dream is prophetic. It simply tells what will happen to the cupbearer in three days' time.

The concept of lifting up someone's head is idiomatic in the Old Testament for the restoration of a person's fortunes or office (see, for instance, 2 Kings 25:27). The opposite, that is, a lowered head, is a symbol of shame and denigration (see Judg. 8:28).[81]

40:14-15. 'But remember me when it goes well for you and please show kindness to me, and mention me to Pharaoh and bring me out of this house. Because I was certainly kidnapped from the land of the Hebrews. And also here I have done nothing that they should put me in the dungeon.'

An interpreter of dreams in ancient Egypt would normally be paid by the dreamer. Joseph merely asks that the chief cupbearer should **'remember'** him when the official is restored to his position. It literally says, 'Remember me with you' — that is, recall to mind this present incident when you are later with Pharaoh. Joseph then asks the officer to **'mention'** Joseph to the King of Egypt: this is the same verb used earlier in the verse for 'remember'. Here it is a Hiphil form that means 'to cause to remember' or 'mention'.

Joseph then pleads his innocence. First, he is a victim because he was stolen from his homeland. The **'land of the Hebrews'** probably simply refers to the area in which his relatives are sojourning in Canaan.[82] (For commentary on the epithet 'Hebrew' see 39:14.)

Secondly, Joseph also says he is a victim because he was unjustly imprisoned in Egypt. The term for **'dungeon'** is literally 'pit', and that is the same word that is used for Joseph's place of imprisonment at the hand of his brothers (37:20,22,28-29). The two events are parallel.

Application

It is interesting to note that Joseph is able to foresee the chief cupbearer's day of deliverance, but he cannot predict his own time of release. He is called to be patient, and to rest on Yahweh and his timing. As George Müller once said, 'You need never to take a step in the dark. If you do, you are sure to make a mistake. Wait, wait, wait till you have light. Remind the Lord Jesus that as He is counsellor to the Church of God, He will be in your particular case Counsellor and Guide, and will direct you. And if you patiently wait, expectantly wait, you will find that the waiting is not in vain, and that the Lord will prove Himself a Counsellor, both wise and good.'

The dream of the chief baker
(Genesis 40:16-19)

After seeing the interpretation that Joseph gave to the chief cupbearer, the chief baker is anxious to hear the meaning of his dream. Joseph's interpretation, however, is the antithesis of what he had said to the cupbearer.

40:16-17. When the chief baker saw that he interpreted a good thing, he said to Joseph, 'Also I was in my dream, and behold three baskets of white bread were on my head. And in the top basket all kinds of baked food for Pharaoh. But the birds were eating them from the basket on my head.'

The opening part of the sentence can also be translated as **'... the chief baker saw that he interpreted well'**. This translation would be a comment upon Joseph's ability and acumen in interpreting dreams. Our translation above is more of a comment on the nature of the dream — the fact that its outcome is good. The latter is more appropriate because the chief baker is eager to have a good report about his dream.

The first words of the chief baker are often rendered by modern translations as 'I also saw in my dream' (NASB), or 'I too had a dream' (NIV). The literal rendering given above is accurate, and it fits with one of the essential characteristics of Egyptian dream omens, which is that, in the dream, the dreamer is a salient figure, and he sees himself doing something.

The term translated as **'white bread'** is uncertain in meaning. It has been variously interpreted as 'wicker', 'holes', or even 'Horite'.[83]

40:18-19. And Joseph answered, and he said, 'This is its interpretation: three baskets are three days; in three days Pharaoh will lift your head from you, and he will hang you on a tree. And the birds will eat your flesh from you.'

Joseph's interpretation of the chief baker's dream begins exactly as had the one for the chief cupbearer, with the words: **'In three days Pharaoh will lift your head...'** But in the present sequence the author adds one Hebrew word at the end of the phrase that completely alters the meaning: '**... from upon you'**! And whereas the first use of the clause was metaphorical (40:13), here it is literal. He is to be decapitated.

Some commentators argue that if he is decapitated, then he cannot be hung. So they say that he is not hung, but rather impaled.[84] However, he may simply be dangled by his hands or feet and not by the neck (see Lam. 5:12).

The chief baker, unlike the chief cupbearer, is not actively serving the pharaoh in his dream. He is merely passive. Thus, he is the one on the receiving end of the actions of both Pharaoh and the birds.

The eating of the flesh of the chief baker would have been seen as particularly reprehensible and demeaning in ancient Egypt. The Egyptians believed that the preservation of the flesh was important for a person to attain to the afterlife. That is why they placed so much emphasis on embalming and other procedures of preservation.

Application

It is clear that Joseph does not hold back in telling the interpretation of the dream. He is direct and tells the truth. According to
rabbinic tradition, his forthright prediction earned him two more
years in prison. But tell the truth he does. He does not give the
baker what he wanted to hear, as did so many false prophets
and interpreters of the day. As Casuerba says, 'The study of truth
is perpetually joined with the love of virtue; for there is no virtue
which derives not its original from truth, as, on the contrary, there
is no vice which has not its beginning in a lie. Truth is the foun-
dation of all knowledge, and the cement of all societies.' Joseph's
telling the truth demonstrates that he is a man of virtue. Oh that
we had men like that in the church today!

The dreams come to pass
(Genesis 40:20-23)

This section demonstrates the fulfilment of Joseph's dream-interpretations. It turns out to be a joyous day for the pharaoh, because it is his birthday, and for the cupbearer. But it is, in contrast, a day of disappointment for Joseph.

40:20. And it came to pass on the third day, Pharaoh's birthday, that he held a feast for all his servants. And he lifted up the head of the chief cupbearer and the head of the chief baker in the midst of his servants.

A special day arrives. It is Pharaoh's **'birthday'**, literally, 'the day of one's being born'. The verb is a Hophal infinitive, and it is found only here and in Ezekiel 16:4-5 (also translated 'on the day of your birth'). It is a day of festivity, when Pharaoh normally would be joyful and inclined to be merciful.

Pharaoh thus **'lifted up the head'** of both courtiers who had been in prison. Only one verb is used for what happens to the two of them — one verb, however, with two different meanings. To 'lift the head' is an idiom in Hebrew that can be a sign of pardon (40:13; 2 Kings 25:27) or a sign of execution (40:19).[85] The following few verses tell the reader which it will be for each official.

40:21-22. And he restored the chief cupbearer to his position. And he placed the cup in the hand of Pharaoh. But he hung the chief baker, as Joseph had interpreted for them.

Pharaoh decides the cases of his two high court officials. First, he restores the chief cupbearer to his station, and the official immediately carries out his duties. **'But'** (a disjunctive *waw*) he has the chief baker executed. The disposition of the two cases is related using the very words of Joseph's interpretations earlier in the chapter. That reiteration underscores the exact and precise fulfilment of what he had said.

The word for **'position'** is literally 'cup-bearing'. The first sentence thus involves a play on words, reading, **'He restored the chief cupbearer to his cup-bearing.'** This is for emphasis, signifying that the officer is not given a different position in the royal court, but he is restored to precisely the same post that he held previously.

40:23. But the chief cupbearer did not remember Joseph, and he forgot him.

Restored to his position of authority, the chief cupbearer promptly forgets the slave who had helped him. The loss of memory of the official is put in a negative way — he **'did not remember'**; and then in a positive way — **'he forgot'**. This negative-positive formula is idiomatic to underscore the total forgetfulness on the part of the chief cupbearer. The lapse is later called an 'offence' or 'sin' by the chief cupbearer himself (41:9).

Application

It is difficult to fathom, but nowhere in the text does it say that Joseph became discouraged or was in despair. Although he worked diligently and uprightly, and he had predicted the future of the chief cupbearer, Joseph is left to serve in the dungeon. And it would be for two more years! How could he not but be despondent in his circumstances? Taylor rightly said, 'It is impossible for that man to despair who remembers that his helper is Omnipotent.' No matter what his external condition, Joseph knew that Yahweh was with him and it was Yahweh who sustained him. Oh that we would be like that in times of trial, fear and despair! It is a true saying of Feltham that 'He that despairs degrades the Deity, and seems to intimate that he is insufficient, or unfaithful to his word...'

Pharaoh's dream
(Genesis 41:1-8)

Pharaoh now finds himself in a situation similar to that of his two officials who were in prison. He dreams a dream, but he does not understand its meaning. He is in need of an interpreter, but no one can interpret for him. In addition, it should be observed that as Joseph's descent into slavery and imprisonment began with a series of dreams, now his rise to a position of honour and power centres on dreams.

41:1. And it came to pass after two full years that Pharaoh dreamed. And, behold, he was standing next to the Nile river.

The verse opens with an event occurring, literally, **'after two years of days'**. This is an idiomatic way of expressing an exact period of time (see 2 Sam. 13:23; 14:28; Jer. 28:3,11). Thus the day of Pharaoh's dream is on his birthday two years later. Because of the dream's timing, it takes on special importance.

As with other ancient Egyptian dream omens, Pharaoh sees himself doing something (see commentary on 40:9-11).[86] He dreams that he is standing next to the Nile river. The Nile was very important to the ancient Egyptian. The Greek historian Herodotus comments 'that Egypt ... is land acquired by the Egyptians, given them by the river'. The ancient Egyptians believed Egypt to be a gift of the Nile, and the river to be the primary source of the nation's existence. In its inundation stage, it is considered 'the lord of sustenance' and 'he who causes the whole land to live through his provisions'. The physical benefits of a Nile with a high water-level are obvious: a supply of water, irrigation, leading to food production, a means of transport, and the like.

The god who was personified in the inundation of the Nile was Hapi, and he was a god of fecundity and fertility. It was he who was thought to sustain Egypt and provide for her. As Pharaoh's dream unfolds this fact needs to kept in mind.

41:2-4. And, behold, from the Nile came up seven cows, beautiful of form and fat; and they pastured in the reeds. And, behold, seven other cows came up after them from the Nile, ugly of form and thin; and they stood next to the [other] cows near the Nile. And the ugly and thin cows ate the seven beautiful and fat cows. And Pharaoh awoke.

Here is Pharaoh's first dream. The first group of cows that he sees are described with the epexegetical phrase **'beautiful of form'**. This is the same expression that was used earlier in the story to describe Joseph (39:6), and it means to be healthy, sturdy and strong. The symbol of the cow is important, for it was a staple element of the ancient Egyptian economy.[87] And the fact that Pharaoh sees **'seven'** cows signifies an abundance or completeness.

The seven healthy cows are seen grazing in the **'reeds'** along the banks of the Nile. That term is an Egyptian loan-word.[88] It originated there and then it filtered into other languages, such as Hebrew and Ugaritic.[89] Such word-colouring accentuates the validity of the Egyptian setting of the passage dealing with the life of Joseph.

41:5-7. And he slept and he dreamed a second time. And, behold, seven ears of grain rose on one reed, fat and good.

Then, behold, seven ears of grain, thin and scorched by the
east wind, sprouting up after them. And the thin ears of grain
swallowed the seven fat and full ears of grain. And Pharaoh
awoke, and, behold, it was a dream.

Here is the second dream of Pharaoh in the same
night. Although the symbols have changed, the basic
thrust of the dream is the same. The first thing the
king sees is a stalk with seven ears of grain — this is
a sure sign of abundance. In fact, the seven ears are
called **'fat'** and **'good'**; the **'good'** here probably
means 'healthy' (see Exod. 2:2).

Pharaoh then sees seven sick and withered ears of
grain **'swallow'** the good ears. The act of swallowing
in the ancient Near East 'can serve a principally
hostile function, whereby "devour" signifies "to destroy"'[90] Thus it is clear that the idea is that the
afflicted will devastate the abundant.

The particle of exclamation, **'behold'**, appears
three times in these verses. It is employed to describe
circumstances that follow immediately one after
another.[91]

41:8. And it came to pass in the morning that his spirit was
disturbed. So he sent and called for all the magicians of
Egypt and all its wise men. And Pharaoh recounted his
dreams to them. But no one could interpret them for
Pharaoh.

Pharaoh has a restless night. Because of his dreams
his **'spirit was disturbed'** within him. That is a rare
verb in Hebrew which bears the basic idea of 'to beat'
or 'thrust'. The point is clear: Pharaoh's faculties are
taking a beating because of his two dreams.

Because of his vexation, the king calls for the
'magicians of Egypt'. The title is an Egyptian loan-
word. It comes from the Egyptian *ḥry-ḥbt*.[92] The Egyptian epithet refers to a chief lector priest, someone

who is not only a magician, but also a member of the priestly caste. Pharaoh also calls for the wise men of Egypt. These officials cannot, however, interpret Pharaoh's dreams. They are impotent in the matter. The story, then, is a polemic against Egyptian magical practice, for, as we shall see, interpretations belong to God (40:8).

Application

In ancient Egypt, and in the ancient Near East in general, people believed that the true power in the universe was magic. They relied on magic (i.e., omens, sorcery, divinations, necromancy, and dream interpretation) to manipulate nature (the gods) for their own benefit. It was a means to determine the future and to provide understanding of reality. The same is true for many today who rely on astrology and other New-Age mechanisms to provide meaning to life. But, as in the story of Joseph, the magicians can provide no answers. Meaning and purpose belong to the Creator, and we must rest in him in order to have significance and satisfaction in life.

The cupbearer remembers Joseph (Genesis 41:9-24)

Because of the similarity of the circumstances, the chief cupbearer remembers what Joseph had done for him by properly interpreting his dream. That had occurred two years previously, although the dream's fulfilment had happened on Pharaoh's birthday. Joseph is thus brought before Pharaoh to hear the dreams.

41:9. And the chief cupbearer spoke with Pharaoh, saying, 'I am remembering my failings today.'

The restlessness and lack of understanding of Pharaoh regarding his dreams remind the chief cupbearer of his own situation two years before. He is struck to the heart, and he realizes his offence. His realization is emphasized in the Hebrew word order, in which the direct object, **'my failings'**, is the first element in the sentence: **'My failings I am remembering today.'**

The Hiphil participle translated **'remembering'** can have a more active thrust, in the sense of 'making known'. It probably bears both ideas here. And what the chief cupbearer is revealing is his **'failings'** — literally in Hebrew the word is 'sins', but we must understand its use here in a more secular sense, such as 'offences' or 'omissions'.

41:10-11. 'Pharaoh was livid with his servants, and he put me in the custody of the house of the captain of the bodyguard, me and the chief baker. And we dreamed a dream in the night; I had one and he had another. Each dream had an interpretation of its own.'

The drama of the episode is increased as the reader wonders how much the chief cupbearer remembers. The truth is that he recalls much of what happened. His statement here is a recapitulation of what was narrated in 40:2-3 — and much of it word for word! The official remembers the incident almost perfectly.

In verse 11, the chief cupbearer begins by saying, **'And we dreamed.'** Attached as a suffix to that verb, there is a final form *–āh*; this serves to give emphasis to the expression.[93] The official is driving home the point concerning the similarities with Pharaoh's present circumstances. He is highlighting the fact that he may have the answer to Pharaoh's problem.

41:12-13. 'And there [was] with us a Hebrew youth, a servant of the captain of the bodyguard. And we told him, and he interpreted our dreams for us. Each dream had its own interpretation. And it came to pass, just as he had interpreted for us, thus it was. He restored me to my position, but he hung him.'

In his account of the events that had taken place two years earlier, the chief cupbearer calls Joseph a **'servant'** of the prison officer. Redford argues that because in some places Joseph is called a prisoner and in other places a servant, we must have here elements of two different stories that have been combined by a redactor.[94] Actually, there is no reason to doubt that Joseph is serving a dual role. Since Potiphar is the captain over the prison-house and Joseph's master, there really is no problem.

The final clause of verse 12, **'each dream had its own interpretation'**, is an asyndeton clause; this is a clause that omits a conjunction that would normally join clauses. It is common in Hebrew, and its purpose is to explain the former clause by the latter clause.

41:14. And Pharaoh sent out and called for Joseph. And they brought him quickly from the dungeon. And he shaved and he changed his clothes. And he came to Pharaoh.

This verse contains six converted imperfect verbs. They come one right after another, and 'The reader easily senses the haste and excitement which attends the summoning of Joseph by Pharaoh.'[95] In fact, the verb translated **'they brought him quickly'** is literally from the Hiphil stem 'to run'; that is, the attendants caused Joseph to run.

Joseph shaves himself in preparation for the meeting with Pharaoh. The Hebrew verb is used for shaving both the face and the head (see Num. 6:9,18; Lev. 21:5).[96] In ancient Egyptian reliefs, Egyptians are usually distinguished from Asiatics by being clean-shaven.

Joseph also changes his clothes. Clothing has been a central motif in Joseph's life. It is symbolic here: new clothes reflect a new life of freedom. He is being brought out of the 'pit' (the literal translation of **'dungeon'**) to stand in Pharaoh's court!

41:15. And Pharaoh said to Joseph, 'I dreamed a dream. And there is no one who can interpret it. And I heard about you, saying, you hear a dream; you can interpret it.'

In the chief cupbearer's account of the story to Pharaoh, he nowhere mentions the part that God had played in the interpretation of his dream. Even in spite of the fact that Joseph explicitly made that point (see 40:8), the officer does not acknowledge it. Now Pharaoh obviously understands that a magical power of dream interpretation resides in the person of Joseph: **'I heard about you … you hear … you can interpret.'** Joseph will correct that misunderstanding in the next verse.

(For commentary on the inability of any seer or magician to interpret Pharaoh's dreams, see 41:8.)

41:16. And Joseph answered Pharaoh, saying, 'Not me! God will answer Pharaoh completely.'

Joseph's response to Pharaoh is quite strong. He first answers with a particle used as an exclamation of deprecation: **'Not me!'** — that is, Joseph claims nothing for himself. He is not a magician or a seer; the power of dream interpretation is not something innate in him. Joseph acknowledges that his ability is totally from God.

The final phrase of the sentence has been translated in various ways: e.g., 'God will give Pharaoh the answer he desires' (NIV); 'God will give Pharaoh a favourable answer' (NASB); etc. The Septuagint was so concerned at the idea of such a positive response that it inserted a negative particle in its translation, so that it reads, 'God will not give Pharaoh…'! In reality, the word *shālōm* often bears the idea of 'completely / perfectly / fully'[97] And that is what it means here, since Joseph does not yet know the content of the dream, or whether its interpretation is favourable or not.

41:17-20. And Pharaoh spoke to Joseph, 'In my dream, behold, I was standing upon the bank of the Nile. And, behold, from the Nile came up seven cows, fat and beautiful of form; and they pastured in the reeds. And, behold, seven other cows came up after them, weak and very ugly of form and lean of flesh. I have not seen [any] like these in all the land of Egypt for ugliness. And the lean and ugly cows ate the first seven fat cows.'

Pharaoh now describes his first dream to Joseph. It ought to be compared with the narration of the dream in 41:1-4. Pharaoh's review of that dream sequence is expanded by subjective comments, vocabulary changes and grammatical alterations. First, he puts the story in the first person. Secondly, the adjectives he uses to describe the cows differ from those used earlier. And, finally, the king adds material to the story for the purpose of emphasis. In verse 19 he employs the word **'very'** to emphasize the ugliness of the cows. Then he adds a whole new statement: **'I have not seen [any] like these in all the land of Egypt for ugliness.'** Why Pharaoh embellishes the original dream is clear: it reflects his earnestness and the fact that the dream needs an immediate interpretation. He elaborates in order to press home the importance of the dream's message.

41:21. 'And [when] they entered into their stomach it was not known that they entered into their stomach. For their appearance was as ugly as in the beginning. Then I awoke.'

Thus ends Pharaoh's narration of the first dream. This entire verse, except for the very last clause, is not part of the original dream narration. The point of the opening sentence of the verse is that the fat, healthy cows are swallowed by the lean cows, but it does not alter the appearance of the latter in the least. Whatever the fat cows symbolize, they do not affect the lean cows at all. The term for **'stomach'** is consistently used in the Old Testament of the inner parts, or entrails, of an animal.[98]

41:22-24. 'Then I looked in my dream and, behold, seven ears of grain arose on one reed, fat and good. Then, behold, seven ears of grain, dry, thin and scorched by the east wind, sprouting up after them. And the thin ears of grain swallowed the seven good ears of grain. Then I spoke to the magicians, but they could not explain it to me.'

In reporting the second dream, Pharaoh does not embellish the account as much as he did in the first dream. He does add the words **'dry'** and **'good'** to this narration, in order to accentuate the drama and the antithesis between the two types of ears of grain. Otherwise, it is almost a word-for-word repetition of the original narrative.

Pharaoh does omit an important statement from 41:5, the one that says, 'He ... dreamed a second time.' It is as if Pharaoh now recognizes that the two dreams are really one, and they only have one interpretation.

Application

At this point Joseph certainly would have sensed that his deliverance was near. How easy it would have been for him to take credit for properly interpreting the dreams he had heard! How easy to be full of pride! Here he was being brought before Pharaoh, the greatest monarch on earth, and before his court, having been given new clothes and having been freshly shaved. Was it not a time for honour and glory?

After having given a particularly devout and moving sermon one Sunday morning, Charles Spurgeon was greeted by members of his congregation. One man said to him, 'Sir, that was the greatest sermon I have ever heard and that you have ever preached!' Spurgeon turned to him and said, 'Yes, the devil told me that ten minutes ago.' There is no room for pride in the pulpit or in the pew. All honour and glory must go to God — for only he is deserving of it.

Joseph gave the glory and the credit to God. No matter that he stood before the greatest earthly king, who could have him executed immediately. He did not hesitate, but he stood tall for his Creator.

Buck tells us of a certain Auxensius who was a notable military commander under the Emperor Lycinius: 'Lycinius came one day into the court of his palace, where there was a great bath, and some vines growing about it, with the image of Bacchus set up among the vines. The emperor commanded Auxensius to draw his sword and cut off a bunch of grapes, which, as soon as he had done, he ordered him to offer it at the feet of Bacchus, which was as much as to acknowledge him to be a god. Auxensius answered, "I am a Christian; I will not do it." "What! Not do it at my command?" saith the emperor; "Then you must quit your place." "With all my heart, sir," said the Christian soldier, and, in token of it, put off his belt, which was the same as giving up his commission, and departed rejoicing that he was enabled to withstand the temptation.'

Joseph interprets Pharaoh's dreams (Genesis 41:25-37)

Joseph now tells the meaning and significance of the dreams to Pharaoh and his courtiers. Once again he emphasizes God's central role in the dreams and their interpretation. But Joseph goes beyond a mere interpretation: he also tells Pharaoh how the king ought to respond to the message of what is coming in the not-too-distant future.

41:25. And Joseph said to Pharaoh, 'Pharaoh's dream is one; what God is going to do, he has made known to Pharaoh.'

Joseph first answers Pharaoh by stating that his two dreams are 'an unambiguous unity'[99] — that is, they both have the same meaning. Apparently Pharaoh had already suspected this (see commentary on 41:22-24), and now Joseph confirms it.

Underscoring God's sovereignty again, Joseph explains that God has revealed to Pharaoh what God is about to do. The participle translated **'going to do'** is a *futurum instans* that signifies the certainty and immanence of the events.[100] They are near at hand!

41:26-27. 'Seven good cows, they are seven years, and the seven good ears of grain, they are seven years. It is one dream. And the seven lean and ugly cows who arise after them, they are seven years, and the seven thin ears of grain,

scorched by the east wind, they will be seven years of a
famine.'

In these two verses Joseph provides the key to the
understanding of Pharaoh's dreams. The four symbols are sets of seven years. Two of them are more
specifically years of famine. And two of them, as will
be seen later (41:29), are years of abundance. He
reiterates, however, that the two dreams are really
'one dream' and, thus, we are dealing with only two
periods of seven years.

With the use of the term **'famine'**, we realize that
this dream is different from the earlier dreams in the
story of Joseph. The significance of those earlier
dreams was concerned primarily with the personal
future of individuals, but Pharaoh's dream has
consequences for the nation as a whole.[101] Since he is
the head and ruler of Egypt, it is no wonder that the
dream should come to him.

41:28. 'It is the word which I have spoken to Pharaoh: what
God is doing he has shown to Pharaoh.'

Joseph now repeats the statement of verse 25. The
only difference is that he employs the verb **'he has
shown'** instead of 'he has made known'. The present
verb highlights the visual imagery and the quality of
a dream revelation. Reiteration here is for the purpose of emphasis — that is, to stress that God has
made known to Pharaoh what he is about to do. It
underscores the imminent action of God in the story.
He is about to act.

41:29-31. 'Behold, seven years of great plenty are coming in
all the land of Egypt. But seven years of famine will come up
after them, and all the plenty in the land of Egypt will be
forgotten. And the famine will waste away the land. And the

plenty in the land will not be known because of that later
famine, for it will be very severe.'

Now Joseph launches into the formal and detailed
interpretation of Pharaoh's dream. First will arrive
seven years of **'plenty'**, which can also be translated
as 'abundance' or 'satiety'.[102] This term is used
throughout the chapter (41:34,47,53), and it reflects
an immense increase in the goods of Egypt. For
example, Proverbs 3:10 employs the word when it
says, 'And your storehouses will be filled with plenty,
and your vats will overflow with new wine.'

Seven more years will follow, but these will be
times of great famine. At the close of the passage the
famine is described as **'very severe'**. This construction is an intensifying adverb based on the Hebrew
noun *kābēd*. The latter literally means that something is 'heavy / weighty', and the word is used here
to underscore the fact that this is not a light famine,
but one that is oppressively strong. It will be so
harsh, in fact, that the former seven years of abundance **'will not be known'**; that phrase is a Hebrew
idiom that signifies that no trace of it will be left.[103]
Not a kernel of grain will remain from before! In
addition, the reiteration of the effects of the famine in
this verse accentuates the reality of the unusual
nature and seriousness of this famine.

41:32. 'Now concerning the dream's being repeated to
Pharaoh, [it is] because the matter has been firmly determined by God, and that God will quickly do it.'

Joseph now explains why Pharaoh had the dream in
duplicate. He gives two reasons: First, it is repetition
for the purpose of emphasis. It demonstrates the
inevitability of the event's taking place. And this is
true because God has **'firmly established'**, or 'se-
curely fixed', it in history. The second purpose of a

double dream is to impress on Pharaoh the rapidity
with which the events will unfold. In other words, the
events are coming swiftly and surely!

41:33. 'And now Pharaoh ought to look for a discerning and
wise man, and place him over the land of Egypt.'

Now that the interpretation of the dream is con-
cluded, Joseph gives advice to Pharaoh regarding
what he ought to do. The phrase **'and now'** signifies
the beginning of a new section: it is distinct from the
dream. He gives three recommendations. The first,
described in this verse, is that Pharaoh should
search for an able, learned leader — one who will
serve at his right hand — who will be in charge of the
entire land of Egypt.

In a document from the Tomb of Rekhmire from
the Eighteenth Dynasty (1550-1307 B.C.) the duties
of the position of vizier in Egypt are described. The
vizier is the 'grand steward of all Egypt' and all the
activities of the state are under his control. Rekhmire
was vizier under Thutmosis III, and he served as
overseer of the treasury, chief justice, chief of police,
minister of war, secretary of the interior and agriculture, and other positions. He ran the state, and
apart from Pharaoh, he was the most powerful person in Egypt. It must be 'this office which the Hebrew
writer has in mind in the story of Joseph'.[104]

41:34. 'May Pharaoh act and appoint commissioners over
the land, and he will take a fifth part of the land of Egypt
during the seven years of plenty.'

In this second recommendation, Joseph duly recognizes Pharaoh's authority by saying, **'May Pharaoh
...'** — this is not a demand or command on Joseph's
part. He is merely giving advice. Joseph suggests to
the king that the vizier would need a large staff in

order to organize and run Egypt in the light of an impending famine.

The duty of the vizier, the **'he'** of this verse, will be to levy on the land of Egypt a tax of one-fifth of the produce of the seven years of abundance. The commissioners, of course, would be an integral part of the tax system and its organization. In fact, some have argued that the verb translated **'he will take a fifth part'** really means 'he will organize / regiment'.[105] That is unlikely, because Joseph later does in fact tax the people of Egypt according to a one-to-five ratio (see 47:24-26).

41:35-36. 'And let them gather all the food of these coming good years. And let them store the grain under the authority of Pharaoh in cities of food and let them guard [it]. And let the food be as a reserve for the land, for the seven years of the famine which will come on the land of Egypt. And the land will not be destroyed by famine.'

In view of the severity of the future famine, Joseph makes a sensible third recommendation: the Egyptian state ought to stockpile grain during the seven good years in order to sustain Egypt during the seven years of scarcity. The word **'reserve'** is used only here and in Leviticus 6:2-4 (5:21-23 in the Hebrew Bible), where it refers to a 'deposit' or 'security'.

Joseph says that **'all the food'** should be gathered. That statement is clearly qualified by verse 34, so that the meaning is that all the grain to be collected in payment of the imposed tax ought to be gathered. How else would Egypt survive the seven good years?

Joseph again defers to Pharaoh by specifically stating that these deposits are, literally, **'under the hand of Pharaoh'**. That is an idiom which signifies authority and control.[106] There is no doubt but that Pharaoh is in charge!

41:37. And the matter was good in the sight of Pharaoh and in the sight of all his servants.

Even though Joseph predicts an impending disaster, Pharaoh and his people determine that it is **'good'**. The reason, of course, is that Joseph does not simply provide a stark interpretation of the king's dreams. He proposes a solution, a way to deal with the predicted doom.

Application

Three times in this section, Joseph has declared that what is happening in Egypt and what is about to take place is due to the providence of God (41:25,28, 32). We have commented much on the doctrine of the sovereignty of God in the account of Joseph. But that is proper because it is central to the story. Nothing is occurring in Egypt apart from God's will. And that is true of all times and all places.

Calvin remarks: 'Hence we maintain that by his providence, not heaven and earth and inanimate creatures only, but also the counsels and wills of men are so governed as to move exactly in the course which he has destined. What, then, you will say, does nothing happen fortuitously, nothing contingently? I answer, it was a true saying of Basil the Great, that fortune and chance are heathen terms; the meaning of which ought not to occupy pious minds. For if all success is blessing from God, and calamity and adversity are his curse, there is no place left in human affairs for fortune and chance.'[107]

Earthly rewards
(Genesis 41:38-45)

Because of his interpretive abilities and his wise counsel, Joseph is made vizier over the land of Egypt. He is second to none, with the exception of Pharaoh himself. Thus God has taken him from being a slave to Potiphar and a prisoner in the jail to a position of great prominence in the government of Egypt. God is the one who causes men to fall and to rise; it is he who is in control of such things.

41:38. Then Pharaoh said to his servants, 'Can we find [anyone] like this man in whom is the spirit of God?'

In response to Joseph's first recommendation, Pharaoh asks a rhetorical question of his servants: is there anyone who fits the bill better than the man standing before them, the one who has displayed great discernment and wisdom? (41:33). Joseph has **'the spirit of God'** within him and thus he is an obvious choice for the position of vizier over Egypt.

Daniel is described in the same way by the Babylonian king Belshazzar: 'Now I have heard about you that the spirit of God is in you, and that illumination, insight, and extraordinary wisdom have been found in you' (Dan. 5:14). The context of the passage in Daniel is quite similar to the story of Joseph. Daniel is able to interpret the handwriting on the wall, after the wise men and magicians of Babylon cannot do it.

After Daniel succeeds, he is raised to a position of great authority over Babylon.

41:39-40. So Pharaoh said to Joseph, 'Because God has made known to you all of this, there is no one as discerning and wise as you. You will be over my house. And all my people will kiss your mouth. Only [in the matter of] the throne will I be greater than you.'

Now we see Pharaoh's assessment of Joseph. He is impressed by one thing above all others: God is with Joseph, and that is why Joseph is **'discerning and wise'** (here Pharaoh repeats the words of Joseph from verse 33). Joseph has made a great impression in stressing that the source of his power is God, and only God.

Pharaoh then rewards Joseph by placing him **'over [his] house'**. The same expression was used back in 39:4 when Potiphar put Joseph in charge of all his estates and business affairs. Joseph is now to perform the same functions for Pharaoh. In addition, Pharaoh says that all his people **'will kiss'** Joseph's **'mouth'**. Numerous scholars believe this to be a corrupt text, and that it ought to be repointed to read something like 'submit to your orders'.[108] This is unnecessary, however, for it is an idiomatic expression. To kiss royalty, an idol, or someone in authority signifies the paying of homage to that person or object (see Ps. 2:12; 1 Kings 19:18). The meaning, then, is that Joseph will be greatly served and admired in Egypt.

41:41. Then Pharaoh said to Joseph, 'See! I am setting you over all the land of Egypt.'

Pharaoh reiterates what he has just said by using an exclamation. He employs the imperative, **'See!'**, to add a touch of the superlative to the announcement.

It is approximately equivalent to the Hebrew demon-strative particle, 'Behold!'[109] Pharaoh is simply mak-ing a grand proclamation that Joseph will now serve as vizier of Egypt.

41:42. Then Pharaoh removed his signet ring from his hand, and he put it on the hand of Joseph. And he clothed him with fine linen clothes. And he put the golden necklace around his neck.

Following the grand announcement of verse 41, Joseph now passes through a ceremony of investi-ture to the office of vizier. The first act of Pharaoh is to give Joseph his ring with the royal seal on it — this is a sign that Joseph now has royal authority over the land of Egypt (cf. Esth. 3:10-12). The word for **'signet ring'** is an Egyptian loan-word and, thus, it gives authenticity to the scene. Pharaoh also **'clothed'** Joseph (a Hiphil causative verb) in **'fine linen'**; this is another Egyptian loan-word (see Ezek. 27:7). As we have seen, garments and clothing play an important role in the story of Joseph; now he wears the finest cloak of all!

Finally, the king bestows on Joseph a **'golden necklace'** or 'collar'. This action is well known from ancient Egypt. Its presentation symbolizes the be-stowing of great reward and favour upon the recipi-ent.[110] Joseph is being greatly honoured in Egypt!

41:43. And he caused him to ride in the chariot of his second-in-command. And they called before him, 'Prostrate yourself!' And he set him over all the land of Egypt.

Numerous translations render the opening phrase as 'his second chariot' rather than **'the chariot of his second-in-command'**. Speiser has convincingly shown that the word **'second'** in Hebrew may be used either as an adjective or as a title (see 2 Chr.

28:7).[111] Thus here it fits the idea of Joseph's having been made vizier, second only to Pharaoh in all Egypt.

As Joseph rides through the Egyptian crowds, a herald commands the spectators to **'prostrate'** themselves. This term in Hebrew appears only in this passage of Scripture. Vergote is right in saying it derives from an Egyptian word meaning 'to do obeisance'.[112] In his early dreams Joseph had seen that his brothers were to bow before him — but now all Egypt bends the knee!

41:44. And Pharaoh said to Joseph, 'I am Pharaoh. Without you a man shall not lift his hand or his foot in all the land of Egypt.'

Pharaoh's proclamation begins with his statement of self-identification: **'I am Pharaoh.'** And that title carries with it all the powers attributed to that position. The ancient Egyptians believed him to be omnipotent because of imputed divine powers. He rules the land as a god, as the incarnation and son of Re, as the Horus, and as a combination of the goddesses of Upper and Lower Egypt. For example, the stele of Sehetep-ib-Re from Abydos enjoins worship of King Ni-Maat-Re (Amenemhat III, 1844-1797 B.C.) as a deity:

> Worship King Ni-Maat-Re, living for ever, within
>   your bodies
> And associate with his majesty in your hearts.
> He is Perception which is in [men's] hearts,
> And his eyes search out everybody.
> He is Re, by whose beams one sees,
> He is one who illumines the Two Lands more
>   than the sun disc...
> He who is to be is his creation,
> For he is Khnum[113] of all bodies.[114]

The Egyptians held that Pharaoh was eternal, worthy of worship, omnipotent and omniscient. He imbued Egypt with existence and power. And, so, the declaration Pharaoh is about to make regarding Joseph has the authority of a divine pronouncement!

The expression **'hand and foot'** is a merism in Hebrew. It means that there will be no activity whatsoever in Egypt without Joseph's approval. This is a hyperbolic statement to underscore the power and authority that have been invested in Joseph by the King of Egypt.

41:45. Then Pharaoh called Joseph by the name Zaphenath-paneah. And he gave him Asenath the daughter of Poti-phera, priest of On, for a wife. And Joseph went throughout the land of Egypt.

To demonstrate the favour that Pharaoh bestows on Joseph, he gives him an Egyptian name. It is Zaphenath-paneah, which literally means, **'God speaks and he lives.'**[115] This name may reflect the event that has brought Joseph to a position of honour in Egypt — that is, God has spoken through him in the interpretation of a dream and now Joseph lives. Or it may signify Joseph's new role and status in Egypt — God will speak through him as vizier, and Egypt will survive.

Pharaoh then presents an Egyptian wife to Joseph. Her name is Asenath. It is Egyptian, meaning the one 'belonging to [the goddess] Neit'. Ironically, she is the daughter of someone called **'Poti-phera'**, a fuller form of the name Potiphar (see commentary on 37:36). This was a common name in ancient Egypt, meaning 'he whom Re gives'. This present character serves as a priest of On. On is Heliopolis in Greek, and it was a city seven miles north-east of modern Cairo. It is well known as a city of seers, interpreters of dreams and priests. Joseph marries into a high caste.

The idea that Joseph **'went through'** the land of Egypt probably indicates that he immediately takes charge and makes himself familiar with the workings of Egypt. He is planning strategy and beginning to implement it.

Application

There is no sense from the text that Joseph was in any way regaled with, or that he indulged in, the accolades, honours and freedoms of his new office. He went directly to work and apparently shunned all the popularity accorded him. This is worthy of emulation.

As Mansfield says, 'It is not the applause of a day, it is not the huzzas of thousands, that can give a moment's satisfaction to a rational being: that man's mind must, indeed, be a weak one, and his ambition of a most depraved sort, who can be captivated by such wretched allurements, or satisfied with such momentary gratification.'

Joseph served his God as he had served him in slavery and in prison. Now he serves him in the court of Pharaoh.

Famine and preparation for it
(Genesis 41:46-57)

There is much repetition of material in the passage before us. We read three times that the famine severely afflicts Egypt. Then we read three times how it directly affects the rest of the countries of the world. The writer's purpose is to emphasize the severity of the famine, and to highlight the fact that what Joseph had prophesied has indeed come to pass.

The episode also lays the groundwork for the remainder of the book of Genesis — it is because of this great famine that Joseph's brothers travel to Egypt and are eventually reunited with him.

41:46. And Joseph was thirty years old when he stood before Pharaoh, King of Egypt. And Joseph went out from before Pharaoh, and he went throughout all the land of Egypt.

In Genesis 37:2, the story of Joseph began by specifying his age as seventeen. Here we are told that he is thirty as he stands in the presence of Pharaoh. Thus he has been in Egypt as either a slave or a prisoner for thirteen years. It was two years before this, when Joseph was twenty-eight years old, that he interpreted the dreams of the chief baker and the chief cupbearer (41:1).

The statement that Joseph travels throughout the land of Egypt is a reiteration of verse 45. It is made for emphasis, stressing that he loses no time in becoming familiar with the ways and customs of

Egypt. And, certainly, it may be assumed that he is diligently checking on the agricultural production of the land in preparation for the coming drought and famine.

41:47. And the land, during the seven years of plenty, produced by handfuls.

Joseph was right when he interpreted the first part of Pharaoh's dream as meaning that seven years of abundance would soon come to Egypt. The phrase **'by handfuls'** explains the plenty as one of super- or great abundance. That noun is used elsewhere only in Leviticus in the context of the priest taking a handful of grain in sacrificial preparations (Lev. 2:2; 5:12; 6:15).

41:48. And he gathered all the food of [the] seven years which was in the land of Egypt. And he put the food in the cities. He put in the city the food from the fields of the city surrounding it.

As vizier, Joseph is made minister over agriculture in Egypt. In that role he manages the production and storage of grain stocks throughout Egypt. For storage practices in the ancient Near East, recent research has been done and ought to be consulted.[116]

The final sentence of the verse is an *asyndeton* clause — that is, it explains the clause that immediately precedes it.[117] Without it the reader may have thought that Joseph had set up regional centres for acquisition and distribution of grain. But we see that Joseph actually has each individual city gather for its own populace.

41:49. So Joseph stored grain like sand of the sea, a great quantity, until he stopped recording [it] for there was no recording [it].

Joseph's interpretation of Pharaoh's dream regarding seven years of plenty comes to pass. It is so abundant, in fact, that the recorders of Egypt are unable to keep up with the amount of grain being produced and stored.

41:50-52. Before the years of the famine arrived, two sons were born to Joseph — Asenath, the daughter of Potiphera, the priest of On, bore [them] for him. And Joseph called the name of the first-born Manasseh, 'For God has made me forget all my trouble and all my father's household.' And he called the name of the second Ephraim, 'For God has made me fruitful in the land of my suffering.'

Before the famine strikes the land of Egypt, the land is producing abundantly, and so is Joseph! He has two sons through his wife Asenath; no other wife is mentioned for Joseph, and so he is depicted as monogamous. Joseph's naming of his two sons demonstrates his joy and gratitude for the turn of events in his life. He has gone from being oppressed and suffering to being fruitful in many ways, such as in position, in agriculture and in progeny.

Joseph names the first-born son **'Manasseh'**. The name sounds like the verb **'forget'** in Joseph's speech. The assonance underscores his elation in forgetting his **'trouble'** and his **'father's household'**. These two terms may serve as a hendiadys, meaning that he has forgotten the trouble from his family which he received when he was in the land of Canaan.

The second son he calls **'Ephraim'**. This name is related to the verb meaning to be **'fruitful'** that Joseph uses in his speech. The name has a dual ending and, thus, it literally means 'twice fruitful'. That construction highlights the elation that he feels. And, especially, it contrasts with **'my suffering'**. Whereas the name Manasseh focuses on troubles in

Canaan, this name deals with Joseph's oppression in
Egypt. The term 'suffering' is later used of the Hebrews in Egypt (Exod. 3:7,17; 4:31). And it is never
used in the Old Testament of deserved suffering, but
only of oppression and abuse.[118]

41:53-54. Then the seven years of plenty in the land of Egypt
came to an end. And seven years of famine began to arrive,
just as Joseph had said. And the famine was in all lands, but
in all the land of Egypt there was food.

Famine was a common occurrence in Egypt in antiquity. It normally arrived because low levels of the Nile
reduced the area of cultivation and limited agricultural productivity.[119] The phenomenon of a seven-
year famine cycle is also known from Egypt and other
ancient Near-Eastern locales.[120] In Hebrew, the
number **'seven'** often reflects completion, and here it
signifies the intense severity of the famine. Examples
of local officials distributing famine relief are also
found in the literature of ancient Egypt, such as the
tomb biography of Ankhtyfy.[121]
    The final sentence is chiastic. It runs as follows:

a	b
famine	in all lands
b[1]	a[1]
in all the land of Egypt	bread

The contrast is further highlighted by the disjunctive
vav in Hebrew, here translated as **'but'**. It is an
anticipatory contrast, because included in the **'all
lands'** is the area of Canaan in which Joseph's family
lives. Chapter 42 demonstrates that the famine is the
catalyst for the reunion of Joseph with his family.

41:55-57. Then all the land of Egypt became famished, and
the people cried out to Pharaoh for food. So Pharaoh said to

all Egypt, 'Go to Joseph. Whatever he says to you, do it.'
Now the famine was on all the face of the earth. So Joseph
opened all the [storehouses] and he rationed [grain] to the
Egyptians. And the famine was severe in the land of Egypt.
And all the earth came to Egypt to get rations from Joseph,
because the famine was severe in all the earth.

The noun **'famine'** derives from the opening verb of
this passage, **'became famished'**. Although Egypt
has been spared up to this point, the famine now
engulfs Egypt in a **'severe'** way. Fortunately for
Egypt, Joseph had stored reserves of grain for seven
years. Pharaoh tells his hungry people to go to Joseph for relief. Joseph is in charge, the authority over
the stores of grain. This fact is anticipatory: later
Joseph's brothers must come to him to receive grain.

The text literally reads that **'Joseph opened all
that was in them'**, but the object is missing. The
Septuagint and the Vulgate render it as 'all the
granaries' to make sense of the passage, and we have
adopted that reading here. The next sentence is
equally difficult. We have inserted the word **'grain'**,
which may have dropped due to scribal haplography:
the last two consonants of the verb **'rationed'** are
b-r, and those are the two consonants of the word for
'grain'. In any event, our translation seems sufficiently warranted.

Many translations say that Joseph sold the grain
to the Egyptians. But the verb literally means 'to
break into parts', which, of course, is the basic idea
behind the concept of rationing.[122] Joseph is frugal
and determined: he needs to provide for Egypt during
several years of famine.

Study Commentary on Genesis

Application

Joseph has now risen to a position of great rank, prestige and authority. Yet he is one who wields virtuous power. First, he clearly recognizes the source of his position and strength as God, and no other. He names his children after that truth: Manasseh ('For God has made me forget all my trouble') and Ephraim ('For God has made me fruitful'). And in wielding his authority, Joseph is sober, diligent and disciplined. He works as hard in his lofty position as he previously worked in his lowly one. Many in the church today need to heed this lesson. How many has God blessed with great ministries and power in the church, and they fall because of their own pride? They forget that God was the one who brought them to that position and that he is the one to be honoured and obeyed.

The brothers come to Egypt for food (Genesis 42:1-17)

Because of a famine in the land of Canaan, Joseph's brothers are sent by Jacob to obtain grain in Egypt. Of course, Joseph is vizier over the land of Egypt, and the one in charge of all the grain stores. In this opening episode of the story, Joseph treats his brothers harshly, subjecting them to harassment and imprisonment. And why does he do this? Is it for vengeance? One would think that to be a natural response by Joseph to his many years of servitude and incarceration. But Joseph later appears to be very forgiving and he realizes that his situation ultimately came from Yahweh. So, then, why does he mistreat his brothers? The primary reason is to subject them to the experiential situation that he underwent — that is, to put them in prison and treat them harshly as he had previously been treated.[123] And his hope is that his brothers may come to a point of repentance for the way they had treated him.

42:1-2. And Jacob saw that there was grain in Egypt. So Jacob said to his sons, 'Why are you looking at one another?' And he said, 'Behold, I have heard that there is grain in Egypt. Go down there and procure some for us from there, so that we may live and not die.'

According to Genesis 41:57, people from all the known lands of the Near East were travelling to Egypt for relief from the famine. That is what is

meant by the statement that Jacob **'saw'** that there
was food available in Egypt. He also sees that his
sons are helpless and inactive: the verb for **'looking
at one another'** is in the Hithpael pattern which
signifies reciprocal action. None of them knows what
to do. In contrast, Jacob takes action and uses his
authority: he commands his sons to **'Go down'** to
Egypt. That verb is an imperative — Jacob is taking
control of the situation. Further force is added to his
command by the final part of the sentence, which
begins positively — **'so that we may live'** — but is
followed by the negative, **'and not die'**, which is not
required for the sense. This is a form of amplification
that emphasizes the positive statement.

Egypt has always been the land of grain for Palestine during rough times (see 12:10-20; cf. 26:1-2). A
good example comes from the time of Pharaoh
Haremhab of the Nineteenth Dynasty in Egypt. It
tells of Asiatics being allowed to come to Egypt to
pasture herds and to obtain food because of times of
distress in the rest of the ancient Near East.[124]

42:3-5. So ten brothers of Joseph went down to obtain
rations of grain from Egypt. But Jacob did not send Benjamin, Joseph's brother, with his brothers. For he said, 'Lest
trouble come on him.' Thus the sons of Israel came among
those who were coming [to Egypt] to get rations because the
famine was in the land of Canaan.

Ten of the eleven brothers of Joseph travel to Egypt
to procure grain for the family of Jacob. Why so
many? Undoubtedly it is so that the caravan will be
able to obtain plenty of foodstuffs and will be able to
bring it to Canaan. There is also a sense of security
in numbers. Many people are on the road to Egypt
and danger thus lurks everywhere (41:57).

Benjamin is not allowed to go with them. He is the
full brother of Joseph, the only son left of the beloved

wife Rachel. Since Joseph's supposed death, Jacob loves Benjamin as he had loved Joseph (44:20). Jacob's adamance in not letting his youngest son go is confirmed by the structure of the Hebrew sentence, which reads: '**... but Benjamin the brother of Joseph he did not send'**. This inversion is emphatic. Jacob is afraid that **'trouble'**, or 'harm', will come to Benjamin. That term in Hebrew is rare, but it clearly denotes some type of bodily injury (see Exod. 21:22-23).

This is the first time in Scripture that the descendants of Jacob are called **'the sons of Israel'**. It anticipates what the progeny of Jacob will become in Egypt: a nation that goes by the name of Israel.

42:6-8. Now Joseph was master over the land; he rationed grain to all the people of the land. And Joseph's brothers came and they bowed down before him to the ground. When Joseph saw his brothers, he recognized them. Yet he acted as a stranger to them, and he spoke harshly with them. And he said to them, 'From where do you come?' And they answered, 'From the land of Canaan in order to obtain a ration of food.' So Joseph recognized his brothers but they did not recognize him.

The opening sentence of this passage is a restatement of Joseph's position of vizier that had been bestowed on him by Pharaoh (41:41). In this role, Joseph has control and authority over all that belongs to Pharaoh. In order to get rations, the brothers come before Joseph and **'they bowed down'** to him. This act is a fulfilment of Joseph's dreams when he was a youth: in Genesis 37:7,9 he had dreamt that his brothers would one day 'bow down' before him.

Joseph's brothers do not **'recognize'** him. That is no surprise since they last saw him when he was seventeen years old (37:2), and he is now at least thirty-seven (see 41:46-48). In addition, he now has

an Egyptian name, he speaks Egyptian, he wears
Egyptian clothing and he is probably clean-shaven
(whereas Asiatics always have beards in Egyptian
portraiture). The same verb appears in Genesis
37:32-33 in which Jacob recognizes Joseph's coat.

The consonantal root of the verb 'to recognize' is
n-k-r; it has the same consonantal root as the verb
which immediately follows — 'to act as a stranger'.[125]
This is a pun to underscore the contrast between
what Joseph knows and how he reacts.

42:9-11. Then Joseph remembered the dreams he had
dreamt about them. So he said to them, 'You are spies. You
have come to see the unprotected parts of the land.' But they
said to him, 'No, my lord! Your servants have come to obtain
rations of food. We are all sons of one man. We are honest
men; your servants are not spies.'

Joseph responds by being difficult and by accusing
his brothers of being spies. The north-eastern border
and frontier were vulnerable throughout the history
of ancient Egypt. Egyptians were afraid of hostile
intervention from that direction. During antiquity the
eastern boundary of Egypt was protected by a huge
canal that appears to have run from Pelusium on the
Mediterranean Sea to Lake Timsah. Its primary
function was for defence and containment — to keep
Asiatics out and slaves in.[126] In addition, a network of
Egyptian fortresses lined the eastern border of Egypt
during various periods in order to protect the land
from Asiatic incursion.[127] No wonder Joseph uses
such a pretence to trap his brothers!

Joseph claims that they have come to spy out **'the
unprotected parts'** of the land. This is a term in
Hebrew that literally means 'nakedness', but here
acts as a figure of personification. It is used in
Hebrew of indecent behaviour (9:22), and of things
thought improper to expose.[128]

The brothers vehemently deny any subterfuge. They respond with a strong negative in Hebrew.[129] They then claim they are **'sons of one man'**. They are so many that they look like a military force, so they tell him that they are of one family. The brothers further argue that they are not spies, men of deception, but rather **'honest'**, 'veritable', or 'just' men.[130]

42:12-13. But he said to them, 'No! Because you have come to see the unprotected parts of the land.' And they answered, 'Your servants are twelve brothers; we are the sons of one man [who is] in the land of Canaan. But, behold, the youngest is with our father today, and the one is no more.'

Joseph responds to his brothers' claim of honesty by snapping out a resounding negative. They are liars, and so he accuses them a second time of spying: here he employs the same wording as in verse 9 to demonstrate that their claims are false and unheeded. The brothers answer Joseph politely and respectfully. They say they are his **'servants'** and, again, the sons of one man — not a military force.

They then provide further information to Joseph. They tell him that one brother did not come with them to Egypt, but he remains with their father in Canaan. He is **'the youngest'**; this is a superlative in Hebrew in which a simple adjective has a definite article.[131] Joseph now knows that it is his full brother Benjamin who has stayed behind in Canaan. The brothers then explain why one of them is missing, for **'The one is no more'**. The Hebrew literally says, 'He is not': it is a particle in the absolute sense that can be used as a euphemism for death (cf. 5:24). Judah later states outright that the other brother is dead (44:20).

42:14-17. Then Joseph said to them, 'It is what I spoke to you, saying, "You are spies." And by this you will be tested:

as Pharaoh lives, you will not go out from this place unless your youngest brother comes here! Send one of you to get your brother, and you will be imprisoned. And your words will be tested [to see] if the truth is in you. And if not, as Pharaoh lives, you are spies.' So he gathered them into custody for three days.

Joseph vigorously rejects their defence. So he is going to put them to a test. The test, however, is really a pretext in order that Joseph's beloved brother Benjamin should be brought to Egypt. The manner in which the test is put to them is one of tremendous gravity: twice Joseph utters the solemn oath, **'as Pharaoh lives ...'** This is an oath formula of kingly divinity; the expression 'as Yahweh lives' is often used in the same way by the Hebrews (see Judg. 8:19; Ruth 3:13; 1 Sam. 14:39,45). Pharaoh was, of course, considered a deity in Egypt, and so Joseph uses an expression which was in common usage.

The phrase, **'You will be imprisoned'**, is a Niphal imperative in Hebrew, which is used grammatically to express distinct assurance. The brothers are going to jail! What an irony! Joseph had been in that jail for years; now we shall see how the brothers handle it. The term for **'in custody'** confirms the ironic parallel — it is used earlier of Joseph's imprisonment (40:3-4). It also denotes the place of confinement for the chief baker and chief cupbearer (41:10).

Application

As was stated in the introduction to this section, Joseph is setting up circumstances in order that the consciences of his brothers might be pricked. This is so that they might have a sense of remorse regarding what they had done to him. Conscience is a mighty tool. To quote Fuller, it '... is God's officer and vicegerent in man; set by him to be, as it were, thy angel, keeper, monitor, remembrancer, king, prophet, examiner, judge — yea, thy lower heaven. If thou slightest it, it will be an adversary, informer, accuser, witness, judge, jailer, tormentor, a worm, rack, dungeon, unto thee — yea, thy upper hell!' Joseph understands that, as Tillotson says, there is 'no man that is knowingly wicked but is guilty to himself; and there is no man that carries guilt about him, but he receives a sting into his soul'.

Returning to Canaan
(Genesis 42:18-38)

The section of Genesis relating to Joseph opened with the account of Jacob sending Joseph to his brothers. They mistreated him and imprisoned him in a pit. Joseph was fully under their control. Now the circumstances are reversed. Jacob has sent the brothers to Joseph, and the latter subjects them to harsh treatment and puts them in prison. In addition, it is clear that Joseph is in total control of the situation. He is manipulating it to his own ends, but those ends are different from what the brothers had in mind: they planned to destroy Joseph, but Joseph wants repentance and reconciliation.

42:18-20. Then Joseph said to them on the third day, 'Do this and live, [for] I fear God: if you are honest men, let one of your brothers be confined in your prison house, and you go taking grain to your hungry families. Then you will bring back your youngest brother to me. Thus your words will be verified, and you will not die.' And thus they did.

Joseph has his brothers incarcerated for three days. This is so that the brothers should consider Joseph's demands and choose one of their number to return to Jacob in Canaan. In addition, all the brothers get a taste of what Joseph had undergone in his years of imprisonment.

At the end of three days, Joseph has a change of heart and is merciful: he decides to keep only one of them in prison, and to send the rest to Canaan. It may be that Joseph realizes that Jacob will be reluctant to send Benjamin to Egypt if so many of the brothers are in prison. In any event, Joseph begins his proposal with back-to-back imperatives: **'Do this and live!'** That construction in Hebrew provides direct assurance that the stated consequence will surely follow the stated action.[132] He also gives this new proposal because he is a man who **'fear[s] God'**. That pronouncement signifies that he is a just and fair man, and he will not unjustly punish them. It should also be noted that he uses the name *Elohim* for God, and not Yahweh. He still does not want to reveal his true identity.

The final statement, **'And thus they did'**, is not a statement of action at this time, but rather one of agreement to the conditions of Joseph's proposal. Indeed, they realize that without grain they will die, and their families will suffer greatly — so they are compliant.

42:21-22. Then they said to one another, 'Surely we are guilty concerning our brother, for we saw the distress of his soul when he pleaded with us; but we did not listen. Therefore, this distress has come on us.' And Reuben answered them, saying, 'Is it not what I said to you, saying, "Do not sin against the boy"? But you did not listen. And, also, behold, his blood must be accounted for.'

The brothers are beginning to realize their responsibility in the treatment of Joseph, and they announce that they are **'guilty'**. That term in Hebrew reflects both the guilt and punishment that have come on them for their wicked deed. They are also discerning enough to understand that it is their sin that is coming back on their own heads. This is an example of retributive justice, in which one is punished by one's own sins. Confirmation of this point is seen in the fact that the word **'distress'** is used twice here, once for Joseph's situation, and once for the brothers' condition. The brothers are so convinced that they begin their statement with **'surely'**, a term with a strong asseverative force.

The brothers obviously believe that Joseph is dead and, therefore, they are guilty of his blood. One exception is Reuben, who claims that he was Joseph's advocate, and he did not want him dead. What he says is an approximate citation of Genesis 37:22. It may be because of his advocacy for Joseph that Reuben, the first-born, is not the one taken hostage. Simeon, the second-born, is the one left behind in Egypt.

42:23-24. And they did not know that Joseph understood because there was an interpreter between them. So he turned away from them and he wept. Then he turned back to them, and he spoke to them. And he took Simeon from them and imprisoned him before their eyes.

The entire time Joseph has spoken Egyptian, and the purpose of this has been to hide his identity. To converse with his brothers he has used an **'interpreter'**. This is the only time that word appears in the Pentateuch. Elsewhere in the Bible it signifies an emissary or ambassador (see Isa. 43:27; 2 Chr. 32:31).[133]

Because of his brothers' remorse, Joseph is moved to tears. Yet he does not allow them to see him weeping because he fully intends to execute his plan. When Joseph turns back to face them he speaks to them; the fact of his speaking stresses that he has regained control of himself.[134]

Joseph then binds and imprisons Simeon, the second-born son of Jacob. It is likely that Reuben is spared because he had tried to protect Joseph from his brothers at the time when he was thrown into the pit and subsequently sold into slavery. In addition, Simeon seems to have been a violent man (34:25-29) and he will later be cursed on account of this (49:5-7). He is bound **'before their eyes'**: he is a hostage, and the brothers are obligated to return for him. The scene is solid proof of the seriousness of the matter.

42:25-26. And Joseph commanded that they fill their sacks with grain, and to return their silver, each man into his own bag, and to give them provisions for the trip. And so they did for them. And they loaded their rations on their donkeys, and they left from there.

The brothers had originally come to Egypt to purchase grain. As they leave, minus one brother, Joseph has their sacks filled with grain and, unbeknownst to them, their silver is included as well. Joseph's motivation does not seem to be sly or cunning. He is merely making the brothers a gift of the grain, treating them as if they had been guests in Egypt. When they discover it, the brothers fear it is a trap and that they will be accused of robbery (43:18). But Joseph is not acting out of trickery, but of generosity.

42:27-28. And one opened his sack to give fodder to his donkey at the lodging-place, and he saw his silver, and, behold, it was in the mouth of his sack. And he said to his brothers, 'My silver has been returned, and, behold, it is in my sack.' And their heart[s] went out [of them], and they trembled, one before his brothers, saying, 'What is this that God has done to us?'

One of the brothers, who remains nameless, opens his sack to feed his pack animal and he discovers his silver. He thought he had left it in Egypt to pay for the grain. When he tells his brothers, **'their heart[s]**

went out [of them]' — this is a hyperbolic expression indicating that their hearts fail them and they feel despair.[135] They realize that at some point they must return to Egypt without having paid for the grain in their sacks. They then physically tremble before each other out of fear: they are anxious that they are now considered thieves on the run.

The brothers conclude with an exclamation of wonder regarding God's part in what has happened. The word **'this'** is a demonstrative which is used here as an enclitic particle for emphasis.[136] In other words, they are deeply distressed that God in his providence has brought this situation on them. But, in reality, can they not see that their own sin is responsible for the problem? As we shall see later, both God's providence and man's responsibility play integral parts in the unfolding of the story before us.

42:29-32. So they came to Jacob their father in the land of Canaan, and they told him all that happened to them, saying, 'The man, the lord of the land, spoke to us harshly, and he treated us like spies in the land. But we said to him, "We are honest men. We are not spies. We are twelve brothers, the sons of our father; the one is no more and the youngest is today with our father in the land of Canaan."'

When the brothers return to their father in Canaan they tell him what happened in Egypt. It is a recapitulation of the events, and at times it is verbatim. Yet the report is laconic and much is missing from their account: matters such as their remorse, the fact that they were put in jail and the continued custody of Simeon are strangely left out.

The back-to-back sentences, **'We are honest men'**, and **'We are not spies'** are set in apposition, a construction that enhances the two opposing concepts.[137] In addition, in the original they are arranged in a chiastic structure:

a	b
honest men	we are
b¹	a¹
we are not	spies

This construction highlights the antithesis between the two clauses.

42:33-34. 'Then the man, the lord of the land, said to us, "In this I will know that you are honest men: leave one of your brothers with me, and take [food] for your hungry households and go! And bring your youngest brother to me. Then I will know that you are not spies because you are honest men. I will give your brother back to you. And you may travel about in the land."'

Much of the brothers' statement is mere reiteration of what has gone before. However, one clause literally reads, **'and take the hunger of your households'**; obviously an object is missing for the verb. Most early translations, such as the Septuagint, add the word **'food'**. The final sentence has been added by the brothers: the verb **'travel about'** is often used in the sense of trading (23:16; 37:28), and so perhaps they are claiming that they will receive *carte blanche* to buy and sell in Egypt.

42:35-36. And it came to pass as they were emptying their sacks that, behold, each man's bag of silver was in his sack! When they and their father saw their bags of silver, they were afraid. Then Jacob their father said to them, 'You have bereaved me of my sons. Joseph is no more. And Simeon is no more. And you would take Benjamin from me. Everything is against me!'

According to Genesis 43:21, all the sons of Jacob had found the silver in their bags on the journey back from Egypt. How then are we to understand this

surprising discovery as the brothers stand before
their father? Redford claims that this present event is
merely an 'editorial interpolation'.[138] But that interpretation is a problem because this so-called redac-
tion does not solve any textual problem or clear up
any matter, but merely causes problems. The reality
is that this is probably a staged event by the brothers
to draw their father's attention to the seriousness of
the matter at hand. Such conspiracy is a trademark
of the dealings of these men (see 37:19,31-32).

Jacob reacts to the situation in various ways.
First, he is **'afraid'** (here is an assonance with the
verb **'saw'**), which is a similar response to that of the
brothers when they first made this discovery (42:28).
He is then deeply distraught. He accuses them of
having **'bereaved'** him: that verb is often used of
making someone childless, or causing barrenness.[139]
Jacob's expression here is emphatic, because it
literally reads from the Hebrew: **'Me you have bereaved'**; so Jacob is focusing on his own loss. Ironically, the shadow of the lost Joseph hangs over the
entire scene: **'Joseph is no more.'**

42:37-38. And Reuben spoke to his father, saying, 'You may
kill my two sons if I do not return him to you. Give him into
my hand, and I will return him to you.' But he answered, 'My
son will not go down with you, because his brother is dead.
And he alone is left. And if harm came to him on the trip you
are taking, then my grey head would go down to Sheol in
grief.'

Reuben, Jacob's eldest son, now intervenes to make
a noble offer. He says he will protect Benjamin on the
trip, and if he does not then Jacob may put Reuben's
two sons to death. They are to act as a pledge that he
will carry out what he has promised. Reuben adds
emphasis to his offer in two ways. First, the wording
of the pledge is, literally, **'My two sons you may kill'**

— that unusual construction highlights what he is
offering. Secondly, the offer in its entirety is structured so that the consequence (or apodosis) precedes
the conditional clause. The normal sentence structure would be: 'If I do not return ... then you may
kill.' But here it is arranged in the opposite order to
underscore the certainty attached to Reuben's
promise.

Jacob responds by calling Benjamin **'my son'** — a
subtle rebuke — and then he refuses to let him
accompany Reuben to Egypt. He is all that is **'left'** —
that is, of Rachel's sons (since Joseph is presumed
dead). But what of Simeon? Clearly Jacob does not
give much thought to him, or at least he does not set
as much stock by him as he does by Benjamin.

Jacob does not want Benjamin hurt, for if that
were to happen, then his **'grey head would go down
to Sheol in grief'**. This is a Hebrew idiom for an
unhappy death (see 44:31). It ought to be contrasted
with a happy death, such as that of Abraham (25:8).

Application

Retributive irony may be defined as when someone is punished
by his or her own sins. It occurs frequently in Scripture. For
instance, in the book of Esther, the evil Haman sets up gallows to
hang the righteous Mordecai; but it is Haman who eventually
hangs on those very gallows. The psalms are replete with such
examples. Psalm 7:15 says of the wicked:

He has dug a pit and hollowed it out,
And has fallen into the hole which he made.
His mischief will return upon his own head,
And his violence will descend upon his own pate.

And in Psalm 37:14-15 we read:

The wicked have drawn the sword and bent their bow,
To cast down the afflicted and the needy,
To slay those who are upright in conduct.
Their sword will enter their own heart,
And their bows will be broken.

A similar principle operates in the world today. I once had a student who cheated on an exam by writing the answers to the test on her hand. Midway through the exam she asked clarification from me on a question, and she pointed to the problem with the hand that was full of answers! The way she attempted to succeed came back to bite her!

Richard Nixon attempted to have a successful presidency through much scheming. And he wanted to keep a record of his achievements — so he had his White House conversations taped. It was those very tapes that made him infamous, rather than famous.

The point is that our sins will find us out. And there is only one remedy — forgiveness that comes through the person and work of Jesus Christ. It is only through his blood that anyone can be redeemed from sin.

The decision to return to Egypt (Genesis 43:1-15)

As the foodstuffs begin to run out, Jacob is forced to relent. A crucial factor in his yielding is a conversation that he has with Judah, who assumes a leadership position among the brothers and speaks for them. Reuben, Jacob's first-born, no longer holds that role. We later learn that Reuben had lost his pre-eminent position because he had lain with one of his father's concubines (49:4; cf. 35:22). In any event, Judah convinces Jacob to send his youngest son Benjamin with the brothers to Egypt.

43:1-2. Now the famine was severe in the land. And it came to pass when they finished eating the rations which they had brought from Egypt, that their father said to them, 'Return, purchase for us a little food.'

The statement describing the severity of the famine in Canaan forcefully interrupts the narrative of events in the family. We have been told twice before of the harshness of this particular famine (41:31,56), but here it serves to cause Jacob and his sons to confront the situation in Egypt. Jacob is pictured in a callous light, acting only when their provisions are coming to an end. What about Simeon?

43:3-5. Then Judah spoke to him, saying, 'The man solemnly warned us, saying, "You will not see my face unless your brother is with you!" If you send our brother with us then we will go down and we will purchase food for you. But if you do not send [him], we will not go down. For the man said to us, "You will not see my face unless your brother is with you!"'

Judah now takes centre stage, whereas Reuben is relegated to the background in the remainder of the story of Joseph. We are not told why, but, as noted above, it may be due to Reuben's sexual indiscretion (see 35:22; 49:4).

Judah is quite forceful in his response to Jacob's command to return to Egypt.

First, his entire statement is accentuated by being arranged in a chiastic structure:

a	b
You will not see ...	If you send ...
b¹	a¹
If you do not send ...	You will not see ...

Secondly, Judah emphasizes the Egyptian's admonition by saying that he **'solemnly warned'**: the Hebrew construction is an infinitive absolute before an imperfective verb of the same root. It literally reads, 'Warning, he warned', and gives added force to the idea conveyed by the verb.

Thirdly, the verbs, **'we will go down'** and **'we will purchase'** are both cohortatives, a form that intensifies the root of the verb in question.

It is important to note that Judah refers to Joseph as **'the man'**. That epithet reflects anonymity, a stated lack of identity. Much of the remainder of the story is concerned with the revelation of the identity of 'the man'.

The clause, **'You will not see my face,'** is the language of the court; to see a person's face is an idiom for having an audience with a ruler or chieftain (see Exod. 10:28).

43:6-7. And Israel replied, 'Why did you cause this trouble for me by telling the man you had another brother?' But they answered, 'The man closely questioned us about ourselves and our relatives, saying, "Is your father still alive? Do you have a brother?" So we answered him by these words. How could we possibly have known that he would say, "Bring down your brother"?'

Jacob now accuses his sons of bringing **'trouble'**, or 'evil', on him by telling the Egyptian vizier about Benjamin. The fact is that Jacob does not know half of it! The sons' evil deeds began when they put Joseph in a pit and sold him to Egypt (that same word 'evil' is used in 37:2,20,33). Here the word is in a verbal form and its pattern is Hiphil, which is the causative stem. In other words, Jacob is placing full blame on his sons.

Jacob's sons attempt to defend themselves. They are vigorous in their denial: the clause, **'How could we possibly have known ...?'** is the familiar imperfect verb followed by an infinitive absolute of the same verb. It has an intensifying effect, and it indicates an excited dialogue.

The questions the brothers say the Egyptian asked them are not found in Genesis 42:8-17, the account of when they stood before Joseph. Is there a discrepancy here? No, Genesis 44:19 indicates that Joseph did ask these questions when the brothers were originally grilled by him. Chapter 42 does not recount that entire conversation; it is merely selective.

43:8-10. So Judah said to Israel, his father, 'Send the youth with me. And we will rise and we will go; and we will live and not die — both we and you and also our children. I will pledge it; from my hand you may exact it. If I do not bring him to you and set him before you, then I will be guilty before you for ever. For if we had not lingered, then we could have [gone and] returned twice.'

In verse 7, the brothers collectively answer their father's accusation. Now Judah specifically intervenes, and adopts an assertive tone. First, he opens with an example of a literary feature called polysyndeton, which is a successive use of 'and' or 'also' at the beginning of a series of phrases. [140] He says, literally:

> And we will rise
> and we will go
> and we will live
> and not die
> also we
> also you
> also our children...

Judah does this to attract his father's attention, and to heighten the effect of his appeal.

To gain his father's approval to take Benjamin to Egypt, Judah makes a pledge that invokes a curse on himself. The two verbs **'pledge'** and **'exact'** are set in apposition for emphasis — the two clauses are essentially saying the same thing. The sentence also begins with the personal pronoun **'I'**; it comes before the verb and thus adds weight to it.

The final sentence begins with, **'For if ...'**, which has an asseverative force and is often used to introduce oaths.[141] The oath is also an emphatic one: the clause, **'then we could have [gone and] returned twice'**, contains a demonstrative particle that is left untranslated, the sole purpose of which is to add emphasis to the oath.

43:11-14. So Israel their father said to them, 'If it is so, then do this: Put some of the choice products of the land into your vessels, and take them down to the man as a gift: a little balsam and a little honey; spice and myrrh; pistachios and almonds. Take double the silver in your hand; you must return in your hand the silver that was returned in the mouths of your sacks. Perhaps it was a mistake. And take your brother and rise up, return to the man. And may El Shaddai give you mercy before the man so that he will send out your other brother and Benjamin with you. And I — if I am bereaved of my sons, I am bereaved of my sons.'

Judah's remarks convince his father that Benjamin must be taken to Egypt. Jacob's entire speech here is one of resignation. He begins with, **'If it is so ...'**, a phrase that offers no resistance to Judah's arguments. The ending of his speech has been described as 'an expression of despairing resignation'.[142] The repetition in that last sentence underscores the depth of Jacob's despondency. Expressions of resignation at the beginning and end act as an *inclusio* for his entire speech.

It was customary for travellers to present gifts to a high official in a foreign land. The gifts to be offered by the brothers to the Egyptian vizier are called **'choice products'**. The Hebrew term occurs only in this passage, and its precise meaning is uncertain. It appears to be related to a noun meaning 'song' or 'praise', or perhaps to another word which means 'strong'.[143] The gift includes three products that formed part of the merchandise carried by the Ishmaelite caravan that took Joseph to Egypt (37:25). It is ironic that he should now be the recipient of those very same products! That a parallel is deliberately being drawn here is confirmed by the fact that two of the products, **'spice'** and **'myrrh'**, are mentioned in the Bible only in these two places.

43:15. So the men took this gift, and they took the double amount of silver in their hand, and Benjamin. Then they rose up, and they went down to Egypt, and they stood before Joseph.

This final verse of the section begins with a chiasmus in the original language. It reads:

a	b
the men took	this gift
b¹	a¹
the double amount of silver	they took

The purpose of this structure is to indicate that the sons take everything their father had specified — nothing has been left out.

It should be observed that the entire trip to Egypt, up to the beginning of the audience before Joseph, is described in a single verse. The narrative is condensed in order to heighten the tension, drama and sense of anticipation. Events are hurtling towards a climax when the identity of the vizier of Egypt is to be revealed to the brothers.

Application

Jacob's response to the events surrounding him is complex. On the one hand, his piety is evident in his prayer: 'May El Shaddai give you mercy'. As Matthew Henry says, 'Those that would find mercy with men must seek it of God, who has all hearts in his hands, and turns them as he pleases.'

On the other hand, Jacob demonstrates a great depth of despair and resignation when he says, 'And I — if I am bereaved of my sons, I am bereaved of my sons.' This sounds like acquiescence to fate — in other words, 'Whatever will be, will be.' And that seems to be a very worldly attitude and thought.

But we ought to have compassion on Jacob here. Are not our thoughts very similar when we undergo the severest of afflictions? On one hand we want to trust in the providence of God, but our flesh is weak. And so we turn to the other side, where despair and hopelessness reign. The answer, of course, is to go to our Creator, and to seek mercy from him. Only then will we be reconciled to our sorest trials.

Festivity in the house of the vizier
(Genesis 43:16-34)

The brothers have returned to Egypt, and they do not know what to expect from the vizier. They are in dread because of the silver that they had found returned in their sacks. They believe they will be accused of theft. Joseph's reception of them, however, is congenial and gracious. Because of his attitude towards them, the brothers let down their guard and relax. Of course, this is all part of Joseph's plan: he lulls them into thinking there is no danger, and then, in the next chapter, the proverbial axe falls on them.

43:16-17. And Joseph saw them with Benjamin. So he said to the one over his house, 'Bring the men into the house, and slaughter an animal and prepare [it] because the men will eat with me at noontime.' Thus the man did as Joseph said, and the man brought the men into Joseph's house.

Joseph sees that the brothers have returned to Egypt, and that they have brought Benjamin. So he gives instructions to his chief steward who is responsible for receiving visitors to the vizier. Joseph himself had held a similar position in the household of Potiphar (39:4). Joseph's orders are in the form of commands: the three verbs, **'Bring ... slaughter ... prepare ...'** are all imperatives. The chief steward does as he is directed, and he brings the brothers into Joseph's house for a meal. It would have been a

great honour for these Asiatic shepherds to dine with
a high-ranking minister of Egypt!

43:18. But the men were afraid because they had been
brought to the house of Joseph. And they said, 'Because of
the silver that was returned into our sacks the first time, we
have been brought [here]; so that he might fall upon us and
crush us and seize us as slaves and [take] our donkeys.'

Being invited into the vizier's house must have been
a frightening experience: it clearly was not a common
occurrence for lowly shepherds to receive such an
invitation. Thus the brothers are uneasy and they are
inwardly very anxious. They simply fear the worst.
They believe that Joseph will **'fall upon'** (literally,
'roll himself on') them — this verb is reflexive (Hithpael pattern), and it bears the idea of assailing another with overwhelming force.[144] They mistakenly
believe they will be treated in this way because the
Egyptians perceive them as thieves. The crime of
robbery in the ancient Near East could mean imprisonment and loss of property, such as animals (see
Exod. 22:1).

43:19-22. So they drew near to the man who was over
Joseph's house, and they spoke to him at the entrance of the
house. And they said, 'Please, my lord, we really came down
the first time to get rations of food. And it came to pass when
we came to the lodging-place that we opened our sacks and,
behold, each man's silver was in the mouth of the sack, our
silver according to its weight. But we have brought it back in
our hand[s]. And we have brought down other silver in our
hand[s] to get rations of food. We do not know who put our
silver in our sacks.'

Before they enter the house of Joseph, the brothers
speak to the chief steward **'at the entrance to the
house'**. They do this in order to speak to him alone,

and not in front of the rest of the people of the house
(including the vizier). They are anxious to find out
their standing before the vizier. No accusation has
been made against them, yet they come up with an
excuse prior to the charge! In addition, the brothers'
language is excited dialogue: their opening statement, **'We really came down,'** contains an imperfect
verb and an infinitive absolute of the same verb for
the purpose of emphasis. They are defending their
honour even before they enter the courtroom.

The translation, **'according to its weight'**, is
accurate because at this time coinage had not been
introduced. Payments made in metal were measured
by weight.[145] The term for **'weight'** has the consonants *sh-q-l* from which the later unit of currency
called the shekel derives its name.

43:23-25. And he answered, 'Peace to you! Do not be afraid.
Your God and the God of your father gave hidden treasure in
your sacks; your silver came to me.' Then he brought
Simeon out to them. So the man brought the men to the
house of Joseph. And he gave [them] water, and they
washed their feet. And he gave [them] fodder for their donkeys. Then they prepared the gift for the coming of Joseph at
noontime, because they heard that they would eat food
there.

The chief steward's response to the brothers' excuses
is to proclaim to them, **'Peace to you!'** The noun in
Hebrew is *shālôm*, a term denoting harmony, well-
being and happiness. When a noun is used in a
direct address like this the effect is exclamatory.[146]
This official is certainly involved in Joseph's scheme,
or ruse. His statement that **'Your silver came to
me,'** is legal language: he is saying, 'Legally, you
have nothing to worry about. As far as I am concerned, the money for the first grain-sale has *already*
been received in full and I have absolutely no claims

against you.'[147] The phrase is employed in a similar way in other ancient Near-Eastern contexts.

The clause, **'The man brought the men to the house,'** is an example of resumptive narrative. It is the same expression that was used in verse 17; the narrative, however, had been interrupted by the conversation between the chief steward and the brothers at the doorway of the house. Once inside the house, the brothers prepare themselves for a meal with the Egyptian vizier: they wash themselves, feed their animals and make ready the various gifts they have for Joseph.

43:26. When Joseph came to the house, they brought to him into the house the gift that was in their hand[s]. Then they bowed before him to the ground.

This opening scene follows official protocol, and Joseph appears in the role of the aristocrat accepting his due.

At this point it may be helpful to deal with the issue of Semites attaining high positions in the Egyptian government. The reality is that it seems to have occurred frequently. In fact, during the Middle Kingdom period (c. 2040-1640 B.C., the patriarchal period) a certain Asiatic named Hur became the Superintendent of the [Royal] Seal or 'Chancellor' of Egypt. He is well known from numerous scarab-seals of the seventeenth and sixteenth centuries B.C.[148] Joseph's appointment is to a position at a similar level to that held by Hur.

43:27-28. Then he asked about their well-being. And he said, 'Is your aged father well, of whom you spoke? Is he still alive?' And they answered, 'Your servant, our father, is well. He is still alive.' Then they paid homage and they bowed down.

Joseph begins his conversation with the brothers with common courtesy, asking about their health. It is touching to see that Joseph focuses particularly on his father's condition: Jacob is old, and it is important for Joseph to know how his father is faring. The brothers respond to these niceties by bowing before Joseph a second time. In the present instance their action is expressed by a hendiadys: the text literally reads, **'They prostrated themselves and they bowed down.'** It is a case of redundant language used for intensification. The brothers are not merely respectful, but they are obsequious, compliant to excess.

43:29-30. So he lifted his eyes and he saw Benjamin his brother, son of his mother; and he said, 'Is this your youngest brother of whom you spoke to me?' Then he said, 'May God show favour to you, my son.' But Joseph hurried out because his compassion grew tender for his brother. And he sought [a place] to cry. And he came to his private room and he cried there.

Joseph sees Benjamin. He is called the **'son of his mother'**: all of the brothers are sons of Jacob, but only Joseph and Benjamin are children of Rachel. Joseph then speaks, asking if the person before him is Benjamin; he does not know for certain because Benjamin was young when Joseph was taken to Egypt. He speaks tenderly to Benjamin, even calling him **'my son'**, a clear expression of endearment.

Joseph is so overcome by emotion that he retires to his apartment to weep. The phrase translated, **'His compassion grew tender,'** literally reads: 'His compassion boiled over.' This latter expression is found elsewhere only in 1 Kings 3:26. There Solomon orders that a child be cut in two in the presence of two women who both purport to be the child's mother. The real mother's 'compassion boils over' —

that is, her heart is deeply stirred. The term for **'compassion'** appears in the Hebrew only as an absolute plural noun — the use of the plural form is for intensification. Finally, it should be noted that Jacob's prayer of Genesis 43:14 is answered: 'the man' has 'compassion'.

Although Joseph is deeply moved, he does not yet reveal his identity. There are still lessons that the brothers need to learn. Joseph's discipline and self-control are highlighted by his refusal to let them know who he is at this point.

43:31-32. Then he washed his face, and he came out. Thus he controlled himself, and he said, 'Serve the food.' So they served him alone, and them by themselves, and the Egyptians who ate with him by themselves. For the Egyptians are not able to eat food with the Hebrews because it is an abomination to Egyptians.

Joseph now hosts a meal for his brothers. Ironically, the brothers sat down to eat a meal after they had thrown Joseph into a pit (37:25). They had callously eaten while Joseph was in despair; now Joseph uses a meal to entrap them. It appears to be a strange meal as Joseph, the Hebrews and the Egyptians are all served separately. Joseph's being seated by himself is a matter of rank and position, for he is not only not eating with the Hebrews, but not with the other Egyptians either.

The Hebrews are separated from all the Egyptians while eating. This is because of racial exclusiveness on the part of the Egyptians. They did not mix with the likes of the Hebrews; they had an ethnic / religious / national sense of superiority. Indeed, the Hebrews are shepherds, and 'Every shepherd of flocks is an abomination to the Egyptians' (46:34). The same term for **'abomination'** is used in the present text: it is a technical term for something strictly forbidden or taboo.

43:33-34. And they sat before him, the first-born according to his birthright and the youngest according to his youth. And the men looked at each other in astonishment. Then he set before them portions from his own [table]; and Benjamin's portions were five times as much as the rest of them. So they feasted and drank freely with him.

Apparently the brothers are seated before Joseph according to their order of birth. The term translated **'before him'** can mean 'at his direction'.[149] No wonder the brothers are dumbfounded! Joseph seats them according to age, and he does not even know them! He must have great powers, or maybe he is one of the renowned magicians of Egypt.

Joseph is cordial in his treatment of them. He even provides food from his own table for them: remember that this is a time of severe famine and, thus, the array of food must have been tempting. The vizier gives Benjamin five times as much food as the other brothers. Benjamin is clearly the favoured one. Why is Joseph partial towards him? It may be to see if the favouritism will arouse envy and jealousy in the brothers. That was, of course, one of the major factors behind their sin in selling Joseph into slavery (37:20).

The result is that the brothers find the time enjoyable. They, literally, **'drank and became drunk with him'**. They are relaxed and sense that the time of danger has passed. How wrong they are! Joseph lures them into this state, and his cordiality provides an extreme contrast to his behaviour in the next chapter in which he adopts a vicious tone and accuses them of theft.

Application

The fraternal affection that Joseph has for Benjamin is touching. It reminds us of Foster's account of the execution of Sir Thomas More. When 'he was being led forth under sentence of death, his daughter Margaret rushed through the guards, threw herself upon her venerable father's neck, and wept in woeful despair. The crowd melted into compassion at the scene. Sir Thomas said, "My dear Margaret, submit with patience; grieve no longer for me, it is the will of God." He embraced her and bade her farewell. After his execution his head was exposed upon London Bridge for fourteen days according to his sentence. It was about to be cast into the Thames, when his daughter was allowed to purchase it. She survived her father only nine years, and died in 1544, in her thirty-sixth year. In compliance with her desire, the head of her father was interred with her, in her arms, as related by some, or, according to others, deposited in a leaden box, and placed upon the coffin.' Such love, compassion and devotion is seen in Joseph's demeanour towards his brother. Yet God's will and purpose must be played out before they can be reunited.

The plot concerning the cup
(Genesis 44:1-17)

Clearly elated after their dinner and revelry with the vizier of Egypt, the brothers pack up and head for home. They have food to stave off the famine in Canaan, and they are returning with their youngest brother Benjamin. What is more, they are leaving with the approval of the highest official of Egypt, the one who ranks just below Pharaoh himself! But this is all part of Joseph's overall strategy, which is to lull them into a false sense of security. Joseph has one more trick up his sleeve.

44:1-2. And he commanded the man over his house, saying, 'Fill the men's sacks with as much food as they are able to carry, and put each man's silver into the mouth of his sack. Then put my cup, the silver cup, into the mouth of the sack of the youngest [brother] with the silver for his rations.' And he did as Joseph had said.

Later that evening, after the feast, Joseph orders the duplicitous chief steward to set a trap for the brothers. He is to place Joseph's cup in the sack belonging to Benjamin. It is not just any cup belonging to Joseph, but through apposition it is specified as the particular **'silver cup'** of his. The word for **'cup'** is an Egyptian loan-word that signifies a vessel used for libations.[150] It is a sacred object that is used as a divining instrument (see 44:5). Thus it is an object of inestimable value, something similar to the sacred

idols that Rachel had stolen from her father (31:32).
The Egyptians used such utensils for lecanomancy
(that is, divining the future by looking into a dish).[151]
Redford concludes that the object was not a small
drinking-goblet or utensil, but that 'Something the
size and with the function of a punch-bowl seems
envisaged here.'[152]

The fact that the cup is made of **'silver'** obviously
underscores the value of the piece. However, it also
adds an ironic twist to the story. The brothers had
originally sold Joseph to Midianites for silver (37:28),
and now he traps them by using an object made of
silver to demonstrate their thievery. The value of the
cup is important in its own right: theft of such a
sacred object would entail severe penalties in the
ancient Near East. Legal rulings current at the time
included the death penalty or enslavement for such
an act.[153]

44:3-5. As the morning became light, the men were sent out,
they and their donkeys. They had gone not very far out of the
city when Joseph said to the one over his house, 'Rise up,
pursue after the men! And when you overtake [them], then
you shall say to them, "Why did you repay evil for good? Is
this not [the cup] from which my master drinks and practises
divination in it? You have done evil by doing this thing."'

Joseph's plan rapidly begins to be played out. As the
brothers go on their way back to Canaan, Joseph
orders his chief steward to track them down (the
verbs here are synchronic — that is, demonstrating
simultaneous action). The chief steward is to interro-
gate the brothers, and to do so in such a way that it
is accusatory. His opening question is one of morality. They have been arguing that they are honest
men. So how could they respond to Joseph's hospi-
tality by stealing his cup? He had provided them with
a feast, and they have stolen one of the utensils on

display at the feast (in today's terms it would be like pilfering the silverware!). The expression **'repay evil for good'** is found only here and in the book of Psalms. It is perhaps a subject of ironic reversal in Genesis 50:20, where Joseph concludes that the brothers meant all their deeds as 'evil against me, but God meant it for good'.

The stolen silver cup was not only for drinking out of, but for divining. Divination by liquids (hydromancy) was a well-attested practice in the ancient Near East.[154] In short, a diviner would pour water on oil, or oil on water, in a divining bowl. The various reactions produced would determine whether an answer was favourable or not. The text is not clear whether Joseph truly used such means of reading omens, or whether he was merely pretending to do so. On the one hand, he clearly had the God-given gift of interpreting dreams. On the other hand, when he seated his brothers at the feast, there was nothing magical about it — although the brothers must have believed it was.

44:6-9. And he overtook them, and he spoke to them these words. And they said to him, 'Why is my lord saying these things? Far be it from your servants to do this thing. Behold, the silver that we found in the mouth of our sacks we returned to you from the land of Canaan. So why would we steal silver or gold from the house of your master? With whoever of your servants it is found, he will die; and we will also become slaves to my lord.'

There is no need for recapitulation of what Joseph had ordered his chief steward to perform. He simply does what Joseph had told him to do. The brothers are stunned by the accusations. Their bewilderment is confirmed by their use of two rhetorical questions in repudiation — that is, to underscore the absurdity of the accusation. And their defence is that they had acted honestly and with integrity on a prior occasion: they had brought back the silver all the way from Canaan. They had not kept that money or spent it.

The brothers are so convinced of their innocence that they pronounce a penalty on themselves if they are found to be guilty. It is a matter of individual liability: if one is found with the cup, then he will die. But it is also collective liability: they will all go into slavery if one of them stole the piece. A self-imposed death penalty is found elsewhere as punishment for stealing a sacred object (see 31:32). Penalties for theft, including the extreme one of capital punishment, are well-known in the ancient Near East.[155]

44:10. And he answered, 'Now, indeed, let it be according to your words! Whoever is found with it will become a slave to me, and [the rest of] you will be free from guilt.'

The first line of the chief steward's response begins in the original with a term meaning **'indeed'**, which is used here to introduce an intensive clause. He is stating emphatically his agreement with the judgement the brothers have called down on themselves. The problem is that in his next statement he declares the penalty to be considerably less severe than the one pronounced by the brothers. The steward does not accept capital punishment as a fitting punishment for the offence, and he also concludes that only the culprit should be arrested. The remainder of the brothers **'will be free from guilt'** — this is judicial terminology meaning that a person is free from responsibility for a crime. How are we to understand the apparent contradiction between the steward's opening remarks and his later words? It is likely that he is agreeing that the penalties presented by the brothers are legitimate, but he is being magnanimous and does not expect to impose the most extreme penalty permitted by the law.

The phrase **'a slave to me'** can only be understood as the chief steward speaking as Joseph's
representative. However, it is also true that slaves
would report directly to, and be under the authority
of, the chief steward.

44:11-13. And each man quickly brought down his sack to
the ground, and each man opened his sack. And [the chief
steward] searched beginning with the oldest and finishing
with the youngest; and the cup was found in the sack of
Benjamin. So they tore their garments. Then each man
loaded his donkey, and they returned to the city.

Believing they are innocent, the men **'quickly'** lower
their sacks to the ground. Joseph's steward then
begins to look through their sacks in a very systematic
way: **'beginning with the oldest and finishing with
the youngest'**. That entire clause is an example of
asyndeton and explains the verb that immediately
precedes it.[156] The order in which the search is carried out is to heighten the suspense and drama: the
brothers think they are all guiltless; the steward
knows that Benjamin, the youngest brother, has the
cup.[157]

Once the silver bowl is discovered in Benjamin's
possession the brothers tear their clothes. This is a
sign of grief and despair. It is also ironic because
they had earlier caused Jacob to do the same thing
over the apparent death of Joseph (37:34). They do
not speak, however. Obviously, the evidence is so
overwhelming that they are stunned and they resign
themselves to the forthcoming consequences.

44:14-15. When Judah and his brothers came to Joseph's
house, he was still there. And they fell before him to the
ground. Then Joseph said to them, 'What is this deed you
have done? Did you not know that a man like me can truly
divine things?'

Judah assumes the leadership role among the brothers. He was the one who had guaranteed Benjamin's safety to his father Jacob; now he acts on his promise by intervening with Joseph. When the brothers, with Judah at their head, return to the vizier's house, he is **'still there'**. Perhaps the statement is made because Joseph should normally have been busy with his work by this time. His being at home is to impress on the brothers his foreknowledge regarding what they had done.

Joseph confirms his prescience by asking the accentuated question: **'Did you not know that a man like me can truly divine things?'** He is boasting here of the Egyptians' reputation for magical skills, which were renowned in the ancient Near East.[158] It may also be a subtle play on the fact that the brothers had not recognized the validity of Joseph's interpretations of dreams in Genesis 37:8.

44:16-17. So Judah said, 'What can we say to my lord? What can we say? How can we justify ourselves? God has found out the iniquity of your servants. Behold, we are my lord's slaves — both we and the one in whose hand was found the cup.' And he answered, 'Far be it from me to do this thing. The man in whose hand the cup was found will be my slave. But [the rest of] you may go up to your father in peace.'

Judah's sense of resignation to the events which have overtaken them is evident as he asks the same question twice, using synonymous verbs. He realizes there is no defence. He asks the rhetorical question: **'How can we justify ourselves?'**[159] That verb is being used in the sense of the brothers' being able to clear themselves of suspicion.[160] As things stand, there is no excuse or justification.

Judah understands their situation as poetic, or retributive, justice from God. The brothers are not paying for the crime of stealing, but they are being called to account for what they had done to Joseph. Their sins are finding them out. This attitude has been seen earlier in the story (see 42:21).

Joseph's response is to reject Judah's offer of collective liability. Only Benjamin will be kept as a slave, but the rest of them are free to go. Joseph is thus attempting to isolate Benjamin from the rest of the brothers. He wants to test them. How will they react? Will they return to Jacob, reporting the loss of another son? Will they act as they had when they told Jacob about Joseph?

Application

Judah is discerning to recognize that God uses retributive irony to punish sinners. One's sins will normally find one out, and they will serve to punish the sinner. God often works that way. Even at the cross there is a sense of retributive irony: there Satan and his followers attempt to destroy the promised one by hanging him on a cross. But it is the very death of the Messiah on the cross that brings about the eternal defeat of Satan and his gang. And, of course, all of that unfolded according to 'whatever your hand and your purpose predestined to occur' (Acts 4:28). Satan and all his thugs meant the cross for evil, but God meant it for good.

But the cross is also an event of restorative irony. That is, through the death of the Messiah life was brought to his people. Through his suffering, his people are made whole and restored to a proper relationship with the Creator.

Judah's speech
(Genesis 44:18-34)

Judah now steps forward before the vizier of Egypt, and he gives one of the most eloquent speeches in the entire Bible. He speaks 'of a family tortured by grief and pain, in need of relief'.[161] It is a family wracked with death and the inevitability of death. And at the end of the oration, Judah, in a selfless gesture, offers himself in the place of his brother Benjamin. He is willing to trade places with his brother; he would go into slavery, and Benjamin would go free. Will this self-sacrifice break the downward spiral of this family? Will it relieve the despair?

44:18. Then Judah approached him, and he said, 'Please, my lord, let your servant speak a word in the ears of my lord. And do not be angry with your servant — because you are like Pharaoh.'

Judah now presents himself before the vizier of Egypt as the spokesman for the brothers. There is nothing defiant here; Judah is fully submissive. His humility before Joseph is obvious: he begins his request with a particle of entreaty, **'please'**. He demonstrates great deference to Joseph, and he pays great homage to him. Judah underscores Joseph's exalted position — he acknowledges that Joseph is virtually equal to Pharaoh (cf. 41:40). Joseph has the power to grant clemency or to enact severe punishment, and so Judah recognizes the one before whom he is speaking.

All of this is so that he would be granted an audience
before Joseph — that is, have a court hearing before
him.

44:19-23. 'My lord asked his servants, saying, "Do you have
a father or a brother?" And we answered my lord, "We have
an aged father, and a young son of his old age. And his
brother is dead. And he is the only one who remains of his
mother, and his father loves him." But you said to your
servants, "Bring him down to me so that I can look on him."
Then we answered my lord, "The youth is not able to leave
his father. If he left his father, then he would die." But you
said to your servants, "If your youngest brother does not
come down with you, you will not see my face again."'

Judah gives an impassioned speech that begins with
a detailed review of what has transpired thus far. His
recitation is somewhat muddled, however. For instance, in the episode he is recounting Joseph did
not ask the brothers about a father or brother; in
reality, they had freely volunteered this information
(42:13). In addition, here Judah uses the forceful
statement regarding Joseph that he **'is dead'**,
whereas in the earlier narrative he had pronounced,
'The one is no more' (42:13). In one sense the scene
is farcical because the 'dead' brother Joseph is
standing directly in front of Judah as the latter
announces his demise!

Judah also adds a phrase that Joseph had pur-
portedly said: **'so that I may look on him'**. That is
an idiom in Hebrew that means to take someone
under another's care, or to have compassion on
someone.[162] Judah includes it because Benjamin is in
dire need of the vizier's compassion and mercy.
Benjamin is the one who stole Joseph's cup!

The last clause attributed to the brothers, **'... then
he would die'**, is ambiguous — does it refer to Jacob
or to Benjamin? Jacob worried that Benjamin would

be harmed if he went to Egypt. Yet Jacob also declared that he would go down to Sheol in despair if
anything happened to Benjamin (42:38). It may be a
purposeful ambiguity — that is, that both of them
may perish if Benjamin goes to Egypt.

44:24-26 'And it came to pass when we went up to your
servant, my father, that we told him the words of my lord.
And our father said, "Return, purchase for us a little food."
But we responded, '"We are not able to go down. If our
youngest brother is with us, then we will go down. For we are
not able to see the man's face if our youngest brother is not
with us."'

Judah continues his retelling of the story. Yet here
his narration is selective. In other words, he omits
some parts of the story, certain facts that would
damage the case he is making to Joseph. Judah fails
to mention that Jacob and his sons allowed Simeon
to languish in an Egyptian jail until they had consumed all the food they had brought back from Egypt
(see 43:2). The famine had been severe (43:1), but so
had their callousness. But Judah frames everything
in a good light.

44:27-29. 'And your servant, my father, said to us, "You
know that my wife bore two sons for me. And the one went
out from me, and I said, 'Certainly he has been torn to
pieces.' And I have not seen him since. If you take this one
also from me and harm comes to him, then my grey head
would go down to Sheol in grief."'

Judah here continues with his recounting of previous
events. He describes Jacob's response to the brothers' suggestion of taking Benjamin to Egypt. The
statement, **'Certainly he has been torn to pieces,'**
is highly emphatic. First, it begins with an adverb
that highlights an unexpected conclusion and is

asseverative.[163] It may be translated 'certainly', 'surely', or 'indeed'. The verb in the sentence is actually an absolute infinitive followed by a finite form of the same root: this is a construction to give emphasis in Hebrew.

Jacob's statement in regard to Joseph that **'I have not seen him since'** is curious considering that Joseph is supposedly dead. Is it possible that there is a lingering doubt in Jacob's mind? Is there a question about his sons and the veracity of their account of years ago? Does he suspect that they indeed are not honest men?

44:30-32. 'So now, when I come to your servant, my father, and the youth, whose soul is bound to his soul, is not with us, then when he sees that the youth is not [with us], he will die. Thus your servants will bring down the grey head of your servant, our father, to Sheol in despair. For your servant made a pledge regarding the youth with my father, saying, "If I do not bring him back to you, then I have sinned against my father for ever."'

Judah now argues that Benjamin must return to Canaan because of the effect it would have on their father if he did not. It would be as if Benjamin had died: interestingly the text literally says he **'is not'**, and that is the same expression used of Joseph's supposed death in Genesis 42:13. In other words, at Benjamin's death, Jacob would also die. Their souls are bound to one another: this is idiomatic for loving another person as one loves oneself (see 1 Sam. 18:1). Thus, in reality, Judah is indirectly blaming Joseph for the anticipated death of Jacob, for it is Joseph who is keeping Benjamin in servitude.

Joseph may have been wondering why Judah should step forward as the spokesman for the brothers; after all, he is not the first-born. That is why

Judah tells the vizier of the pledge he had made to his father to return Benjamin to Canaan.

44:33-34. 'So now please let your servant stay in place of the youth, a slave to my lord; and let the youth go up with his brothers. For how can I go up to my father and the youth not be with me, lest I see the evil which will come on my father?'

Judah now makes a noble offer. He proposes that he should be a substitute for Benjamin; in other words, Judah should become a slave in his youngest brother's stead. The overture is made in an emphatic way: first, the verb **'stay'** is a jussive followed by a particle of entreaty (**'please'**) that strengthens the request. The offer is given in chiastic form, as follows:

a	b
let your servant stay	in place of the youth
b¹	a¹
let the youth	go up with his brothers

This construction further accentuates Judah's petition.

In Genesis 42:37, Reuben had offered two of his sons as surety for the return of Benjamin. That was not enough, and clearly Reuben was attempting to deflect any retribution from coming on him personally.[164] Only now, after Judah offers his own life in his place, is Benjamin freed and the story brought to a happy and satisfying climax.

There is also an irony attached to Judah's offer: he was the one responsible for Joseph's being sold into slavery (37:26-27). Now he asks to be sent into slavery in place of his brother Benjamin. Thus we see that the brothers have passed Joseph's test — they do not abandon Benjamin, but rather they seek to protect him. The brothers have clearly changed, and this sets the stage for Joseph to reveal his own identity. As we shall see, then, there is also a dramatic change in Joseph.[165]

Application

It was indeed a virtuous action on Judah's part to offer himself in his brother's place. As Jesus stated, 'Greater love has no one than this, that one lay down his life for his friends' (John 15:13). It reminds us of the story of Xerxes, King of Persia, when he was fleeing from Greece. The boat he was on was so crowded with people that it threatened to sink. Xerxes exclaimed to his men, 'Since upon you, O Persians, depends the safety of your king, let me know how far you take yourselves to be concerned therein.' As soon as he had spoken, most of the men had jumped into the sea to save the life of their king.

It is a noble deed to sacrifice oneself for one's brother or for a king. But how much more so when the king sacrifices himself for the lowliest in the kingdom! And, indeed, that is what King Jesus has done for his people: although he was undeserving, he came to earth to be a substitute for his people. Although they deserved death for their sins, Christ went to the cross in their stead. Is that not a King worthy of following? Will you follow him this day?

The reunion
(Genesis 45:1-15)

The brothers have passed the test Joseph set up for them. Now it is time for him to unveil his own identity. The story of Joseph reaches its crescendo in this section; everything that has gone before has been heading towards this supreme climax. Joseph will be reunited with his brothers and, in particular, with his full brother Benjamin.

45:1-2. And Joseph was not able to restrain himself in front of everyone standing before him. Thus he cried out, 'Have every man leave my presence!' So no man stood with him when Joseph made himself known to his brothers. And he wept so loudly that the Egyptians heard [it], and the house of Pharaoh heard [it also].

When Joseph had first seen his brother Benjamin, he was able to 'control himself' (43:31), but now he is so overcome he can no longer **'restrain himself'**. These two expressions are the same verb and the same verbal pattern in Hebrew. Joseph's inner emotions have reached a point of climax, and he will now reveal his identity to his brothers.

Joseph clears the room of all his attendants. The revelation of his identity is an intimate moment not to be shared with outsiders. In addition, it may be to slow down the breaking news so that Pharaoh and others may not intervene. Joseph will be able to present it to him as a *fait accompli*. He may well be worried regarding Pharaoh's view of so many Asiatics in the land. But, most importantly, Joseph's standing alone before his brothers is a reversal of the situation in Genesis 37.[166] There they had been in power and he had been destitute — and they took advantage of him, selling him into slavery. Now the roles have been reversed. How will Joseph treat them?

45:3. Then Joseph said to his brothers, 'I am Joseph! Is my father still living?' But his brothers were unable to answer him because they were alarmed at his presence.

Up to this point, Joseph has been employing an interpreter in his conversations with his brothers. He has been speaking Egyptian, and his words have been translated into Hebrew (42:23). Now, however, Joseph clears the room and he speaks Hebrew to them: **'I am Joseph!'** Their response is to be **'alarmed'**. The latter term in Hebrew means 'to be panic-stricken / terrified /astonished'.[167] Thus, the brothers are absolutely thunderstruck and rendered silent. They are stunned.

Joseph asks about the well-being of his father Jacob. He has made this enquiry previously (43:27), and so the present instance is a question of assurance. Judah's plea to Joseph had centred on the welfare of Jacob, and this had penetrated Joseph's soul. And so he naturally asks about him again.

45:4-7. Then Joseph said to his brothers, 'Draw near, now, to me.' And they drew near. And he said, 'I am Joseph your brother, whom you sold into Egypt. Do not be grieved and do not be angry with yourselves because you sold me here, because God sent me before you in order to save lives. For two years now the famine has been in the land, and there are still five years in which there will be no ploughing or reaping. But God sent me before you to preserve for you a remnant on the earth and to save your lives with a great deliverance.'

The brothers' stunned silence indicates that they need further convincing. So Joseph draws them closer, and he repeats his claim: **'I am Joseph.'** He adds proof to the statement by giving the information that they had sold him into Egypt — only Joseph and the brothers would have known that fact.

Joseph does not relieve the brothers of responsibility for their sinful activity. They are guilty, yet he has compassion on them and comforts them. Even after all he has been through, Joseph forgives his brothers. He is able to do so because he understands that God's hand is behind it all. God's providence has directed everything, even the misdeeds of the brothers. It underscores the true purpose of the entire account of Joseph: God is the subject of the story, and he is moving all things to the end and goal that he has decreed (cf. 50:20).

That goal is the preservation of a **'remnant'**, or seed on the earth. That, of course, has been the primary purpose of the book of Genesis since the prophetic announcement of Genesis 3:15. It is so that God's people would not be destroyed but saved with a **'great deliverance'**.

As a grammatical aside, the two terms **'ploughing'** and **'reaping'** are a merism meaning that no agricultural activity of any kind is taking place in Egypt. The famine is that severe.

45:8-11. 'So now, you did not send me here, but God did. And he put me as a father to Pharaoh and as lord over all his house and as one who rules over all the land of Egypt. Go up quickly to my father, and say to him, "Thus says your son Joseph: God has put me as lord over all Egypt. Come down to me; do not linger. You will live in the land of Goshen so that you will be near to me — you and your sons and your grandsons, and your flocks and your herds, and everything that belongs to you. And I will support you there because there are still five years of famine; lest you and your house and all that belongs to you becomes impoverished."'

Joseph again highlights the fact of the sovereignty and providence of God. He states emphatically that the true source of his coming to Egypt is not the brothers' evil activity. The independent personal pronoun **'you'** is added for force.[168] The negative, which normally is used directly before a verb, is here placed right in front of the personal pronoun to emphasize it: **'you did not'** could easily be translated as 'it was not you!'[169] Rather, it was the will of God that brought about the present circumstances: this opening statement clearly proclaims the doctrine of providence.

It was God who placed Joseph in these various official positions. The title **'father [of] Pharaoh'** is reminiscent of the name 'father of god' used of vizier Ptahhotep in the twenty-fourth century B.C. in Egypt.[170] The 'god' referred to in the latter name is probably a reference to the Egyptian king. It demonstrates that the vizier exerts a paternal influence over Pharaoh. The epithet **'lord over all his house'** was a common title in the ancient Near East for the royal steward of the court. Joseph's final title, **'the one who rules over all the land of Egypt'**, is not known to have been applied to any vizier in Egyptian literature — it actually may be a satirical statement for the brothers' benefit. They were the ones who had said, 'Will you really rule over us?' (37:8).

Joseph then sends a message by the hands of the brothers. It begins with the standard epistolary formula of a royal court official: **'Thus says ...'** (cf. Exod. 5:10). Joseph makes the request to Jacob: **'Come down to me; do not linger.'** These two clauses are set in apposition in order to enhance their opposition — an imperative is immediately followed by a strong prohibition with no conjunction tying them together.

The Egyptian vizier announces that the Hebrews may live in the land of Goshen. That region is widely understood to have been located in the area of the Wadi Tumilat in the eastern part of the Nile Delta. It was well known for its pasturelands. The Egyptian document Papyrus Anastasis VI, for example, tells of Pharaoh Merneptah allowing Edomite nomads to settle in Goshen 'to keep themselves and their flocks alive in the territory of the king'.[171] This event occurred around 1220 B.C.

45:12-13. 'And, behold, your eyes have seen, and so have the eyes of my brother Benjamin, that my mouth has been speaking to you. So report to my father all my honour in Egypt, and everything you have seen. Thus go quickly and bring my father down here.'

Now Joseph gives his brothers instructions to go and fetch Jacob and bring him to Egypt. They carry with them direct evidence of Joseph's existence and how God has blessed him greatly in Egypt. The strength of the evidence is that they have seen Joseph face to face. In addition, he has spoken to them directly, and in Hebrew! This is incontrovertible proof.

45:14-15. Then he fell on the shoulders of his brother Benjamin, and he wept. And Benjamin wept on his shoulders. Then he kissed all his brothers, and he cried over them. And afterwards his brothers spoke with him.

Verse 14 is highlighted drama because of the appearance of a chiasmus, as follows:

                 a   b
he fell on the shoulders   he wept

$$b^1 \qquad\qquad\qquad a^1$$

Benjamin wept   on his shoulders

Thus the long-anticipated reunion of the two full blood-brothers has come to pass. It is followed by an emotional embrace between Joseph and the rest of the brothers. They had been silent up to this point, but now they finally gain courage to speak with Joseph. It is a happy conclusion to a lengthy biblical story.

Application

Joseph, as Najpaver puts it, is 'making peace with his past'.[172] After all that has been done to him by his brothers, he does not retaliate. From a human perspective, he has every right and reason to avenge what they had done to him. He had been sold into slavery, and had lived as a slave or a prisoner for thirteen years! Yet he responds to his brothers with compassion and forgiveness. He embraces them and loves them. But how could he do that — something that is so much against human nature? It is simply that he believes in the sovereignty of God. He understands that God was working through all the painful events, and that his purposes are coming to pass.

What an example of Christ-likeness! When Peter came to Jesus, he asked him, 'Lord, how often shall my brother sin against me and I forgive him? Up to seven times?' Jesus responded by saying, 'I do not say to you, up to seven times, but up to seventy times seven' (Matt. 18:21-22). Dear Christian, is there a person in your life whom you need to forgive, or from whom you need to receive forgiveness? Take care of it now so that Christ may be honoured. For how can we not forgive others when Christ has forgiven us?

The invitation to Jacob
(Genesis 45:16-28)

When Pharaoh hears that Joseph's brothers have been reunited with him, the Egyptian king is glad. Pharaoh gives an invitation to the Hebrews: they are to return to Canaan and gather all their possessions and people, and then return to Egypt. There Pharaoh will allow the Hebrews to live off the fat of the land. When the brothers go to Jacob, their father is at first sceptical but later joyful. And the basis of his joy is that he will see his son Joseph one more time before he dies.

45:16-18. When the news was heard in the house of Pharaoh, saying that Joseph's brothers had come, it was good in the eyes of Pharaoh and in the eyes of his servants. Then Pharaoh said to Joseph, 'Speak to your brothers: "Do this: load your animals, and go [and] enter the land of Canaan. Then take your father and your households and come to me. And I will give to you the best of Egyptian land, and you will eat the fat of the land."'

These verses pick up on verse 2, in which the house of Pharaoh had heard about Joseph weeping and wailing. Now the reason for this display of emotion is relayed to Pharaoh: Joseph's brothers have arrived in Egypt. Pharaoh, however, gives no formal audience to the Hebrews; instead he speaks and gives an invitation to them through Joseph. His invitation is to endorse Joseph's offer of a move to Egypt for the

Hebrews. Pharaoh does not specify Goshen, but only the **'best'** of Egyptian land — that is an abstract noun in the construct state, which conveys a super-lative. The region is so rich and lush that the Hebrews will be able to eat **'the fat of the land'**. The latter is an expression denoting the best products of the land, including oil, corn, wine and wheat (see its use in Num. 18:12). Considering that it is a period of severe famine, this is a very generous offer by the Egyptian king.

The brothers must act quickly. The back-to-back verbs **'go'** and **'enter'** are constructed in such a way as to urge them not to delay. They are to lose no time, and to get to Canaan as soon as possible.

45:19-20. 'Now you have been commanded, "Do this: take wagons for yourselves from the land of Egypt for your children and for your wives. Then get your father and come. And do not let your eye look with regret on your belongings because the best of all the land of Egypt is for you."'

The clause, **'Now you have been commanded,'** conveys that this is an official royal edict of authori-zation. In order for the Hebrews to secure wagons in Egypt, they need the pharaoh's standing instruc-tions. In addition, the decree provides royal protec-tion for the brothers' trip to Canaan. The Egyptian king further orders them not to take all their goods with them on the journey. This would obviously slow them down, and the pharaoh does not want them to delay. This circumstance once again underscores the severity of the famine in the ancient Near East at this time, and it demonstrates Pharaoh's care and con-cern for Joseph's relatives.

Pharaoh tells Joseph's brothers not to **'look with regret'** on the possessions that they leave behind. That verb means to have a great longing for something.[173] There is no need for such feelings because they will find their goods waiting for them when they return to Egypt.

45:21-22. And the children of Israel did so. And Joseph gave them wagons according to the word of Pharaoh. And he gave them provisions for the journey. To all of them he gave a change of clothes. But to Benjamin he gave three hundred [pieces of] silver and five changes of clothes.

Joseph obeys Pharaoh's command by giving the Hebrews wagons and provisions for their trip to Canaan. Over and above that, he gives each brother a change of clothes. Benjamin, who is favoured over the other brothers, receives five sets of garments. Obviously, these are good-quality outfits since the same expression 'change of clothes' was used for Joseph when he entered the presence of Pharaoh for the first time (41:14). It is indeed fitting that the story of Joseph begins with hostility over clothing — his ornamental robe — and now reconciliation is symbolized by his gifts of clothing!

The phrase, **'according to the word of Pharaoh'**, includes a figure of speech called a metonymy, in which the instrument is put in place of the thing produced. The term for **'word'** is literally 'mouth': the word of Pharaoh, or that which proceeds from his mouth, was law in ancient Egypt.

45:23-24. And to his father he sent the following: ten donkeys loaded with good things from Egypt, and ten female donkeys loaded with grain and food and provisions for his father for the journey. So he sent his brothers, and they went. And he said to them, 'Do not quarrel on the journey.'

Joseph now acts explicitly on the royal command. In verse 17, Pharaoh had directed the brothers (through

Joseph) to load their animals and return to Canaan. As Pharaoh ordered, so Joseph has done. As he sends his brothers to Canaan, Joseph gives them only one charge: **'Do not quarrel'** on the way. This verb carries a wide range of meaning in Hebrew. On the one hand, it means 'to tremble / quake', and so some commentators argue that Joseph is telling his brothers not to be afraid on their journey.[174] They are under Egyptian royal protection. On the other hand, the verb can mean 'to be agitated / angry / argumentative'. If that is the sense here, Joseph is warning them not to argue with one another or to blame one another for their present circumstances. It then is to be understood as a directive against mutual recrimination.[175]

45:25-26. Thus they went up from Egypt, and they came to the land of Canaan, to their father Jacob. And they reported to him, saying, 'Joseph is still alive! And he is ruling over all the land of Egypt!' But his heart grew cold because he did not believe them.

When the brothers arrive in Canaan they announce to their father that Joseph is still living and that he is governing the entire land of the pharaohs. Jacob's initial response is that his **'heart grew cold'** — this is a verb that literally means 'to grow numb'.[176] He is indifferent and apathetic to the message of his sons. The reason is clear: he does not **'believe'** them. This latter verb also bears a sense of trust.[177] The fact of the matter is that Jacob does not place any value on the word of his sons — their history is one of untruthfulness. And, furthermore, the news they bring is simply too incredible.

45:27-28. When they told him all the words of Joseph which he spoke to them, and he saw the wagons that Joseph sent to carry him, then the spirit of Jacob their father revived. And

Israel said, 'Enough! My son Joseph still lives. I will go and I will see him before I die.'

Now Jacob's response to the evidence of his sons is lively, in contrast to his cold heart in verse 26. His eagerness to go to Egypt is accentuated by the brevity of his vocal response: it is not a time to talk but a time to hurry, especially if Jacob's death is imminent. In addition, his pronouncement, **'I will go,'** is a cohortative of resolve — he is clearly intent on seeing his son. And the latter point needs to be emphasized. He is not concerned with the famine, or with Joseph's position in Egypt. No, he simply wants to see Joseph one last time before his death.

No confession of the sons to Jacob regarding their part in the crime is narrated. That is because the forthcoming reunion of the family now dominates the scene.

Application

When Pharaoh and all his court heard that Joseph's brothers had come to Egypt it was good in their sight. However, these men were Asiatics and shepherds, who would normally be despised by the Egyptians (46:34). So how is it that such a visit was seen as a good thing by the Egyptian court? It is clearly a testimonial to the character and work ethic of Joseph. He was noted for his skill, honesty and piety. He had, therefore, earned the respect of the Egyptians, and those who were related to him would be treated well.

Christians today ought to display a similar type of work ethic. God wants workers for his glory and honour! We need more saints in the workshops! John Wesley preached three sermons a day for fifty-four years, rode 290,000 miles on horseback or in a carriage, wrote more than eighty different works and edited a fifty-volume library. Samuel Johnson commented on Wesley's routine by saying, 'His conversation is good, but he is never at leisure. He always has to go at a certain hour. This is very disagreeable to a man who loves to fold his legs and have his talk out as I do.' Such striving for God can be a great witness to the truth of the gospel.

Jacob's vision and migration
(Genesis 46:1-27)

The biblical author now describes the move of Jacob and all his possessions to the land of Egypt. It is important to note that Jacob departs from the town of Beersheba, the place where so much patriarchal activity was centred. Now Jacob leaves the promised land for a heathen land: his departure marks the end of the patriarchal period. A major theological issue of Genesis is highlighted again, and that is, how will the seed of the woman survive among the seed of the serpent? How will the promised seed receive the land of promise?

The genealogy of Jacob is catalogued here, prior to their departure for Egypt. That is important because later that same genealogy is traced just before Israel is to enter the land of Canaan (Num. 26). The registers are essentially the same, except for a few scribal variations. The one in Numbers, of course, is much longer because it includes many more generations descended from Jacob. The point is to see the increase in the people of Israel — that is, the descendants of Jacob — while they are in Egypt.

46:1-2. So Israel, with all that belonged to him, set out, and he came to Beersheba, and he offered sacrifices to the God of his father Isaac. Then God spoke to Israel in a night vision, and he said, 'Jacob, Jacob.' And he answered, 'Here I am.'

Jacob sets out from Hebron (37:14) and he arrives at Beersheba, a place on the natural route from the hill-country of Canaan to Egypt. Beersheba was an important location in the life of Isaac, Jacob's father. Here God appeared to Isaac in the night and spoke to him words of promise and comfort (26:23-24). In response, Isaac built an altar there and called on the name of Yahweh (26:25). Perhaps it is on this same altar that Jacob now offers sacrifices to God.

The patriarch is afraid to go to Egypt (see 46:3). This may be because he knows of the incident involving Abraham in that land (12:10-20), or the fact that God had previously told Isaac not to go there during a time of famine (26:2). Or perhaps Jacob does not know what to expect in Egypt, and so he hesitates. In any event, God comes to him in a **'night vision'** in order to encourage and to comfort him. The Hebrew word for **'vision'** is plural in order to intensify the idea of the word (called the plural of amplification).[178] Then God calls to the patriarch using iteration, or duplication: **'Jacob, Jacob'**. This repetition of his name calls special attention to the solemnity of the event.[179]

46:3-4. And he said, 'I am God, the God of your father. Do not fear going down to Egypt because I will make you into a great nation there. I will go down with you to Egypt, and, indeed, I will certainly bring you back. And Joseph will lay his hand on your eyes.'

God begins his statement with the common formula of royal self-disclosure: **'I am'** (see 15:7; 26:24). A clause in apposition immediately follows: its purpose is to provide a clear and distinct identification of the opening formula — **'the God of your father'**. There is to be no question as to who is speaking to Jacob.

Jacob is afraid to go to Egypt. One aspect of his fear may be an apprehension about forfeiting the promise given to him of a land and a people. God, however, allays his misgivings by saying that he will make a nation of Jacob in Egypt, and that they will return to the land of Canaan. God's words here are emphatic: first, the clause, **'I will go down with you,'** begins with the independent personal pronoun **'I'**. In that position the particle has an accentuating effect. In addition, the promise, **'Indeed, I will certainly bring you back,'** is strengthened by the insertion of the particle **'indeed'** into the grammatical construction of an imperfective verb followed by an infinitive absolute of the same verb, so that the clause literally reads: 'I will bring you back, indeed, bringing back!'

Another promise to Jacob is that Joseph will outlive him and will lay his hands on the eyes of Jacob. The latter is an idiom referring to the closing of a person's eyes at death. How comforting for Jacob to know that the one he thought dead will be with him at his death!

46:5-7. Then Jacob arose from Beersheba, and the sons of Israel carried their father and their children and their wives in the wagons that Pharaoh had sent to carry him. And they took their herds and their possessions which they had acquired in the land of Canaan, and they came to Egypt — Jacob and all his seed with him. His sons and his grandsons and his daughters and his granddaughters and all his seed he brought with him to Egypt.

These verses record the emigration of Jacob and his clan to Egypt. The description presented reflects the all-inclusive nature of the move. It is reminiscent of the journey of Abram from Haran to Canaan in which he brought everything with him (12:5). The move is simply en masse.

Included in the people travelling with Jacob are **'daughters'**. However, the text seems to indicate that

Jacob only has one daughter, whose name is Dinah (46:15). The plural noun is probably being used as a synecdoche, to denote both his daughter and his daughters-in-law.

Some commentators have tried to point out a discrepancy in the story of Joseph regarding who it was that authorized the wagons that were sent to Canaan.[180] Some passages say that Pharaoh sent the wagons (45:19) and others that Joseph sent them (45:27). This is not a problem since Joseph is explicitly obeying a royal command, and Joseph's word is to be equated with that of Pharaoh (41:40-44).

46:8-15. And these are the names of the sons of Israel, Jacob and his sons, who came to Egypt: Jacob's first-born was Reuben. And the sons of Reuben: Hanoch and Pallu and Hezron and Carmi. And the sons of Simeon: Jemuel and Jamin and Ohad and Jacin and Zohar and Shaul, the son of a Canaanite woman. And the sons of Levi: Gershon, Kohath and Merari. And the sons of Judah: Er and Onan and Shelah and Perez and Zerah. But Er and Onan died in the land of Canaan. And the sons of Perez: Hezron and Hamul. And the sons of Issachar: Tola and Puah and Job and Shimron. And the sons of Zebulun: Sered and Elon and Jahleel. These are the sons of Leah whom she bore to Jacob in Paddan Aram, including his daughter Dinah. In all, his sons and daughters were numbered thirty-three.

The biblical author now provides a genealogical list of the people who travelled with Jacob to Egypt. It begins with a common introductory formula for a genealogy: **'And these are the names of ...'** (Exod. 1:1). This registry is not, however, based on the order of birth of the sons of Jacob, but rather according to the one who gives birth. The first six sons listed are children of the first wife Leah; the next two belong to Zilpah; Rachel is the mother of the following two sons; and, finally, the last two sons belong to Bilhah.

In these verses we witness a catalogue of the sons and grandsons of Jacob and Leah. It is similar to the genealogy recorded in Numbers 26:4-62, although the latter includes later generations as well. There are a few differences between the two lists, although most of them can be explained as dialectical variations. So, for example, the first son of Simeon is named **'Jemuel'** (also in Exod. 6:15), but his name appears as Nemuel in Numbers 26:12 and 1 Chronicles 4:24. This is not a scribal error, but rather a variation in pronunciation or spelling.

The last son of Simeon is called **'the son of a Canaanite woman'**. This phrase may perhaps have been inserted as a stinging rebuke of Simeon and of his relations with a pagan woman. Ironically, it was Simeon (and Levi) who killed the Shechemites for dishonouring his sister Dinah (34:25-31).

The descendants of Jacob and Leah listed here are said to number **'thirty-three'**. The problem is that if we include Dinah in the list, then it numbers thirty-four. She probably is to be included because the text says his **'sons and daughters'** added up to thirty-three. If, on the other hand, we eliminate Er and Onan (because God had eliminated them!), then the number of children is thirty-two. Perhaps there is an unnamed daughter or son who has not been specifically mentioned in the text.

46:16-18. And the sons of Gad: Zephon and Haggi, Shuni and Ezbon, Eri and Arodi and Areli. And the sons of Asher: Imnah and Ishvah and Ishvi and Beriah and Serah their sister. And the sons of Beriah: Heber and Malkiel. These are the children of Zilpah whom Laban gave to Leah his daughter. And she bore these [children] for Jacob, sixteen lives.

Now are listed the descendants of Zilpah, the handmaid of Leah: included are two sons, eleven grandsons, one granddaughter and two great-grandsons.

This section of the genealogy is very similar to what appears in Numbers 26. The only differences are that in the latter Ezbon is called Ozni (probably a dialectical distinction) and Ishvah has been omitted for some unknown reason (although he is included in the registry of 1 Chr. 7:30).[181]

46:19-22. The sons of Rachel, the wife of Jacob: Joseph and Benjamin. And born to Joseph in the land of Egypt, whom Asenath, the daughter of Potiphera, the priest of On, bore for him: Manasseh and Ephraim. And the sons of Benjamin: Bela and Beker and Ashbel, Gera and Naaman, Ehi and Rosh, Muppim and Huppim and Ard. These are the sons of Rachel born to Jacob: fourteen lives in all.

Rachel is called **'the wife of Jacob'**, a description reserved for her and not applied to any of the other women in this genealogy.[182] It is an appositional phrase that probably indicates her favoured status in Jacob's eyes (cf. 44:27).

Benjamin has ten sons according to this register. However, in Numbers 26:38-40, three of the sons of Benjamin are missing, and two of the sons are listed as his grandsons. How are we to understand these apparent discrepancies? Hamilton says, 'The genealogy need not be pressed for historical exactness.'[183] In reality, the term **'sons'** in Numbers 26 may be used multi-generationally. And the practice of omitting names from earlier genealogies is quite common.

Benjamin's age is also at issue. How could he have so many children if he were merely a **'lad'**? (43:8). The problem is not as difficult as it appears. First, Benjamin was born before Joseph was sold into Egypt (35:16-18). Joseph went to Egypt when he was seventeen (37:2); he spent thirteen years in slavery or prison (41:46). And seven years of plenty have passed, followed by two years of famine (Gen. 45:6). Joseph is at least thirty-nine years old at this point of the story — Benjamin, therefore, is at least twenty-two years old.

46:23-25. And the sons of Dan: Hushim. And the sons of Naphtali: Jahziel and Guni and Jezer and Shillem. These are the sons of Bilhah, whom Laban gave to Rachel his daughter. And she bore these to Jacob, seven lives in all.

The final section of the registry catalogues the sons and grandsons of Bilhah, the handmaid of Rachel (29:29; 30:3). The opening entry speaks of **'the sons of Dan'**, but only one son is listed. This is nothing more than the genealogist persisting in using a genealogical formula for introducing a person's descendants (cf. Num. 26:8,42). The names and number of Naphtali's descendants are the same as in Numbers 26:48-49.

46:26-27. Every life that came from Jacob to Egypt, who came out of his loins, not including his sons' wives, were sixty-six lives. And the sons of Joseph who were born to him in Egypt were two. All the lives of the household of Jacob who came to Egypt were seventy.

These verses offer the concluding totals of the preceding genealogy of Jacob. The first figure includes all that **'came from Jacob to Egypt'**, a clause reporting the status of the people at the time of the departure from Canaan. The figures of the genealogy are as follows:

Leah	=	33 persons
Zilpah	=	16 persons
Rachel	=	14 persons
Bilhah	=	7 persons
Total	=	70 persons

The total of **'sixty-six'** lives in verse 26 does not include Judah's sons Er and Onan because they had died in the land of Canaan (46:12). And the sons of Joseph must be deducted because they are already in Egypt.

The clause, **'not including his sons' wives'**, is an example of the figure called epitrechon. It is a parenthetical addition that helps to explain Acts 7:14, which says that seventy-five persons came to Egypt with Jacob. There it is said that 'all his relatives' came with him, and this number appears to include Jacob's daughters-in-law.

The final number of **'seventy'** in verse 27 denotes the amount of people who arrived in, or were already in, Egypt. The additions are Jacob himself, the two sons of Joseph and perhaps Dinah (46:15). The number seventy is one that also symbolizes fulness or completion; in other words, Jacob's entire clan has made the journey to Egypt (see Deut. 10:22; Exod. 1:5).

Application

Authors often comment on how great and awesome was God's work to deliver Israel out of Egypt, and how he bore them on eagle's wings to the promised land of Canaan. And, indeed, that redemption is a wonderful event, and it should be celebrated. What is not often noticed is the fact that it was God who put them in Egypt in the first place. He tells Jacob in our passage not to fear because the Lord will make a great nation of Jacob in Egypt (46:3). But they have to undergo such misery and hardship in Egypt for four hundred years. Why would God, by his own decretive will, set Israel in such hard circumstances and then deliver them out of the situation?

But is that not how God often works? Why does he work this way? First, it is obviously for the benefit of his people. Bowes remarks that 'There is no saint in the Bible, of whose history we have any lengthened record, who was not called to endure trouble in some form; and very frequently the most eminent saints were most tried. Those who were called to important services, were generally trained in the school of affliction.' Secondly, and most importantly, it is so that God would be honoured as the matchless sovereign Lord of the universe. The truth is that nothing happens in heaven or on earth apart from his decretive will — they whys, the whens, the whats and the hows all proceed from his hand.

Jacob meets Joseph and settles in Goshen (Genesis 46:28 – 47:12)

Jacob, at the head of the entire clan of the Hebrews, now enters the land of Egypt. He remains in Goshen until his son Joseph comes to meet him. The Hebrews, however, do not have permission to stay in Goshen permanently. Joseph therefore sets up an audience for them before the Egyptian pharaoh.

46:28-29. And he sent Judah before him to Joseph in order to point out [the way] before him to Goshen. And they came to the land of Goshen. Then Joseph harnessed his chariot, and he went up to meet his father in Goshen. And when he appeared to him, he fell on his shoulders and wept on his shoulders for a long time.

Jacob sends Judah ahead to get directions to Goshen.[184] The verb translated **'to point out'** derives from the basic Hebrew verb meaning 'to teach / instruct / direct'.[185] The problem is that it carries no object — in our translation we have supplied **'[the way]'**. The Septuagint translates it as 'to present oneself', but that is probably based on a corruption. The important point is that Judah has been assigned this task. Earlier he had become spokesman for the brothers (see 43:3-10; 44:18-34); now Jacob appears to recognize Judah's leadership.

Joseph leaves only when he hears that his family has arrived in Egypt. And he prepares quickly: the text says that he **'harnessed his chariot'** — hardly a thing he would do himself, but it is written that way to show great haste on his part. The chariot symbolizes his high position to his father — all that was told to Jacob is true. And when they meet there are no words, only copious tears. Here is the son whom Jacob truly loves!

46:30. Then Israel said to Joseph, 'I can die at last, after I have seen your face, for you are still alive.'

Jacob finally utters some words: **'I can die at last.'** In Hebrew, the verb is a cohortative, and it is used here to express self-encouragement.[186] Joseph has been thought dead for twenty-two years, and now he has been found alive. The father's heartache has come to a good end, and now he is ready and willing to die. The son he loves is here to carry on and protect the clan.

46:31-32. Then Joseph said to his brothers and to his father's household, 'I will go up, and I will report to Pharaoh, and I will say to him, "My brothers and my father's household who were in the land of Canaan have come to me. And the men are shepherds, for they have been men of livestock. And they have brought their herds and their flocks and everything that belongs to them."'

The question of where the Hebrews will settle has not yet been answered. Joseph wants them to live in Goshen (45:10), but Pharaoh has not given his approval. In order to receive royal assent, an audience before the Egyptian king is required. Joseph, who is familiar with the ways of the royal court, instructs his family on how the audience will proceed. He shrewdly rehearses the speech that he will give to Pharaoh, and then tells his family how to respond to Pharaoh's questions (46:33-34).

Joseph's report to Pharaoh puts pressure on the monarch to make a decision. First, Asiatics are suspect in Egypt, especially so many with all their herds and other possessions — they could appear to be a threat to Egypt. So what is Pharaoh to do with such a mass of people? On the other hand, the Hebrews are Joseph's relatives, and Joseph has been loyal to the king and a deliverer of Egypt from famine. Thus the king probably wants them close, but not too close. A place like Goshen, in Joseph's mind, clearly fits the bill. But why Goshen? Gunkel says, 'The fact that he goes to such effort for Goshen can probably be explained by the fact that Goshen is on the border where it would be possible for his brothers to leave Egypt again if they want.' The passage, then, 'looks ahead to the exodus narrative. It was later possible for Israel to escape Egypt precisely because they dwelt near the border.'[187]

46:33-34. 'And when Pharaoh calls to you, and he says, "What is your occupation?", you will say, "Your servants have been men of livestock, from our youth even unto now, both we and our fathers," so that you might dwell in the land of Goshen; for every shepherd is an abomination to the Egyptians.'

When answering Pharaoh's question about their occupation, the Hebrews are to reply with one accord that they are herders of animals. This will demonstrate to the king that they are useful for nothing else and, therefore, they ought to be set apart for their rightful task. Joseph wants their separation from the Egyptians, and he understands that the Egyptians will want it as well because of the Hebrews' occupation. Shepherding was **'an abomination'**, or 'anathema', to the Egyptians. This is the same term that was used in Genesis 43:32, where we were told that Joseph did not eat bread with the Hebrews because it was 'an abomination' to the Egyptians to do so. Both customs signify racial exclusiveness on the part of the Egyptians: they did not mix with Asiatics.

Many commentators argue that this conception of hatred cannot be substantiated from Egyptian sources.[188] However, it is known that cattle-herders were despised in Egypt, and they lived in the northern marshes, separated from the common population.[189] In addition, Herodotus mentions a haughty attitude towards those who herded swine.[190] Such an attitude towards herders should not surprise us, as Redford comments that it simply 'seems to be a reflection of the age-old fear and hatred the Egyptians entertained for the *bedu* of the desert'.[191] The reality is that historically townspeople have looked down on shepherds and held them in low esteem.

47:1-2. So Joseph came and he reported to Pharaoh, and he said, 'My father and my brother and their flocks and their herds and everything that belongs to them have come from the land of Canaan; and, behold, they are in Goshen.' And from all his brothers he took five men and he presented them before Pharaoh.

Now we see a formal audience before the royal court of Egypt. Pharaoh learns of Joseph's family having arrived in Egypt from the mouth of Joseph.[192] In the original language Joseph highlights this family migration by placing the verb **'have come'** after the subjects of the verb, a common linguistic means of emphasis. This report is important because Pharaoh had previously extended an invitation for the Hebrew clan to come to Egypt (45:17-18), and now they have arrived.

Joseph has cleverly arranged that the Hebrews should be in Goshen before Pharaoh learns of it or approves it. He is subtly attempting to bring about

his clan's settlement in this area. When he tells
Pharaoh, **'They are in Goshen,'** perhaps Pharaoh
might consider that a good place for them to stay.
Joseph's intention all along has been for his family to
settle there (45:10; 46:28).

Joseph then introduces several of his brothers to
the royal Egyptian court. He selects only five of them
to participate. The text says that Joseph chose **'from
all'** his brothers; in Hebrew it literally reads: 'from
the edge / end / extremity'. This vocabulary suggests
that Joseph selects the outstanding ones, the brothers who would make a good impression.[193] The same
term is employed in 1 Kings 12:31 in which Jeroboam purposefully chooses non-Levites for the
priesthood of Israel. It is not a random selection, but,
in a manner fitting with the context of the story,
Joseph plans his way carefully.[194]

47:3-4. Then Pharaoh said to [Joseph's] brothers, 'What is
your occupation?' And they answered Pharaoh, 'Your
servants are shepherds of flocks, both we and our fathers.'
Then they said to Pharaoh, 'We have come to sojourn in the
land because there is no pasture for the flocks of your
servants because the famine is severe in the land of Canaan. And now, please, let your servants dwell in the land of
Goshen.'

Pharaoh, as sovereign of the Egyptian court, opens
the conversation with the Hebrew brothers. He asks
them a universal question of identification: 'What do
you do for a living?' This is a proper question since
Pharaoh knows little about them; he has not met
them prior to this audience. The brothers answer
Pharaoh according to the instructions of Joseph
(46:34).

The Hebrews claim that they are **'shepherds'**. In
Hebrew, that term is in the singular, and so it is
serving as a collective in order to represent a class of

people. It is not as if they have various trades among them that Pharaoh may utilize. They are shepherds, and only shepherds. This fact is confirmed by the statement that literally reads, **'also we and also our fathers'** (the word **'also'** appears twice as inclusive co-ordinators). Their trade as shepherds has been handed down the generations.

Joseph's brothers desire **'to sojourn'** in Egypt. That is a legal term signifying only temporary residence in the land. They do not want to be fully-fledged citizens. This is the fulfilment of God's promise to Abraham in Genesis 15:13: 'Know certainly that your seed will be a sojourner in a land that does not belong to them.'

The specific region of Egypt where they wish to settle is Goshen, and they boldly ask for it. Joseph's speech to Pharaoh in verse 1 had ended with the name **'Goshen'**, and now the brothers' statement concludes with the same name. The point has been clearly made to the Egyptian king.

47:5-6. Then Pharaoh spoke to Joseph, saying, 'Your father and your brothers have come to you. The land of Egypt is before you; settle your father and your brothers in the best parts of the land. They may settle in Goshen. And if you know that there are among them men of ability, then set them as overseers of my livestock.'

Pharaoh responds directly to Joseph, not to the brothers. He is acting in a regal manner, and he speaks to Joseph as the official in charge of the present situation. In addition, the king's speech is given in staccato tones; he employs asyndeton, omitting conjunctions between the various clauses. His speech is clipped as if he is giving a set of instructions.[195]

The King of Egypt's opening statement to Joseph is not intended to impart information, but rather it is

an acknowledgement of the fact. He, then, is magnanimous to the Hebrews: they may choose to live
anywhere in Egypt, even in the land of Goshen!
Joseph has thus been offered all that he had hoped
for.

Surprisingly, Pharaoh makes a final offer to Joseph: if there are **'men of ability'** among the Hebrews, then he is to choose them to be superinten-
dents of Pharaoh's cattle. It is well known from
ancient records that the pharaoh owned many herds
of cattle (some intended for his court and some for
the gods), and that there was a complex adminis-
tration associated with the livestock. Papyrus Harris
records the words of Rameses III (Twentieth Dynasty,
early twelfth century B.C.) as he extols his own
virtues in regard to serving the god Amon: 'I made for
thee herds in the South and North containing large
cattle, fowl, and small cattle by the hundred-
thousand, having overseers of cattle, scribes, overseers of the horns, inspectors, and numerous shepherds in charge of them; having cattle fodder; in
order to offer them to thy *ka* at all my feasts, that thy
heart may be satisfied with them, O ruler of gods.'[196]
The official position of 'overseer of cattle' is commonly
used in Egyptian texts.[197]

47:7-10. Then Joseph brought Jacob his father and presented him before Pharaoh. And Jacob blessed Pharaoh.
Then Pharaoh said to Jacob, 'How long have you lived?' And
Jacob answered Pharaoh, 'The days of my sojourning have
been 130 years. The days of my life have been few and
troubling. And the days of my life have not reached the days
of my fathers' sojournings.' So Jacob blessed Pharaoh, and
he went out from his presence.

The presentation of Jacob to Pharaoh is set in a
chiastic structure, as follows:

a	b
Joseph brought / presented	Jacob blessed Pharaoh
b¹	a¹
Jacob blessed Pharaoh	he went out

So at the beginning and end of the audience Jacob
'blessed' Pharaoh. This is nothing more than a
salutation on Jacob's part, and it is used in Scripture
that way both when one is arriving (1 Sam. 13:10;
2 Kings 4:29; 10:15) and leaving (Gen. 24:60; 1 Kings
8:66).[198]

When Pharaoh asks Jacob how long he has lived,
he literally says, **'How long are the days of the
years of your life?'** Jacob responds three times
using the same expression as Pharaoh: **'the days of
the years of'**. This is an example of pleonasm for the
purpose of amplification. Jacob thus equates the
days of his life with the days of his **'sojourning'**: the
latter term signifies that he has lived a transient
existence with no land ownership or settlement. In
addition, his days have been fewer than those of his
fathers: he will not live as long as Abraham (175
years — 25:7) or Isaac (180 years — 35:28). And they
have been **'troubling'**. Indeed, we may underscore
Jacob's conflicts with Esau and Laban, Rachel's
death and Joseph's supposed death, among other
problems. Jacob's statement is one of tragedy.[199]

47:11-12. So Joseph settled his father and his brothers. And
he gave them property in the best parts of the land of Egypt,
in the region of Rameses, as Pharaoh had commanded. And
Joseph supported his father and his brothers and all his
father's household with food according to the number of
children.

Joseph takes charge in providing for his family. He
first **'settled'** them in the land of Goshen — this verb
is in the Hiphil causative pattern in Hebrew. He

locates them specifically in **'the region of Rameses'** (obviously a synonym for Goshen). The name of the area stems from a city located in the region (Exod. 1:11). 'Widely accepted today is the belief that Rameses is located at Qantir (Tell ed-Dab'a), about seventeen miles south-west of Tanis. Excavations of the site in the last twenty-five years have confirmed that identification. Qantir was an important city in the eastern Nile delta during the second millennium B.C. In the Second Intermediate Period (c. 1640-1532 B.C.) the city witnessed a massive influx of foreigners, and it probably served as the capital of the Hyksos (Dynasty 15).'[200] A factory has been discovered at the site that produced decorated glazed tiles and some 'ostraca discovered in the factory bear the name of Rameses'.[201]

The famine is still under way, so Joseph supplies food for his family. The last phrase, translated, **'according to the number of children'**, is literally 'by the mouth of the children'. The expression probably means 'in full measure' — that is, he supports his family liberally with foodstuffs.[202]

Application

Joseph took great pains to ensure that his brethren settled in Goshen. Matthew Henry comments: 'He would have them to live by themselves, separate as much as might be from the Egyptians, in the land of Goshen, which lay nearest to Canaan, and which perhaps was more thinly peopled by the Egyptians, and well furnished with pastures for cattle. He desired they might live separately, that they might be in the less danger both of being infected by the vices of the Egyptians and of being insulted by the malice of the Egyptians.' Thus Joseph did not want the Hebrews to be assimilated into Egyptian culture (as he himself had been!), but rather not to lose their identity as the people of God.

Acculturation is as much a problem for the church today as it was for the church of the Old Testament. Often one can see no difference between the way people behave and think within the church from those outside it. Recent studies, for example, indicate that sexual promiscuity and adultery occur as often among church-goers as the unchurched. Christians, however, are called to be set apart and holy. God says, 'You shall be holy, for I am holy' (1 Peter 1:16). J. Wilbur Chapman, who wrote the hymn 'Jesus, What a Friend for Sinners', once said, 'Anything that dims my vision of Christ or takes away my taste for Bible study or cramps my prayer life or makes Christian work difficult is wrong for me, and I must, as a Christian, turn away from it. This simple rule may help you find a safe path for your feet along life's road.'

The famine becomes more severe (Genesis 47:13-26)

The famine that has ravaged the lands of Canaan and Egypt now increases and becomes more oppressive. The people of Egypt are forced to spend all their money, sell all their livestock and lands and, finally, sell themselves into slavery in order to obtain food. Joseph is the one who oversees the government's sale of grain to the people. It basically is a centralization of power in the royal court and, in particular, in the position of vizier, which Joseph holds. The Egyptians are glad to have food to eat, even though it means they have to relinquish much of their freedom.

47:13-15. Now there was no food in all the land because the famine was very severe. And the land of Egypt and the land of Canaan languished on account of the famine. So Joseph collected all the silver that was found in the land of Egypt and in the land of Canaan for the grain which they were purchasing. And Joseph brought the silver to Pharaoh's palace. Thus the silver from the land of Egypt and from the land of Canaan was exhausted. And all the Egyptians came to Joseph, saying, 'Give us food. Why should we die in your presence? For the silver is used up.'

The severity of the famine in the ancient Near East continues to be a major theme of the story of Joseph. It is so oppressive that both Egypt and Canaan are **'languishing'** — that verb occurs only in this passage, and it may be related to a verb meaning 'to be

wearisome' or 'tiresome'.203 The land is simply exhausted and it is full of hungry, desperate people. So
Joseph sells the people grain, as it would seem he
has been doing since the beginning of the famine (see
41:56), and he then puts the money into the treasury
of Pharaoh.

But now a problem arises: the people's money is
exhausted. And they are desperate because they are
hungry. So they appear before Joseph and demand
that he **'give'** them food; that verb is an imperative of
demand. How will Joseph respond?

It ought to be noted that **'the land of Canaan'** is
mentioned by name three times in the passage. The
repetition is intended to remind the reader that it is a
good thing that Jacob and his family left that land for
Egypt. They are now under Joseph's care during a
very trying time.

47:16-17. Then Joseph said, 'Give up your livestock, and I
will give [food] in exchange for your livestock, since [your]
silver is used up.' So they brought their livestock to Joseph,
and Joseph gave them food in exchange for the horses, and
the flocks of sheep and goats and cattle and donkeys. And
he led them through that year with food in exchange for all
their livestock.

The Egyptian people have no means to pay for food
from the government. So Joseph offers grain in
exchange for their livestock; in this manner, all
Egyptian livestock comes into the possession of
Pharaoh.204 Among the animals brought to Joseph
are **'horses'** — this is the first mention of this crea-
ture in the Bible. Interestingly, ancient Egypt is well
known for its mastery of the horse, at least from the
beginning of the Eighteenth Dynasty, and probably
much earlier.205 The Egyptians also plied their craft in
horsemanship by trading horses to western Asia.206

Even Solomon imported horses from Egypt (1 Kings 10:28-29).

The verb translated **'he led them through'** is normally used only for leading flocks of animals.[207] Here it is used of Joseph as a shepherd who is guiding the people through a dangerous and difficult period. Perhaps its use reflects the fact that Joseph's actions are not harsh or greedy, but he has the people's best interests in mind.[208]

The term **'that year'** probably refers to the third year of the famine (see 45:6).

47:18-19. When that year had ended, they came to him the following year, and they said to him, 'We will not hide from our lord that the money is gone, and the herds of cattle belong to our lord. There is nothing left for our lord except our bodies and our lands. Why should we die before your eyes — both we and our lands? Buy us and our lands in exchange for food, and we and our lands will be slaves of Pharaoh. And give [us] seed that we may live and not die, and that the land may not be devastated.'

The grain given in exchange for livestock lasts to the end of the year. Yet, in **'the following year'**, the people come to Joseph for more grain. That chronological phrase literally says 'the second year', and some have argued that it refers to the second year of the plague. But, in reality, it denotes the fourth year of the famine (see 47:17). Others believe it signifies the last year of the famine, because the Egyptians are asking for seed in the belief that the famine is at an end. Yet we know that farmers sow every year, even during times of famine.

All of their moveable possessions have been exhausted, so the people offer themselves and their lands in exchange for food. They literally propose putting themselves and their lands into bondage to Pharaoh. Yet they ask for seed because they will continue to work the land even though it will now belong to Pharaoh. This is a form of serfdom that is well known from documents of the ancient Near East.

47:20-22. So Joseph purchased all the lands of the Egyptians for Pharaoh, because the Egyptians sold their fields for the famine was hard on them. Thus the land belonged to Pharaoh. And he moved the people into cities from one end of the border of Egypt to the other. Only he did not purchase the land of the priests because the priests had an allotment from Pharaoh, and they ate their allotment that Pharaoh gave to them. Therefore they did not sell their lands.

The shift from privately owned land in Egypt to a centralized governmental ownership under Pharaoh is now related. Such centralization is known to have happened a few times in ancient Egyptian history. Von Rad says, 'The decline of free peasantry which owned its own land began in the so-called new kingdom, and only the Pharaoh was nominal owner and lord of all agricultural land.'[209] This shift began after the demise of the Hyksos in the sixteenth century B.C.[210]

Not all lands came under the rule of Pharaoh; verse 22 begins with the particle **'only'**, which is the chief exclusive conjunction in Hebrew and it introduces a sentence specifying what is excluded from the previous statement. The priestly lands are not included in the royal right of possession. The priests were supported by fixed royal endowments of food — a stipend — so they did not have to sell their lands. One Egyptian text tells us that Rameses II (thirteenth century B.C.) made an annual grant of 185,000 sacks of grain to the temples; this was in addition to the fact that the temples owned their own fields.[211]

The beginning of verse 22 is peculiar: it literally reads: **'And the people he moved them to the cities.'** This is an example of extraposition (or Latin *casus pendens*) in which a prominent word is isolated at the beginning and then followed by a sentence in which it is resumed by a pronoun.[212] It highlights the introduction of a new topic: the author has been speaking about the land; now he turns to consider the people. Here is a major population transfer. But, for what purpose? It may simply be to shift the farmers off the national lands, or to get them to work other national lands, or to bring them to the city to work on national building projects.

47:23-24. Then Joseph said to the people, 'Behold, I have purchased you and your fields today for Pharaoh; here is seed for you so that you can plant the ground. And it will be when [the crop] comes in that you shall give a fifth of it to Pharaoh. And the other four parts shall be for you as seed for the field and food for yourselves, and for your households, and for your children.'

Apparently the government does not move everyone into the cities. But it sets up a state-controlled system in which former landowners work the land and pay a 20% tax on crops produced. The practice is a form of tenant farming or share-cropping. The amount of tax is not excessive according to ancient Near-Eastern standards. In fact, Joseph is merely continuing the practice he had begun during the seven years of harvest (41:34). In addition, it was a common practice in Egypt to impose a tax on the harvest.[213]

The term translated **'here'** is found only in this verse and in Ezekiel 16:43. Its meaning is uncertain, although a Mishnaic analogue means 'behold'.[214] It seems to be an exclamatory particle to strengthen the idea conveyed by the verb. It would then be in parallel with the **'behold'** earlier in the sentence.

The phrase, **'for your children'**, perhaps harks back to verse 12, which also mentions the feeding of children. There it had the sense of 'in full measure', meaning that Joseph will supply enough food for his family. It probably bears a similar sense in the present passage.

47:25-26. And they answered, 'You have saved our lives! May we find favour in the eyes of our lord. And we will be slaves to Pharaoh.' So Joseph established it as a statute, even to this day, over the land of Egypt that a fifth belongs to Pharaoh. Only the land of the priests alone did not belong to Pharaoh.

The severity of the famine has caused the people of Egypt to be desensitized to the consequences of their plight. They have lost almost everything to the royal government — all their money, their lands and their freedom — yet they are grateful to Joseph! The Egyptians' gratitude ought to be seen in contrast to their fears in verses 15 and 19. Joseph is thus hailed as the deliverer of Egypt. It is ironic that Moses is later acclaimed as the deliverer of Israel because he frees his people from bondage.

The phrase, **'even to this day'** is an editorial comment by Moses. He is saying that in his time, Egypt was still operating by royal ownership of all land, except for the land owned by the priesthood. (See comments on verses 20-22, in which such a condition is shown to have been common throughout the history of Egypt.)

The declaration, **'You have saved our lives ... we will be slaves to Pharaoh,'** is the language of a legal formula in the ancient Near East. It has Mesopotamian parallels dealing with persons selling themselves due to famine.[215]

Application

It may be difficult to understand why the Holy Spirit preserved this story for the church. What is the purpose and significance of Joseph's agrarian policy? In Genesis 15:13-14, God made the following promise to Abram: 'Know certainly that your seed will be a sojourner in a land that does not belong to them; and they will be enslaved and afflicted for four hundred years. But, also, the nation which they serve I will judge. And afterwards they will come out with great possessions.' Joseph is a tool of God in the fulfilment of this promise. As Ron comments, 'Genesis 47:13-27 actually describes an important step in the realization of God's words to Abraham at the Covenant of Parts, and the future of the children of Israel. Joseph was acting as the agent of God in more ways than even he was able to fathom.'[216] The fact that Joseph protects his family and feeds them allows them to survive. The survival of the seed of the woman is such a central story in the book of Genesis that we should not be surprised to see it here as well.

The blessing of Ephraim and Manasseh (Genesis 47:27 – 48:22)

Genesis 48 is normally analysed as a unit by itself. But, in company with Seebass, I would argue that the final verses of Genesis 47 belong to that section.[217] First, verses 27-28 serve as a transition from what has gone before — that is, the arrival in the land of Egypt. Now we see Jacob near the end of his life, and he is about to bless Joseph and his two sons. That blessing concludes at the end of chapter 48.

The central scene of the passage is the formal adoption of the two sons of Joseph, Ephraim and Manasseh, as sons of Jacob. That event explains why these two and their descendants come to be listed among the twelve tribes of Israel. But, more than that, it shows that Joseph will receive a double portion of Jacob's inheritance. Finally, Jacob's act clearly honours the memory of his wife Rachel (see 48:7).[218]

47:27-28. So Israel settled in the land of Egypt, in the land of Goshen. And they took possession of property in it, and they were fruitful and they multiplied greatly. And Jacob lived in the land of Egypt seventeen years. So the days of Jacob's life were 147 years.

The nature of these two verses as a summary statement belies the fact that they contain three rather important themes of the Joseph story. First, in the opening two sentences there is a change in the verbal forms: the first verb, **'settled'**, is in the singular, whereas the next three verbs are all in the plural. Yet they all have the same subject — **'Israel'**. The author certainly intended this shift in order to demonstrate the change that is now taking place from the individual Israel / Jacob to a people named Israel.[219]

Secondly, in Genesis 35:11-12, God had told Jacob to 'be fruitful' and 'multiply', and had promised that God would give him a land to possess. Here in Egypt, Jacob and his descendants are fulfilling that mandate; yet the reader knows that Egypt is not the land that is to be given to Israel as a possession (15:18; 35:12). Thus we anticipate that God has yet to act to fulfil that promise.

Finally, the text says that Jacob lives seventeen more years in Egypt, although he did not expect to live much longer after his arrival (46:30). **'Seventeen years'** is the length of time that Joseph had lived in Canaan with his father prior to being sold into slavery (37:2). This period of time, therefore, serves as an *inclusio* for the Joseph story — it borders both ends of the account.

47:29-31. When the days of Israel drew near to death, he called for his son Joseph, and he said to him, 'If, indeed, I have found favour in your eyes, [then] put your hand beneath my thigh, and deal with me in covenant loyalty and in truth. Do not bury me in Egypt. But when I lie down with my fathers then you shall carry me out of Egypt, and [you shall] bury me in their burial place.' And he answered, 'I will do as you have spoken.' Then he said, 'Swear to me.' And he swore to him. Then Israel bowed on the top of [his] staff.

As his death approaches, Jacob asks Joseph to make a promise that will be hard to keep — he demands that Joseph swear to take his corpse back to Canaan for burial in the family tomb in Hebron. Because of the difficulty involved, Jacob places Joseph under oath. The sign of the pledge is that Joseph is to put

his **'hand beneath'** the **'thigh'** of Jacob; the thigh
here ought to be equated with the genital organ, a
fact that highlights the seriousness of the act. (The
idiom is discussed in detail in the commentary on
24:2 — vol. 1, p.412).

Jacob's final action is hard to understand. The
Masoretic Text renders the phrase by saying, 'Israel
bowed at the head of the bed' — what that signifies is
uncertain. The consonants of the word for **'bed'** can
also mean 'staff / rod'; thus a simple repointing of
the term (following the Septuagint and Syriac versions) denotes something different. But what is the
significance of 'bowing on the top of his staff'? The
staff was a symbol of authority and power in the
ancient Near East.[220] Thus this may be an act of
submission on Jacob's part — not necessarily to
Joseph, but rather to God, who is the one who ultimately will see that the covenant is kept.

48:1-2. And it came to pass after these things that it was said
to Joseph, 'Behold, your father is sick.' So he took his two
sons, Manasseh and Ephraim, with him. Then it was reported to Jacob, and it was said, 'Behold, your son Joseph
has come to you.' So Israel strengthened himself and he sat
up in the bed.

The time reference, **'after these things'**, clearly
refers back to Genesis 47:28. The story now jumps to
the end of Jacob's seventeen years in Egypt. He is at
the end of the line of life, and death is soon to occur.
Jacob's impending death is anticipated as coming
quickly — the particle **'behold'** is used twice in this
passage, and it reflects vivid immediacy.[221]

The text is focusing here on the imminent death of
Jacob. That is confirmed by the use of three indefinite personal subjects: **'it was said'** (twice) and **'it
was reported'**. The names and positions of the
speakers are not given; they are superfluous to the

main point of the story. They are minor supporting
actors in a larger unfolding drama.

48:3-4. Then Jacob said to Joseph, 'El Shaddai appeared to
me in Luz in the land of Canaan, and he blessed me. And
he said to me, "Behold, I will make you fruitful, and I will
multiply you, and I will make you an assembly of people,
and I will give this land to your seed after you as an eternal
possession."'

Now Jacob recounts to his son Joseph what was
perhaps the most important event of his entire life:
the appearance of God to him in a dream at Bethel
(28:10-22). There at Bethel (originally called **'Luz'**)
God confirmed that Jacob was the true heir of the
promises to Abraham. God had promised him that
his descendants would be many, and that they would
inherit the land of Canaan. The latter will be **'an
eternal possession'** — this phrase should be contrasted with Genesis 47:11 and 27, in which the land
of Egypt is Israel's immediate possession. But that
will not last; the true inheritance is in Canaan.

48:5-6. 'And now, your two sons who were born to you in the
land of Egypt before I came to you to Egypt, they belong to
me. Ephraim and Manasseh are like Reuben and Simeon:
they will be mine. And the ones born to you after them, they
will be yours. They will be called by the name of their brothers in their inheritance.'

Now we witness the act of a formal adoption. Here
Jacob adopts two grandchildren, the sons of Joseph,
to bestow on them the status of his two eldest children, Reuben and Simeon. In the Hebrew the language is emphatic, thus Jacob literally says, **'To me
they belong!'** Ephraim and Manasseh are thus
elevated to the status of full membership in the tribal
league. As an aside, it ought to be noted that

Ephraim, the younger son, is mentioned before the first-born, Manasseh (see 41:51). This is a reversal of the order in verse 1 of the chapter: it is anticipatory of what is about to happen.

The children born to Joseph after Ephraim and Manasseh will not receive their own tribal allotments. Rather, they will share in the inheritance of their two eldest brothers: that is what is meant by the last sentence of the passage. These children, however, are mentioned nowhere else in the Bible.

48:7. 'And when I came from Paddan, Rachel died, to my sorrow, in the land of Canaan on the way, yet some distance to go to Ephrath. And I buried her there on the way to Ephrath, that is, Bethlehem.'

Jacob now mentions the death and burial of Rachel. How does this statement relate to what has gone before or after? It does not appear to fit the flow of Jacob's speech. Some commentators believe that Jacob inserts it here as further encouragement to Joseph to bury him in Canaan in the cave of Machpelah. Jacob had not done that for Rachel, his beloved wife and Joseph's mother, and apparently he now regrets it. Perhaps there is some value to this interpretation, although it still seems to make Jacob's narrative choppy and fragmented.

It may be that Jacob includes it because it reflects the chronology and structure of the events as recorded in Genesis 35:9-20.[222] There Jacob had his vision at Luz / Bethel (vv. 9-15), and it is immediately followed by the death and burial of Rachel (vv. 16-20). The parallel looks like this:

	Genesis 35			Genesis 48
vv. 9-15	Vision at Luz	vv. 3-4	Vision at Luz
vv. 16-20	Death of Rachel	v. 7	Death of Rachel

Jacob, therefore, views the events as occurring one after the other, and so he includes them in his re-telling in Genesis 48.

48:8-11. **Then Israel saw the sons of Joseph, and he said, 'Who are these?' And Joseph answered his father, 'They are my sons, whom God has given to me in this place.' And he said, 'Bring them to me that I might bless them.' Now the eyes of Israel were heavy because of age; he was not able to see. And he brought them to him, and he kissed them and he embraced them. Then Israel said to Joseph, 'I did not expect to see your face. But, behold, God has also caused me to see your seed.'**

It is not that Jacob does not know his grandsons, but he is having difficulty recognizing them due to poor vision. The text literally says that he has **'heavy'**, or 'weighty', eyes: that adjective is used of other sense organs in Scripture (Exod. 4:10; Isa. 59:1) to indicate dullness. Here it bears the idea of dimness. This problem is further enhanced by the statement, **'he was not able to see'** — here a negative with an appositional clause accentuates the idea of opposi-tion. He simply cannot see very well.

The motif of a blind patriarch giving a blessing to his descendants is reminiscent of Genesis 27:1-45. Jacob's own father Isaac was in this condition, and thus Jacob was able to fool him so that he could steal the blessing of the first-born. In the present episode, once again the first-born will not receive the blessing — but this time it is the patriarch who causes the unexpected to occur.[223]

At the close of Jacob's speech, he acknowledges and praises God for bringing his life to such a fine conclusion. It has exceeded anything he had expected or hoped for. It is a recognition of God as the one who turned his sorrow into joy!

48:12-14. Then Joseph took them from off his knees, and he bowed with his face to the ground. So Joseph took the two of them, Ephraim with his right hand at Israel's left side and Manasseh with his left hand at Israel's right side. And he brought [them] near to him. And Israel stretched out his right hand and set it on the head of Ephraim, although he was the younger, and his left hand on the head of Manasseh, crossing his hands, although Manasseh was the first-born.

The act of having Ephraim and Manasseh on Jacob's knees is a formal, legal rite of adoption. (For a discussion of this practice, see the commentary on Genesis 30:3 and 50:23.) Jacob is simply taking them as his own. Joseph responds to this solemn ceremony with a deep and profound reverence: he bows down before his father.

A scene of blessing is about to occur. The Hebrews believed that a person in authority could bestow an irrevocable blessing on another. Joseph understands the custom, so he organizes the event so that his first-born, Manasseh, should receive the blessing conferred by Jacob's right hand. The right hand in Hebrew belief is symbolic of power, pre-eminence and strength (see Exod. 15:6; Ps. 98:1). The one receiving blessing from that hand gets a superior blessing.

Jacob, however, does something unexpected. He bestows the greater blessing on the younger son by **'crossing his hands'**. The latter is a verbal circumstantial clause the primary purpose of which is to clarify what is happening. And it is clear: Jacob blesses Ephraim above Manasseh.

48:15-16. Then he blessed Joseph, and he said:
  'May the God with whom my fathers, Abraham and
    Isaac, walked before him;
  The God who has been my shepherd ever since I had
    being to this day;
  The Angel who has redeemed me from all evil —

> May he bless the young men.
> And may my name be called on them, and the name
>   of my fathers, Abraham and Isaac.
> And may they multiply greatly on the earth.'

The blessing of Jacob on Ephraim and Manasseh is said to be given to Joseph. Some critics argue that the phrase 'sons of' has dropped out of the text (following the Vulgate), and others say the name **'Joseph'** is an error and that it should really read 'them' (following the Septuagint).[224] In reality, there is no need of such gymnastics: Joseph is simply being blessed through and in his offspring.

The content of the blessing begins with a tripartite invocation. A threefold address to God is not uncommon in the Bible (e.g. Ps. 50:1; see especially Num. 6:24-26). The number three in such instances symbolizes completeness, power and effectiveness (cf. Isa. 6:3). The first line of the blessing underscores the historical tie between God and the Hebrews. The second line of the invocation indicates a more immediate presence — the fact that God has been with Jacob and his family ever since Jacob's birth (the clause **'since I had being'** is rare, but see its use in Num. 22:30). And, finally, Jacob invokes the name of God as an **'Angel'** who delivered him from evil. This is clearly the Angel of Yahweh who is one and the same as Yahweh himself (see 16:7-8; Exod. 3:2; Judg. 13:17-22). His statement here highlights the work of redemption of God through the Angel of Yahweh: certainly this is a foreshadowing of the work of the Messiah, Jesus Christ!

The blessing on Ephraim and Manasseh is in two parts. First, Jacob pronounces that his name (Israel) and the names of Abraham and Isaac shall **'be called on them'**. The idea is that they should always be a part of the people of Israel. Although they have an Egyptian mother, they are to be of the covenanted people. And, secondly, Jacob bestows the blessing of a great posterity on them; Numbers 1:32-35 indicates that during the wilderness wanderings, these two tribes together numbered 72,700 adult males.

48:17-18. When Joseph saw that his father put his right hand on the head of Ephraim it was troubling in his eyes. So he grasped his father's hand to move it from the head of Ephraim to the head of Manasseh. And Joseph said to his father, 'Not so, my father, for this one is the first-born. Set your right hand on his head.'

Obviously Joseph believes that because Jacob has such poor sight he lays his right hand on the wrong son. Such an act goes against the customs of primogeniture in which the first-born should receive the blessing. Jacob's act is **'troubling'** to Joseph; this verb is strong in Hebrew, normally carrying the idea of something that is evil or bad.[225] Jacob's placement of his hand essentially bestows the rights of the first-born on Ephraim.

48:19-20. But his father refused, and he said, 'I know, my son, I know. He also will become a people, and he also will become great. However, his youngest brother will become greater than he, and his seed will become a multitude of nations.' Then he blessed them on that day, saying,
'In you Israel will pronounce a blessing, saying,
"May God make you like Ephraim and like Manasseh."'

Jacob answers his son with the emphatic **'I know … I know'**. Joseph thinks that his father is blind, but, in reality, Jacob sees into the future with great clarity. He sees that Manasseh will become a great people, but Ephraim an even greater one. Ephraim will evolve into **'a multitude of nations'** — this term bears the idea of 'a quantity sufficient for many nations'.[226] It is similar to the promise God gave to

Jacob in Genesis 35:11; Jacob now makes a similar promise to Ephraim. Indeed, Ephraim over the years multiplies greatly as a tribe (Num. 1:33), and takes on a leadership role in the northern tribes of Israel.[227]

Jacob's prescient view is seen in the benediction he gives. He sees **'Israel'** as a nation pronouncing a blessing on Ephraim and Manasseh. The content is reminiscent of Ruth 4:11-12, in which it is said, 'May your family be like that of Perez.' It is a great honour to receive such an accolade. Significantly, the name of Ephraim appears before that of Manasseh in the benediction. That fact seals their places in the history of the tribes of Israel.

48:21-22. Then Israel said to Joseph, 'I am about to die, but God is with you and he will bring you to the land of your fathers. And I give to you Shechem, as one over your brothers, which I took from the hand of the Amorites with my sword and my bow.'

Now at the point of death, Jacob gives a bequest to Joseph. The first part of the endowment is for all the people of Israel: the two pronouns **'you'** in verse 21 are plural, thereby signifying many more than just Joseph. It is the assurance of a future return to the land of Canaan. Here is a promise of an exodus in very broad and generic terms.

The second gift is for Joseph alone — the singular pronouns **'you'** and **'yours'** are used in verse 22. The exact nature of the bequest is a matter of dispute. The Hebrew term used of the gift literally means 'shoulder'.[228] Some have argued that it refers to a shoulder or slope of land in Canaan (see NIV), although that would be a unique usage of the word. Also without philological support is the rendition 'one portion' (see NASB), although early versions such as the Vulgate and the Targums read it that way.[229] The word in Hebrew is *sheꞎkem*, which is also the name for

the city of Shechem. That city has played an important role in the lives of the patriarchs. It was the first
place that Abram visited in the land of Canaan
(12:6). Jacob himself had settled in the city, and had
purchased a plot of land there (33:18-19). The sons
of Jacob had looted Shechem, and taken many of the
inhabitants as prisoners (34:1-31). These brothers
apparently often pastured their flocks in the region of
Shechem (37:12-13).

The gift of the city of Shechem to Joseph came to
pass: within the tribal boundaries of Israel, it sits
near the border of two tribes — Ephraim and
Manasseh, the two sons of Joseph (Josh. 17:7). In
fact, Joseph himself has his final resting-place in
Shechem (Josh. 24:32).

Application

The promise that the Hebrews would one day return to the land
of their fathers, and that it would be an eternal possession for
them, is a central and significant one in the present story — and
in the whole of the book of Genesis, for that matter. Yes, the
Hebrews were able to take possession of some property and
land in Egypt, but that was not the promised land — they were
not to settle down there and think that it was! The Hebrews were
to understand that they were aliens and sojourners in a foreign
land (see, especially, Acts 7:6; Heb. 11:13).

The Scriptures teach that the church today is in a similar
situation. Christians are merely pilgrims on this earth (see
1 Peter 2:11, in which Peter calls believers 'aliens and strangers'). The world is not our true inheritance or home. Something
greater awaits us! As the apostle Peter so wonderfully announces, 'Blessed be the God and Father of our Lord Jesus
Christ, who according to his great mercy has caused us to be
born again to a living hope through the resurrection of Jesus
Christ from the dead, to obtain an inheritance which is imperishable

and undefiled and will not fade away, reserved in heaven for you' (1 Peter 1:3-4).

So let us not build mansions on the earth as if this were our permanent residence. Let us live in tents until we are called to the great mansion that God has prepared for his people for eternity.

Jacob blesses his sons
(Genesis 49:1-28)

Many, if not a majority of biblical scholars today, believe that this chapter has no literary unity, but is just a collection of sayings brought together by a later redactor.[230] They deny that it has any historical context in the life of Jacob, but claim that it was merely a piece inserted later, probably for political reasons. Westermann, for example, says these sayings were added at a time when Israel was attempting to organize itself into one, unified nation, and this chapter was collated in order to substantiate that one nation.[231] In short, critical scholars understand Genesis 49 as political propaganda written late in the history of Israel.

The traditional perspective, which I hold, argues that Genesis 49 is a series of blessings given by Jacob to his sons just prior to his death. They are prophetic: the character of each son of Jacob finds an outgrowth in the future existence of the twelve tribes of Israel. In addition, the blessings are clear predictions of the environment in which the various tribes will live when they settle in the land of Canaan.

49:1-2. Then Jacob called for his sons, and he said, 'Gather together so that I might tell you that which will happen to you in later days:

Assemble yourselves and listen, O sons of Jacob;
And listen to Israel your father.'

As with much poetical literature of the Old Testament, this poem opens with a superscription (see
many of the psalms). The title is verse 1, in which the
speaker is identified and the basic thrust of the
poem's purpose is given. It is a summons on the part
of Jacob to his sons in order to tell them what will
happen to them **'in later days'**. This expression is
common in the prophetic literature to signify the end
times. In the Pentateuch, however, it rarely has that
meaning; rather it denotes days that will occur in the
distant future (see Deut. 4:30; 31:29).

Verse 2 serves as the introduction to the poem, and
it is part of the poem. The two lines are in parallel:

a	b
Assemble your-selves and listen	O sons of Jacob

	b¹	c¹
	and listen	to Israel your father

The 'a' element of the first line is assumed to continue in the second line. Such a repetition is used to
drive home a point: the Hebrews are to listen closely
to their father's words.

49:3-4.
'Reuben, you are my first-born,
my strength and the beginning of my vigour,
pre-eminent in dignity and pre-eminent in power.
Uncontrollable as the waters, you will not have pre-
     eminence,
because you went up on your father's bed,
then you defiled [it].
He went up [on] my couch!'

As is customary, Jacob deals first with his first-born,
Reuben.[232] The opening verse indicates what Reuben

should have been in the family, that is, **'pre-eminent'**. However, he has merely caused Jacob pain — it should be noted that the Hebrew word for **'vigour'** has a homonym meaning 'pain' or 'suffering'.[233] That homonym was part of the name that Rachel originally gave to Benjamin (see commentary on 35:18). Jacob uses it here as a play on words to highlight the fact that Reuben has really caused him much pain.

The second verse relates what Reuben had done: he had slept with Jacob's concubine Bilhah (see 35:22). This whole verse is exclamatory. For instance, the last line switches to the third person as an emphatic construction. Jacob simply cannot believe what his eldest son has done. Reuben's sexual violation now becomes his lasting legacy (see 1 Chr. 5:1). The descendants of Reuben eventually settle the area east of the Dead Sea in Transjordan, and there they fade from history without making any significant impact on the history of the nation of Israel.[234]

49:5-7.
'Simeon and Levi are brothers,
their swords are implements of violence.
Do not let my soul enter their council,
do not let my being join their assembly,
for in their anger they killed mankind,
and in their own will they hamstrung oxen.
Cursed is their anger because it is strong
and their fury because it is harsh!
I will divide them among Jacob,
and I will scatter them among Israel.'

A severe indictment is now handed down from Jacob to his two sons, Simeon and Levi. They are the only two sons dealt with at the same time. The reason for this is the occasion in Genesis 34 when they acted together in carrying out blood-vengeance on the

Shechemites in response to the violation of Dinah.[235]
Jacob uses the word **'cursed'** in his judgement: this
is a very strong negative word in Hebrew, the one
that has been used in Genesis to censure the serpent
(3:14), Cain (4:11) and Canaan (9:25).

Jacob wants no part in these two sons. He says he
does not want his **'soul'** or his **'being'** to be involved
with them in any way. The Hebrew word translated
as **'being'** literally means 'weight', 'heaviness' or
'glory'. It has a qualitative application in Scripture
which signifies a moral quality that primarily defines
a person (see Exod. 33:18). In other words, Jacob
refuses to have the very core and essence of his being
in league with these two scoundrels.

The main consequence of their deed is that they
will be scattered among the other tribes of Israel.
Neither will receive an allotment or parcel of land
that will last. Thus they will be refused one of the
major covenant blessings promised by God to the
patriarchs (see 15:18-20). And here, in the last two
lines of the passage, Jacob speaks as if he were God
— this is prophetic, Jacob speaking on God's behalf.
The tribe of Simeon is the smallest tribe in the census of Israel during the wilderness wanderings (Num.
26:12-14). And they are soon swallowed up by the
tribe of Judah (Josh. 19:1). The Levites, of course,
receive no land inheritance (Josh. 18:7). Yet God
redeems the Levites and calls them to serve the
cultus of Israel for 'The priesthood of Yahweh is their
inheritance' (Josh. 18:7). It is ironic that God would
take such a violent and warlike tribal leader and then
turn his descendants into the priestly tribe!

49:8-12.
'You, Judah: your brothers will praise you;
your hand will be on the neck of your enemies;
the sons of your father will bow down to you.
Judah is a lion's cub;

you ascend to the prey, my son;
he crouches, he lies down like a lion;
like a lion who can rouse him?
The sceptre will not depart from Judah,
or the ruler's staff from between his feet,
until Shiloh comes
and the obedience of the peoples belongs to him.
He tethers his donkey to the vine,
and to the branch the colt.
He washes his garment in the wine,
and his robes in the blood of grapes.
His eyes are darker than wine,
and his teeth are whiter than milk.'

Jacob now turns to deal with his son Judah. The judgement here contrasts sharply with what has gone before: the first three sons received negative reports, but now Judah is given positive promises. The first element of the blessing is that the brothers of **'Judah ... will praise'** him. Here is a clear word-play involving the verb 'to praise'. When Judah was born, Leah named him 'This time I will praise Yahweh' (29:35 — that is the meaning of the name 'Judah'). Not only will Judah be praised, but his hand will be on the neck of his enemies; this is a Hebrew idiom signifying authority, dominion and subjugation (Josh. 10:24). In this manner, Jacob gives Judah the position of honour among his sons.

In verse 9 Jacob employs a simile to describe Judah. His son is like a lion: he is strong and power-ful. Who dare wake him? This figure is obviously Messianic; as Sarna states, 'Under the influence of this verse the "lion of Judah" became a favourite motif in Jewish art and acquired messianic expect-ations.'[236] In Revelation 5, John relates an incident regarding the one worthy of opening the book with seven seals. One of the elders then says to John, 'Stop weeping; behold, the Lion that is from the tribe of Judah, the Root of David, has overcome so as to open the book and its seven seals' (Rev. 5:5). The lion of Judah in Genesis 49 is a shadow of the coming one, Christ Jesus.

Verse 10 begins with an incomplete synonymous parallelism, as follows:

a	b	c
It will not depart	the sceptre	from Judah
	b¹	c¹
	nor the ruler's staff	from between his feet

This parallelism highlights the official mark and symbol of authority throughout the ancient Near East — the rod or staff.[237] This dominance will continue **'until'** Shiloh comes: that word in Hebrew is actually an adverbial clause, and Gesenius points out that 'Clauses such as this sometimes express a limit which is not absolute (terminating the preceding action), but only relative, beyond which the action or state described in the principal clause still continues.'[238]

The meaning of **'Shiloh'** is a matter of great dispute. Perhaps it is a proper noun (a city in ancient Israel had that name), although the sense of the verse would then be uncertain. Another possibility is to translate it as 'he whose it is', although a few changes of consonants and vowels are necessary to meet that translation.[239] The manuscript evidence strongly confirms that the reading of the Masoretic Text is the correct one. Another option is to separate the term into two words, which would then mean 'tribute to him' — thus the entire clause would read: 'until tribute shall come to him'.[240] There are difficulties with all three interpretations, and so the meaning remains an enigma.[241]

Verse 11 is loaded with hyperbolic language. For instance, the figure in which Judah is depicted as washing his garments and robes in wine obviously reflects a great degree of abundance for his tribe. In other words, there is so much wine in Judah that the people can even wash their clothes in it! Some have attempted to draw a Messianic parallel with this verse — for example, with the triumphal entry.[242] Such parallels seem to be stretching the meaning of the passage.

The element of hyperbole continues into the last verse. The contrast of **'darker'** / **'whiter'** is a merism. The abundance enjoyed by Judah will simply be comprehensive and complete.

49:13.
'Zebulun will dwell by the seashore,
and he will be a haven for ships;
and his border will be near Sidon.'

One would expect to read now the blessing upon Dan since he is the fifth son of Jacob (30:6). Yet the chronology here is not according to birth but according to the birth mother: the first six sons of Jacob described in the poem are children of Leah, the first wife (see 35:23). But even allowing for that order, a problem remains: Issachar, who is dealt with in verses 14-15, is older than Zebulun and by right ought to appear first. Moses similarly blesses Zebulun before Issachar in Deuteronomy 33:18. The reason for this switch is unknown.

The location of Zebulun in the tribal allotment is also a problem. Although Jacob proclaims that Zebulun will live by the seashore, Zebulun's inheritance contains no shoreline (Josh. 19:10-16). This may be explained by the fact that the Phoenicians stand between Zebulun and the sea, and perhaps Zebulun carries on maritime trade *through* the

Phoenicians. In addition, the border of Zebulun is not **'near'** the city of Sidon. Yet the term **'Sidon'** is used in the Scriptures to refer to all the land of Phoenicia (Isa. 23:4; Ezek. 28:22), and Zebulun's land does abut Phoenicia.

49:14-15.
'Issachar is a strong ass,
lying down between the sheepfolds.
And he saw a resting-place that was good,
and that the land was pleasant.
And he will bend his shoulder for the load,
and he will become a slave of forced labour.'

Issachar is a **'strong ass'**; he is powerful and mighty, one who could get his way. However, he prefers **'lying down'** in the **'sheepfolds'** — the latter term is found elsewhere only in Judges 5:16, where it is also used with regard to Issachar. The point signifies that Issachar is strong but indifferent and lazy. His main aim appears to be to find a good resting-place and a land that is pleasant. Indeed, Issachar's tribal allotment is the lush, fertile land of Lower Galilee (Josh. 19:17-23).

Issachar's apathy will result in the tribe's slavery to the Canaanites.[243] They become vassals to the peoples of the land — their oppression will be so severe that it is described as **'forced labour'**, a term used of Israel's servitude in Egypt (Exod. 1:11).

49:16-18.
'Dan will judge his people
as one of the tribes of Israel.
Dan will be a serpent on the way,
a viper on the path.
The one biting horse's heels
so that its rider will fall backwards.
For your salvation I wait, O Yahweh.'

There are two parts to the blessing Jacob gives to
Dan. The first, in verse 16, begins with a pun: the
name **'Dan'** means 'judge'; thus he will live up to his
name (see commentary on 30:6). Judging is a good
activity, and it bears the sense of helping to achieve
justice. The point of the opening line, then, is that
Dan will remain independent and the Danites will
care for their own people. Dan will be **'as one of the
tribes of Israel'** — even though he is the son of a
concubine (Bilhah), Dan will have equal status in the
tribal hierarchy.

Jacob resorts to metaphor to make his second
point. It may signify that, although Dan is a small
tribe (see Judg. 18:11), through means of guerrilla
warfare they will overcome their enemies. It may also
indicate that in conflict the tribe will be as cunning
as a viper.

At first glance, the final line of praise to Yahweh
appears out of place. Such an invocation would seem
more appropriate at the end of all the blessings. Yet
it fits here in the following sense: the Danites may
conquer their enemies through guile and subtlety,
but true deliverance only comes from the hand of
Yahweh! One tribe may boast of its military exploits,
but the reality is that victory only comes from the
Lord!

49:19.
'Gad: a raiding band will raid him;
but he will raid [at] their heels.'

This brief blessing is constructed on a word-play: the
name **'Gad'** in Hebrew sounds like the noun **'raiding
band'** and the verb **'raid'** (used twice). His name as
originally given means 'good fortune /luck' (see
30:11). Yet he will be attacked by a marauding band.
This probably refers to the settlement when Gad
takes possession of land east of the Jordan, and they

are constantly under attack from their neighbours.
But Gad will indeed fight back: according to later
texts the Gadites are proven warriors (see, for example,
1 Chr. 12:8-14).

49:20.
'From Asher: his food will be rich,
and he will provide royal delicacies.'

Jacob's prophecy for the tribe of Asher certainly
comes true when the people settle in Canaan (Josh.
19:24-31). Asher's allotment is in the western Galilee
hill-country, an area famed for its lushness and
fertility (cf. Deut. 33:24-25).[244] In fact, the produce of
Asher will be so fine that the tribe will provide **'delicacies'** for the royal court in Jerusalem. That term in
Hebrew refers to luxurious and delightful things (see
2 Sam. 1:24), especially food that gives pleasure
(Lam. 4:5). Thus the descendants of Asher will live up
to their forebear's name, which means 'the happy
one' (see commentary on 30:13).

49:21.
'Naphtali: a hind let loose,
giving [birth] to beautiful offspring.'

The metaphor Jacob uses to describe Naphtali has
been variously interpreted. Its meaning depends on
the lexical understanding of the two words translated
as **'a hind'** and **'offspring'**. The Septuagint has
determined that the metaphor is an image taken
from forestry, rather than from animal husbandry, so
the translators render the first term as 'terebinth'
and the second as 'tops / crests'.[245] So it would read
something like: 'Naphtali: a tree stretched out, providing beautiful tops [of the trees].' This translation is
possible only when both of the Hebrew words are
pointed differently from the prevailing Masoretic Text

reading. I lean towards an animal metaphor because of the predominance of such imagery throughout the entire blessing: Judah is described as lion's cub, Issachar as a strong ass and Dan as a serpent.[246]

Throughout the Bible the **'hind'** is a symbol of one who is sure-footed (Ps. 18:33; Hab. 3:19). It appears to denote that Naphtali as a tribe will be secure, and they will produce beautiful children (see Deut. 33:23).

49:22.
'Joseph is a fruitful vine,
a fruitful vine near a spring,
whose branches climb over a wall.'

These opening lines of the blessing on Joseph relate the prosperity that Joseph has enjoyed while in Egypt. The term **'a fruitful vine'** is often used in the Bible to signify great productivity and fruitfulness (see Ps. 128:3; Ezek. 19:10). The fact that the vine is planted next to water and its branches are creeping over a wall also underscores the idea of lushness and success. Some scholars, on the basis of on a cognate word in Ugaritic, think the reading should be 'cow' or 'heifer'.[247] While an animal metaphor would be in keeping with the extended use of such imagery in the passage as a whole, that reading makes the present verse all but incomprehensible.

H. Stevenson has made a proposal that is worthy of consideration. He says that the Hebrew word for **'wall'** 'can either be a noun meaning "wall" or a proper noun indicating a location called "Shur"... the location south-west of Palestine on the eastern border of Egypt. Shur often refers to the "wall" or line of fortresses built by Egyptian kings across the isthmus of Suez.[248] There may be an intentional play on words here indicating that Joseph was a fruitful vine behind the "wall" between Egypt and Canaan. Even so, his branches have reached over the wall of adversity in order to bear fruit back in Canaan for his family.'[249]

49:23-24.
'And the archers showed bitterness towards him,
and they shot and they assaulted him.
But his bow remained fixed,
and his arms were agile.
Because of the hands of the Mighty One of Jacob,
because there is the Shepherd, the Stone of Israel.'

Joseph's life is now compared to a hostile conflict between enemy archers. The identity of the archers is disputed by scholars. Perhaps they symbolize foes from Joseph's past, including his brothers and Potiphar's wife. Or, maybe, the imagery refers to the future existence of the tribes of Ephraim and Manasseh, the sons of Joseph: they certainly come under great attacks as part of the nation of Israel. Against such odds, Joseph remains strong, firm and **'agile'** — the latter term appears elsewhere only in 2 Samuel 6:16, in which David leaps and dances before the ark of the covenant. Thus Joseph withstands the assaults of his foes.

But what is the source of Joseph's strength? The last two lines of the passage tell us that he does not stand in his own power, but it is the hands of Yahweh that sustain him. This truth is confirmed by a chiastic construction in lines 4-5, as follows:

a	b
they were agile	the arms of his hands (literal)
b¹	a¹
because of the hands	of the Mighty One of Jacob

Joseph's agility and success simply come from the
hands of Yahweh. And this God who is with Joseph
is the God who is with Jacob. Jacob calls him the
'Shepherd'; this calls to mind Jacob's earlier blessing
of Joseph when he had proclaimed the name of
Yahweh as 'the God who has been my Shepherd'
(48:15). In addition, the naming of Yahweh as the
'Stone of Israel' is to remind his hearers of the
episode in Genesis 28:18-22 where Jacob set up a
pillar of stone because of his meeting with God. Both
Jacob and Joseph are being led by the same God
who is shepherding and strengthening them.

49:25-26.
'From the God of your father,
who will help you,
And with the Almighty,
who will bless you:
With blessings of the heavens above,
[with] blessings of the deep lying below;
[with] blessings of breasts and womb.
The blessings of your father are mightier
than the blessings of the ones conceiving me
even to the desires for the ancient hills.
May they be on the head of Joseph,
and on the crown of the prince of his brothers.'

Not only is God the source of Joseph's strength
(49:23-24), but God is the one who ultimately blesses
him. The scope and breadth of the blessings on
Joseph are astonishing. Jacob employs figures of
speech that express the depth of these blessings.
First, the reference to the **'heavens above ... deep
lying below'** is a merism, and therefore all-inclusive.
Secondly, the phrase **'blessings of breasts and
womb'** is another merism conveying a picture of
great fecundity in the line of Joseph. And, finally, in
the Hebrew there is alliteration between the words

'**heavens**' and '**breast**' and between '**deep**' and '**womb**': this echo again highlights the completeness of God's promises to Joseph of great blessing on him and his descendants.

Many commentators want to emend the difficult clause, '**the blessings of the ones conceiving me**' to read, 'the blessings of the ancient mountains'. Thus it would parallel the next line, which reads '**the desires for the ancient hills**' (so reads the Septuagint).[250] But, in reality, as the Masoretic Text stands it makes perfectly good sense: it simply means that the blessings coming on Joseph will be even greater than the ones that came on his ancestors, including Abraham, Isaac and Jacob!

The final lines of the blessing serve as an *inclusio* to the life of Joseph. At the beginning of his story Joseph had dreamt that he would rule over his brothers (37:5-11). Now he is told by Jacob that God's blessings will come on him as '**prince of his brothers**'. What Joseph dreamt has indeed come to pass and will continue to be the case.

The history of the two tribes of Joseph, Ephraim and Manasseh, confirms that great blessings came on Joseph's descendants. Both tribes were to become prosperous, and they would be very influential among the tribes of the northern kingdom. Samaria, the capital of Israel, lies within these tribal allotments. Major leaders in Israel's history, such as Joshua (Num. 13:8) and Gideon (Judg. 7:24), came from these tribes.

49:27.
'Benjamin: a ravenous wolf.
In the morning, he will eat the prey;
and in the evening he will divide the plunder.'

Animal metaphors continue to abound. Here Jacob compares his youngest son Benjamin to a '**ravenous wolf**': the text literally reads 'a wolf that will tear', and the sense is clear. His activity is not intermittent, however. The last two lines are structured as a merism, **'morning ... evening'**, which highlights the all-inclusiveness of Benjamin's activity.

Fulfilment of this prophecy is found in the settlement in the period of the conquest. The tribe of Benjamin receives a land allotment in Canaan situated between the tribes of Ephraim and Judah. It remains a war-zone throughout Israel's history. The Benjamites themselves become well known as a warrior tribe (see 1 Kings 12:21; 2 Chr. 14:8; 17:17).

49:28. All these are the twelve tribes of Israel, and this is what their father said to them when he blessed them, blessing them each with a blessing appropriate to him.

The blessing of Jacob began with a superscription (49:1), and now it concludes with a colophon, a closing statement that summarizes what has gone before. And here the summarization focuses on **'the twelve tribes of Israel'**. This is the first time this entity is mentioned in Scripture (cf. 49:16). A twelve-tribal system is common in Genesis: the Aramaeans (22:20-24), the Ishmaelites (25:16) and the people of Esau (36:10-14) are all structured that way. The amphictyony system in ancient Greece was also founded on a twelve-tribal structure.

Application

The blessings that Jacob gives to his children are to remind the church of the wondrous and rich blessings that all the people of the covenant receive down through the ages. But how much greater are the covenant blessings on the church today because of the work of Jesus Christ? The apostle Paul proclaimed, 'Blessed be the God and Father of our Lord Jesus Christ, who has blessed us with every spiritual blessing in the heavenly places in Christ' (Eph. 1:3). As Matthew Henry says, '… as long as we have an interest in God's covenant, a place and a name among his people, and good hopes of a share in the heavenly Canaan, we must account ourselves blessed.'

The death and burial of Jacob
(Genesis 49:29 – 50:14)

Jacob had previously made Joseph swear that he would not bury his father in the land of Egypt, but would return his body to Canaan (47:29-31). Now Jacob repeats that command to all his sons in order to ensure that his instructions would be carried out. The first section of Genesis 50 demonstrates that they did what they had promised.

49:29-30. Then he commanded them, and he said to them, 'I am about to be gathered to my people. Bury me with my fathers in the cave which is in the field of Ephron the Hittite, in the cave which is in the field of Machpelah, near Mamre, in the land of Canaan, the field which Abraham bought from Ephron the Hittite for a burial plot.'

The blessing that Jacob has just given to his sons turns out to be his last will and testament. For death now comes to him. Jacob's statement, **'I am about to be gathered...'** is a participial phrase that is a *futurum instans* (that is, it serves to show certainty and immanency).[251] It also begins with the independent personal pronoun **'I'**, which is emphatic.

For the expression **'gathered to my people'**, see the commentary on Genesis 25:8. The description of the burial site is almost word for word the same as that in Genesis 23:17-20.

49:31-32. 'There they buried Abraham and Sarah his wife, and there they buried Isaac and Rebekah his wife, and there I buried Leah. The field and the cave which are in it were bought from the sons of Heth.'

The fact that Rebekah and Leah have been buried in the cave of Machpelah is nowhere mentioned prior to this reference to it. It demonstrates that the site has truly become a family plot and burial area.

49:33. When Jacob finished commanding his sons he gathered his feet to the bed and he expired. And he was gathered to his people.

The expression, **'he gathered his feet to the bed,'** is a unique one in the Bible. Its meaning is uncertain. On the one hand, it could simply be describing a physical gesture — that is, he lifts his feet onto the bed after having been in a sitting position; so he lies down to die. Or perhaps it is a lost idiom: the Hebrew writer may merely be using it as a euphemism for death. The verb 'to gather' is also used in verse 1 of the chapter and, thus, it may serve as an *inclusio* for the entire section relating to the blessing.

50:1-3. Then Joseph fell on the face of his father and he wept on him and he kissed him. So Joseph commanded his servants, the physicians, to embalm his father. And the physicians embalmed Israel. Forty days was required for him because it is the requisite number of days for embalming. And the Egyptians wept over him for seventy days.

The process of embalming in ancient Egypt became a complex and scientific process during the Middle Kingdom period (c. 2040-1640 B.C.). It first involved the removal of the internal organs of the deceased which were then placed in canopic jars. The body was treated with *natron,* a dehydrating sodium carbonate; the skin was also treated with resin and spices. (It ought to be noted that the Hebrew verb for **'embalming'** means 'to make something spicy'.)[252] The body was then wrapped in many layers of linen, and finally placed in a wooden coffin. By the time of the New Kingdom (c. 1550-1070 B.C.) the process of embalming (mummification) became quite refined: it often preserved the hair, flesh and nails of the deceased.[253] Why the Egyptians did this is clear: they '... believed that death was not the end of life; rather, life could be everlasting. Because of that perspective they laid great emphasis on the preservation of the dead in as close to lifelike form as possible. The survival of the body was a necessary requirement for continual existence beyond death.'[254]

Jacob and Joseph (50:26) are the only Hebrews mentioned in the Bible as having been embalmed in an Egyptian fashion. For them it was a more practical solution to a difficult problem: how were they to be preserved for the long transport for burial in Canaan? These Hebrews in no way agreed with the Egyptians' concepts of the afterlife.

According to the text, the preparation of Jacob's body took forty days and the Egyptians mourned him for seventy days: in all probability the forty days are to be included in the seventy days.[255] There are numerous Egyptian texts which refer to such a seventy-day period. Ancient authors such as Herodotus and Diodorus say the process took more than thirty days and as much as seventy days.[256] In any event, the biblical reference accords well with what we know of ancient Egyptian funerary practices.

50:4-5. When the days of mourning for him had passed, Joseph spoke to the house of Pharaoh, saying, 'If I have found favour in your eyes, speak now in the ears of Pharaoh, saying, "My father made me swear, saying, 'Behold, I am dying. In the grave that I hewed out for myself in the land of

Canaan, bury me there.' Now, please, let me go up and let me bury my father, and I will return."'

Joseph now makes a request of Pharaoh regarding the funeral arrangements for his father. He does so, however, not in person, but through the intermediation of the palace court. This appears odd since Joseph is the closest person to Pharaoh. Perhaps he needs to avoid the palace and the presence of Pharaoh since he has just been in a period of mourning.[257] Or it is possible that he wants the court officials on his side to sway Pharaoh to let him go.

It is strange that Jacob should say that he **'hewed out'**, or, literally, 'cut', the grave at Machpelah, when it had been used since the time of Abraham. Redford argues that what we see here is really two burial traditions combined into one.[258] Yet the idea of 'cutting' a grave for oneself appears to be idiomatic for preparing a grave for oneself (see 2 Chr. 16:14). The verb does stem from the word for 'to hew', but it has probably taken on a more general significance.

Joseph's request to Pharaoh is strongly worded. The last three verbs he employs are cohortatives. They are used here as a forceful type of entreaty putting pressure on the king.[259]

50:6-9. And Pharaoh said, 'Go up and bury your father as he made you swear.' So Joseph went up to bury his father, and all the servants of Pharaoh went up with him — the elders of his house and all the elders of the land of Egypt; and all the house of Joseph and his brothers and the house of his father. Only their children and their flocks and their herds were left in the land of Goshen. Also chariots and horsemen went up with him. And it was a very large company.

Pharaoh grants permission for Joseph to bury his father in Canaan. The king's statement begins with two imperatives that serve the purpose of giving a final definitive answer: **'Go up and bury...!'**

Once permission is given, the biblical writer describes the pomp of the funeral procession. It is a vast throng that includes three basic groups. First mentioned are the dignitaries and senior officials of Egypt; the term **'elders'** is used to underscore the seniority of the court officials. This is a funeral sanctioned by the royal court. The second group is Jacob's family members, including Joseph's brothers, who have been forgiven by him. And, finally, there is a military escort: the chariot force is there to provide security while in Canaan, but perhaps also to ensure the return of the Hebrews to Egypt.

The children and animals of the Hebrews are excluded from the procession and funeral. It may be that the children are too young to participate, and that the animals have no business at a funeral. On the other hand, their being left behind in Egypt makes certain that the Hebrews will return there. A later pharaoh attempted to use the same tactic to keep the Hebrews in Egypt (see commentary on Exod. 10:9-10,24).

50:10-11. And they came to the threshing floor of Atad, which is across the Jordan, and they wailed a great and very strong lamentation there. And he observed a seven-day period of mourning for his father. When the Canaanites who dwelt in the land saw the mourning at the threshing floor of Atad, they said, 'This is a great period of mourning for the Egyptians.' Therefore, its name is called Abel Mizraim, which is across the Jordan.

On the way to the burial site in Hebron the funeral entourage stops at a place where there is a prominent threshing floor. The term for **'threshing floor'** in Hebrew is *gōrĕn*, and this may be part of the place-name, that is, the site may be called Goren-ha-Atad.

Here the people hold a ceremony of mourning that lasts seven days. It is quite vigorous and vibrant. The text literally reads: **'they wailed a great and very strong wailing'** — the construction is a verb followed by its cognate noun for the purpose of unusual force. The length of the period of mourning appears to have been typical of the Hebrews (see 1 Sam. 31:13).

The site 'Atad' is renamed because of the event that occurred there. **'Abel Mizraim'** literally means 'the river bed of the Egyptians'; however, the word **'Abel'** is a pun on the term for **'mourning'** (they have the same consonants). Thus it plays on the sense of the event as the place of the 'mourning of the Egyptians'. It is located **'across the Jordan'**. One needs to be careful here because many commentators assume that it lies in Transjordan. However, that geographical designation can refer to either east or west of the Jordan river depending on where one stands (see, in particular, Deut. 3:25; 11:30). It is likely that this site is somewhere between Egypt and Hebron on the way to Canaan, and not in Transjordan.

50:12-14. And his sons did for him as he had commanded them. So his sons carried him to the land of Canaan, and they buried him in the cave in the field of Machpelah, the field which Abraham had bought as a burial plot from Ephron the Hittite near Mamre. Then Joseph returned to Egypt, he and his brothers and all who went up with him to bury his father, after he buried his father.

The focus of the passage now shifts back to Jacob's sons. It is transitional because the next section, verses 15-21, centres on them as they stand before Joseph. The content of the present verses demonstrates that the brothers fulfilled the instructions that Jacob had given to them in Genesis 49:29-32. The whole passage has a repetitive quality, which strengthens the fact that the action has taken place.

For instance, the last line, **'after he buried his father'**, is so obvious and repetitive that the Septuagint omits it from its translation. There is no reason to emend the text that way, however, because the repetition serves the purpose of eliminating any doubt concerning the chronology. What is about to happen (50:15-21) occurs only after the burial of Jacob and the Hebrews' return to Egypt.

Application

Ecclesiastes 3:11 says that God has 'set eternity' in the hearts of men. That means that God has ingrained in mankind the ability to perceive and have a basic understanding of their condition on the earth. Humans can contemplate where they have been and where they are going. In this regard, humans are different from animals. Neibhur used to use the illustration of cows who are fattened up in the fields while trains go by. They are eventually herded onto the trains and taken to the stock-yards where they are slaughtered. Let us suppose that there are humans in those fields: they can figure out what is going on, what has happened to the others, and where the trains are going. They understand what awaits them.

And so it was with the ancient Egyptians. They understood that there is an afterlife, and so they attempted to preserve their bodies so that they could function in eternity. Of course, they were deluded in their attempts to deal with an afterlife; yet they clearly believed that there is an afterlife. And it is true. The question for each of us today is whether we are ready to face that afterlife or not? And the Scriptures teach that the only secure way to attain to heaven is by having a trusting relationship with Jesus Christ. Will you trust him today?

The fear of the brothers (Genesis 50:15-21)

The story of Joseph began with a description of the strained relations between Joseph and his brothers. Now it nears its end on the same note. Now that Jacob is dead, how will Joseph deal with his brothers? Was he merely being kind to them on account of their father? Or has he truly forgiven them?

50:15-17. When Joseph's brothers saw that their father was dead they said, 'What if Joseph should bear a grudge against us and fully pay us back for all the evil which we dealt to him?' So they sent to Joseph, saying, 'Before his death, our father gave a command, saying, "Thus you will say to Joseph, 'Ah, now, forgive the iniquity of your brothers and their sin for they did evil to you.'" And, now, forgive the iniquity of the servants of the God of your father.' And Joseph wept when they spoke to him.

Soon after the death of Jacob, the brothers show a great deal of anxiety and fear. In their imaginations they conjure up a terrible situation. They begin with the exclamatory particle **'what if...?'** introducing a conditional sentence. The hypothetical nature of what is proposed is highlighted by the fact that only the protasis, or conditional clause, is spelled out — the apodosis is left to one's imagination. The brothers now lack their father's protection, and they do not know what Joseph will do to them.

The brothers are afraid that Joseph may **'bear a grudge'** against them. Ironically, that is the same verb used in Genesis 49:23 (translated there as 'showed bitterness') to describe the manner in which the brothers had treated Joseph back in Genesis 37. They expect Joseph to act in the same way that they did when outside of their father's oversight. It is clear that the brothers have not dealt thoroughly with their own guilt, and they have not fully understood Joseph's forgiveness of them. They do not believe that they have been completely exonerated.

Their sending of a third party to speak with Joseph confirms their trepidation. The verb translated **'they sent'** is literally 'they commanded', and it is used in the Hebrew Bible of sending someone else in one's place (see Esth. 3:12; 8:9). In addition, in their message the brothers call to Joseph's attention the fact that they are **'servants of ... God'**: by including the name of God they are attempting to play on Joseph's religious sensibilities for their own ends. Since they all serve the same God, no harm should come to them.

50:18. So his brothers also came and they fell down before him, and they said, 'Behold, we are your servants.'

Hearing of Joseph's reaction to their words — that is, his tears — the brothers feel brave enough to face him in person. They come to him in humility, bowing before him and announcing their servitude. Here is another stark and direct statement that Joseph's dreams back in Genesis 37:5-10 have indeed come true (cf. 44:14). This statement thus serves as part of an *inclusio* for the entire account of Joseph.

50:19-20. Then Joseph said to them, 'Do not be afraid, for am I in the place of God? And you meant evil against me,

[but] God meant it for good; so that he might act, as it is this day, to preserve many people alive.'

Joseph's response to his brothers at this point serves as the climax to his entire story. He begins by reassuring the brothers that they have nothing to fear; he will in no way seek revenge. He understands that he is not **'in the place of God'**: he realizes that he is not sovereign. Indeed, everything that has happened occurred because of the providence of God — how could he, a mere human, alter it? The point is so clear to Joseph that he employs a rhetorical question in order to emphasize it. Jacob used the very same phrase to make exactly the same point regarding Rachel's barrenness (30:2).

But Joseph goes deeper still by viewing his brothers' evil activity in the light of God's providence: he did this previously in Genesis 45:5-8, and the reader ought to consult the commentary on that passage.[260] Joseph simply believes that God even uses the sinfulness of humans to bring about his good purposes for the world. This theological concept is no stranger to the rest of Scripture (see Prov. 16:1; 20:24; Ps. 37:23; Jer. 10:23). As Proverbs 16:9 says, 'The heart of man plans his way, but Yahweh directs his steps.' There is no stronger statement regarding the true meaning of the sovereignty of God in Scripture than what Joseph says here to his brothers.

50:21. 'So, now, do not be afraid. I will support you and your children.' Thus he comforted them, and he spoke to their heart[s].

As this speech began with Joseph's encouragement to the brothers not to fear, so now he ends it with the same words (an example of an *inclusio*). He also eases their anxiety by announcing that he will continue to support them despite his father's death. The independent personal pronoun **'I'** adds force to his words. His **'support'** of his brothers has nothing to do with the famine, for that has been over for some years (see 47:28). Perhaps it hints at the situation of the Hebrews in Egypt as being a tenuous one; possibly their condition may have deteriorated. Joseph's demeanour is caring and kind — **'he spoke to their heart'** is a Hebrew idiom for an act of tenderness (see 34:3).

Application

There is no doctrine so clearly taught in the Bible as the sovereignty of God. God is grandly portrayed as the 'blessed and only Sovereign, the King of kings and Lord of lords... To him be honour and eternal dominion!' (1 Tim. 6:15-16). Berkhof summarizes the doctrine as follows: 'The sovereignty of God is strongly emphasized in Scripture. He is represented as Creator and His will as the cause of all things... He is clothed with absolute authority over the hosts of heaven and the inhabitants of the earth. He upholds all things with His almighty power, and determines the ends which they are destined to serve. He rules as King in the most absolute sense of the word, and all things are dependent on Him and subservient to Him.'[261] The Bible teaches that at this very moment God sits enthroned over the universe. He is preserving and maintaining his creation by his sovereign hand. Everything in the universe — the whens, the wheres, the hows and the whys — is determined and directed by the matchless, supreme God.

The death of Joseph
(Genesis 50:22-26)

The book of Genesis ends with a mixed message. On the one hand, Joseph lives a very full life in which he sees his great-grandchildren born to him. Yet, on the other hand, like any man, Joseph dies. The Hebrews are in Egypt and there is a great sense of foreboding in the text. But Joseph prophesies that they will one day be delivered from Egypt and brought to the land of promise. So the reader is left seeing the Hebrews in Egypt and knowing that they will be enslaved. However, the reader also anticipates that God will act in a marvellous way and bring them forth to the land that he promised to Abraham, Isaac and Jacob.

50:22-23. So Joseph dwelt in Egypt, he and his father's household. And Joseph lived 110 years. And Joseph saw the children of the third generation of Ephraim. And also the children of Makir, the son of Manasseh, were born on Joseph's knees.

In these two verses, the biblical author describes how God favours Joseph during the remainder of his life. First, he lives to the ripe old age of **'110 years'**. The Egyptians viewed this figure as the ideal lifespan.[262] In addition, Joseph is so blessed as to see his great-grandchildren.[263] In fact, his great-grandchildren through Manasseh **'were born on Joseph's knees'**; this is an idiom that, as we have seen, signifies a

formal rite of adoption (see commentary on 30:3 and
48:12).

The mention of Makir is anticipatory. He is the
most important son of Manasseh, and he becomes
the progenitor of the Gileadites (Num. 26:29; 32:39;
Deut. 3:15; Josh. 13:31). His descendants settle the
areas of Gilead and Bashan on the eastern side of the
Jordan river (Josh. 17:1). His descendants are
famous for being warlike (see Judg. 5:14).

50:24. And Joseph said to his brothers, 'I am about to die;
but God will certainly visit you and bring you up from this land
to the land which he swore to Abraham, to Isaac and to
Jacob.'

In his final statement, Joseph tells his brothers of his
impending death, and the fact that there will one day
be an exodus out of Egypt. The content is the same
as that of Jacob's speech at the end of his life (see
commentary on 48:21). Joseph's language is forceful
when he announces that God **'will certainly visit'**
them; this phrase is constructed of an infinitive and
an imperfective of the same verb and literally reads,
'Visiting, he will visit.' Such a construction is emphatic in Hebrew. Here is a prophecy that Joseph
believes will be fulfilled. And that fulfilment occurs
during the period of the Exodus: when God tells
Moses to deliver Israel, he instructs him to gather the
elders and say on God's behalf 'I have certainly
visited you'! (Exod. 3:16).

Hebrews 11:22 confirms the prophetic word and
its fulfilment at the Exodus. The biblical writer says,
'By faith Joseph, when he was dying, made mention
of the exodus of the sons of Israel ...'

The phrase, **'to Abraham, to Isaac, and to
Jacob'**, is found here for the first time in the Bible. It
becomes idiomatic for the promises of the covenant

that God made to the patriarchs — see commentary on Exodus 2:24; 3:6,15; 4:5.

50:25. Then Joseph made the children of Israel swear, saying, 'God will certainly visit you, and you shall bring up my bones from this place.'

Here too the dying man requires an oath from the living. Joseph makes his brothers swear to **'bring up my bones'** from Egypt to Canaan. This promise is fulfilled in Exodus 13:17-19 and in Joshua 24:32, in which Joseph's bones are interred at Shechem in Canaan. It is a similar request to the one made by Jacob (49:29-30). Burial in the land of Canaan appears to have been very important to the Hebrews (see, for example, 1 Sam. 31:11-13; 2 Sam. 21:12-14), and especially the preservation of a person's bones (see 1 Kings 13:29-31; 2 Kings 23:16-20). Interment in the land of promise may be in anticipation of a resurrection there (2 Kings 13:20-21; Ezek. 37:1-14). Joseph himself may have believed in the bodily resurrection of the dead (Heb. 11:17-22).[264]

50:26. So Joseph died at the age of 110. And they embalmed him, and he was placed in a coffin in Egypt.

Like all men, Joseph dies — but he expires at a full, ripe old age. Yet it is interesting to note a contrast with the death and funeral of Jacob. For Joseph no pomp or festive ritual is recorded. He is merely embalmed and placed in a sarcophagus, both particularly Egyptian rituals. Thus, the book of Genesis ends on a note filled with foreboding — in fact, the final words of the text are **'in Egypt'**!

Application

Joseph's anticipation of a bodily resurrection is a mere shadow of things to come. He gave directions concerning his bones because he believed that God could raise men even from the dead. Jesus Christ is the fulfilment of what Joseph merely anticipated. He taught, 'Do not marvel at this; for an hour is coming, in which all who are in the tombs will hear his voice, and will come forth; those who did the good deeds to a resurrection of life, those who committed the evil deeds to a resurrection of judgement' (John 5:28-29). The first-fruits of his work occurred at the event of the crucifixion: 'And behold, the veil of the temple was torn in two from top to bottom; and the earth shook and the rocks were split. The tombs were opened, and many bodies of the saints who had fallen asleep were raised; and coming out of the tombs after his resurrection they entered the holy city and appeared to many' (Matt. 27:51-53). Those many saints raised from the dead are a sign to us of a final resurrection, when believers will be raised to eternal life with Christ, and unbelievers to eternal death. Oh to be part of the resurrection that leads to life!

List of abbreviations

ABD	D. N. Freedman, ed., *Anchor Bible Dictionary* (6 vols, 1992)
ANEP	J. B. Pritchard, ed., *The Ancient Near East in Pictures* (1954)
ANET	J. B. Pritchard, ed., *Ancient Near Eastern Texts Relating to the Old Testament* (3rd ed., 1969).
ARE	J. H. Breasted, ed., *Ancient Records of Egypt* (5 vols, 1906)
BA	*Biblical Archaeologist*
BAR	*Biblical Archaeology Review*
BASOR	*Bulletin of the American Schools of Oriental Research*
BDB	F. Brown, S. R. Driver and C. A. Briggs, *A Hebrew and English Lexicon of the Old Testament* (1907)
BR	*Bible Review*
BS	*Bibliotheca Sacra*
BT	*Bible Translator*
BTB	*Biblical Theology Bulletin*
CBQ	*Catholic Biblical Quarterly*
CTQ	*Concordia Theological Quarterly*
ET	*Expository Times*
HS	*Hebrew Studies*
HTR	*Harvard Theological Review*
HUCA	*Hebrew Union College Annual*
JANES	*Journal of the Ancient Near Eastern Society*
JAOS	*Journal of the American Oriental Society*
JBL	*Journal of Biblical Literature*
JBQ	*Jewish Bible Quarterly*
JBR	*Journal of Bible and Religion*
JEA	*Journal of Egyptian Archaeology*

JETS   *Journal of the Evangelical Theological Society*
JNES   *Journal of Near Eastern Studies*
JQR   *Jewish Quarterly Review*
JSOT   *Journal for the Study of the Old Testament*
JSS   *Journal of Semitic Studies*
JTS   *Journal of Theological Studies*
NEAEHL   E. Stern ed., *The New Encyclopedia of Archaeological Excavations in the Holy Land* (4 vols, 1992)
NIDOTTE   W. A. Van Gemeren, ed., *The New International Dictionary of Old Testament Theology and Exegesis* (5 vols, 1997)
NTS   *New Testament Studies*
PEQ   *Palestine Exploration Quarterly*
RB   *Revue Biblique*
RR   *Reformed Review*
TAPS   *Transactions of the American Philosophical Society*
VT   *Vetus Testamentum*
WTJ   *Westminster Theological Journal*
ZAW   *Zeitschrift für die alttestamentliche Wissenschafft*

Notes

Chapter 8 — The story of Jacob and Esau

1. R. J. Clifford, 'Genesis 25:19-34,' *Interpretation* 45 (1991): 398.

2. See M. D. Turner, 'Rebekah: Ancestor of Faith,' *Lexington Theological Quarterly* 20 (1985): 44-5.

3. B. K. Waltke and M. O'Connor, *An Introduction to Biblical Hebrew Syntax* (Winona Lake, IN: Eisenbrauns, 1990), pp.389-90.

4. *BDB*, p.647.

5. *Rashi Commentary*, p.115; *Genesis Rabba* 63.

6. For a study of this poetical structure, see R. A. Kraft, 'A Note on the Oracle of Rebekah (GEN. xxv. 23),' *JTS* 13 (1962): 318-20.

7. E. A. Speiser, Genesis (Garden City, NY: Doubleday, 1964), vol. 1, pp.194-5.

8. *BDB*, p.796.

9. Speiser, *Genesis,* p.195.

10. For ironic word-plays in this story, see V. H. Mathews and F. Mims, 'Jacob the Trickster and Heir of the Covenant: A Literary Interpretation,' *Perspectives in Religious Studies* 12 (1985): 185-95.

11. See J. Terino, 'A Text Linguistic Study of the Jacob Narrative,' *Vox Evangelica* 18 (1988): 45-62.

12. *BDB*, p.1071.

13. *Rashi Commentary*, p.116.

14. *BDB*, p.542.

15. E. W. Bullinger, *Figures of Speech Used in the Bible* (London: Eyre & Spottiswoode, 1898), p.189.

16. I. Mendelsohn, 'On the Preferential Status of the Eldest Son,' *BASOR* 156 (1959): 38-40.

17. *ANET*, p.220.

18. Bullinger, *Figures of Speech Used in the Bible*, p.211.

19. Waltke and O'Connor, *An Introduction to Biblical Hebrew Syntax*, p.22.

20. Abraham's keeping of God's law by faith is discussed by J. Sailhamer, 'The Mosaic Law and the Theology of the Pentateuch,' *WTJ* 53 (1991): 241-61.

21. An important article comparing the three incidents is D. Gordis, 'Lies, Wives, and Sisters: The Wife-Sister Motif Revisited,' *Judaism* 34 (1985): 344-59.

22. Speiser, *Genesis,* p.203; and see M. Biddle, 'The "Endangered Ancestress" and Blessing for the Nations,' *JBL* 109 (1990): 599-611.

23. See the discussion in the introduction to the commentary on Genesis 20:1-18, and its relevant bibliography.

24. G. Nicol, 'The Chronology of Genesis: Genesis XXVI 1-33 as "Flashback",' *VT* 46 (1996): 330-38.

25. *BDB,* p.850.

26. J. C. L. Gibson, *Davidson's Introductory Hebrew Grammar: Syntax* (Edinburgh: T. & T. Clark, 1994), p.176.

27. Waltke and O'Connor, *An Introduction to Biblical Hebrew Syntax,* p.493.

28. Clines, *The Dictionary of Classical Hebrew,* vol. I, pp.415-16.

29. *ANET,* pp.162, 171.

30. Gesenius, *Hebrew Grammar,* 2nd English ed. (Oxford: Clarendon Press, 1910), p.344.

31. *Rashi Commentary,* p.118 (*Gen. Rabba* 64).

32. *BDB,* p.636.

33. For a study of pastoralism as it relates to the region of Gerar, see Mathews, 'The Wells of Gerar,' pp.118-26.

34. N. Sarna, *The JPS Torah Commentary: Genesis* (Philadelphia: Jewish Publication Society, 1989), p.186.

35. *BDB,* p.966.

36. H. Gunkel, *Genesis* (Macon: Mercer University Press, 1997 reprint), p.296.

37. See discussion in John Currid, *Study Commentary on Exodus* (Darlington: Evangelical Press, 2001), vol. 2, p.35.

38. At Mari, for example, the official with this name was the supervisor of the royal pasturage (See J. Safran, 'Ahuzzath and the Pact of Beer-Sheba,' *ZAW* 101:2 (1989): 184-98).

39. *BDB,* p.46.

40. See discussion in Currid, *Study Commentary on Exodus,* vol. 2, p.139.

41. G. von Rad, *Genesis: A Commentary* (Philadelphia: Westminster, 1961), p.267.

42. Safran, 'Ahuzzath and the Pact of Beer-Sheba,' p.185.

43. Esau later marries his cousin named Mahalath (see 28:8-9; 36:2-3). This may have been to please his family over against their displeasure with his Hittite wives. For an interesting discussion of the issue, see J. Abraham, 'Esau's Wives,' *JBQ* 25 (1997): 251-9.

44. Gesenius, *Hebrew Grammar,* p.382.

45. *Rashi Commentary,* p.122.

46. Sarna, *Genesis,* p.190.

47. Waltke and O'Connor, *An Introduction to Biblical Hebrew Syntax,* p.493.

48. Speiser, *Genesis,* pp.208-9.

49. See J. Rackman, 'Was Isaac Deceived?', *Judaism* 43 (1994): 37-45.

50. S. Gevirtz, 'Of Patriarchs and Puns,' *HUCA* 46 (1975): 33-54.

51. Sarna, *Genesis,* p.191.

52. Turner, 'Rebekah: Ancestor of Faith,' p.46.

53. Waltke and O'Connor, *An Introduction to Biblical Hebrew Syntax,* p.670.

54. Sarna, *Genesis,* p.191.

55. Waltke and O'Connor, *An Introduction to Biblical Hebrew Syntax,* pp.312, 326.

56. *BDB,* p.648.

57. Cf. Speiser, *Genesis,* p.209.

58. B. Uval, 'The Dew of Heaven,' *JBQ* 26 (1998): 117-18.

59. H. Brongers, 'Alternative Interpretationen des Sagennanten Was Copulativum,' *ZAW* 90 (1978): 273-7.

60. Waltke and O'Connor, *An Introduction to Biblical Hebrew Syntax,* p.134.

61. Gesenius, *Hebrew Grammar,* p.464.

62. To show Esau in a vulgar light, the Targum of Genesis 27:31 says that he brought his father cooked dog (See R. Hayward, 'Targum Pseudo-Jonathan to Genesis 27:31,' *JQR* 84 (1993-94): 177-88).

63. *BDB,* p.169.

64. Gesenius, *Hebrew Grammar,* p.342.

65. *BDB,* p.724.

66. Gesenius, *Hebrew Grammar,* p.475.

67. For the importance and weight of blessing, see S. Abegunde, 'Curses and Blessings in Genesis in the Light of the Extension of Personality,' *BT* 42 (1991): 242-7.

68. For a different view see T. Muraoka, *Emphatic Words and Structures in Biblical Hebrew* (Jerusalem: Magnes, 1985), pp.63-5, 141-6.

69. Muraoka, *Emphatic Words,* pp.63-5, 141-6.

70. *BDB,* p.784.

71. For a discussion of Esau's speech, see J. Joosten, 'The Syntax of *haberakah 'ahat hi leka 'abi,' JSS* 36 (1991): 207-21.

72. Waltke and O'Connor, *An Introduction to Biblical Hebrew Syntax,* p.214. It has been suggested that the preposition is actually being used in a partitive sense — that Esau is really sharing in the wealth of the earth. Such an interpretation goes against the entire force and flow of the passage (See Speiser, *Genesis,* p.210).

73. *BDB,* p.525.

74. Turner, 'Rebekah: Ancestor of Faith,' p.47.

75. Called a *dativus commodi* by Gesenius, *Hebrew Grammar,* p.381.

76. See the discussion of Haran in *ABD,* vol. III, pp.58-9.

77. V. Mathews and F. Mims, 'Jacob the Trickster and Heir of the Covenant: A Literary Interpretation,' *Perspectives in Religious Studies* 12 (1985): 188.

78. *BDB,* pp.880-81.

79. Speiser, *Genesis,* p.215.

80. *BDB,* p.139.

81. W. F. Albright, 'The Names *Shaddai* and *Abram,' JBL* 54 (1935): 173-204.

82. *BDB,* p.874.

83. *Rashi Commentary,* p.130.

84. J. Abraham, 'Esau's Wives,' *JBQ* 25 (1997): 251-9.

85. Waltke and O'Connor, *An Introduction to Biblical Hebrew Syntax,* p.217.

86. O. P. Robertson, *Understanding the Land of the Bible* (Phillipsburg, NJ: Presbyterian and Reformed, 1996), p.73.

87. Gesenius, *Hebrew Grammar,* p.407.

88. J. Currid, *Ancient Egypt and the Old Testament* (Grand Rapids: Baker, 1997), pp.224-8.

89. A. Ross, 'Jacob's Vision: The Founding of Bethel,' *BS* 142 (1985): 224-37.

90. *BDB,* p.700.

91. Z. Weisman, 'National Consciousness in the Patriarchal Promises,' *JSOT* 31 (1985): 55-73.

92. Waltke and O'Connor, *An Introduction to Biblical Hebrew Syntax,* p.670.

93. Sarna, *Genesis,* p.199.

94. *ANET,* p.33.

95. *Ibid.,* p.52.

96. *BDB*, p.531.
97. Sarna, *Genesis*, p.201.
98. Waltke and O'Connor, *An Introduction to Biblical Hebrew Syntax*, p.414. See E. Jenni, *Syntaktisch-semasiologische Untersuchung einen Verbalform im Alten Testament* (Zurich: EVZ, 1968).
99. M. Pamment, 'The Son of Man in the Fourth Gospel,' *JTS* 36 (1985): 56-66.
100. Ross, 'Jacob's Vision,' p.234.
101. Gesenius, *Hebrew Grammar*, p.476.
102. *BDB*, p.932.
103. *Rashi Commentary*, p.135.
104. Speiser, *Genesis*, p.223.
105. Von Rad, *Genesis*, p.284.
106. Gesenius, *Hebrew Grammar*, p.424.
107. See discussion in M. Seelenfreund and S. Schneider, 'Leah's Eyes,' *JBQ* 25 (1997): 18-22.
108. Sarna, *Genesis*, p.204; Von Rad, *Genesis*, p.286.
109. *BDB*, p.940. Cf. W. G. Kendrick, 'Selected Translation Problems in Genesis,' *BT* 41 (1990): 425-31.
110. *ANET*, pp.171-3; cf. Sarna, *Genesis*, p.204.
111. Speiser, *Genesis*, pp.44-5.
112. *Ibid.*, pp.226-7.
113. Waltke and O'Connor, *An Introduction to Biblical Hebrew Syntax*, p.265.
114. G. W. Coats, *Genesis with an Introduction to Narrative Literature* (Grand Rapids: Eerdmans, 1983), p.215.
115. Von Rad, *Genesis*, p.289.
116. *BDB*, p.971.
117. J. Calvin, *Genesis* (Grand Rapids: Eerdmans, 1948 reprint), vol. II, p.134.
118. Many of the statements made by the women throughout these birth narratives are later reflected in the literature of the Psalms (See J. Ross-Burstall, 'Leah and Rachel: A Tale of Two Sisters,' *Word and World* 14 (1994): 162-70).
119. Throughout the entire passage the name given to each child is determined by the circumstances of the mother (See G. W. Ramsey, 'Is Name Giving an Act of Domination in Genesis 2:23 and Elsewhere?', *CBQ* 50 (1988): 24-35).
120. *BDB*, p.530.
121. For how rabbinic Judaism attempted to explain this problem, see S. Dresner, 'Rachel and Leah,' *Judaism* 38 (1989): 151-9.

122. Speiser, *Genesis,* p.230.

123. K. Grosz, 'Dowry and Brideprice in Nuzi,' in M. Morrison and D. Owen, eds. *Studies on the Civilization and Culture of Nuzu* (Winona Lake, IN: Eisenbrauns, 1981), pp.161-82.

124. F. I. Andersen, 'Note on Genesis 30:8,' *JBL* 88 (1969): 200.

125. Bullinger, *Figures of Speech Used in the Bible,* p.276.

126. D. Winton Thomas, 'A Consideration of Some Unusual Ways of Expressing the Superlative in Hebrew,' *VT* 3 (1953): 209-24.

127. Sarna, *Genesis,* p.208.

128. Waltke and O'Connor, *An Introduction to Biblical Hebrew Syntax,* p.490.

129. Gesenius, *Hebrew Grammar,* p.312.

130. C. F. Keil and F. Delitzsch, *Commentary on the Old Testament* (Grand Rapids: Eerdmans, 1981 reprint), vol. 1, p.289.

131. However, see the caveat of M. Zohary, *Plants of the Bible* (Cambridge: Cambridge University Press, 1982), pp.188-9.

132. Some of the rabbis argue that the word 'tonight / night' is figurative for 'death'. When Rachel made her proposal it became a curse on herself: she would not be buried with Jacob, but Leah alone would share his grave (See D. Daube, 'The Night of Death,' *HTR* 61 (1968): 629-32).

133. In the Hebrew text, there are variant readings of certain texts that the Masoretes wished to preserve. The desired reading appears in the margin of the text (called *qere*) — the reading in the text is called *kethib* (See B. Kittel, V. Hoffer, and R. Wright, *Biblical Hebrew: A Text and Workbook.* New Haven: Yale University Press, 1989, pp.366-7).

134. Sarna, *Genesis,* p.211.

135. Gesenius, *Hebrew Grammar,* p.498.

136. Von Rad, *Genesis,* p.295.

137. Currid, *Ancient Egypt and the Old Testament,* pp.219-28. Consider, on the other hand, the argument of N. Waldman, that the verb is actually related to the Akkadian *naḥāšu*, which means 'to become wealthy' ('A Note of Genesis 30:27b,' *JQR* 55 (1964): 164-5. See also W. Chomsky, 'The Case of Genesis 30:27b,' *JQR* 55 (1965): 365-6).

138. *BDB,* p.919.

139. Von Rad, *Genesis,* p.296.

140. *ANET,* p.75. See also Genesis 22:4; 31:22; 42:18 (Cf., Sarna, *Genesis,* p.361).

141. Van Haitsma, *The Supplanter Undeceived,* p.61, quoted in R. Harback, *Studies in the Book of Genesis* (Grandville Protestant Reformed Church, 1986), p.605.

142. J. Calvin, *Commentary on the Book of Genesis,* pp.155-6. For a concise study of the history of interpretation regarding this moral problem, see J. Thompson, 'The Survival of Allegorical Argumentation in Peter Martyr Vermigli's Old Testament Exegesis,' in R. Muller and J. Thompson, eds., *Biblical Interpretation in the Era of the Reformation* (Grand Rapids: Eerdmans, 1996), pp.262-4.

143. Speiser, *Genesis,* p.237.

144. Gesenius, *Hebrew Grammar,* pp.335-6.

145. Waltke and O'Connor, *An Introduction to Biblical Hebrew Syntax,* p.296.

146. Bullinger, *Figures of Speech Used in the Bible,* pp.251-2.

147. Gesenius, *Hebrew Grammar,* p.496.

148. J. Greenfield, 'Našū-nadānu and its Congeners,' in M. de Jong Ellis, ed. *Ancient Near Eastern Studies in Memory of J. J. Finkelstein* (Hamden: Connecticut Academy of Arts and Sciences, 1977), pp.90ff. Cited in Sarna, *Genesis,* pp.365-6.

149. Bullinger, *Figures of Speech Used in the Bible,* p.709.

150. Keil and Delitzsch, *Genesis,* p.295.

151. Waltke and O'Connor, *An Introduction to Biblical Hebrew Syntax,* p.586.

152. This is a legal situation. See M. Burrows, 'The Complaint of Laban's Daughters,' *JAOS* 57 (1937): 259-76.

153. Sarna, *Genesis,* p.217.

154. J. Currid, 'Travel and Transportation,' in *Dictionary of the Old Testament: Pentateuch* (Downers Grove, IL: InterVarsity, 2003), pp. 870-74.

155. For various proposals for the rationale of Rachel, see K. Spanier, 'Rachel's Theft of the Teraphim: Her Struggle for Family Primacy,' *VT* 42 (1992): 404-12.

156. See J. Huehnergard, 'Biblical Notes on Some New Akkadian Texts from Emar (Syria),' *CBQ* 47 (1985): 428-34.

157. Sarna, *Genesis,* p.216.

158. Bullinger, *Figures of Speech Used in the Bible,* p.682.

159. C. R. Krahmalkov, 'Exodus Itinerary Confirmed by Egyptian Evidence,' *BAR* 20.5 (1994): 54-62.

160. H. Murrow, 'God's Gift of the Law,' *The Cumberland Seminarian* 22 (1984): 18.

161. Sarna, *Genesis,* p.215.

162. See the example from Tell Halaf in the ninth century B.C. in *ANEP,* pp.59, 271. On the subject of camels in the Levant, see R. Bulliet, *The Camel and the Wheel* (Cambridge, MA: Harvard University Press, 1975); I. Kohler-Rollefson, 'Camels and Camel

Pastoralism in Arabia,' *BA* 56 (1993): 180-8; W. G. Lambert, 'The Domesticated Camel in the Second Millennium — Evidence from Alalakh and Ugarit,' *BASOR* 160 (1960): 42-3; and P. Wapnish, 'Camel Caravans and Camel Pastoralists at Tell Jemmeh,' *JANES* 13 (1981): 101-21.

163. *BDB*, p.936.

164. *ANET*, p.177.

165. W. F. Albright proposed the translation, 'the kinsman of Isaac,' based on ancient Near-Eastern cognates. See his *From the Stone Age to Christianity* (Baltimore: Johns Hopkins, 1946), p.324. The suggestion has been appropriately criticized by D. R. Hillers, 'PAḤAD YIṢḤĀQ,' *JBL* 91 (1972): 90-92.

166. M. Malul believes the phrase should be translated as 'the thigh of Isaac', based on an Aramaic cognate. He argues that it 'symbolizes the family and ancestral spirits of Isaac. In it is reflected the custom of the oath by the thigh twice attested in the stories of the patriarchs, an oath to which one had recourse when the continuity and cohesion of the family were at stake' (See his 'More on PAḤAD YIṢḤĀQ (Genesis XXXI 42, 53) and the Oath by the Thigh,' *VT* 35 (1985): 192-200).

167. *ANET*, pp.199-206.

168. Speiser, *Genesis*, pp.247-8.

169. Garcia-Treto attempts to solve the problem by saying that the word 'witness' actually means 'pact/covenant' — so that the sentence should read, 'Let us make a covenant, you and I, and let there be a pact between you and me' (See his 'Genesis 31:44 and "Gilead",' *ZAW* 79:1 (1967): 13-17).

170. Many scholars see the two acts of ratification as reflecting the combination in the text before us of material from two different sources (See, for example, Von Rad, *Genesis*, p.307).

171. Keil and Delitzsch, *Genesis*, p.299.

172. Waltke and O'Connor, *An Introduction to Biblical Hebrew Syntax*, p.216.

173. *ANET*, p.223; Speiser, *Genesis*, p.248.

174. *BDB*, p.776.

175. N. H. Snaith, 'Genesis XXXI 50,' *VT* 14 (1964): 373.

176. *ANET*, pp.200, 205.

177. Gesenius, *Hebrew Grammar*, p.472.

178. Calvin, *Genesis*, vol. 1, p.181.

179. E. M. Curtis, 'Structure, Style and Context as a Key to Interpreting Jacob's Encounter at Peniel,' *JETS* 30 (1987): 129-37.

180. Speiser, *Genesis*, p.254.

181. D. Pardee, 'An Overview of Ancient Hebrew Epistolography,' *JBL* 97 (1978): 329.

182. B. Jacob, *Das erste Buch der Tora, Genesis* (Berlin, 1934); quoted in Von Rad, *Genesis,* p.312.

183. Sarna, *Genesis,* p.224.

184. Waltke and O'Connor, *An Introduction to Biblical Hebrew Syntax,* p.266.

185. Gesenius, *Hebrew Grammar,* p.396.

186. See the important study of D. Judisch, 'Propitiation in the Language and Typology of the Old Testament,' *CTQ* 48 (1984): 221-43.

187. *BDB,* p.670.

188. To be identified with modern Telul ed-Dhahab el-Garbi (See discussion in J. Simons, *The Geographical and Topographical Texts of the Old Testament.* Leiden: Brill, 1959, pp.229-32).

189. See H. Knight, 'Meeting Jacob at the Jabbok: Wrestling with a Text — A Midrash on Genesis 32:22-32,' *Journal of Ecumenical Studies* 29 (1992): 451-60.

190. S. Levin, 'Jacob's Limp,' *Judaism* 44 (1995): 325-7.

191. See the discussion of J. McKenzie, 'Jacob at Peniel: Gn 32,24-32,' *CBQ* 25 (1963): 73.

192. H. McKay, 'Jacob Makes It Across the Jabbok: An Attempt to Solve the Success / Failure Ambivalence in Israel's Self-Consciousness,' *JSOT* 38 (1987): 3-13.

193. *BDB,* p.7.

194. See W. T. Miller, *Mysterious Encounters at Mamre and Jabbok* (Atlanta: Scholars, 1984).

195. For a study of the Hosea passage and its relationship with Genesis, see S. L. McKenzie, 'The Jacob Tradition in Hosea XII 4-5,' *VT* 36 (1986): 311-22.

196. F. Holmgren, 'Holding Your Own Against God! Genesis 32:22-32,' *Interpretation* 44 (1990): 5-17.

197. The difference in spelling between Peniel and Penuel merely reflects alternative old case-endings (See Waltke and O'Connor, *An Introduction to Biblical Hebrew Syntax,* p.127; Gesenius, *Hebrew Grammar,* pp.251-2).

198. Sarna, *Genesis,* p.227.

199. *Ibid.,* p.229.

200. E. Tov, *Textual Criticism of the Hebrew Bible* (Minneapolis: Fortress, 1992), p.56.

201. Speiser, *Genesis,* p.259.

202. Von Rad, *Genesis,* p.322.

203. Z. Zevit, 'Expressing Denial in Biblical Hebrew and Mishnaic Hebrew, and in Amos,' *VT* 29 (1979): 505-9.

204. *BDB*, pp.624-5.

205. See G. Van Der Kooij, 'Tell Deir 'Alla,' *NEAEHL* (New York: Simon and Schuster, 1992), vol. I, pp.338-42.

206. *BDB*, pp.108-9.

207. For important studies of Shechem, see G. E. Wright, *Shechem: The Biography of a Biblical City* (New York: McGraw-Hill, 1965); E. F. Campbell, *Shechem II: Portrait of a Hill Country Vale* (Atlanta: Scholars Press, 1991).

208. Von Rad, *Genesis*, p.323.

209. L. Berkhof, *Systematic Theology* (Grand Rapids: Eerdmans, 1977), p.513.

210. M. Kessler, 'Genesis 34 — An Interpretation,' *RR* 19 91965): 3-8.

211. *BDB*, p.776.

212. M. M. Caspi, 'The Story of the Rape of Dinah: The Narrator and the Reader,' *HS* 26 (1985): 33.

213. *BDB*, p.615.

214. *NEAEHL*, vol. II, p.503.

215. *BDB*, p.1034.

216. *BDB*, p.105.

217. Sarna, *Genesis*, p.238.

218. Speiser, *Genesis*, pp.265-6.

219. R. J. Bull, 'A Re-examination of the Shechem Temple,' *BA* 23 (1960): 110-19; E. F. Campbell and J. F. Ross, 'The Excavation of Shechem and the Biblical Tradition,' *BA* 26 (1963): 2-27.

220. An article by L. Bechtel argues that Levi and Simeon are really the guilty party. She says, 'Ironically, if there is rape in this story, it is Simeon and Levi who "rape" the Shechemites. It is their behaviour that is violent and hostile, carried out for the purpose of exploitation.' She says that Dinah is not raped but merely wants to interact with outsiders — the brothers' authority is thus threatened and so they retaliate ('What if Dinah is Not Raped? (Genesis 34),' *JSOT* 62 (1994): 19-36). Such a view has little, if any, justification from the text.

221. Von Rad, *Genesis*, p.331.

222. V. Horowitz has made the suggestion that these are the earrings of the idols and not the people ('Who Lost an Earring? Genesis 35:4 Reconsidered,' *CBQ* 62 (2000): 28-32).

223. *ANEP*, p.22.

224. J. A. Soggin, 'Jacob in Shechem and in Bethel,' in M. Fishbane and E. Tov, *Sha'arei Talmon* (Winona Lake, IN: Eisenbrauns, 1992), pp.195-8.

225. It may be argued that the use of the name *Elohim*, or 'God' here is not a title but merely a way of expressing the superlative, i.e., 'a mighty terror' (See D. W. Thomas, 'A Consideration of Some Unusual Ways of Expressing the Superlative in Hebrew,' *VT* 3 (1953): 209-24).

226. Gesenius, *Hebrew Grammar*, p.463.

227. *Ibid.*, p.399.

228. *Ibid.*, p.405.

229. For a discussion of the structure and content of passages that tie together sanctuaries and theophanies, see B. Otzen, 'Heavenly Visions in Early Judaism: Origin and Function,' in W. Barrick and J. Spencer, eds. *In the Shelter of Elyon* (Sheffield: JSOT Press, 1984), pp.199-215.

230. Speiser, *Genesis*, p.271.

231. Sarna, *Genesis*, p.242.

232. D. D. Luckenbill, *The Annals of Sennacherib* (Chicago: University of Chicago Press, 1924), p.130.

233. G. R. Driver, *Canaanite Myths and Legends* (Edinburgh: T. & T. Clark, 1971 reprint), p.87.

234. *BDB*, p.460.

235. Speiser, *Genesis*, p.273.

236. It has been argued that the conditions of the birth reflect a breech delivery. See M. and S. Blondheim, 'Obstetrical and Lexicographical Complications: The Birth of Benjamin and Death of Rachel,' *JBQ* 27 (1999): 15-19.

237. *BDB*, p.20.

238. *BDB*, p.19.

239. The verb 'called' here is a disjunctive form that stresses contrast (See Ramsey, 'Is Name-Giving an Act of Domination,' p.29).

240. Von Rad, *Genesis*, p.336.

241. See the discussion of Sarna, *Genesis*, pp.244-5.

242. Tov, *Textual Criticism*, pp.53-4.

243. Gibson, *Davidson's Introductory Hebrew Grammar: Syntax*, p.178.

244. Bullinger, *Figures of Speech Used in the Bible*, p.637.

245. See the calculations in Keil and Delitzsch, *Commentary on the Old Testament: Pentateuch*, p.320; cf. *Rashi Commentary*, p.173. For the opposite view, see S. Levin, 'Isaac's Blindness: A Medical Diagnosis,' *Judaism* 37 (1988): 81-3.

246. Curiously there are no accounts given in Genesis of the death and burial of either Rebekah or Leah.

247. Speiser, *Genesis*, p.279.

248. J. Abraham argues that these are the same women, but Esau has changed their names to gain sympathy from his parents ('Esau's Wives,' *JBQ* 25 (1997): 251-9).

249. R. Williams, *Hebrew Syntax: An Outline* (Toronto: University of Toronto, 1976), p.55.

250. Waltke and O'Connor, *An Introduction to Biblical Hebrew Syntax,* p.131.

251. Gibson, *Davidson's Introductory Hebrew Grammar,* p.1.

252. Speiser, *Genesis*, p.282.

253. D. A. Clines, ed. *The Dictionary of Classical Hebrew* (Sheffield: Sheffield Academic Press, 1993), vol. 1, pp.288-9.

254. Speiser, *Genesis*, pp.279-80. A Beeston draws the unlikely conclusion that what Anah saw was a mirage and, therefore, that this is a comment of ridicule (See his 'What Did Anah See?', *VT* 24 (1974): 109-10).

255. It has long been argued that the text really denotes the kings of Edom before an Israelite king ruled over Edom, in which case perhaps David is meant (See J. Skinner, *A Critical and Exegetical Commentary on Genesis.* Edinburgh: T. & T. Clark, 1910, p.434).

256. J. R. Bartlett, 'The Edomite King list of Genesis XXXVI. 31-39 and I Chronicles I. 43-50,' *JTS* 16 (1965): 301-14.

257. E. A. Knauf, 'Alter und Herkunft der edomitischen Königsliste Gen. 36:31-39,' *ZAW* 97 (1985): 245-53.

258. For good studies of the Edomites, see J. R. Bartlett, *Edom and the Edomites* (Sheffield: JSOT, 1989); and, B. Dicou, *Edom, Israel's Brother and Antagonist* (Sheffield: JSOT, 1994).

259. *NEAEHL,* vol. I, pp.264-6.

260. Bartlett, *Edom,* p.50.

261. *Ibid.,* p.49.

Chapter 9 — The story of Joseph

1. *BDB,* p.655 and Sarna, *Genesis,* p.255. See also Num. 22:22; Judg. 7:10-11, etc.

2. E. Hilgert, 'The Dual Image of Joseph in Hebrew and Early Jewish Literature,' *Biblical Research* 30 (1985): 17; cf., J. Peck, 'Note on Genesis 37:2 and Joseph's Character,' *ET* 82 (1971): 342-3.

3. Gesenius, *Hebrew Grammar,* p.430.

4. *BDB,* p.821.

5. A. L. Oppenheim, 'The Golden Garments of the Gods,' *JNES* 8 (1949): 172-93; see Speiser, *Genesis,* p.290.
6. A. L. Oppenheim, 'The Interpretation of Dreams in the Ancient Near East,' *TAPS* 46.3 (1956): 179-353. For dreams in Egypt, in particular, see Currid, *Ancient Egypt and the Old Testament,* pp.224-8.
7. *BDB*, pp.728-9.
8. *Ibid.,* p.244.
9. See the discussion in Lambdin, *Introduction to Biblical Hebrew,* pp.170-71.
10. A. H. Gardiner, *Hieratic Papyri in the British Museum* (London: British Museum, 1935); cf., S. Israelit-Groll, 'A Ramesside Grammar Book of a Technical Language of Dream Interpretation,' in *Pharaonic Egypt,* ed. S. Israelit-Groll (Jerusalem: Magnes, 1985), pp.71-118.
11. *ANET,* p.495.
12. *NIDOTTE,* vol. II, p.1137.
13. Sarna, *Genesis,* p.257.
14. *Ibid.*
15. For analysis of both biblical and environmental contexts of the Shechem area, see E. F. Campbell and J. F. Ross, 'The Excavation of Shechem and the Biblical Tradition,' *BA* 26 (1963): 2-27; and E. F. Campbell, *Shechem II — A Portrait of a Hill Country Vale: The Shechem Regional Survey* (Atlanta: Scholars Press, 1991).
16. The Shechem area is part of the Mediterranean weather zone that is characterized as a subtropical wet zone. It receives about fourteen inches of rain per year. Because of its high precipitation, it is an area of many forests (See J. Currid, 'Climate and Vegetation,' in O. P. Robertson, *Understanding the Land of the Bible.* Phillipsburg, NJ: Presbyterian and Reformed, 1996, pp.55-62).
17. Gesenius, *Hebrew Grammar,* p.456.
18. See R. E. Cooley and G. D. Pratico, 'Dothan,' in *NEAEHL,* vol. I, pp.372-4.
19. *BDB*, p.647.
20. *Ibid.,* p.247.
21. See J. Currid and J. Gregg, 'Why Did the Early Israelites Dig All Those Pits?', *BAR* 14:5 (1988): 54-7; J. Currid and A. Navon, 'The Tell Halif (Lahav) Grain Storage Project,' *ASOR Newsletter* 37:2 (1986): 7; J. Currid and A. Navon, 'Iron Age Pits and the Lahav (Tell Halif) Grain Storage Project,' *BASOR* 273 (1989): 67-78.

22. Speiser, *Genesis,* p.291. See, in particular, H. C. White, 'Reuben and Judah: Duplicates or Complements,' in *Understanding the Word,* eds. J. Butler, E. Conrad and B. Ollenburger (Sheffield: JSOT, 1985), pp.73-97.

23. Gesenius, *Hebrew Grammar,* p.372.

24. F. Deist misunderstands this point. He believes the author is being intrusive, and Reuben did not really say these words ('A Note on the Narrator's Voice in Gen. 37,20-22,' *ZAW* 108:4 (1996): 621-2).

25. See the important work of E. Knauf, 'Midianites and Ishmaelites,' in *Midian, Moab and Edom,* eds. J. Sawyer and D. Clines (Sheffield: JSOT, 1983), pp.147-62.

26. O. P. Robertson, *Understanding the Land of the Bible* (Phillipsburg, NJ: Presbyterian and Reformed, 1996), p.23.

27. Speiser, *Genesis,* p.291. Redford says, 'Generations of Bible students have utilized this discrepancy as a show piece for demonstrating the validity of the Documentary Hypothesis' (See D. B. Redford, *A Study of the Biblical Story of Joseph.* VTS, 20; Leiden: Brill, 1970, p.145).

28. Another possibility is presented by E. Fry, who says, 'My guess is that "Ishmaelite" and "Midianite" were both understood as general terms for nomadic people thought to be descended from Abraham, and the two terms were therefore recognized as referring to the same group' (See his, 'How Was Joseph Taken to Egypt? (Genesis 37:12-36),' *BT* 46:4 (1995): 445-8).

29. J. M. Sasson, ed. *Civilizations of the Ancient Near East* (New York: Scribner's, 1995), vol. I, p.229.

30. Sarna, *Genesis,* p.261.

31. *Ibid.,* p.262.

32. Waltke and O'Connor, *An Introduction to Biblical Hebrew Syntax,* p.584.

33. V. P. Hamilton, *The Book of Genesis: Chapters 18-50* (Grand Rapids: Eerdmans, 1995), p.428.

34. Sarna, *Genesis,* p.255.

35. For the various positions, see Currid, *Ancient Egypt and the Old Testament,* pp.75-7.

36. G. E. Kadish, 'Eunuchs in Ancient Egypt?' in *Studies in Honor of John A. Wilson,* ed. G. E. Kadish (Chicago: University of Chicago Press, 1969), p.59.

37. See the discussion of E. Curtis, 'Genesis 38: Its Context(s) and Function,' *Criswell Theological Review* 5 (1991): 247-57.

38. S. Mathewson, 'An Exegetical Study of Genesis 38,' *BS* 146 (1989): 373-92.

39. J. Currid, 'The Deforestation of the Foothills of Palestine,' *PEQ* (1984): 1-11.

40. *Rashi Commentary,* p.186.

41. Sarna, *Genesis,* p.266.

42. *BDB,* p.386.

43. Gesenius, *Hebrew Grammar,* p.336; Gibson, *Davidson's Introductory Hebrew Grammar: Syntax,* p.154.

44. *BDB,* p.1008.

45. Gesenius, *Hebrew Grammar,* p.482.

46. J. Rook, 'Making Widows: The Patriarchal Guardian at Work,' *BTB* 27 (1997): 10-15.

47. Simons, *Geographical and Topographical Texts of the Old Testament,* pp.150,172.

48. Waltke and O'Connor, *An Introduction to Biblical Hebrew Syntax,* p.675.

49. Gunkel, *Genesis,* pp.399-400.

50. J. Currid, 'Cosmologies of Myth,' in W. A. Hoffecker, ed., *Building a Christian World View* (Phillipsburg, NJ: Presbyterian and Reformed, 1988), vol. II, p.17. See M. Astour, 'Tamar the Hierodule,' *JBL* 85 (1966): 185-96; cf. J. Westenholz, 'Tamar, Qedesa, Qadistu, and Sacred Prostitution in Mesopotamia,' *HTR* 82 (1989): 245-65.

51. See D. Collon, ed., *7000 Years of Seals* (London: British Museum Publications, 1997).

52. J. Currid, 'The Rod of Moses,' *Buried History* 33:4 (1997): 107-14.

53. Gunkel, *Genesis,* p.400. Cf., Von Rad, *Genesis,* p.355.

54. G. Coats, 'Widow's Rights: A Crux in the Structure of Genesis 38,' *CBQ* 34 (1972): 461-6.

55. Sarna, *Genesis,* p.270.

56. According to G. Rendsburg, the purpose of this episode has more to do with David than with Judah ('David and His Circle in Genesis XXXVIII,' *VT* 36 (1986): 438-46). See also C. Ho, 'The Story of the Family Troubles of Judah and David: A Study of Their Literary Links,' *VT* 49 (1999): 514-31.

57. C. Westermann, 'Structure and Intention of the Book of Ruth,' *Word and World* 19 (1999): 285-302.

58. *BDB,* p.280.

59. Gesenius, *Hebrew Grammar,* p.455.

60. *BDB,* p.1058.

61. S. C. Layton, 'The Steward in Ancient Israel: A Study of Hebrew ['ăšer] 'al-habbayit in its Near Eastern Setting,' *JBL* 109 (1990): 633-49.

62. T. D. N. Mettinger, *Solomonic State Officials: A Study of the Civil Government Officials of the Israelite Monarchy* (Lund: Gleerup, 1971), pp.73-9.

63. D. B. Redford, *A Study of the Biblical Story of Joseph* (VT XX, Leiden: Brill, 1970), p.75.

64. *ANET,* p.83.

65. J. M. Sasson, ed. *Civilizations of the Ancient Near East,* vol. 1 (New York: Scribner's, 1995), p.375.

66. *BDB,* p.93; Sarna, *Genesis,* p.274.

67. Gesenius, *Hebrew Grammar,* p.8.

68. For example, see J. H. Breasted, *ARE* (London: Grassmill, 1988 reprint), vol. III, pp.268-73.

69. *ANET,* pp.23-5.

70. N. Glueck, *Hēsĕd in the Bible* (Cincinnati: Hebrew Union College Press, 1967 ed.).

71. K. Sakenfeld, *The Meaning of Hēsĕd in the Hebrew Bible* (Cambridge, MA: Harvard Semitic Monographs, 1978).

72. H. Tadmor, 'Rab-saris or Rab-shakeh in 2 Kings 18,' in C. Meyers and M. O'Connor, eds., *The Word of the Lord Shall Go Forth* (Winona Lake, IN: Eisenbrauns, 1983), pp.279-85.

73. Redford, *A Study of the Biblical Story of Joseph,* p.47.

74. Gesenius, *Hebrew Grammar,* p.449.

75. On the general subject of dreams, see Currid, *Ancient Egypt and the Old Testament,* pp.224-8.

76. Gesenius, *Hebrew Grammar,* p.420.

77. This application section is taken from Currid, *Study Commentary on Exodus,* vol. 2, p.203.

78. F. F. Bruce, *The Epistle to the Hebrews* (Grand Rapids: Eerdmans, 1964), p.3.

79. Currid, *Ancient Egypt and the Old Testament,* pp.224-8.

80. *ANET,* p.495.

81. H. Hollis believes that, when Jesus spoke of 'being lifted up' in the Gospel of John (3:14; 8:28; 12:32,34), he had in mind this story of the lifting up of the cupbearer and the baker ('The Root of the Johannine Pun,' *NTS* 35 (1989): 475-8).

82. D. B. Redford argues unconvincingly that the phrase 'land of the Hebrews' supports a late date for the Joseph story ('The 'Land of the Hebrews' in Gen. XL 15,' *VT* 15 (1965): 529-32).

83. Speiser, *Genesis,* p.307.

84. *Ibid.*

85. E. A. Speiser, 'Census and Ritual Expiation in Mari and Israel,' *BASOR* 149 (1958): 21.

86. For a good study of Egyptian dreams in comparison with the accounts of dreams in the story of Joseph, see S. Israelit-Groll, *Pharaonic Egypt* (Jerusalem: Magnes Press, 1985), pp.71-118.

87. In the book of Exodus, the destruction of the livestock (Exod. 9:1-7) is a devastating blow to the economy of Egypt.

88. T. O. Lambdin, 'Egyptian Loan Words in the Old Testament,' *JAOS* 73 (1953): 146.

89. C. Gordon, *Ugaritic Handbook* (Rome: Pontificium Institutum Biblicum, 1965), p.534.

90. R. Ritner, *The Mechanics of Ancient Egyptian Magical Practice* (Studies of Ancient Oriental Civilization, 54; Chicago, 1993), p.103; and S. Noegel, 'Moses and Magic: Notes on the Book of Exodus,' *JANES* 24 (1997): 45-59.

91. Waltke and O'Connor, *An Introduction to Biblical Hebrew Syntax,* pp.625-6.

92. See J. Quaeqebeur, 'On the Egyptian Equivalent of Biblical ḤARṬUMMÎN,' in *Pharaonic Egypt,* ed. by Israelit-Groll, pp.162-72. For a contrary view, see Lambdin, 'Egyptian Loan Words,' pp.150-51.

93. Gesenius, *Hebrew Grammar,* p.134.

94. Redford, *A Study of the Biblical Story of Joseph,* p.146.

95. *Ibid.,* p.76.

96. *BDB,* p.164.

97. *Ibid.,* pp.1023-4.

98. *Ibid.,* p.899.

99. Redford, *A Study of the Biblical Story of Joseph,* p.60.

100. Waltke and O'Connor, *An Introduction to Biblical Hebrew Syntax,* p.627; Gesenius, *Hebrew Grammar,* p.360.

101. Redford, *A Study of the Biblical Story of Joseph,* p.165.

102. *BDB,* p.960.

103. Speiser, *Genesis,* p.313.

104. Breasted, *ARE,* vol. II, p.672.

105. Speiser, *Genesis,* p.313.

106. Waltke and O'Connor, *An Introduction to Biblical Hebrew Syntax,* p.221.

107. Calvin, *Institutes,* I, xvii, I, p.179.

108. Speiser, *Genesis,* pp.311-14; Sarna, *Genesis,* p.286.

109. *BDB,* p.907.

110. J. Vergote, *Joseph en Égypte* (Louvain: Publications Universitaires, 1959), pp.121-35. For a different view see Redford, *A Study of the Biblical Story of Joseph,* pp.208-26.

111. Speiser, *Genesis,* p.314.

112. Vergote, *Joseph en Égypte,* pp.135-41.

113. Khnum was one of the creator gods of ancient Egypt. In the 'Great Hymn to Khnum' he is portrayed as 'forming all on his potter's wheel ... he made mankind, created gods, he fashioned flocks and herds. He made birds, fishes, and reptiles all.'
114. *ANET,* p.431.
115. See W. F. Albright, 'New Light on Early Recensions of the Hebrew Bible,' *BASOR* 140 (1955): 31; cf., Redford, *A Study of the Biblical Story of Joseph,* p.230; and Vergote, *Joseph en Égypte,* pp.141-3.
116. See J. Currid, 'The Beehive Buildings of Ancient Palestine,' *BA* 49:1 (1986): 20-25; J. Currid and A. Navon, 'Iron Age Pits and the Lahav (Tell Halif) Grain Storage Project,' *BASOR* 273 (1989): 67-78.
117. Redford, *A Study of the Biblical Story of Joseph,* p.38.
118. Currid, *Study Commentary on Exodus,* vol. 2, p.93.
119. Sasson, *Civilizations of the Ancient Near East,* vol. I, p.185.
120. An extensive discussion occurs in Sarna, *Genesis,* p.290.
121. Sasson, *Civilizations of the Ancient Near East,* vol. III, p.1383.
122. *BDB,* pp.990-91.
123. S. Schimmel, 'Joseph and His Brothers: A Paradigm for Repentance,' *Judaism* 37 (1988): 62.
124. Breasted, *ARE,* vol. III, pp.6-8.
125. *BDB,* pp.648-9.
126. A. Sneh, T. Weissbrod and I. Perath, 'Evidence for an Ancient Egyptian Frontier Canal,' *American Scientist* 63 (1975): 542-48; and W. Shea, 'A Date for the Recently Discovered Eastern Canal of Egypt,' *BASOR* 226 (1977): 31-8.
127. A. Gardiner, 'The Ancient Military Road between Egypt and Palestine,' *JEA* 6 (1920): 107-9.
128. *BDB,* p.789; Isa. 20:4.
129. Z. Zevit, 'Expressing Denial in Biblical Hebrew and Mishnaic Hebrew, and in Amos,' *VT* 29 (1979): 505-9.
130. *BDB,* p.467.
131. Gesenius, *Hebrew Grammar,* p.431.
132. Williams, *Hebrew Syntax: An Outline,* p.35.
133. *BDB,* p.539.
134. Redford, *A Study of the Biblical Story of Joseph,* p.31.
135. Bullinger, *Figures of Speech Used in the Bible,* p.423.
136. Williams, *Hebrew Syntax: An Outline,* p.24.
137. Gibson, *Davidson's Introductory Hebrew Grammar: Syntax,* p.178.
138. Redford, *A Study of the Biblical Story of Joseph,* p.152.

139. *BDB*, p.1013.
140. Bullinger, *Figures of Speech Used in the Bible*, pp.208-11.
141. Williams, *Hebrew Syntax: An Outline*, p.73.
142. Gesenius, *Hebrew Grammar*, p.313.
143. *BDB*, p.275.
144. *Ibid.*, p.164.
145. See Currid, 'Weights and Measures in the Pentateuch,' in *Dictionary of the Old Testament: Pentateuch*, eds. D. W. Baker and T. D. Alexander (InterVarsity Press).
146. Gibson, *Davidson's Introductory Hebrew Grammar: Syntax*, p.188.
147. Y. Muffs, 'Two Comparative Lexical Studies,' *JANES* 5 (1973): 289.
148. K. A. Kitchen, 'Genesis 12-50 in the Near Eastern World,' in *He Swore an Oath: Biblical Themes from Genesis 12-50*, eds. R. Hess, P. Satterthwaite, and G. Wenham (Cambridge: Tyndale House, 1993): 86-7.
149. Von Rad, *Genesis*, p.329.
150. L. Koehler, 'Hebraische Etymologien,' *JBL* 59 (1940): 36.
151. Currid, *Ancient Egypt and the Old Testament*, pp.222-3.
152. Redford, *A Study of the Biblical Story of Joseph*, p.48.
153. D. Daube, *Studies in Biblical Law* (New York: KTAV, 1969), pp.235-57.
154. F. H. Cryer, *Divination in Ancient Israel and Its Near Eastern Environment* (Sheffield: JSOT Press, 1994), pp.145-7.
155. *ANET*, p.167, Law no. 22.
156. Redford, *A Study of the Biblical Story of Joseph*, p.38.
157. Similar drama is found in the story of David's anointing in 1 Sam. 16:6-11.
158. See R. K. Ritner, *The Mechanics of Ancient Egyptian Magical Practice* (Chicago: University of Chicago Press, 1993).
159. This verb is in the Hithpael pattern with an 'inflexed t', that is, two consonants of the verb have been subject to metathesis (See Waltke and O'Connor, *An Introduction to Biblical Hebrew Syntax*, p.425).
160. *BDB*, p.843.
161. J. Harris, 'Genesis 44:18-34,' *Interpretation* 52:2 (1998): 178-81.
162. *BDB*, p.963.
163. Waltke and O'Connor, *An Introduction to Biblical Hebrew Syntax*, p.670.

164. J. Levenson, *The Death and Resurrection of the Beloved Son: The Transformation of Child Sacrifice in Judaism and Christianity* (New Haven: Yale University Press, 1993), pp.162-3.

165. M. O'Brien, 'The Contribution of Judah's Speech, Genesis 44:18-34, to the Characterization of Joseph,' *CBQ* 59 (1997): 429-47.

166. Redford, *A Study of the Biblical Story of Joseph*, p.72.

167. Clines, *The Dictionary of Classical Hebrew*, vol. II, p.97.

168. Gibson, *Davidson's Hebrew Introductory Grammar: Syntax*, pp.2, 140-41.

169. G. Whitney, 'Alternative Interpretations of LO in Exodus 6:3 and Jeremiah 7:22,' *WTJ* 48 (1986): 151-9.

170. For a different view see Redford, *A Study of the Biblical Story of Joseph*, p.191.

171. Von Rad, *Genesis*, p.394.

172. T. Najpaver, 'Making Peace with Your Past,' *Preaching* 13 (1997): 38-41.

173. *BDB*, p.299.

174. *Ibid.*, p.919.

175. Speiser, *Genesis*, p.339.

176. *BDB*, p.806.

177. Clines, *The Dictionary of Classical Hebrew*, vol. I, p.316.

178. Gesenius, *Hebrew Grammar*, pp.397-8.

179. Currid, *Study Commentary on Exodus*, vol. 1, p.82; cf., Gen. 22:11.

180. See Redford, *A Study of the Biblical Story of Joseph*, pp.158-9.

181. M. Zipor, 'Two Textual Notes (PS. LXXIV 11; LXX GEN. XLVI 17),' *VT* 49 (1999): 553-7.

182. Speiser, *Genesis*, p.345.

183. V. Hamilton, *The Book of Genesis, Chapters 18-50* (Grand Rapids: Eerdmans, 1995), p.599.

184. For verbs of direction used in this passage, see S. Shibayama, 'Notes on *Yarad* and *'Alah*: Hints on Translating,' *JBR* 34 (1966): 358-62.

185. *BDB*, p.435.

186. Gesenius, *Hebrew Grammar*, p.319.

187. Gunkel, *Genesis*, p.440.

188. Von Rad, *Genesis*, p.399.

189. Gunkel, *Genesis*, p.441.

190. Herodotus, ii, 47.

191. Redford, *A Study of the Biblical Story of Joseph*, p.235.

192. Regarding the identity of this pharaoh, see J. Battenfield, 'A Consideration of the Identity of the Pharaoh of Genesis 47,' *JETS* 15 (1972): 77-85.

193. Von Rad, *Genesis,* p.350.

194. For a different view see Sarna, *Genesis,* p.317.

195. The Ten Commandments are structured by asyndeton, and they are indeed a list of directives. The Seputagint misses this figure in the present text and it, therefore, attempts to repair the text, with gruesome results (See Von Rad, *Genesis,* pp.401-2).

196. Breasted, *ARE,* vol. IV, pp.120-21.

197. *Ibid.,* vol. II, p.427; vol. IV, pp.87, 269-70.

198. *BDB,* p.139.

199. F. Landy, 'Are We in the Place of Averroes? Response to the Articles of Exum and Whedbee, Buss, Gottwald, and Good,' *Semeia* 32 (1984): 131-48.

200. Currid, *Ancient Egypt and the Old Testament,* pp.127-8; for the excavation report, see M. Bietak, *Tell el-Dab'a,* vol. 2 (Vienna: Oesterreichische Akademie der Wissenschaften, 1975).

201. Currid, *Ancient Egypt and the Old Testament,* p.128.

202. S. R. Driver, quoted by Redford, *A Study of the Biblical Story of Joseph,* p.52.

203. *BDB,* pp.521, 529.

204. Ramban argues that Joseph does this in order to demonstrate his loyalty to Pharaoh (47:14).

205. A. R. Schulman, 'Egyptian Representations of Horsemen and Riding in the New Kingdom,' *JNES* 16 (1957): 263-71.

206. Y. Ikeda, 'Solomon's Trade in Horses and Chariots in Its International Setting,' in *Studies in the Period of David and Solomon and Other Essays,* ed. T. Ishida (Winona Lake, IN: Eisenbrauns, 1982), pp.215-38.

207. *BDB,* pp.624-5.

208. As opposed to the view of B. Lerner, 'Joseph the Unrighteous,' *Judaism* 38 (1989): 278-81, who portrays Joseph as a tyrannical ruler.

209. Von Rad, *Genesis,* p.406.

210. For a different view see Redford, *A Study of the Biblical Story of Joseph,* p.236, n.2.

211. Gunkel, *Genesis,* p.444.

212. Gibson, *Davidson's Introductory Hebrew Grammar: Syntax,* p.180.

213. Sasson, ed. *Civilizations of the Ancient Near East,* vol. I, p.320.

214. Waltke and O'Connor, *An Introduction to Biblical Hebrew Syntax,* p.684, n. 44.

215. V. Hurowitz, 'Joseph's Enslavement of the Egyptians (Genesis 47:13-26) in Light of Famine Texts from Mesopotamia,' *RB* 101 (1994): 355-62.

216. Z. Ron, 'The Significance of Joseph's Agrarian Policy,' *JBQ* 28:4 (2000): 256-9.

217. H. Seebass, 'The Joseph Story, Genesis 48 and the Canonical Process,' *JSOT* 35 (1986): 29-43.

218. G. Tucker, 'Jacob's Terrible Burden,' *BR* 10 (1994): 20-28, 54.

219. Sarna, *Genesis,* p.323.

220. J. Currid, 'The Rod of Moses,' *Buried History* 33:4 (1997): 107-14.

221. Waltke and O'Connor, *An Introduction to Biblical Hebrew Syntax*, p.675.

222. Redford, *A Study of the Biblical Story of Joseph,* p.22.

223. Z. Ron, 'The Preference of Ephraim,' *JBQ* 28:1 (2000): 60-61.

224. Speiser, *Genesis,* p.357.

225. *BDB,* p.949.

226. Speiser, *Genesis,* p.358.

227. E. C. Kingsbury points out, in addition, that Ephraim gains a cultic superiority over Manasseh ('He Set Ephraim Before Manasseh,' *HUCA* 38 (1967): 129-36).

228. *BDB,* p.1014.

229. B. Zion Katz, 'Judah Hasid: Three Controversial Commentaries,' *JBQ* 25 (1997): 23-30.

230. See the important work of J. Heck, 'A History of Interpretation of Genesis 49 and Deuteronomy 33,' *BS* 147 (1990): 16-31.

231. C. Westermann, *Genesis*, 3 vols. (Neukirchen-Vluyn: Neukirchener, 1974), vol. I, pp.277-8.

232. See the study of S. Gevirtz, 'The Reprimand of Reuben,' *JNES* 30 (1971): 87-98.

233. *BDB,* pp.19-20.

234. Wenham, *Genesis,* p.473.

235. M. Dahood, argues that the word I have translated as 'swords' actually refers, specifically, to knives used for circumcision. Jacob's polemic against the act recorded in Genesis 34 would thus be heightened ('MKRTYHM in Genesis 49,5,' *CBQ* 23 (1961): 54-56).

236. Sarna, *Genesis,* p.336.

237. Currid, 'The Rod of Moses,' pp.107-14.

238. Gesenius, *Hebrew Grammar,* p.503.

239. M. Treves, 'Shiloh (Gen. 49:10),' *JBL* 85 (1966): 353-6. An example of even greater butchering of the text can be seen in B. Margulis, 'Gen. XLIX 10/Deut. XXXIII 2-3,' *VT* 19 (1969): 202-10.

240. Sarna, *Genesis,* p.336.

241. E. Good attempts to link Shiloh with Judah's son Shelah ('The "Blessing" on Judah, Gen. 49:8-12,' *JBL* 82 (1963): 427-32), but this is highly improbable.

242. J. Blenkinsopp, 'The Oracle of Judah and the Messianic Entry,' *JBL* 80 (1961): 55-64.

243. I. Mendelsohn, 'State Slavery in Ancient Palestine,' *BASOR* 85 (1942): 14-17; for a contrasting perspective, see J. Heck, 'Issachar: Slave or Freeman?', *JETS* 29 (1986): 385-96. See, also, C. Carmichael, 'Some Sayings in Genesis 49,' *JBL* 88 (1969): 435-44.

244. S. Gevirtz argues that 'his food will be rich' actually means the opposite when the Hebrew is properly understood. He repoints the text so that it reads 'who rations his bread', as if Asher were poor in produce ('Asher in the Blessing of Jacob,' *VT* 37 (1987): 154-63).

245. *BDB,* p.1018.

246. S. Gevirtz, 'Naphtali in "The Blessing of Jacob",' *JBL* 103 (1984): 513-21.

247. Hamilton, *The Book of Genesis, Chs. 18-50,* p.678.

248. A. Gardiner, 'The Ancient Military Road Between Egypt and Palestine,' *JEA* 6 (1920): 99-116.

249. Unpublished Th.M paper, Reformed Theological Seminary (December, 2001).

250. Sarna, *Genesis,* p.345.

251. Waltke and O'Connor, *An Introduction to Biblical Hebrew Syntax,* p.627.

252. *BDB,* p.334.

253. For an excellent study of mummification, see A. Lucas, *Ancient Egyptian Materials and Industries* (London: Histories & Mysteries of Man Ltd, 1989), pp.270-326.

254. Currid, *Ancient Egypt and the Old Testament,* p.36.

255. J. Davis, *Mummies, Men and Madness* (Grand Rapids: Baker, 1972), p.99.

256. Von Rad, *Genesis,* p.425.

257. Gunkel, *Genesis,* p.463.

258. Redford, *A Study of the Biblical Story of Joseph,* p.162.

259. Gibson, *Davidson's Introductory Hebrew Grammar: Syntax,* p.82.

260. Consider also the work of W. Brueggemann, 'Genesis L
15-21: A Theological Exploration,' in J. Emerton, ed. *Congress
Volume: Salamanca* (Leiden: Brill, 1985), pp.40-53.
261. Berkhof, *Systematic Theology*, Part 1, p.76.
262. Vergote, *Joseph en Égypte*, pp.200-201. The Hebrews seem
to put the ideal number at 120 years (Deut. 31:2; 34:7).
263. For a different view see Gesenius, *Hebrew Grammar*, p.418.
264. See the important study of M. Wilcox, 'The Bones of Joseph:
Hebrews 11:22,' in B. Thompson, ed. *Scripture: Meaning and
Method* (Hull University, 1987), pp.114-30.